OCEANIC ENCOUNTERS

exchange, desire, violence

OCEANIC ENCOUNTERS

exchange, desire, violence

edited by
MARGARET JOLLY,
SERGE TCHERKÉZOFF & DARRELL TRYON

E PRESS

Published by ANU E Press
The Australian National University
Canberra ACT 0200, Australia
Email: anuepress@anu.edu.au
This title is also available online at:
http://epress.anu.edu.au/oceanic_encounters _citation.html

National Library of Australia
Cataloguing-in-Publication entry

Title: Oceanic encounters : exchange, desire, violence / editors, Margaret Jolly ; Serge Tcherkézoff ; Darrell Tryon.

ISBN: 9781921536281 (pbk.) 9781921536298 (pdf)

Notes: Includes index.
Bibliography.

Subjects: Pacific Islanders--First contact with Europeans.
Cultural relations.
Pacific Area--Colonization.
Pacific Area--History.
Pacific Area--Discovery and exploration.

Other Authors/Contributors:

Jolly, Margaret.
Tcherkézoff, Serge.
Tryon, Darrell.

Dewey Number: 305.80099

All rights reserved. No part of this publication may be reproduced, stored in a retrieval system or transmitted in any form or by any means, electronic, mechanical, photocopying or otherwise, without the prior permission of the publisher.

Cover photo: *A watery shot of the island of Ambae under cloud and sunburst* by John Patrick Taylor

The editors acknowledge with gratitude the financial support received from the Australian Research Council and the Pacific Editorial Board of ANU E Press.

This edition © 2009 ANU E Press

*In fond memory of Greg Dening
and Epeli Hau`ofa*

Table of Contents

Preface		ix
Acknowledgements		xi
Contributors		xiii
List of Figures and Tables		xvii
List of abbreviations and acronyms		xix
Chapter 1.	Oceanic Encounters: A Prelude *Margaret Jolly and Serge Tcherkézoff*	1
Chapter 2.	Linguistic Encounter and Responses in the South Pacific *Darrell Tryon*	37
Chapter 3.	The Sediment of Voyages: Re-membering Quirós, Bougainville and Cook in Vanuatu *Margaret Jolly*	57
Chapter 4.	A Reconsideration of the Role of Polynesian Women in Early Encounters with Europeans: Supplement to Marshall Sahlins' Voyage around the Islands of History *Serge Tcherkézoff*	113
Chapter 5.	Uncertain Times: Sailors, Beachcombers and Castaways as "Missionaries" and Cultural Mediators in Tonga (Polynesia) *Françoise Douaire-Marsaudon*	161
Chapter 6.	In the Event: Indigenous Countersigns and the Ethnohistory of Voyaging *Bronwen Douglas*	175
Chapter 7.	Watkin Tench's Fieldwork: The Journal of an "Ethnographer" in Port Jackson, 1788-1791 *Isabelle Merle*	199
Chapter 8.	The Art of Encounter: Verisimilitude in the Imaginary Exploration of Interior New Guinea, 1725–1876 *Chris Ballard*	221
Chapter 9.	Black Powder, White Magic: European Armaments and Sorcery in Early Mekeo and Roro Encounters *Mark S. Mosko*	259
Chapter 10.	A Measure of Violence: Forty Years of "First Contact" Among the Ankave-Anga (Papua New Guinea) *Pascale Bonnemère and Pierre Lemonnier*	295
Subject Index		335
People and Places Index		339

Preface

Scientific collaboration between France and Australia in the social sciences and humanities has really forged ahead since 2000, with collaborative agreements covering a wide range of disciplines across a broad spectrum of French and Australian institutions of higher learning.

In 2001 an International Program of Scientific Collaboration (Programme International de Coopération Scientifique, PICS) was initiated between the National Centre of Scientific Research (Centre National de la Recherche Scientifique, CNRS), France's national research body, and The Australian National University (ANU), Canberra. This program bears the title "Early Encounters in the Pacific."

Within this framework, this volume, *Oceanic Encounters*, is the first fruit of ongoing collaboration between the Research School of Pacific and Asian Studies (RSPAS) at The Australian National University and the Centre of Research and Documentation on Oceania (Centre de Recherche et de Documentation sur l'Océanie, CREDO), a research centre within an Institute of Asia-Pacific (Maison de l'Asie-Pacifique), located at the University of Provence in Marseilles, incorporating members of the Centre National de la Recherche Scientifique (CNRS), and the School for Advanced Studies in the Social Sciences (École des Hautes Études en Sciences Sociales, EHESS).

This multidisciplinary research program, initiated by Serge Tcherkézoff in Marseilles and myself in Canberra, has flourished since its inception, involving twenty researchers and research students in France and Australia. Thus far it has resulted in two symposia, held in Marseilles and Canberra, examining the connections between history and anthropology in the early days of exploration and colonial contact with the indigenous peoples of the Pacific.

A second series of multidisciplinary symposia is looking at contemporary issues such as socio-political upheaval in Oceania. The first symposium of the series has already taken place in La Ciotat, organized by CREDO, with the second set to take place in Canberra. It is planned that this will lead to a volume on contemporary issues in Oceania, perhaps as a special number of the *New Pacific Review/La Nouvelle Revue du Pacifique*, itself a product of French-Australian collaboration in the social sciences.

While scientific collaboration between the Centre National de la Recherche Scientifique (CNRS) and the Research School of Pacific and Asian Studies (RSPAS) at The Australian National University is now becoming well established, there is an urgent need to make Francophone research more accessible to the English-speaking world. This was one of the principal findings of the French, Assises de la Recherche Française dans le Pacifique – a French government review of French research in the Pacific over the last twenty years, held in Nouméa in 2004.

In response to this, and partly as a result of Serge Tcherkézoff's appointment as Linkage International Fellow in the Gender Relations Centre in 2004–05, we have seen the recent publication of *The Changing South Pacific: Identities and Transformations* (Pandanus Books 2005), edited by Serge Tcherkézoff and Françoise Douaire-Marsaudon, itself an English translation of *Le Pacifique-sud aujourd'hui: identités et transformations culturelles* (CNRS 1997); *"First contacts" in Polynesia: the Samoan case (1722–1848): Western misunderstandings about sexuality and divinity* (Macmillan Brown Centre for Pacific Studies and *The Journal of Pacific History* Monograph 2004); and *Tahiti—1768: Jeunes filles en pleurs: la face cachée des premiers contacts et la naissance du mythe occidental* (Au Vent des Îles 2004), the latter two both authored by Serge Tcherkézoff.

Oceanic Encounters represents a further step in Australia-France collaboration in multidisciplinary research in the social sciences and the humanities in the Pacific. At the same time, our broader French-Australian collaboration is building for the future through the increasing involvement of younger scholars as the program develops.

Darrell Tryon
The Australian National University
Canberra, January 2009

Acknowledgements

Many people and institutions have made this volume possible. As Darrell Tryon explains in his preface, we must first acknowledge the innovative funding which came from the French National Centre for Scientific Research (CNRS) as part of the International Program of Scientific Collaboration (PICS). This has been a very successful program. We also acknowledge the "Fonds Pacifique" of the French Ministry of Foreign Affairs which, most recently, funded a week-long symposium in Suva, Fiji in December 2008 bringing biologists, archaeologists, historians and anthropologists together to debate the distinction between Melanesia and Polynesia in Oceania. Darrell Tryon and Serge Tcherkézoff were the main co-organisers of that important event.

There have also been significant contributions from the Australian side – from The Australian National University and particularly from several parts of the Research School of Pacific and Asian Studies: ANU Cartographic Services, Anthropology, Pacific and Asian History and the Gender Relations Centre (all now located in the College of Asia and the Pacific). The Gender Relations Centre has invested much in this volume through the work of research assistants and administrative staff as well as my own time. Also on the Australian side we must acknowledge the generous funding from the large Australian Research Council Discovery Project (2004–08, DP0451620). This bears the same name as this volume, *Oceanic Encounters* but a different subtitle: *Colonial and Contemporary Transformations of Gender and Sexuality in the Pacific*.

We must also thank the several institutions which have allowed images to be reproduced in electronic and hard copy form: All of these are acknowledged in detail in the captions which accompany the images. We warmly thank John Taylor for the use of his superb photograph of Ambae, Vanuatu, which we have reproduced on the cover.

We gratefully acknowledge the professionalism of Duncan Beard and his team at ANU E Press in the final design and production of this volume and Professor Stewart Firth, Chair of the Pacific Editorial Board of ANU E Press, who provided funds for final production and for securing permissions for reproduction of images.

We thank all of the contributors not just for the quality of their scholarship but for their prompt and thoughtful responses to the processes of peer review and copyediting; that has made the final stages of editing this large volume easier and even pleasurable. The comments of two anonymous reviewers were generous, cogent and extremely helpful. We thank each other as editors and contributors for the stimulating collaborative intellectual journey of which this is a part.

We especially thank several members of the Gender Relations Centre staff who have brought this volume to fruition: Annegret Schemberg who did preliminary work in editorial preparation just prior to her retirement, Josie Stockdill who did early work with the images and much later work in the preparation of the final manuscript, and Janet Beard who assisted in the compilation of abbreviations and acronyms, unusual symbols and the all-important index. But most of all we thank Michelle Antoinette whose final copyediting and work in securing images for this volume has been, to use a favourite phrase of Ian Chubb, our Vice Chancellor at the ANU, "superlatively good". She has been both meticulous and gracious in this crucial role.

Finally we dedicate this volume to the cherished memory of Greg Dening and Epeli Hau`ofa, two stellar scholars, whose inspirational ideas about the "beach" of Oceanic encounters and the concept and value of Oceania have proved formative for all of us.

Margaret Jolly
The Australian National University
Canberra, January 2009

Contributors

Chris Ballard is a Fellow in Pacific History at The Australian National University in Canberra. He has conducted long-term research as an archaeologist, historian and anthropologist in Papua New Guinea, Indonesian Papua and Vanuatu. His current research interests include land reform in Vanuatu, the history of racial science in Oceania, and indigenous historicity and cultural heritage in the Pacific. His publications include edited and co-edited collections on anthropology (*Fluid Ontologies*, 1998; *Myth and History in the New Guinea Highlands*, 1999), agriculture (*Agricultural Intensification in New Guinea*, 2001; *The Sweet Potato in Oceania*, 2005), history (*Historical Perspectives on West New Guinea*, 1999; *Race to the Snow*, 2001; *Foreign Bodies*, 2008), and mining (*Mining and Mineral Resource Policy in Asia-Pacific*, 1995; *The Ok Tedi Settlement*, 1997).

Pascale Bonnemère is a member of the Centre of Research and Documentation for Oceania team (CREDO, Centre de Recherche et de Documentation sur l'Océanie) based in Marseilles, and Director of research at the National Centre of Scientific Research (Centre National de la Recherche Scientifique, CNRS). She has been engaged in long-term fieldwork among the Ankave-Anga of Papua New Guinea since 1987. Her published works include *Le pandanus rouge: Corps, différence des sexes et parenté chez les Ankave-Anga* (1996) and, with Pierre Lemonnier, *Drumming to Forget: Ordinary Life and Ceremonies among a Papua New Guinea Group of Forest-Dwellers* (2007), as well as the edited volumes *Women as Unseen Characters: Male Ritual in Papua New Guinea* (2004) and, with Irène Théry, *Ce que le genre fait aux personnes* (2008).

Françoise Douaire-Marsaudon is an anthropologist, a Director of research at the National Centre of Scientific Research (Centre National de la Recherche Scientifique, CNRS) in France, and a member of the Centre of Research and Documentation on Oceania (Centre de Recherche et de Documentation sur l'Océanie, CREDO-Maison Asie-Pacifique) in Marseilles. Her research interests include the formation and transformation of political systems in Polynesia (Tonga, Wallis and Futuna) and their relationship with the construction of the person (self, body, gender and sexuality), processes of Christianisation and relations between memory and history. Among her publications are: *Les premiers fruits: Parenté, identité sexuelle et pouvoirs en Polynésie occidentale (Tonga, Wallis et Futuna)*, Paris, CNRS Editions, Editions de la MSH, 1998; The Kava ritual and the Reproduction of Male Identity in Polynesia, in Monique Jeudy-Ballini and Bernard Juillerat eds., *People and Things. Social Mediations in Oceania*, Durham, Carolina Academic Press, 2002; *The Changing South Pacific. Identities and Transformations*, Canberra, Pandanus Publications, RSPAS and ANU, co-edited with Serge Tcherkézoff, 2005; and *Grand-mère, grand-père. La grandparentalité* *en Asie et dans le Pacifique* ed., Aix-Marseilles, Publications de l'Université de Provence, 2008.

Bronwen Douglas is Senior Fellow in Pacific and Asian History at The Australian National University. Her major research interest is in the history of race, especially the interface of metropolitan discourses, field encounters, and local agency in the representation and classification of indigenous Oceanian people. She is the author of *Across the Great Divide: Journeys in History and Anthropology* (1998); editor of *Women's Groups and Everyday Modernity in Melanesia* (2003); and co-editor of *Tattoo: Bodies, Art and Exchange in the Pacific and the West* (2005) and *Foreign Bodies: Oceania and the Science of Race 1750–1940* (2008).

Margaret Jolly is Professor and Head of the Gender Relations Centre in the Research School of Pacific and Asian Studies, College of Asia and the Pacific at The Australian National University. Her work has focused on gender and sexuality across the Pacific, in the context of exploratory voyages, Christianity, the politics of tradition, nationalisms and feminisms and visual anthropology. Her major books include *Women of the Place* (Harwood 1994), *Sites of Desire, Economies of Pleasure* (Chicago 1997, with Lenore Manderson), *Maternities and Modernities* (Cambridge 1998) and *Borders of Being* (Michigan 2001, both with Kalpana Ram). Recently she published *Re-membering Oceanic Masculinities* for *The Journal of the Contemporary Pacific* (January 2008) and papers on the politics of commemorating "discoverers" like Quirós and Cook. She has been a Visiting Professor at the University of Hawai`i at Mānoa (1998), École des Hautes Études en Sciences Sociales (EHESS), Paris (2001, 2009), Centre de Recherche et de Documentation sur l'Océanie/Centre of Research and Documentation for Oceania (CREDO), Marseilles (2001, 2008–09), and the University of California at Santa Cruz (2001–02).

Pierre Lemonnier is a Director of research at the National Centre of Scientific Research (Centre National de la Recherche Scientifique, CNRS) at the Centre of Research and Documentation on Oceania/Centre de Recherches et de Documentation sur l'Océanie (CREDO, Marseilles) and he teaches at the University of Provence. After having conducted repeated field research among the various Anga groups of Papua New Guinea, he chose an Ankave valley for long-term anthropological fieldwork where he regularly returns. He has published books on the anthropology of technology including *Elements for an Anthropology of Technology* (1992) and *Technological Choices* (1993); and has also published on the anthropology of Papua New Guinea including *Guerres et festins* (1990); *Le sabbat des lucioles* (2006); and with Pascale Bonnemère, *Drumming to Forget: Ordinary Life and Ceremonies among a Papua New Guinea Group of Forest-Dwellers* (2007).

Isabelle Merle, historian and member of the French National Centre for Scientific Research (Centre National de la Recherche Scientifique, CNRS, IRIS, Paris), is a specialist in Pacific History and has worked intensively on British and French colonial history in the Pacific since the 1990s, especially regarding Australia, New Zealand, New Caledonia and French Polynesia. *Experiences coloniales. La Nouvelle Calédonie. 1853–1920* (Paris, Belin, 1995), her published PhD, focused on the "fabric" of the French settler society in New Caledonia in the nineteenth century and first part of the twentieth century. She then turned her attention to a comparative exploration of indigenous status and conditions across Australia, New Zealand, New Caledonia, and French Polynesia, focusing on land problems, legal status and derogatory regimes (such as the *Regime de l'indigénat* in French colonial contexts). In 2006, she introduced and published in French the two volumes of Watkin Tench's Australian experiences: *Botany Bay. La fondation de l'Australie coloniale* (Anacharsis, Marseilles). In collaboration with Eric Wittersheim, Merle is currently writing a volume for a world collection published by the German Publisher, Fisher World History entitled, *Australia, New Zealand and Oceania*.

Mark S. Mosko is Professor of Anthropology in the Research School of Pacific and Asian Studies at The Australian National University. Over the last thirty-five years, he has conducted four years of ethnographic research among the North Mekeo peoples of the Central Province of Papua New Guinea. He is author of *Quadripartite Structures: Categories, Relations and Homologies in Bush Mekeo Culture* (Cambridge UP, 1985) and numerous journal articles and chapters exploring North Mekeo symbolism, ritual and religion, social organisation, chiefly leadership, personhood, gift exchange, and change. He is co-editor (with Fred Damon) of *On the Order of Chaos: Social Anthropology and the Science of Chaos* (Berghahn 2005). His most recent volume, *Gifts that Change: Personal Partibility, Agency and Christianity in a Changing Melanesian Society* (Berghahn, forthcoming) adapts recent theoretical developments in the ethnography of Melanesian sociality to the analysis of historical transformation.

Serge Tcherkézoff is Professor of Anthropology at École des Hautes Études en Sciences Sociales (EHESS) of Paris-Marseilles (the French Institute of Advanced Studies in Social Sciences). He has co-founded, with Maurice Godelier and Pierre Lemonnier, the Centre of Research and Documentation for Oceania/Centre de Recherche et de Documentation sur l'Océanie (CREDO), organised by the National Centre of Scientific Research (Centre National de la Recherche Scientifique, CNRS), EHESS, and University of Provence. After working on African ethnography in the 1970s, he has been engaged in fieldwork in Polynesia from the early 1980s. Besides his publications on the theory of anthropology and holism since the early 1980s, and on the transformations of Samoan society in the 1980–90s, his more recent books bring together the results of his field studies and an ethnohistorical critique of European narratives about early encounters in Polynesia.

Darrell Tryon is Emeritus Professor of Linguistics in the Research School of Pacific and Asian Studies, ANU College of Asia and the Pacific, at The Australian National University. He has published extensively on the languages and sociolinguistics of the region, including his *Comparative Austronesian Dictionary* (1995), *Atlas of Languages of Intercultural Communication* (1997) (with Stephen Wurm & Peter Mühlhäusler) and *Pacific Pidgins and Creoles* (2004) (with Jean-Michel Charpentier).

List of Figures and Tables

Front Cover

"A watery shot of the island of Ambae under cloud and sunburst." Photograph by John Patrick Taylor. Reproduced with kind permission of the photographer.

Figures

Figure 1.1	Map of *Terra Australis Incognita (Polus Antarcticus)*. Amsterdam: De Wit, 1666
Figure 1.2	Man of the Island of Mallicollo by William Hodges, first version
Figure 1.3	Man of the Island of Mallicollo, final version, engraving by J. Caldwall after William Hodges
Figure 1.4	Map of *Océanie* by Levasseur after d'Urville's ethnic divisions. *Océanie,* map attribution to Emile Levasseur, from *Atlas universel de géographie physique* (Paris: 1854)
Figure 2.1	Australia and the Pacific, showing conventional contemporary divisions of Micronesia, Melanesia and Polynesia
Figure 2.2	Recorded South Pacific voyages 1788–1840
Figure 2.3	Languages of the Eastern Outer Islands
Figure 2.4	Trade networks in the Santa Cruz Island group
Figure 3.1	Map of Vanuatu
Figure 3.2	Detail from "New Hebrides, Banks and Duff Groups, showing Discoveries of Quiros in 1606"
Figure 3.3	The Site of La Nueba Hierusalem and the Bay of San Felipe y Santiago. Detail from *"Planos de las Bahías descubiertas el año de 1606, en las islas del Espíritu Santo y de Nueva Guinea y Dibujadas por D. Diego de Prado y Tovar en Igual Fecha"* (Soc. Georgr. De Madrid, 1878)
Figure 3.4	"Modern time/space: distancing" – Fabian's Plotting of the Other in the Pre-Modern and Modern Periods
Figure 3.5	Bougainville's Tracks in 1768
Figure 3.6	Pandanus red textile from Ambae, plaited and dyed by women but worn by men ("Men's mat *singo tuvegi*, Ambae, Vanuatu")
Figure 3.7	The tracks of the *Resolution* and *Adventure* on Cook's Second Voyage, 1774 ("Vanuatu/New Hebrides Islands, showing Cook's track in 1774")
Figure 3.8	"Woman of the Island of Tanna, drawn from Nature by William Hodges, engraved by James Basire" (likely William Blake in Basire's studio).
Figure 3.9	"Omai. Drawn from Nature by William Hodges, engraved by James Caldwall". London: Wm. Strahan & Thos. Cadell, 1777
Figure 3.10	The late Bong or Bumangari Kaon of Bunlap in the 1970s

Figure 6.1	Map of d'Entrecasteaux's voyage, 1791–4
Figure 6.2	*"Sauvage des îles de l'Amirauté"* (engraving)
Figure 6.3	*"Homme du Cap de Diemen; Finau, chef des guerriers de Tongatabu"* (engraving)
Figure 6.4	*"Sauvage de la Nouvelle-Calédonie lançant une zagaie"* (engraving)
Figure 8.1	Map of Papua or New Guinea
Figure 8.2	Detail from "Sketch Map of a Journey across the Island of Papua by J.A. Lawson"
Figure 8.3	"Mount Hercules"
Figure 10.1	The Anga groups in Papua New Guinea
Figure 10.2	The Ankave country

Tables

Table 2.1	Oceanic indigenous languages
Table 2.2	Eleven languages of the Santa Cruz Group
Table 2.3	Example possessive noun classes for "Papuan" languages *Nendö* and *Äiwoo*
Table 2.4	Sample of Polynesian borrowings into the non-Polynesian languages of the Santa Cruz Group
Table 2.5	Queensland plantation labour 1863–1906
Table 10.1	Administrative patrols in or around Ankave country (1929–1972)

List of abbreviations and acronyms

ANU	The Australian National University
ASAO	Association for Social Anthropology in Oceania
CAP	College of Asia and the Pacific
CORAIL	Coordination pour l'Océanie des Recherches sur les Arts, les Idées et les Littératures
CNRS	Centre National de la Recherche Scientifique
CRA	Conzinc Riotinto of Australia
CREDO	Centre de Recherche et de Documentation sur l'Océanie
EHESS	École des Hautes Études en Sciences Sociales
IRIS	Institut de recherche interdisciplinaire sur les enjeux sociaux
LMS	London Missionary Society
MSC	Missionaries of the Sacred Heart
MSH	Maison des sciences de l'homme
ORSTOM	Office de la Recherche Scientifique et Technique d'Outre-Mer
PICS	Programme International de Coopération Scientifique
PNG	Papua New Guinea
PNGNA	Papua New Guinea National Archives
RNB	Retrospective National Bibliography of Australia
RSPAS	Research School of Pacific and Asian Studies
SELAF	Société des Études Linguistiques et Anthropologiques de France
SHM	Sacred Heart Mission
UNESCO	United Nations Educational, Scientific and Cultural Organization

Chapter 1

Oceanic Encounters: A Prelude

Margaret Jolly and Serge Tcherkézoff

This volume explores encounters, those encounters between indigenous peoples of the Pacific and foreigners during that *longue durée* of exploration, colonisation and settlement, from the sixteenth century to the twentieth century. By highlighting the idea of encounter we hope to stress the mutuality inherent in such meetings of bodies, and of minds. This is not to say that such encounters were moments of easy understanding or pacific exchanges. As many of the chapters in this volume attest, such encounters, from Quirós' sojourn in Espiritu Santo in 1606 (see Jolly 2007) to Australian patrols in the Highlands of Papua New Guinea from the late 1920s, were often occasions of tumultuous misunderstanding and extreme violence. But, even in the midst of massacre and revenge, there was a meeting of meanings, of bodies and minds, whereby pre-existing understandings, preconceptions from both sides of the encounter, were engaged, brought into confrontation and dialogue, mutual influence and ultimately mutual transformation. We thus prefer the notion of "encounter" to the more common sobriquet – "first contact" – for several reasons (see Connolly and Anderson 1987; Schieffelin and Crittenden 1991; and compare Ballard 2003 [1992]).

Prior Indigenous Encounters: Language, Culture and Power

Firstly, the idea of "first contact" privileges the meeting of Pacific peoples and Europeans, by perceiving these as unprecedented, as "first." This risks occluding all previous cross-cultural encounters between Pacific peoples such as those between Papuan- and Austronesian-speaking peoples or between Fijians and Tongans. As Tryon (this volume) stresses, the past and present patterning of Pacific languages suggests a long history of intensive contact in trade and exchange between Pacific peoples and through the complex processes of indigenous migration and settlement. Such enduring contacts over many millennia brought Pacific peoples speaking very different languages into conversation.

Especially notable here was the contact between the speakers of Papuan and Austronesian languages. As Tryon (this volume) observes, Papuan languages are thought to be ancient: archaeological evidence of Papuan-speaking peoples is dated to 50,000 BP in the interior of Papua New Guinea (PNG); 30,000 in New

Ireland; and 20,000 in Bougainville. Austronesian-speaking peoples by contrast migrated from Taiwan or southern China only about 6,000 years ago, were in New Britain and New Ireland about 4,000 years ago and subsequently dispersed across the islands of Melanesia, Polynesia and Micronesia (see Spriggs 1997). Although clearly two distinct language families, Tryon stresses the pivotal importance of encounters between the people speaking these separate languages, and in that process their mutual influence and transformation, in both vocabulary and grammar. He cites a good instance of this from the Santa Cruz archipelago of the Solomon Islands, where three Papuan and eight Austronesian languages still coexist and where language contact has induced some striking symbioses in grammar. So, the languages Nendö and Äiwoo retained a typically Papuan verb morphology but adopted the four possessive noun classes which characterise Austronesian languages in Island Melanesia. Similar patterns are clear in the way in which Polynesian Outlier languages in the Solomons and Vanuatu have mutually influenced proximate Melanesian languages.

Such examples of indigenous linguistic encounters raise a key conceptual theme for all cross-cultural encounters: they can generate not just superficial exchanges of meanings, manifest in loan words, but deep transformations in the grammar of understanding the world. So, Tryon (this volume) adjudges that it is hard to confidently classify Äiwoo and Nendö as either Papuan or Austronesian. Thus, the mutual influence and imbrication born of encounter can be so profound that it is impossible to disentangle the pre-existing elements as indubitably one or the other. This linguistic process mirrors broader processes of cross-cultural encounter and exchange, described through concepts such as creolisation, syncretism and hybridisation.

In the process of such indigenous linguistic and cultural encounters, as in later colonial encounters, power was crucial. This is graphically illustrated in another example alluded to by Tryon: the encounter between Fijians and Tongans in the course of trade, cultural exchange and colonisation. Geraghty (1983) has discerned a simplified register of Fijian, "foreigner-talk" used to trade with Tongan neighbours to the east. These trade contacts combined with increasing cultural exchange and patterns of marital alliance. But these Tongan traders/neighbours were also colonists. Tongan chiefs, like Ma`afu, extended the range of their influence to the eastern islands of the Fiji group (Spurway 2001) and, in the process, transformed the indigenous chiefly hierarchy, being later recognised by the British as having legitimate sovereignty in this region.

Such earlier encounters between the indigenous peoples of the Pacific in the context of trade, exchange and settlement were perhaps formative in how later strangers or foreigners were perceived and dealt with, although there is much debate as to whether Europeans were perceived as living humans, divine beings, demonic ancestral spirits or simultaneously all three (see Ballard 2003 [1992];

Borofsky 2000; Connolly and Anderson 1987; Jolly 1992a; Sahlins 1985, 1995; Salmond 1991, 1998, 2003; Schieffelin and Crittenden 1991; Tcherkézoff 2004a; 2004b). We consider this debate below.

Before the Brush of Bodies – European Visions

This leads into the second problem we highlight in the concept of "first contact," namely that, by focusing on physical contact as the critical originary moment, we can forget all those imaginative and mediated encounters which preceded the brush of bodies. There has been much written on "European vision" apropos the way in which the Pacific was imagined prior to and during the first European voyages of exploration. As Douaire-Marsaudon (this volume) expresses it: the islands of the South Seas were "invented" before they were "discovered"[1] by Europeans. Cartographies of the fifteenth and sixteenth century not only envision a great south land, the perduring Terra Australis of European imagination, but a variety of monstrous forms, hybrids of people and beasts (see Hodgen 1964; Smith 1992; Spate 1979).

Figure 1.1. Map of "Terra Australis Incognita (Polus Antarcticus)." Amsterdam: De Wit, 1666.

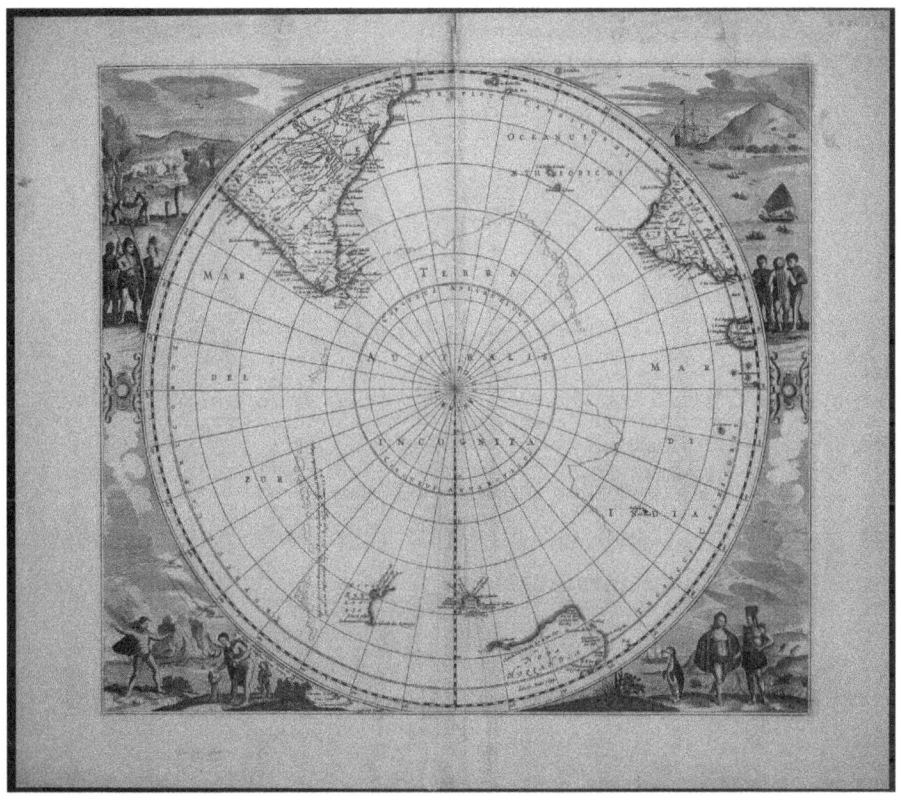

Reproduced with permission of the National Library of Australia, Canberra – nla.map-nk2456-13-v.

The Dutch and Hispanic voyagers who traversed the Pacific Ocean during the sixteenth and seventeenth centuries had to confront and reconcile the distance between their imaginary cartographies and the actual island archipelagoes they encountered, as was evidenced by the continuing debates which raged about the size, location and indeed the very existence of the great south land. It has been argued, particularly for the Hispanic voyages of this period, that the simultaneous fervour about finding gold and saving souls so saturates the records, that it imparts to them a rather hallucinatory, dream-like quality (Greenblatt 1991; Spate 1979). Still, as Margaret Jolly (this volume) suggests, this Anglophonic reading of the Hispanic period is questionable (see also Luque and Mondragón 2005). For instance, in the texts and maps of Quirós' voyage in 1606, rather than an exoticist distantiation, we can perceive precipitate attempts at incorporation of these new lands and peoples. The very naming of the island of Terra Austrialia del Espiritu Santo (in the archipelago now called Vanuatu), suggests its rapid absorption into a Christian imaginary, an absorption amplified by the naming of the European settlement La Nueba Hierusalem (New Jerusalem) and the contiguous river Jordan (see figure 3.3). A similar process of peremptory incorporation pertains to relations with indigenous peoples: they are perceived not so much as distant others but as lost souls who must be saved by the hybrid rituals of salvation and conquest.

Fictional narratives such as Robinson Crusoe (Defoe 1859 [1719]) drew on such knowledges of "real" voyages, to plot novel encounters with Pacific places and peoples, and powerfully moulded Western preconceptions (see Lamb 2001). So Daniel Defoe was inspired by the voyage narratives of William Dampier (1967 [1709]) and the story of Alexander Selkirk, the marooned sailor (1712). As Chris Ballard (this volume) argues, travel narratives, such as Robinson Crusoe, with its compelling conjunction of shipwreck realism and redemptive allegory, were immensely influential, spawning future generations of creative fictions (witnessed in the genre of Robinsonades) and often proving more popular with readers than the narratives of real voyages. Moreover, later narrators of real voyages were in turn influenced by these travel fictions; their narrative conventions and rhetorical devices converged, even as the real world travellers were insisting that their works were not fictions, but rather derived from the painful and arduous processes of "being there" and their careful, disciplined acts of exploration and observation (see, for instance, Johann Reinhold Forster's critiques of metropolitan theorists in his *Observations* (1996 [1778]).

So, from the late eighteenth century, fantastic visions of the medieval and Renaissance epochs were slowly changing in response to the secular sciences of the Enlightenment with their stress on observation, and on the centrality of embodied experience in uncovering the truth of "the other." Such narratives value the I/eye witness and through their use of the genre of the diary or journal, and detailed description of places, peoples and things, stress their critical distance from the "closet speculations" of metropolitan savants. So, in her consideration of Watkin Tench's famous narrative of the settlement at Port Jackson in 1788 (now Sydney), Merle demonstrates how Tench (1789) creates "reality effects" by writing an "as if" journal and by melding depictions of events to which he was an eyewitness, with those to which he was not (see Merle, this volume). Although these are distinguished between an "I" and a "we" in the voice of the author, they alike stress the central value of embodied experience and witness in what Dening (1998) has called "the season of observing."

These values were also central to the changing genres of visual representation, in landscapes, views and portraiture, in which, as Bernard Smith (1985 [1960], 1992; Joppien and Smith 1985, 1988) suggests, neoclassical modes were increasingly challenged by the values of naturalism, realism and ethnographic fidelity (see also Douglas, this volume). So, in the representation of Oceanic peoples, there were passionate debates as to whether portraits were faithful. The case of the *Man of the Island of Mallicollo* is one famous example (see Joppien and Smith 1985, ii: 87–92; Jolly 1992a). The original, "drawn from nature" by William Hodges, presents a man with a bare torso with an arm band and a bracelet holding a bow and arrow (see figure 1.2). In several textual accounts from Cook's second voyage we are told that Malakulan men wear a large pandanus sheath covering their penes (*nambas* in Bislama), the ends of which are tucked up in a bark belt. Rev Canon Douglas' sanitised edition of Cook's journal of the second voyage alludes to this rather as a "wrapper." Perhaps simultaneously responding to this textual euphemism and to the prevailing neoclassical modes of representing the tapa robes of Polynesian peoples as togas, the final version of the engraving by Caldwall depicts the man wearing another kind of "wrapper": a *tapa toga* enveloping his robust chest (see figure 1.3). Both Forsters, Johann and Georg (the father and son naturalists on Cook's second voyage), fiercely criticised such lack of fidelity in this portrait and many other portraits and landscapes (but see Jolly 1992a, 347–8).

Oceanic Encounters

Figure 1.2. Man of the Island of Mallicollo, William Hodges, first version.

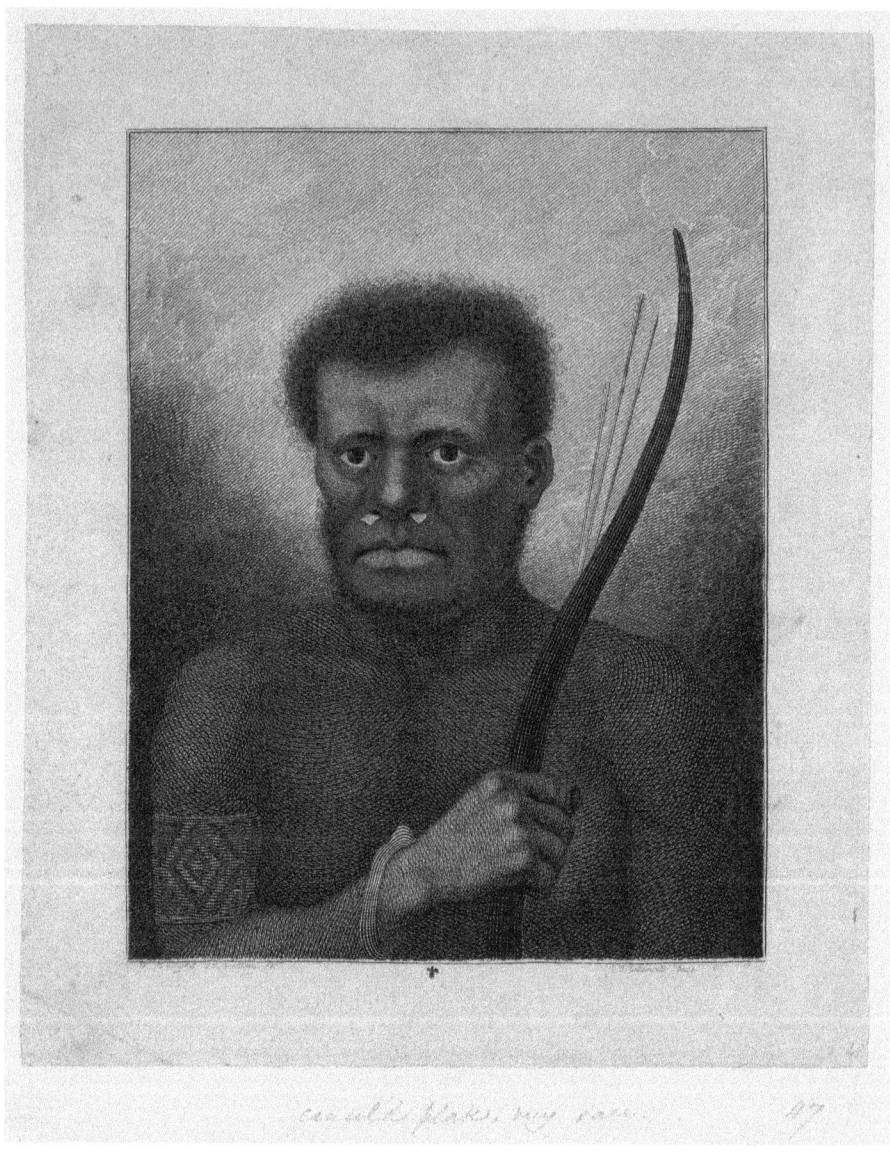

From *Three voyages round the world, being a complete set of plates of the three voyages* ... Engraved by Francesco Bartolozzi. Reproduced with permission of the Mitchell Library, State Library of NSW [PXD 59/1].

Figure 1.3. Man of the Island of Mallicollo, final version, engraving by J. Caldwall after William Hodges.

From *Three voyages round the world, being a complete set of plates of the three voyages* ... Reproduced with permission of the Mitchell Library, State Library of NSW [PXD 59/1].

And so the question becomes whether, from the late eighteenth century, influenced by the values of an empirical science, European visions were more open to transformation through Oceanic experience than they were in previous periods. Following the early lead of Smith (1985 [1960]), Douglas stresses the "mobile dialectic of discourse and experiences" in her reading of the voyages of d'Entrecasteaux (1791–94) and suggests that it was not so much prejudicial preconception as the contingent experiences of encounter which shaped the diverse but differential assessments of the peoples of the Admiralty Islands, Van Diemen's Land, Tonga and New Caledonia on that voyage. Rather than a racial plot which anticipated a clear path to Dumont d'Urville's invidious contrast between Melanesians and Polynesians (1832, 3, 19), she stresses the volatility and fluidity of the notions of "variety" or "nation" (see Jolly 1992a on the Forsters; and Douglas 2003, 2005, 2006). Moreover, she argues that voyage narratives and images often linked a pacific reception by indigenous peoples with good character and good looks, and a hostile, intransigent reception with wickedness and unappealing appearance. So, in some accounts of this voyage, a contrast emerges between the good and simple Tasmanians, and the cunning and treacherous Tongans, which owes more to the contingencies of encounter than any proto-evolutionary presumption about a hierarchy of "races" or "nations." While acknowledging the ethnocentricism of Enlightenment representations, Douglas contends that references to skin colour, hair and physiognomy are circumstantial and shifty, compared to the "complacent, racially-based assumption of European superiority evident in the nineteenth-century equation" (this volume). This, then, poses the question as to whether rigid racial discourse and prejudicial presumption prevailed over the experiences of actual encounters in later epochs of settlement and thoroughgoing colonisation in the nineteenth and twentieth centuries (see Stepan 1982; Douglas 1999a, 2005, 2006, 2008, and this volume). Perhaps, as with Anglophonic assessments of earlier Hispanic voyages, we should be wary of ever imputing a closed discourse, which is impervious to experience.

Metropolitan imaginaries and Oceanic experiences were surely always in dialectical relations of mutual influence, and the borders of European fictional fantasies and factual accounts were permeable. So, Chris Ballard (this volume) attests to how late nineteenth- century imaginary explorations of the interior of New Guinea preceded physical exploration. The fictional accounts of Lawson (1875) and Trégance (1892 [1876]) transposed the tropes of colonial travel narratives in Africa to this new locale: imagining fabulous mountains, extensive lakes and exotic communities in hidden valleys, enriched by veins of gold. So, Trégance evokes an "ecological potpourri" of American, Asian and African fauna: tigers, elks, antelopes, buffalo, bison, striped ponies and eagles flying amongst New Guinea's real "birds of paradise." The interior peoples he encounters, the "Orangwŏks" are shorter, fairer and more civilised than the more boisterous and blacker Papuans of the coast. Their golden armour protects an inner kingdom with rich but badly managed goldmines. Trégance as hero combines mining acumen and Christian zeal, but also embodies what Ballard (this volume) sees as the preferred protagonist of the period: the explorer-scientist.

Ballard contrasts the naïve form of verisimilitude in Trégance (illustrated in Trégance's map, see figure 8.1) with the fully blown claims to veracity in Lawson's account. In *Wanderings in the Interior of New Guinea* (1875) he finds "parodic" precision, a sustained satire of the conventions of verisimilitude found in the textual narratives and maps of real explorers. His ascent of Mount Hercules, his traversing of savannah plains, his crossing of Lake Alexandrina, his sporadic but violent contacts with Papuans, are all evoked in the cool, remote language of the scientist. Unlike Wallace's Papuans, his Papuans are described as squat and "yellowish," with monkeyish manners and polygamous marriage preferences. They trade with Malay and Chinese and speak a language of Asian origin but, although still respectful of the elderly, have been corrupted and oppressed by the Dutch.

These late nineteenth-century fictions with their exoticist spatial and racial plots proved popular but were vituperated by contemporary reviewers as fraudulent exploitations and subversions of the hard work of serious explorers. So, Captain Moresby, recently returned from his own surveying on the southeast coast of New Guinea in 1875, wrote a long letter to the *Athenæum*, where he "laboured, point by point and page by page, through the least plausible of Lawson's claims" (Ballard, this volume). But, Ballard adjudges, Moresby plummeted into Lawson's trap. Lawson's narrative in its minute detail, restraint and bluff, plain prose mimics the rhetoric and the assumed authority of real travellers, and satirises their pretensions and, indeed, all the gentlemen of the learned societies. And, as in earlier epochs of exploration, such persuasive fictions mould the narratives of the real world travellers, they "play off and plagiarise each other" (Ballard, this volume). As both Ballard and Mosko (this volume) attest, the stories of "real travellers," like the naturalist d'Albertis, Captain Moresby and the Assistant Resident Magistrate Monckton, were indebted to this earlier generation of imaginary explorers. Thus, we may conclude with Ballard that "a diffuse but all-pervasive colonial imaginary draws its strength from the permeability of the boundaries between fictional and factual writing" (Ballard, this volume).

Oceanic Visions

But, there were not just "European visions" and colonial imaginaries but "Oceanic visions" and indigenous imaginaries brought to such early encounters. And we can surely discern similar dialectical processes in the relations of cosmological preconception and the unfolding events of successive encounters from the perspective of Pacific peoples. So Marshall Sahlins (1981, 1982, 1985, 1989, 1995) has argued, in a series of influential, magisterial works, that we have to consider voyage narratives not as fabulations or imperialist imaginaries, but offering "truths" about the actual events of encounters, and affording insights not just about how foreigners saw and related to Oceanic peoples, but about how Oceanic peoples saw and related to strangers. Contemporaneous voyage narratives can moreover be juxtaposed with indigenous oral traditions (as transmuted into texts by later indigenous authors, missionaries or anthropologists). So, on the basis of Hawaiian oral traditions and nineteenth-century Hawaiian texts as much as the European archive, Sahlins consistently and ever more trenchantly insisted that Cook was seen by Hawaiians as a manifestation of the god Lono. This interpretation has, of course, been hotly disputed by Obeyesekere and others (Obeyesekere 1992; Bergendorff et al. 1988; and see Borofsky 1997 for a review of the debate).

But, as Tcherkézoff (2004b, ch. 9) has demonstrated, that protracted debate has been predicated on mistranslations and misconceptions. The division between humans and gods, fundamental to Judeo-Christian religion is, he argues, inappropriate to the holistic ontology of ancestral Polynesian cosmology. Obeyesekere (1992) had taken Sahlins too literally, as if Hawaiians had equated Cook the man with the god Lono, whereas what Sahlins had rather attempted to show was how Cook had been incorporated as but one manifestation of the divine principle of Lono, a partial and visible manifestation, alongside many other evanescent material embodiments which Hawaiians already deployed in the annual rituals of the Makahiki (Tcherkézoff 2004b, 124–8, 134–9).

The consequences of so incorporating strangers into indigenous cosmologies had real world effects. At its most obvious, the Hawaiian perception that Cook was an embodiment of Lono, and his return at an inauspicious moment in their annual ritual cycle, led ultimately to his death. But, Sahlins has argued for a more generalised model of how foreign powers were mediated and incorporated, and became crucial to indigenous transformations of the socio-political configurations of the "people of the place." So, he earlier suggested (Sahlins 1985) that congress between European men and Hawaiian women, at the table rather than in bed, was crucial to the disruption of *kapu*, and especially those *kapu* that forbade certain foods to women and enshrined the commensal segregation of men and women. Successive waves of Christian conversion across the Pacific have been seen by Sahlins and many others as the appropriation and indigenisation of sacred powers which first came from "beyond the horizon" (see Jolly 2005a; cf. Robbins 2004).

But can we transpose Sahlins' arguments about Hawai`i and Fiji to other parts of the Pacific? Were foreigners always seen as embodiments of divine or dangerous forces, if not deified like Lono, then perceived as more modest "ancestral spirits," "ghosts" or "goblins," which is how the Maori first perceived the Dutch, according to Salmond (1991, 87–8). We hope to suggest the risks of undue extrapolation from experiences in Hawai`i or New Zealand to other Oceanic sites, such as Samoa (Tcherkézoff, this volume), Papua New Guinea (Bonnemère and Lemonnier, and Mosko, this volume) and Vanuatu. So, Jolly (this volume) queries Salmond's confident claim that the people of the archipelago Cook called the New Hebrides (now Vanuatu) so certainly identified Cook and his men as "the ghosts of their forebears and approached them with caution, for such spirits could be malevolent" (Salmond 2003, 265). She suggests that the linguistic and ethnographic evidence is far more uncertain than Salmond allows, and that the word *tomarr* she translates as "ancestor" or "ghost" might equally be the word for peace.

Double Visions and Alternative Senses

Can we, then, combine a European vision with an Oceanic vision to generate the sharpness, stereoscopy, depth of perspective and three-dimensionality appropriate to looking with both eyes, from both sides? Or will this "double vision" generate the other meaning of that term: a visual disturbance, a blurring of view with the haunting spectre of one eye's vision hanging in a visual field remote from the other? There has been a tremendous stress on vision in cross-cultural encounters in the Pacific from the earliest works of Bernard Smith (1985 [1960]) to those writings of postcolonial theorists preoccupied with the gaze, and others who privilege the visual arts in the histories of such encounters. There is no doubt that vision is a crucial sensibility and that visual materials from both sides of encounters need to be considered alongside words both written and spoken. But, as has been often alleged, vision, the privileged Western sense, is intimately linked to power and control, most notably in those analyses of colonial power, inspired by Foucault, that see the power of the panopticon of Western asylums transplanted into the architectonics of colonial space (Mitchell 1988) and textual and visual encyclopedia of races or castes (see Pinney 1992). Those who have critiqued the more facile uses of theories of the colonial gaze (e.g. Kelly 1997) have often queried an undue or anachronistic association between looking and power, or have insisted on the process of "looking back" or returning the gaze (see Jolly and Manderson 1997, 1–26; Jolly 1997b).

And there may be a larger cross-cultural problem here. The European stress on the visible and the controllable is dramatically at odds with dominant Oceanic philosophies which perceive the visible as but one manifestation, materialisation or embodiment of invisible and ultimately uncontrollable forces (see Thomas 1995 on this, in the context of Oceanic art). So, Tcherkézoff (2004b) argues in his review of the debate between Sahlins and Obeyesekere apropos ancient Hawaiians' perceptions of Cook that there has been a constant mis-recognition even by anthropologists and linguists of the way in which human beings and material images (*ata*) of gods (*atua*), although in a sense themselves *atua*, "remain partial and temporary manifestations of the *atua*-as-a-principle" (2004a, 6). Thus, despite the Polynesian celebration of the world of light and form over the realm of darkness and chaos, the truth of the visible can be eclipsed by powerful invisible forces, divine creative and destructive principles. But for Europeans, from the eighteenth century onward, the visible was increasingly becoming linked to the power of the real.

Given this problem of divergent philosophies and values of vision, might we explore other senses in the process of encounter? The trope of "first contact" highlights touch, the brush of bodies. John Kelly (1997) in his analysis of the sexualised violence which Indo-Fijian women experienced at the hands of Europeans and Australians stressed the importance of "grasping" rather than gazing. And more recently, in relation to the global connections of the present, Anna Tsing (2005) has used the metaphor of friction to convey the "grip" of cross-cultural encounters, presumably more mutual and less violent than a "grasp" and suggestive of both attraction and repulsion, of connection and of difference.

The brush of bodies, violent and sensual, is a crucial dimension of most of the encounters we explore. And, as well as looking and touching, there are those other senses which move between and beyond bodies: the oral/aural, the kinesthetic and the senses of taste and smell, often diminished in Western sensoria. The oral/aural perhaps moves encounters away from the distance implicit in "looking" – and especially "gazing" – to listening and speaking, to the processes of faltering translation in understanding speech, music and song.

The narratives of early Enlightenment voyages evince a keen interest in trying to learn the languages of Pacific peoples. Early attempts at recording, classification and analysis, such as that by Johann Reinhold Forster in his *Observations*, laid the foundations of Oceanic linguistics (see Forster 1996 [1778]). On such voyages Tahitian guides such as Tupaia, crucial as navigators and translators in the Polynesian islands where languages were fewer and closely cognate, became far less help in understanding the diverse languages of archipelagoes like Vanuatu or New Caledonia and, of course, Australia (see Dening 2004, 171–5; Salmond 2003, 116–34, 141–5, 153–8; Thomas 1997a, 1ff.). Still, Europeans early attempted to record word lists, such as the word "*Tanna*", which they wrongly interpreted to be the specific name of this island, rather than the generic name for ground or earth (see Lindstrom 2009).[2] This island is still known by this word today. Often superficial translations of indigenous words and concepts generated confusion and conflict. So, early in the passage of European voyagers in the Polynesian part of the Pacific, they encountered a variant of the word *taio*. This was interpreted into English as "friend," but entailed much more than the European understanding of that word, since it implied a ritual closeness of identity marked by exchanging names and by free use of the others' possessions (Salmond 2003, 193–4, 198–9). So, Europeans were shocked on occasion when their *taio* took their iron tools or their cloth, thinking them no longer friends, but duplicitous, treacherous thieves.

Europeans also speculated as to the meanings of words constantly uttered in their presence and thus about indigenous perceptions of themselves (see Jolly, this volume, on *tomarr*). A common trope in the celebration of mutual understanding was the sharing of song: as in the performance of indigenous chants alongside German lieder during Cook's second voyage on Tanna, or in alternate performances of dance. Although the figure of "dancing with strangers" has been deployed by Inga Clendinnen (2003) as an icon for cross-cultural exploration in Australia, in the Pacific, dance was more often witnessed than imitated by strangers from Europe. And, as Tcherkézoff (2004a, pt 3; 2004b, ch. 10) has shown, the canonical Polynesian dances like the *hula* of Hawai`i or the *heiva* of Tahiti were wrongly perceived as lascivious or lewd. Rather, such displays of nakedness signalled respect for the strangers, catalysing and even celebrating divine unions with them to secure sacred and potent progeny.

Perhaps least explored of all have been the senses of taste and smell, which suggest the permeability of the body and, thus, the risk of cultural mixing or contagion. Europeans had, from the start, adjudged Polynesian fragrances and body oils attractive, while the same navigators had, for instance, expressed a strong disgust when they made contact with the "Patagons" (Bougainville, quoted in Tcherkézoff 2004a, ch. 7). Still, not all Polynesians were thought so alluring. So, in Georg Forster's account of meeting Maori on Cook's second voyage we find a lament about undue mixing, threatened by an unwanted "odoriferous present" of an unguent (possibly seal oil), conferred on the artist William Hodges (Forster 2000 [1777], 1: 98).[3]

The Passage of Time: Contingent Chronologies, Not Teleological Temporality

The third and final problem which we stress apropos this idea of "first contact" is the problem of temporality per se. What counts as *first*? The nature of subsequent encounters was no doubt influenced by those which came before. So, from the moment of Bougainville's "first contacts" in Tahiti, Europeans had certain preconceptions about that place, of tropical beauty and abundance and of sensuality and "sexual hospitality." It is clear that those voyagers who came later (like Cook on his second voyage) expected to find a place and a people similar to that depicted by Bougainville. But in this case the actual chronological sequence of "first contacts" proves less significant than the sequence of publications of narratives of encounters. Thus, although Wallis "discovered" Tahiti a year before Bougainville did, his narrative was published two years after Bougainville's text. What if the dominant or lasting impression for the

Tahitians was rather that generated in the first days of Wallis' sojourn, when relations were pervaded by violence and war? Indeed, it can be argued that Tahitian women were offered to Wallis and his crew precisely to placate them and to avoid further carnage (see Tcherkézoff 2004a). If Bougainville's men were presented with such sexual "offerings" in an apparently peaceful context it is certainly because Tahitian men had experienced Wallis' cannons shortly before. But Bougainville did not know this and genuinely thought that he had found a land of peace and love, a Garden of Eden that was to dominate European visions for many years (see Tcherkézoff 2004a). As Bougainville's narrative was published first, his vision set the tone for all subsequent ones and when Wallis' narrative appeared, the description of the violence at the start of his earlier visit became an aberrant anecdote, discordant with the depictions of love and peace in the second part, which echoed Bougainville.

Thus, any encounter, "first" or subsequent, moves through a dialogical process which combines preconception with interactive experience, which can confound prior expectations. As Bernard Smith (1985 [1960]) suggested long ago, his intellectual project was not primarily about the projection of European images, such as that of the "noble savage" onto Pacific peoples, but rather a process of showing how European visions changed as a result of experiences in the Pacific and Australia, how exploratory voyages proved crucial in the valorisation of a science of nature and an emergent evolutionism. And, as Tcherkézoff (2004b and this volume) argues, there can be a precipitate passage of phases, whereby the events or understandings of the first moment are confounded or betrayed in later moments, which, given the brevity of many encounters (such as La Pérouse's very brief sojourn in Samoa in December 1787), can induce a heady process of transformation in mutual perceptions. The process of encounter is then not a certain teleology determined by the logic of "first contact" but an emergent and contingent process, which unfolds through the transforming dialectic of action and interaction.

In many European accounts, such as the canonical texts of the Enlightenment period, we can distinguish between generalising typifications (which are often articulated at the moment of voyagers' leaving certain islands) and more dedicated depictions of events and interactions with local people. So, Tcherkézoff (this volume) has discerned a huge gap in the accounts of La Pérouse, between La Pérouse's authoritative summations that Samoan women were "mistresses of their own favours," freely offering sexual hospitality, and his graphic depiction in sentences immediately preceding (and in other accounts) of the forced defloration of young virgin girls in marriages with the strangers (cf. Jolly 1993, 1997a). Whether we see the latter genre of writing as more faithful to the truth of events of the encounter or more likely to yield "countersigns" of "indigenous agency" (see Douglas 2006 and this volume), there is no doubt that unfolding events were never predictable from preconception, on either side.

Thus, to continue with that *longue durée* in the history of sexual encounters in Polynesia, we can witness a transformation from such early attempts to make sacred marriages with strangers in pursuit of divine progeny to exchanges which came to resemble more closely the barter of sex for iron and cloth, the "prostitution" which Europeans wrongly perceived from the outset (see Ralston 1989; Jolly 1997a). By Tcherkézoff's account (this volume), Samoans and Tahitians did not in the very first sexual exchanges presume a return, but, since Europeans soon offered nails, beads and cloth for the "favours" of young virgin girls, they soon came to expect presents in return for what were initially "sacrifices" enjoined on these girls by their elders. No doubt the increased potency and fertility which Polynesians hoped would be the sequelae to consorting with powerful foreign men was confounded by the dreadful evidence of "the venereal," which not only brought sickness and death but which starkly reduced the reproductive capacity of women in islands across the Pacific: from Hawai`i and Tahiti to Fiji, Vanuatu, PNG and the Solomons (see Jolly 1997a; Stannard 1989; Bayliss-Smith 2005).

The Unsettled Ground of Knowing: Histories and Ethnographies

Some stories in this volume start with a consideration of those encounters between Pacific peoples that have been usually relegated to "pre-history" (but see Hau`ofa 1992; 2000 for a critique of this division between history and pre-history). We have already distilled some of Tryon's insights about the deep time of indigenous encounters, as revealed by linguists from the patterns of past and present languages or by archaeologists from traces in the ground. The deep time revealed by archaeological research can sometimes complement but sometimes confound the profundity of genealogical history recounted in the oral traditions of most Oceanic peoples (see Kame`eleihiwa 1992; and Sahlins and Kirch 1992 for Hawai`i; on the interaction between archaeological and oral historical knowledge amongst both Huli of the PNG Highlands and ni-Vanuatu, especially apropos Roi Mata, see Ballard 1995, 2006).

Most stories in this volume go back to the early appearance of European voyagers in Pacific waters. Margaret Jolly returns to the seventeenth and eighteenth centuries, comparing Quirós', Bougainville's and Cook's voyages in Vanuatu; Serge Tcherkézoff looks at some moments in the eighteenth century in the details of Bougainville and La Pérouse's encounters in Tahiti and Samoa; Isabelle Merle reads Watkin Tench's narrative of his stay at Port Jackson in 1788; Bronwen Douglas considers d'Entrecasteaux's expedition of 1791–94, examining his calls in the Admiralty Islands (PNG), Tasmania, Tonga and New Caledonia; Françoise Douaire-Marsaudon deals with "uncertain times" in Tonga, between 1796 and 1826, a period which postdates early encounters but predates missionary influence.

A trio of chapters deals with more recent moments in the nineteenth or early twentieth centuries, but, given the later arrival of Europeans, these are still early encounters for those regions. Chris Ballard considers the way in which fictional narratives by Trégance and Lawson preceded the physical exploration of PNG, by Moresby, d'Albertis and others from the 1870s. Mark Mosko takes up the story in southern PNG, where the Mekeo and Roro encountered and creatively responded to the violence of d'Albertis' and Monckton's exploratory surveys toward the end of the nineteenth century. Similarly, Pascale Bonnemère and Pierre Lemonnier juxtapose the stories of violent encounter as revealed in both oral histories and early patrol reports, between the 1920s and the 1970s, in Ankave-Anga territory, at the borders of the Eastern Highlands, Morobe and Gulf Provinces. As this period of time is much closer to the present, they were also able to record the memories of living witnesses who discovered for themselves the nature of Europeans.

Bonnemère and Lemonnier's contribution to this volume is based both on Australian government archives and remembered oral histories. It poignantly poses the question about the relation between different ways of knowing the past, and between the methods respectively privileged by history (reading the archive), and by anthropology (ethnography in the field). Are the chapters which follow only historical research, based on archives and with knowledge derived only from European texts? No, since most of the authors of this volume are also anthropologists, who derive their knowledge from ethnography as much as archives and who have spent many years living with the peoples they write about. Moreover, most authors claim that their ethnographic knowledge of contemporary Oceanic societies has enabled them to gain a better understanding of the situations alluded to in narratives generated by early European "discoverers."

The possibilities of combining archival evidence with indigenous oral history is, of course, greater when the local witnesses to events are still alive, or they remember stories as told by their parents or grandparents who were such witnesses (as in Bonnemère and Lemonnier's study of the violence of early encounters with the Ankave-Anga of the PNG Highlands). Still, even when events occurred in a past too distant for the oral testimonies of living witnesses, ethnographic and linguistic knowledge acquired more recently brings a different lens to those events, which helps to recuperate indigenous agency, even if we have to hazard speculations about past motivations and strategies. Thus, most authors aspire to a sort of "ethno-history," a history which moves dialogically between the archive and the field.

Reading "Against the Grain": Partial Truths?

Authors of this volume assume that there is a possibility to read past European narratives "against the grain" and to there discern glimpses of what the people of the place thought when they first encountered newcomers, whom they called *haole, papalagi, popa`a, waet* man or *salsaliri*.[4] If the potential of a dialogical use of later ethnography and early narratives is posited, it means that, in part, early European narratives can convey, at least sometimes, in some passages, even if in highly mediated form, indigenous insights.

This may seem a rather presumptuous or naïve assertion for two reasons. Firstly, how can we assume the possibility of interpreting what Oceanic people thought about the first Europeans and their strategies in relation to them when we are talking of the years 1606 or 1768, or even 1929? Is this not again succumbing to the Eurocentric view that exotic societies remain immobile, that their cultures are unchanging, frozen in eternal traditions (see Jolly 1992b) and that we can interpret events of the seventeenth, eighteenth or nineteenth centuries through cultural schemes elaborated from ethnographic research in the twentieth or twenty-first centuries?

The answer to this first objection is difficult and complex. Oceanic societies have doubtless always been dynamic, but the velocity of transformation and the rhythms of sociocultural change may differ by epoch and social domain (Tcherkézoff 2005). So, in the Samoan case, the study of the chiefly system suggests marked discontinuity, with major ruptures during the nineteenth century, when "chief" became gradually equivalent to "family head," during the German colonial period and then during the New Zealand mandate and, again, when chiefly suffrage was abolished in the 1990s (Tcherkézoff 2000). In contrast, Tcherkézoff contends that the material and symbolic structures of the Samoan house have remained virtually unchanged since the first European descriptions (in 1787 by La Pérouse) and the first Western graphic representations (in 1838 by Dumont d'Urville) until the 1980s at least. Thus, Tcherkézoff (this volume) felt authorised to use some contemporary clues about the house, derived from his own ethnography from the 1980s, to reinterpret one aspect of the La Pérouse narratives of the first sexual encounters with the French, as they transpired inside a Samoan house in 1787.

Moreover, sometimes, the "later ethnography" which is used to interpret voyage texts comes not from professional anthropologists but from traders, settlers or missionaries, who were resident shortly after the brief sojourns of the first "discoverers." So, in the case of Tahiti and Tonga, Morrison and Mariner were Europeans who were there for a long time, mastered the language and were integrated into local society, only a few decades after the early French or British voyagers. In the Tahitian case, the knowledge derived from Morrison's stay in 1789–91 allowed Tcherkézoff to critically evaluate assertions made by Wallis, Bougainville and Cook on their brief sojourns in 1767–69 (Tcherkézoff 2004a).

A second reason which seems to preclude the possibility of gaining any knowledge from past European narratives is of course their ideological and

Eurocentric bias. No doubt, all of them were written in the service of an authority: the Spanish court who desired to find new lands filled with gold and unsaved souls (see Jolly, this volume); the French and British navigators, naturalists and naval officers, with their "enlightened" but proto-imperialist views (see Douglas, Jolly, Merle, and Tcherkézoff, this volume); and the more overtly colonial and racist agendas of the nineteenth-century fictions and expeditions in PNG (see Ballard, Mosko, Bonnemère and Lemonnier, this volume). Does this mean that these narratives are so biased that each sentence was determined by the Eurocentric agenda of the expedition? This is more or less what Gananath Obeyesekere has implied when, discussing the topic of "cannibalism in the South Seas," he imputed (1998, 2003) that nothing factual could be sustained, since all such ethnographic information was derived from European narratives of voyagers, missionaries, administrators and, we might add, anthropologists.[5]

But, as some of the chapters of this volume demonstrate, all such narratives yield ethnographic insights, albeit episodically and even if such "descriptions" are insinuated as curiosities, as exotic interludes. Moreover, we can discriminate between genres of writing, between the official, authorised narratives written for the King, the Navy, the colonial administration, the mission congregation or a learned public and those journals written without intention of publication, sometimes as intimate notes for friends and families, which often seem less burdened by preconceived agendas and more open to unfolding and expected events. There is much that can be done by comparing different or rival narratives (see Jolly 1992a; and Jolly, this volume, on Quirós' 1606 voyage and Cook's second voyage in Vanuatu); by comparing passages within the same text (as between the generalising depiction and the narration of specific events, for instance, in La Pérouse on Samoa mentioned above and Tcherkézoff, this volume) and by comparing representations between texts and images (see Jolly 1992a; Douglas 1999a and this volume). As Tcherkézoff suggests, often the most useful passages or images are those where the author or artist admits that he (it is almost always he) does not understand what is going on, and their textual and visual authority is suffused with, or even subverted by, greater reflexivity and uncertainty.

Many chapters in this volume demonstrate the potential of reading and looking "against the grain," revealing through deconstructive exercises how "facts" are created from Oceanic experiences and how authorial positions are made authoritative. Such exercises do not entail a nihilistic rejection of the "truths" of such experiences, but the insistence on the partiality of any representation, as both incomplete and inclined to a certain view (see Thomas 1997b). The authors in this volume try to avoid the reinscription of the excessive power of Europeans by seeing Europeans as the authors of compelling illusions or mere fabulations. Such reinscriptions not only risk crediting Europeans with more power than they had but occlude the potent visions of Oceanic peoples, as Sahlins (1995) has argued so passionately in debate with Obeyesekere.

But what of Douglas' argument about "indigenous countersigns" in colonial texts and images? She elaborates an argument long ago advanced by Smith (1985 [1960]) that the events of Oceanic encounters are central to emergent and changing European representations. She argues that whether the reception of Europeans was pacific or violent was crucial in determining the positive or negative evaluation of the morality and beauty of different peoples, and that indigenous countersigns are "camouflaged" in European representations. So the resistance of Kanak to Europeans (and their alleged cannibalism) is represented in Piron's pencil drawing of "Man of Balade" and Copia's re-presentation as "Savage of New Caledonia hurling a spear" (see figure 6.4). The confrontational pose of the warrior, his penis and testicles prominently displayed, is not just a sign of individual bellicosity but, for Douglas, represents a "countersign of confrontational collective agency," surely an ideal type, though grounded in the facts of Kanak resistance. But although this was contrasted with the hospitality and sociality of the inhabitants of the "Friendly Islands" (Tonga), the open opposition of the Kanak was adjudged more favourably than the stealth and cunning of the Tongans (Douglas, this volume).

Douglas' reading of d'Entrecasteaux's voyage is almost solely derived from the primary voyage sources and contemporaneous metropolitan texts (with some allusions to later secondary sources). Unlike many other authors in this volume she does not articulate these with subsequent historical or ethnographic materials, authored by Europeans or indigenous peoples, since, as she argues, "[t]he details of indigenous motivations, the content of their strategies, the meanings of their words and actions reported in long-ago encounters with European voyagers are now difficult, if not impossible, to recover, even where rich local traditions subsist" (this volume).

Yet, other authors in this volume suggest that this task, though necessarily speculative, is not impossible, as Douglas' argument about "countersigns" here and her attempts elsewhere to recuperate the indigenous agency of Pacific women surely suggests (Douglas 1999b). Tcherkézoff's radically different reading of early sexual encounters in Samoa and Tahiti would not have been possible without the suggestive ethnographic insights of later missionaries and settlers and his own linguistic and cultural knowledge derived from decades of ethnographic research with Samoans. Moreover, it is important to stress that the difference is not just between the European archive and indigenous oral history, since from the nineteenth century, and primarily as part of the process of Christian conversion, Pacific people have also been the authors of written texts, both in Oceanic and introduced metropolitan languages. Noenoe Silva (2004) has recently rewritten the history of Hawaiian resistance to the overthrow of the monarchy in the 1890s on the basis of the rich local traditions of Hawaiian language newspapers, and Kame`eleihiwa (1992) earlier used Hawaiian language texts as well as European sources in her retelling of Hawaiian history and the dispossession of Hawaiian land.

Douaire-Marsaudon (this volume) explores the complicated ways in which Tongans embraced writing. Not only missionaries but also the beachcombers they deplored were central to the status that writing assumed. Not only the Christian message but also the medium of the Bible, written hymns and catechisms were appropriated and indigenised. Writing, with its power to communicate and control at a distance, was connected to the sacred power of the chiefs and, indeed, invested with a mystical status, as having the capacity to heal as well as reveal. Further west in the Pacific, others have observed how channelling the power of writing has been fundamental to anticolonial and millennial movements in Fiji and PNG (Kaplan 1995; Derlon 1997) and how suspicions that certain parts of texts have been withheld by Europeans or crucial documents have been lost is still a central tenet of many local movements for reparation for past colonial wrongs or restitution of imagined futures (Lattas 1998; Miyazaki 2004).

Graphic Materialities and the Violence of Exchange

In some parts of the Pacific, European writing is linguistically linked to indigenous systems of graphic representation such as sand-drawing, cats' cradle designs, tattooing and designs on textiles and pottery, many of which were also invested with sacred power (see Zagala 2002; Thomas et al. 2005). This raises the further question of how indigenous agency is not only distilled in the words of oral or textual histories but in material forms, which may prove less evanescent than the word. So, as Tcherkézoff suggests, the perduring materiality of the Samoan house and its associated symbolic logic is crucial to his interpretation of early sexual encounters of Europeans in Samoa as enforced sacrificial marriage with virgin girls (cf. Sahlins' (1976) analysis of the link between house form and hierarchy in Fiji). And, in another context, Taylor (2008) has argued for the integral connection between the "two sides" of material forms, the architectonics of the Sia Raga house and the canonical form of red pandanus textiles, with ideas of moiety divisions, of the complementary differentiation between men and women, and indigenes and Europeans.

Material exchanges between Pacific peoples and Europeans were crucial from the first moments, when food, water, wood and indigenous artifacts were exchanged for European cloth, beads, nails or iron tools, to the later patterns of commodification of Pacific products. Early and later exchanges were the origins of the huge collections of Oceanic artifacts and arts that now reside in the museums of Europe, America, Australia and New Zealand (see Jolly 2008b). And these stunning objects can communicate indigenous concepts and values; indeed, they are often celebrated as embodiments of ancestral power and as articulating the voices of the "ancestors." The selection of objects for collection was partly moulded by European perceptions and their views of particular peoples (e.g. that ni-Vanuatu were more antagonistic and martial than Tongans – as reflected in the dominance of bows and arrows and spears over textiles from these different archipelagoes in the Cook-Forster collection from Göttingen, for example; cf. Thomas 1997a, 93ff.). But indigenous agency was also crucial in determining which objects were given in exchange. Often, despite the loudest and most violent entreaties, "curiosities" desired by Europeans were not on offer. Moreover, from the earliest encounters we see Oceanic peoples desiring not just European goods (like calico and iron tools) but valued Oceanic things (see Newell 2006). So *tapa* (barkcloth) circulated around the Pacific on the boats of European navigators, whalers and traders. Polynesian barkcloth was especially sought in exchanges on the islands of Malakula and Tanna, indeed more desired than European iron tools, which Tannese, unlike Polynesians, found unappealing (Jolly 1992a). Yet, in later periods, European collecting often transformed into looting, with forceful appropriation of indigenous artifacts and local flora and fauna, often in the context of violent incursions (see Mosko, this volume).

Two chapters in this volume consummately explore the relation between European texts and indigenous oral histories, in their exploration of the violence of early encounters in PNG: Mark Mosko on the coastal Mekeo, and Pascale Bonnemère and Pierre Lemonnier on the Ankave-Anga of the Highlands. Mosko combines a meticulous rereading of the texts by the naturalist d'Albertis (1875) and the Assistant Resident Magistrate Monckton (1998), with deep insights derived from his own long-term engagement with the Mekeo. This is not to suggest a perduring, eternal tradition but, rather, a radical reconfiguration of Mekeo culture consequent on the "pacification" and depopulation that ensued from colonial control. Contrary to other accounts, which take the superior power of European firearms as brutally self-evident, Mosko reveals that Mekeo invested guns with mystical efficacy and identified such strangers with unprecedented spiritual powers akin to sorcerers. He deftly shows how both d'Albertis and Monckton intuited and exploited Mekeo beliefs in their spiritual powers, combining a circus-like showmanship with fearful snakes, threats of poisoned water, the illusory magic of false teeth and the pyrotechnics of gunpowder, with a mythopraxis they owed to Mekeo people. The decimation of indigenous people by introduced disease and firearms was seen by Mekeo as a mystical, moral contest. The dynamics of these early encounters radically transformed Mekeo culture and its hierarchies of chiefs and sorcerers in particular, but ironically also conferred on Mekeo a reputation as culturally conservative and as "traditionally preoccupied with magic and sorcery" (Mosko, this volume).

Bonnemère and Lemonnier offer an exhaustive account of the forty years of "first contacts" between Ankave-Anga and Europeans (primarily Australians) in pursuit of gold, and later government patrols conducting a census of people, establishing "law-and-order" and trying to spread the cultural influence of the administration. These patrols were sporadic and punctuated by violence from both sides. The peoples of this region, earlier labelled Kukukuku, were thought dangerous and untrustworthy (their resistance was contrasted with the hospitality and open character of other coastal peoples; cf. Douglas, this volume). In some oral histories collected by Bonnemère and Lemonnier, European violence also looms large. But in a meticulous "matching" of the successive events as recorded in European journals and patrol reports, they discern intriguing patterns in the articulation of violence in texts and in different oral accounts drawn from memory. The European accounts in general minimise violence, through keeping silent or diminishing the numbers of dead and wounded (cf. Merle, this volume, on Watkin Tench). The Ankave-Anga accounts, by contrast, differ by generation. Older women who were alive at the time of such encounters talk openly with graphic personal details about experiences of European violence, their firearms and the punitive character of many patrols. But their children who retell their mothers' stories diminish the violence and rather emphasise the goods that fell from planes in the sky: food, knives and cowrie shells. Indeed, these material exchanges were thought symptomatic of the humanity of Europeans. The authors speculate that this failure to transmit narratives of violent early encounters may have been partly due to the context of elicitation – a deference to their own being European, and even a fear of revenge. The difference between the authority of eyewitness testimonies and secondary retellings might also be crucial (see Ballard 2003 [1992]). Moreover, these later narratives more often link the violence between Ankave-Anga and police patrols to violence with their own neighbours, since outside force was often entangled with and manipulated in internal vendettas and land disputes (especially in relation to the airstrip). The more positive emphasis on material exchanges with Europeans in later narratives perhaps heralds a more welcoming attitude to modernity, although, as the authors stress at the outset, this valley is not only still exceedingly remote and difficult to access, but compared to the neighbouring Baruya, without many marks of modernity or development.

The Place and Time of Oceania

There is a vast and resonating chasm between stories of late twentieth-century encounters in the remote valleys of the New Guinea Highlands and those encounters on the voyages of Hispanic, British and French explorers of the seventeenth and eighteenth centuries with which we open this volume. The papers here collected traverse vast crossings in time and place, a vastness which we hope to echo in our use of the word "Oceanic" (see below). But given that the borders and values of this regional designation have shifted over time, we should briefly explicate our use of it. Up until the 1830s and indeed, well into the nineteenth century, the "South Seas" was the usual designation of the region we explore in this volume. The word *Oceania* derives from the French designation *Océanie*, used in the texts and accompanying maps of Dumont d'Urville (1832) and reproduced by de Rienzi (1836–37). Debate has focused on how from the 1830s, stronger distinctions were being drawn between the regions of Polynesia, Micronesia and Melanesia, and how this cartography related to the mapping of Oceanic races, of how place and race were connected. Since this is the subject of much published and forthcoming research (Clark 2003; Jolly 2007b; Tcherkézoff 2003, 2009; Thomas 1997c; Douglas and Ballard 2008) we do not elaborate on this issue here. Rather we highlight how the generic word Oceania/Océanie stressed the vastness and centrality of the ocean in this human environment.

Yet, the designation of Oceania in this period also included the large land masses of what became PNG and Australia. Melanesie in Dumont d'Urville's map did not terminate at the islands of New Caledonia or even the Torres Strait, but rather extended to include Australia (see figure 1.4). Australia was also included in the map of Océanie attributed to Levasseur (1854) in a French atlas (following Dumont d'Urville's map of 1832), which, as Thomas notes, was regularly reprinted throughout the nineteenth century (1997c, 146–7). The use of the label "Oceania" in English to include Australia and New Zealand persisted long into the twentieth century, as the naming of the Sydney-based journal *Oceania* (founded in 1930 and continuing into the twenty-first century makes clear). Up until the 1970s, collected works with titles like *Anthropology in Oceania* (e.g. Hiatt and Jayawardena 1971) typically included articles on indigenous Australians as well as the Pacific.

But another region appears on the map attributed to Levasseur – Malaisie – following again Dumont d'Urville's map of 1832, embracing the islands of what is now the Philippines, Indonesia, Malaysia and Singapore. So, as Ballard has argued elsewhere (2008), distinctions eastward between Malays and Papuans were, in the nineteenth century, perhaps equally important to the geographic and ethnological borders drawn between Melanesia, Polynesia and Micronesia. Ballard's chapter (this volume) on the relation between the fictional and physical exploration of PNG reminds us of the centrality of that Malay/Papuan contrast in the work of both the naturalist Wallace and purveyors of travel fiction.

Figure 1.4. Map of *"Océanie"* by Levasseur after d'Urville's ethnic divisions.

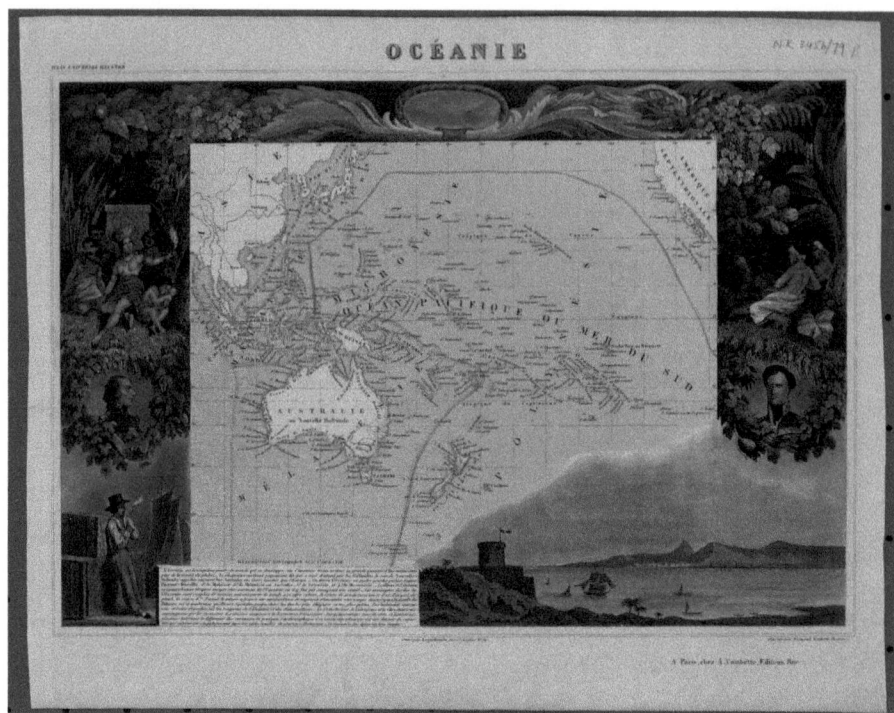

Océanie, map attribution to Emile Levasseur, from *Atlas universel de géographie physique* (Paris: 1854). Reproduced with permission of the National Library of Australia, Canberra – nla.map-nk2456-79.

Similarly two chapters in this volume (Merle on Watkin Tench; Douglas on d'Entrecasteaux) remind us that Australia was an integral part of the European vision of Oceania in both the eighteenth and nineteenth centuries. Merle observes how profoundly Tench's ethnography of the settlement of the First Fleet at Port Jackson was influenced by the genres and the rhetorical canons of observation established during Cook's three voyages of exploration. And Douglas, in tracing the narrative arc of d'Entrecasteaux's (1791–94) voyage through dissolution and disillusion, faithfully follows his itinerary from the Admiralty Islands (now in PNG), through Van Diemen's Land (now Tasmania) and Tongatapu to New Caledonia.

Other contributors use a more restricted sense of Oceanic. So, in his survey of the languages of Oceania, Tryon (this volume) includes the Papuan and Austronesian languages, pidgins and creoles and those introduced metropolitan languages like English, French, German and Hindi. He does not discuss the indigenous languages of Australia however, given their linguistic distance from those indigenous to the Pacific. Still, his map of linguistic transformations in the Pacific highlights the significance of the port of Sydney, in relation to Nouméa,

Suva and Papeete in connecting not just the exchanges of goods and people but also, of words and meanings across the Pacific.

This raises the important question of how the region of Oceania has been reimagined and revalorised in our present epoch, by processes of globalisation which are connecting Pacific island and Pacific rim, and by the critical reflections on such processes in the visionary works of the Tongan scholar Epeli Hau`ofa (1994, 1998, 2000, 2008). Hau`ofa evokes the expansive language of the ocean to oppose those discourses of both academy and policy which diminish the Pacific as a series of tiny remote islands or poor failing microstates (as in the perspective of contemporary Australian foreign policy ranged in an "arc of instability"; see Larmour 2005). In defiance of the diminution implicit in developmentalist projects or the partitions created by highlighting the differences between Melanesians, Polynesians and Micronesians, Hau`ofa stresses the connections between Pacific peoples. He deploys the ocean as both material medium of passage and metaphor, stressing the affinities between ancient canoes and jumbo jets as vessels of "world travelling" for Islanders, especially for those Polynesian and Micronesian migrants who constitute such large diaspora in the countries of the Pacific rim (see also Jolly 2001, 2005b, 2007a, 2007b, 2008a).

In conclusion, then, we want to applaud the way in which Hau`ofa has reimagined Oceania, not as a category in European thought, not as an ethnonym conferred by distant others, but as an inclusive and embracing self-identification on the part of Oceanic peoples, which stresses their relations with each other, rather than with Europeans who have been our focus here. We are intensely aware of how a constant stress on the "beach crossings" (Dening 2004) between Europeans and Pacific peoples, as narrated in this volume, can reinscribe colonial relations in the present, and perceive relations between Pacific peoples as always mediated through their connections with Europeans, rather than with each other (see Jolly 2009). This has been powerfully argued apropos the relation between Maori and Pacific Islanders in the context of the contending bicultural and multicultural values in contemporary Aotearoa New Zealand (Teresia Teaiwa and Mallon 2006). Thus we laud parallel projects (e.g. Katerina Teaiwa 2007) that rather highlight indigenous encounters and relations in the pasts, presents and futures of Oceania.

References

Ballard, Chris

1995 The death of a great land: Ritual, history and subsistence revolution in the Southern Highlands of PNG. PhD thesis, Archaeology and Natural History, The Australian National University, Canberra.

2003 [1992] First contact as non-event. Invited paper prepared for session "Early Contact in Melanesia" at the 91st Annual Meeting of the American Anthropological Association, San Francisco, 2–6 December 1992. Published in French as "La fabrique de l'histoire: événement, mémoire et récit dans les Hautes Terres de Nouvelle-Guinée [Making history: Event, memory and narrative in the New Guinea Highlands]." In *Les rivages du temps: Histoire et anthropologie du Pacifique*, eds Isabelle Merle and Michel Naepels, 111–34. Cahiers du Pacifique Sud Contemporain no. 3. Paris: L'Harmattan.

2006 The once and future chief: Roi Mata and the politics of land in central Vanuatu. Paper presented at Association for Social Anthropology in Oceania conference, San Diego, February.

2008 "Oceanic Negroes": British anthropology of Papuans, 1820–1869. In *Foreign Bodies: Oceania and the Science of Race 1750–1940*, eds Bronwen Douglas and Chris Ballard, 157–201. Canberra: ANU E-Press. http://epress.anu.edu.au/foreign_bodies_citation.html

Bayliss-Smith, Tim

2005 Fertility and depopulation: Childlessness, abortion and introduced disease in Simbo and Ontong Java, Solomon Islands. In *Population, Reproduction and Fertility in Melanesia*, ed. Stanley J. Ulijaszek, 13–52. Oxford: Berghahn Books.

Bergendorff, Steen, Ulla Hasager, and Peter Henriques

1988 Mythopraxis and history: On the interpretation of the Makahiki. *Journal of the Polynesian Society* 97 (4): 391–408.

Borofsky, Robert

1997 Cook, Lono, Obeyeskere and Sahlins. *Current Anthropology* 38: 255–65.

2000 ed., *Remembrance of Pacific Pasts: An Invitation to Remake History*. Honolulu: University of Hawai`i Press.

Clark, Geoffrey, ed.

2003 'Dumont d'Urville's Oceanic Provinces: Fundamental Precepts or Arbitrary Constructs?' *Journal of Pacific History* 38 (2). Special issue.

Clendinnen, Inga

2003 *Dancing with Strangers*. Melbourne Australia: Text Publishing.

Connolly Bob, and Robin Anderson

1987 *First Contact: New Guinea's Highlanders Encounter the Outside World*. New York: Viking.

Dampier, William

1967 [1709] *A New Voyage Round the World*, with an introduction by Sir A. Gray. Fascimile of the 1st edition. London: Argonaut Press.

Defoe, Daniel

1859 [1719] *The Adventures of Robinson Crusoe*, by Himself. London: Nelson.

Dening, Greg

1998 *Readings/Writings*. Melbourne: Melbourne University Press.

2004 *Beach Crossings: Voyaging across times, cultures and self*. Carlton, Vic.: Miegunyah Press/Melbourne University Publishing.

Derlon, Brigitte

1997 *De mémoire et d'oubli: Anthropologie des objets malanggan de Nouvelle-Irelande*. Paris: Editions de la Maison des sciences de l'homme.

Douglas, Bronwen

1999a Science and the art of representing "savages": Reading "race" in text and image in South Seas voyage literature. *History and Anthropology* 11: 157–201.

1999b Provocative readings in intransigent archives: Finding Aneityumese women. *Oceania* 70 (2): 111–29.

2003 Seaborne ethnography and the natural history of man. *The Journal of Pacific History* 38: 3–27.

2005 Notes on "race" and the biologisation of human difference. *The Journal of Pacific History* 40: 331–8.

2006 Slippery Word, Ambiguous Praxis: "Race" and Late-18th-Century Voyagers in Oceania. *The Journal of Pacific History* 41: 1–29.

2008 "*Novus Orbis Australis*": Oceania in the science of race, 1750–1850. In *Foreign Bodies: Oceania and the Science of Race 1750–1940*, eds Bronwen Douglas and Chris Ballard, 99–155. Canberra: ANU E-Press. http://epress.anu.edu.au/foreign_bodies_citation.html

Douglas, Bronwen and Chris Ballard, eds

2008 *Foreign Bodies: Oceania and the Science of Race 1750-1940*. Canberra: ANU E Press. http://epress.anu.edu.au/foreign_bodies_citation.html

Dumont d'Urville, Jules-Sébastien-César

1832 Sur les îles du Grand Océan. *Bulletin de la Société de Géographie* 17: 1–21.

Forster, Georg

1777 *A Voyage Round the World in His Britannic Majesty's Sloop* Resolution, *Commanded by Capt. James Cook, during the Years 1772, 3, 4 and 5*. London: B. White.

2000 [1777] *A Voyage Round the World by George Forster*, eds Nicholas Thomas and Oliver Berghof. 2 vols. Honolulu: University of Hawai`i Press.

Forster, Johann Reinhold

1778 *Observations Made during a Voyage Round the World on Physical Geography, Natural History and Ethic Philosophy*. London: G. Robinson.

1996 [1778] *Observations Made during a Voyage Round the World, on Physical Geography, Natural History and Ethic Philosophy*. New edition, eds Nicholas Thomas, Harriet Guest, and Michael Dettelbach; with a linguistic appendix by Karl H. Rensch. Honolulu: University of Hawai`i Press.

Geraghty, Paul

1983 *The History of the Fijian Languages*. Oceanic Linguistics Special Publication 19. Honolulu: University of Hawai`i.

Greenblatt, Stephen Jay

1991 *Marvellous Possessions: The Wonder of the New World*. Chicago: Chicago University Press.

Hiatt, Lester R., and Chandra Jayawardena, eds

1971 *Anthropology in Oceania: Essays Presented to Ian Hogbin*. Sydney: Angus and Robertson.

Hau`ofa, Epeli

1994 Our Sea of Islands. *The Contemporary Pacific* 6 (1): 148–61

1998 The Ocean in Us. *The Contemporary Pacific* 10: 391–410.

2000 Epilogue – Pasts To Remember. In *Remembrance of Pacific Pasts: An Invitation to Remake History,* ed. Robert Borofsky, 453–71. Honolulu: University of Hawai`i Press.

2008 *We Are the Ocean: Selected Works*. Honolulu: University of Hawai`i Press.

Hodgen, Margaret Trabue

1964 *Early Anthropology in the Sixteenth and Seventeenth Centuries.* Philadelphia: University of Pennsylvania Press.

Jolly, Margaret

1992a "Ill-natured comparisons": Racism and relativism in European representations of ni-Vanuatu from Cook's second voyage. In *Colonialism and Culture,* ed. Nicholas Thomas. *History and Anthropology* 5 (3–4): 331–64. Special issue.

1992b Specters of Inauthenticity. *The Contemporary Pacific* 4 (1): 49–72.

1993 Lascivious ladies, beasts of burden and voyaging voyeurs: Representations of women from Cook's voyages in the Pacific. Paper presented to 9th David Nichol Smith Memorial Seminar "Voyages and Beaches, Discovery and the Pacific 1700–1840," University of Auckland, New Zealand, August 24–28.

1997a Desire, difference and disease: Sexual and venereal exchanges on Cook's voyages in the Pacific. In *Exchanges: Cross-cultural Encounters in Australia and the Pacific,* ed. R. Gibson, 187–217. Sydney: Museum of Sydney/Historic Houses Trust of New South Wales.

1997b From Point Venus to Bali Ha`i: Eroticism and exoticism in representations of the Pacific. In *Sites of Desire, Economies of Pleasure: Sexualities in Asia and the Pacific,* eds Lenore Manderson and Margaret Jolly, 99–122, 303–6. Chicago: University of Chicago Press.

2001 On the edge? Deserts, oceans, islands. In *Native Cultural Studies in the Pacific,* eds Vicente Diaz and J. Kehaulani Kauanui. *The Contemporary Pacific* 13 (2): 417–66. Special issue.

2005a Beyond the horizon? Nationalisms, feminisms, and globalization in the Pacific. In *Outside Gods: History Making in the Pacific,* ed. Martha Kaplan. *Ethnohistory* 52 (1): 137–66. Special issue.

2005b Serene and unsettling journeys: Reflections on the Oceanic in Robin White's *Time to Go.* In *Les cultures à l'œuvre: Rencontres en art,* eds Michèle Coquet, Brigitte Derlon, and Monique Jeudy-Ballini, 273–93. Paris: Maison des sciences de l'homme/Biro éditeur.

2007a Unsettling Memories: Commemorating "Discoverers" in Australia and Vanuatu in 2006. In *Pedro Fernández de Quirós et le Vanuatu. Découverte mutuelle et historiographie d'un acte fondateur 1606,* ed. Frédéric Angleviel, 197–219. Port Vila: Groupe de Recherche sur l'Histoire Océanienne Contemporaine / Délégation de la Commission Européenne au Vanuatu / Sun Productions.

2007b Imagining Oceania: Indigenous and Foreign Representations of a Sea of Islands. *The Contemporary Pacific*, 19 (2): 508–45.

2008a The South in Southern Theory: Antipodean Reflections on the Pacific. *Australian Humanities Review* 44.
http://epress.anu.edu.au/ahr/o44/pdf/essay05.pdf

2008b Moving Objects: Reflections on Oceanic Collections. Distinguished Lecture, European Society for Oceanists Conference, Verona, Italy, 10–12 July 2008.

2009 Beyond the Beach? The limen of Oceanic pasts, presents and futures. In *Changing Contexts, Shifting Meanings*, ed. Elfriede Hermann. Honolulu: University of Hawai`i Press and Honolulu Academy of Arts, in press.

Jolly, Margaret and Lenore Manderson

2007 Introduction. In *Sites of Desire, Economies of Pleasure: Sexualities in Asia and the Pacific*, eds Lenore Manderson and Margaret Jolly, 1-26, 293-296. Chicago: University of Chicago Press.

Joppien, Rudiger, and Bernard Smith

1985 *The Art of Captain Cook's Voyages,* vols 1 and 2. London and New Haven: Yale University Press.

1988 *The Art of Captain Cook's Voyages*, vol. 3. Melbourne: Oxford University Press.

Kame`eleihiwa, Lilikala

1992 *Native Land and Foreign Desires, Pehea La E Pono Ai? How Shall We Live in Harmony?* Honolulu: Bishop Museum Press.

Kaplan, Martha

1995 *Neither Cargo nor Cult: Ritual Politics and the Colonial Imagination in Fiji.* Durham: Duke University Press.

Kelly, John D.

1997 Gaze and grasp: Plantations, desires, indentured Indians, and the colonial law in Fiji. In *Sites of Desire, Economies of Pleasure: Sexualities in Asia and the Pacific*, eds Lenore Manderson and Margaret Jolly, 72–98. Chicago: University of Chicago Press.

Lamb, Jonathan

2001 *Preserving the Self in the South Seas, 1680–1840*. Chicago: University of Chicago Press.

Larmour, Peter

2005 *Foreign Flowers: Institutional Transfer and Good Governance in the Pacific Islands*. Honolulu: University of Hawai`i Press.

Lattas, Andrew

1998 *Cultures of Secrecy: Reinventing Race in Bush Kaliai Cargo Cults*. Madison: University of Wisconsin Press.

Lawson, John A.

1875 *Wanderings in the Interior of New Guinea*. Chapman & Hall.

Lindstrom, Lamont

2009 Naming and memory on Tanna, Vanuatu. In *Changing Contexts, Shifting Meanings*, ed. Elfriede Hermann. Honolulu: University of Hawai`i Press and Honolulu Academy of Arts, in press.

Luque, Miguel, and Carlos Mondragón

2005 Faith, fidelity and fantasy: Don Pedro Fernández de Quirós and the 'foundation, government and sustenance' of *La Nueba Hierusalem* in 1606. *Journal of Pacific History* 40 (2): 133–48.

Mitchell, Timothy

1988 *Colonising Egypt*. Cambridge: Cambridge University Press.

Miyazaki, Hirokazu

2004 *The Method of Hope: Anthropology, Philosophy and Fijian Knowledge*. Stanford: Stanford University Press.

Newell, Jennifer

2006 Collecting from the collectors: Pacific Islanders and the spoils of Europe. In *Cook's Pacific Encounters: The Cook-Forster Collection of the Georg-August University of Göttingen*, 29–47. Exhibition catalogue. Canberra: National Museum of Australia.

Obeyesekere, Gananath

1992 *The Apotheosis of Captain Cook: European Mythmaking in the Pacific*. Princeton New Jersey/ Honolulu: Princeton University Press/Bishop Museum Press.

1998 Cannibal feasts in nineteenth-century Fiji: Seamen's yarns and the ethnographic imagination. In *Cannibalism and the Colonial World*, ed. F. Barker, 63–86. Cambridge: Cambridge University Press.

2003 Cannibal talk: Dialogical misunderstandings in the South Seas. Huxley Memorial Lecture, Manchester University, during Decennial Conference of the Association of Social Anthropologists

Pinney, Christopher

1992 The parallel histories of anthropology and photography; and Underneath the banyan tree: William Crooke and photographic depictions of caste. In *Anthropology and Photography, 1860–1920*, ed. Elizabeth Edwards, 74–95; 165–73. New Haven and London: Yale University Press, in association with the Royal Anthropological Institute, London.

Ralston, Caroline

1989 Changes in the lives of ordinary women in early post-contact Hawaii. In *Family and Gender in the Pacific: Domestic Contradictions and the Colonial Impact*, eds Margaret Jolly and Martha Macintyre, 45–64. Cambridge: Cambridge University Press.

Robbins, Joel

2004 *Becoming Sinners: Christianity and Moral Torment in a Papua New Guinea Society*. Berkeley: University of California Press.

Sahlins, Marshall

1976 *Culture and Practical Reason*. Chicago: Chicago University Press.

1981 *Historical Metaphors and Mythical Realities: Structure in the Early History of the Sandwich Islands Kingdom*. ASAO Special Publication 1. Ann Arbor: University of Michigan Press.

1982 The apotheosis of Captain Cook. In *Between Belief and Transgression: Structuralist Essays in Religion, History and Myth*, eds M. Izard and P. Smith. Chicago: University of Chicago Press.

1985 *Islands of History*. Chicago: University of Chicago Press.

1989 Captain Cook in Hawaii. *Journal of the Polynesian Society* 98 (4): 371–423.

1995 *How "Natives" Think. About Captain Cook, For Example*. Chicago and London: University of Chicago Press.

2003 Artificially maintained controversies: Global warming and Fijian cannibalism. In *Anthropology Today* 19 (3): 1–5.

Sahlins, Marshall, and Patrick V. Kirch

1992 *Anahulu: The Anthropology of History in the Kingdom of Hawai`i*. Chicago: Chicago University Press.

Salmond, Anne

1991 *Two Worlds: First Meetings between Maori and Europeans 1642–1772*. Auckland: Viking.

1998 *Between Worlds*. Auckland: Viking.

2003 *The Trial of the Cannibal Dog: Captain Cook in the South Seas*. London: Allen Lane, Penguin Books.

Schieffelin, Edward, and Robert Crittenden, eds

1991 *Like People You See in a Dream: First Contact in Six Papuan Societies*. Stanford: Stanford University Press.

Silva, Noenoe

2004 *Aloha Betrayed*. Durham: Duke University Press.

Smith, Bernard

1985 [1960] *European Vision and the South Pacific, 1768–1850*. Second Edition. Sydney: Harper and Rowe.

1992 *Imagining the Pacific: In the Wake of the Cook Voyages*. Carlton, Vic.: Miegunyah Press/Melbourne University Publishing.

Spate, Oskar H.K.

1979 *The Spanish Lake: The Pacific since Magellan*, vol. 1. London: Croom Helm.

Spriggs, Matthew

1997 *The Island Melanesians*. Oxford: Blackwell.

Spurway, John

2001 Ma`afu: the making of the Tui Lau. PhD thesis, Pacific and Asian History, The Australian National University, Canberra.

Stannard, David E.

1989 *Before the Horror: The Population of Hawai`i on the Eve of Western Contact*. Honolulu: Social Science Research Institute.

Stepan, Nancy

1982 *The Idea of Race in Science: Great Britain 1800–1960*. London: Macmillan.

Taylor, John P.

2008 *The Other Side: Ways of Being and Place in Vanuatu*. Pacific Islands Monographs Series. Honolulu: University of Hawai`i Press.

Tcherkézoff, Serge

2000 Are the Samoan chiefs Matai "out of time"? Tradition and democracy: Contemporary ambiguities and historical transformations of the concept of chief. In *Governance in Samoa: Pulega i Samoa*, eds Elise Huffer and Asofou So`o, 113–33. Canberra: Asia Pacific Press; Suva, Fiji: Institute of Pacific Studies, University of the South Pacific.

2003 A long and unfortunate voyage toward the invention of the Melanesia/Polynesia opposition (1595–1832). In 'Dumont d'Urville's

Oceanic Provinces: Fundamental Precepts or Arbitrary Constructs?', ed. Geoffrey Clark. *Journal of Pacific History* 38 (2): 175–96. Special issue.

2004a *"First Contacts" in Polynesia: The Samoan Case (1722–1848). Western Misunderstandings about Sexuality and Divinity.* Canberra/Christchurch: Journal of Pacific History Monographs/Macmillan Brown Centre for Pacific Studies.

2004b *Tahiti 1768—Jeunes filles en pleurs: La face cachée des premiers contacts et la naissance du mythe occidental.* Papeete: Au Vent des Îles.

2005 Culture, nation, society: Secondary changes and possible radical transformations in Samoa. Towards a model for the study of cultural dynamics. In *The Changing South Pacific: Identities and Cultural Transformations*, eds Serge Tcherkézoff and Françoise Douaire-Marsaudon, 245–301. Canberra: Pandanus Books.

2009 *Polynésie-Mélanésie, l'invention française des "races" et des régions de l'Océanie (XVIe-XXe siècles).* Papeete: Au Vent des Îles.

Teaiwa, Katerina, ed.

2007 *Indigenous Encounters.* Honolulu: Center for Pacific Island Studies, University of Hawai`i.

Teaiwa, Teresia, and Sean Mallon

2006 Ambivalent Kinships? Pacific People in New Zealand. In *New Zealand Identities, Departures and Destinations*, eds James Liu, Tim McCreanor, Tracey McIntosh and Teresia Teaiwa, 207–29 Wellington: Victoria University Press.

Tench, Watkin

1789 *A Narrative of the Expedition to Botany Bay: with an account of New South Wales, Its Productions, Inhabitants, etc: to which is subjoined a list of the Civil and Military establishments at Port Jackson.* London: Printed for J. Debrett.

Thomas, Nicholas

1995 *Oceanic Art.* London: Thames and Hudson.

1997a *In Oceania: Visions, Artefacts, Histories.* Durham: Duke University Press.

1997b Partial Texts: Representation, Colonialism, and Agency in Pacific History. In *In Oceania: Visions, Artefacts, Histories*, by Nicholas Thomas, 23–49. Durham: Duke University Press.

1997c Melanesians and Polynesians: Typifications Inside and Outside Anthropology. In Nicholas Thomas, *In Oceania: Visions, Artefacts, Histories*, 133–55. Durham: Duke University Press.

2003 *Discoveries: The Voyages of Captain Cook*. London: Allen Lane, Penguin Books.

Thomas, Nicholas, Anna Cole, and Bronwen Douglas, eds

2005 *Tattoo: Bodies, Art and Exchange in the Pacific and the West*. Durham: Duke University Press.

Trégance, Louis

1892 [1876] *Adventures in New Guinea: The Narrative of Louis Trégance, a French Sailor, Nine Years in Captivity among the Orangwŏks, a Tribe in the Interior of New Guinea*, ed. Rev. Henry Crocker. London: Sampson Low, Marston and Company.

Tsing, Anna

2005 *Friction: An Ethnography of Global Connection*. Princeton, NJ: Princeton University Press.

FILMOGRAPHY

Zagala, Stephen

2002 *Vanuatu Sand Drawings*. Submission to UNESCO Intangible Heritage Committee. Port Vila: Vanuatu Cultural Centre.

Notes

[1] We put this in inverted commas throughout, given that it was rather Oceanic peoples who, millennia before Europeans, "discovered" the places of the Pacific.

[2] As Lindstrom (2009) notes, this has become a just-so story, repeated in many contemporary and later sources (G. Forster 2000 [1777]). The original name *Ipare* (meaning "inland" in deictic opposition to "seaward") was supplanted by Tanna both in European and indigenous naming.

[3] "The man pulled out a little leather bag, probably of seals skin, and having, with a great deal of ceremony, put in his fingers, which he pulled out covered with oil, offered to anoint captain Cook's hair; this honour was however declined, because the unguent, though perhaps held as a delicious perfume, and as the most precious thing the man could bestow, yet seemed to our nostrils not a little offensive; and the very squalid appearances of the bag in which it was contained, contributed to make it still more disgustful. Mr Hodges did not escape so well; for the girl, having a tuft of feathers, dipt in oil, on a string round her neck, insisted upon dressing him out with it, and he was forced to wear the odoriferous present, in pure civility" (G. Forster 2000 [1777], 1: 98).

[4] These are respectively the words for white foreigners in Hawai`i, Tonga, Tahiti and the Cook Islands, the pidgins of PNG, the Solomons and Vanuatu, and the Sa language of South Pentecost, Vanuatu.

[5] We quote from an earlier discussion by Serge Tcherkézoff:

"As Sahlins warns us, we should not indulge in this 'post-modernist' strategy of 'creating doubts about apparent "truths" by arguing that their status as truths is derived [only] from the regime of power on whose behalf they have been constructed' (Sahlins 2003, 1). Sahlins further cautions us that for any pre-contact or early contact practice (as for instance in the case of 'cannibalism' evoked by Sahlins in this recent article) this deconstructive attitude only obscures the historical practices, without delivering any alternative conclusion:

> The allegation that good descriptions of Fijian cannibalism are really bad prejudices of European imperialists has submerged its historical practice in a thick layer of epistemic murk. The deconstructive strategy [followed by Obeyesekere] is not to deny the existence of cannibalism altogether ... rather to establish doubt about it. Not that there was no cannibalism, then, only

that the European reports of it are fabrications (Obeyesekere 1998). Even so, not all such reports need be questioned. It is enough to create sufficient uncertainty about a few of them so as to cast suspicion on all the rest, and thus dismiss the whole historical record by implication (*ibid.*, 64–5). Literary criticism of one or two European texts, reducing them to some fictional genre such as sailors' yarns, serves the purpose of obscuring the factuality of scores of cannibal events, which then remain unmentioned and unexamined (Sahlins 2003: 1)" (Tcherkézoff 2004a, 201–2).

Chapter 2

Linguistic Encounter and Responses in the South Pacific

Darrell Tryon

Introduction

In terms of encounters, what characterises the Pacific is the multiplicity and variety of its indigenous languages, perhaps the highest language density in the world. Prior to European contact, the vehicles of communication between communities which did not share the same mother tongue were many and varied, ranging from sign language, a tradition of multilingualism in Oceanic languages, foreigner talk, or simplified language registers, including pidgin varieties of indigenous languages. Pacific Islanders of different language backgrounds came together for purposes of forming alliances or for trade and exchange, or later, in the context of settlement or colonisation.

When the first encounters took place between Europeans and Oceanic populations, as far back as the sixteenth century, it was during voyages of discovery, quickly followed by trade and commerce, evangelisation and ultimately colonisation. After initial encounters, some of the indigenous Pacific Islander groups interacted with their visitors on their home ground, as with suppliers of sandalwood, beche-de-mer and salt pork, while many others had their encounters with Europeans in a maritime environment, far from home, as crewmen on ships around the Pacific or as plantation labourers overseas. These encounters between speakers of different languages resulted in the development of a number of Pacific pidgins and creoles whose lexicon is principally derived from English, as well as simplified registers of indigenous languages.

Language Distribution in the Pacific

A necessary first step in explaining these developments is a brief overview of the distribution and groupings of the indigenous languages of the Pacific region.

There are approximately 6,000 distinct languages spoken in the world today, of which nearly 25 percent, or 1,500, are spoken in the Pacific Islands region (here defined as the great island of New Guinea and all the islands of Oceania to the east, as far as Easter Island). For purposes of this discussion, Australia and its indigenous languages are excluded. All that needs be said about them here is that they constitute a group of genetically related languages, but are unrelated to the languages of New Guinea and Greater Oceania.

In the island Pacific there are two major language groups. The first group is known as Papuan, a group of some 750 languages which extends right along the central mountain chain of the great island of New Guinea. To the west, Papuan languages are also found on the Indonesian islands of Alor, Pantar and Halmahera, and in newly independent East Timor. To the east, Papuan languages are also found in the Bismarck Archipelago, in New Britain, New Ireland and Bougainville. There are also Papuan languages spoken in the Solomon Islands. It has now been demonstrated that roughly 450 of the Papuan languages are genetically related (Pawley 1998), members of the Trans New Guinea Family of languages, first identified by Wurm, McElhanon and Voorhoeve in the 1970s. While it remains to be proved that the remaining 300 Papuan languages are genetically related to each other and to the languages of the Trans New Guinea Family, linguists are optimistic that all of the Papuan languages will ultimately be shown to be genetically related. The Papuan languages are considered to be quite ancient, as archaeological evidence indicates that mainland New Guinea has been settled for approximately 50,000 years, while dates of more than 30,000 have been demonstrated for New Ireland, and more than 20,000 for Bougainville and parts of the Solomon Islands (Spriggs 1997).

Figure 2.1. Australia and the Pacific, showing conventional contemporary divisions of Micronesia, Melanesia and Polynesia.

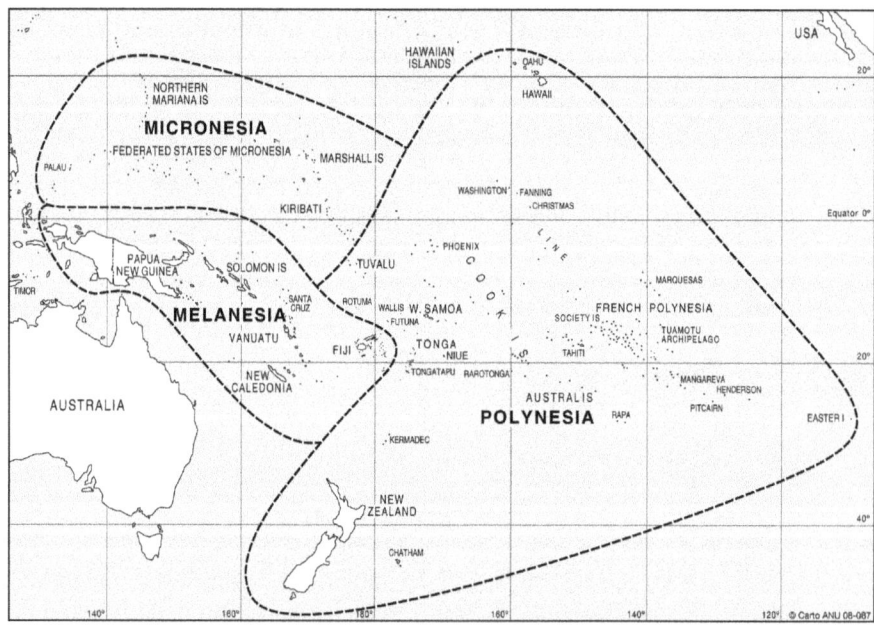

Map courtesy ANU Cartographic Services, RSPAS, ANU, Canberra.

Linguistic Encounter and Responses in the South Pacific

The Austronesian languages, on the other hand, are believed to be much younger, having had their origins in Taiwan and/or the south coast of mainland China about 6,000 years ago. The Austronesian languages, more than 1,000, extend from Taiwan (where they are spoken by the indigenous population), through the Philippines, Indonesia, Malaysia and Singapore, pockets of mainland Southeast Asia, Madagascar and then eastward around the coasts of the great island of New Guinea, down through the Melanesian chain as far as Fiji, then further eastward to include all of the indigenous languages of Polynesia and Micronesia (see figure 2.1). The Austronesian languages are all genetically related, roughly half of them belonging to a single Oceanic subgroup, which includes all of the Austronesian languages east of Geelvinck Bay, about 130 degrees east longitude. The Austronesian-speaking peoples migrated from Southeast Asia to the New Britain/New Ireland area about 4,000 years ago, before moving rapidly southeast about 3,500 years ago to people first, the islands of the Melanesian chain, and then the islands further east and north, Polynesia and Micronesia (Spriggs 1997).

What characterises the Oceanic region is the number and diversity of indigenous languages. A summary table will suffice for present purposes, as follows:

Table 2.1. Oceanic indigenous languages.

Country	Austronesian	Papuan	Total
PNG	220	540	760
Solomons	56	7[1]	63
Vanuatu	110	0	110
N. Caledonia	28	0	28
Fiji	2	0	2
Polynesia	35	0	35
Micronesia	15	0	15

The major subgroups of the Oceanic subgroup of Austronesian are discussed in Tryon (1995) and Ross (1995). They are not relevant to this discussion except to note that nearly half of the Polynesian languages are spoken *outside* Polynesia, in Melanesia and Micronesia, where they are known as Polynesian Outlier languages. These languages are considered to have been present in their current locations for approximately 800 years.

The language diversity which marks the Oceanic region is considered to be the result not only of long-term isolation, due to geographical factors, and inter-group hostility, but also because of the considerable language contact between Papuan and Austronesian languages, between Papuan languages themselves, and also between Polynesian Outlier and stay-at-home Austronesian languages in Island Melanesia (Lynch 1981; Pawley 1981).

The Vectors of Pacific Encounters with Outsiders

Trade and commerce in its various guises was the first and perhaps the major catalyst which brought Pacific Islanders and outsiders together. The port of Sydney was of singular importance in this regard, as the whaling and sealing industry in the Pacific began there as early as 1794. Between 1788, the date of the founding of the Colony of New South Wales, and 1840 there was extremely busy maritime traffic criss-crossing the Pacific (summarised in figure 2.2). Ships came to Sydney from London, via the Cape of Good Hope, bringing colonists, administrators and convicts. On the return journey they sailed north to Canton and Manila, via Fiji or Pohnpei (Ponape), to pick up cargoes of tea and silk. It was obviously unprofitable to sail empty from Sydney to Canton, so the British sought a lucrative cargo to sell to the Chinese. This took the form of sandalwood, beche-de-mer and mother-of-pearl, collected in the Pacific Islands and often brought back to Sydney for loading into larger ships for the voyage to China.

So it was that sandalwood was collected in large quantities in Fiji from the turn of the nineteenth century. As stands were exhausted there by 1811, the traders went as far as the Marquesas as early as 1817 in a rush to obtain this most lucrative commodity. The sandalwood trade was to become a major industry in Melanesia too, after the discovery of large stands on Erromango (Vanuatu) in 1826, its heyday being from approximately 1840–60, both in Vanuatu and New Caledonia (Shineberg 1967). Labourers came from Micronesia and Polynesia to cut and stack the wood ready for shipment, mixing and communicating with Island Melanesians. Apart from whaling and sealing, and the beche-de-mer trade mentioned above, another long distance trade connected Tahiti and Sydney: between 1804 and 1830 more than 3,000,000 pounds of salted pork were imported to Australia from curing plants in today's French Polynesia.

One of the major ports of call in the Pacific was Pohnpei in the Caroline Islands of Micronesia, a convenient lay-over stop between Sydney and Canton, and a very popular lay-over choice with the Pacific whaling fleet (Hezel 1979). Pohnpei was a real melting pot, with a large cosmopolitan population by 1840, consisting of maritime crewmen of many races and Pacific Islanders from all corners of Oceania (Tryon and Charpentier 2004). Communication was carried out mainly in a developing Pacific Pidgin English or South Seas English. There were many other commercial centres in the South Pacific, such as Kosrae, Nauru, Suva and Honolulu, for example.

Figure 2.2. Recorded South Pacific voyages 1788–1840.

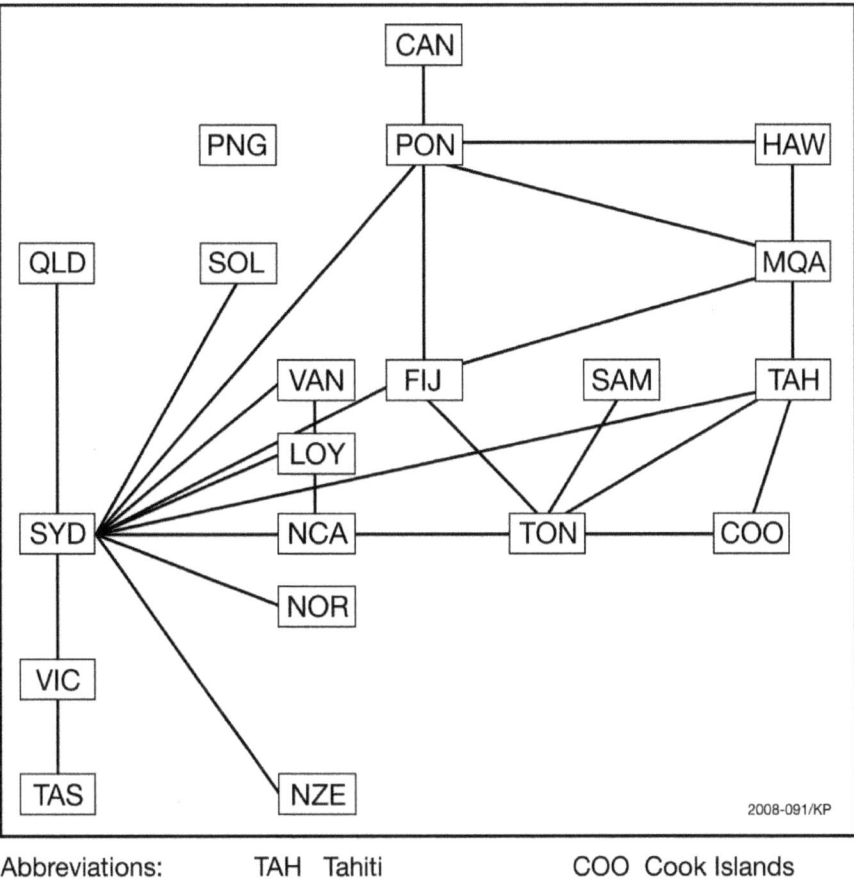

Abbreviations:
QLD Queensland
TAS Tasmania
VAN Vanuatu
NOR Norfolk Island
PON Ponape
TON Tonga
TAH Tahiti
SYD Sydney
PNG Papua New Guinea
LOY Loyalty Island
NZE New Zealand
FIJ Fiji Is
HAW Hawaii
COO Cook Islands
VIC Victoria
SOL Solomon Islands
NCA New Caledonia
CAN Canton
SAM Samoa
MQA Marquesas Islands

Drawing courtesy ANU Cartographic Services, RSPAS, ANU, Canberra. Originally published in *Pacific Pidgins and Creoles: Origins, Growth and Development*, co-edited by Darrell T. Tryon and Jean-Michel Charpentier. Berlin and New York: Mouton de Gruyter, 2004, 80. Reproduced with permission of Mouton de Gruyter.

Of course the greatest movement of Pacific Islanders from their home islands occurred from 1863 until 1906, the so-called "blackbirding" period. This was occasioned first by the American Civil War, which created a severe cotton shortage in Europe. Melanesian recruits, first from southern Vanuatu (formerly the New Hebrides) and the Loyalty Islands, went to work on the plantations in Queensland, Fiji, Samoa and New Caledonia. Once the Civil War was over, planters turned to sugarcane and plantations expanded rapidly, as far as remote North Queensland. Melanesian labourers were recruited for a contract period of three years, beginning in southern Vanuatu and slowly moving north to the Solomon Islands by 1870 and the Bismarck Archipelago of today's Papua New Guinea by 1880. During the forty years of the recruiting period, some 100,000 Melanesians were displaced from their home islands, many for the duration of several contracts (Moore 1985; Shineberg 1999).

As we have seen above, Island Melanesia is characterised by a multiplicity of local distinct vernacular languages, with over one hundred spoken in Vanuatu alone. The recruiters were well aware of this and used to communicate with their charges in what was to become Pacific Pidgin English. They also had a policy of deliberately separating groups of same-language speakers and putting them with speakers of languages from other islands, on the well-known "divide and rule" principle. This had the effect of creating very favourable conditions for the growth and development of Pacific Pidgin, to such an extent that by the mid-1880s a generalised form of Pidgin was spoken across much of the Pacific.

Other vectors which resulted in contact between Pacific Islanders of different language backgrounds were indigenous voyages of exploration, settlement or even conquest. For archaeologists have told us, and linguistic evidence has demonstrated, that there were many deliberate voyages and quite a number of drift voyages around and across the Pacific, the most striking being the surprisingly high number of Polynesian languages spoken in Melanesia and Micronesia, often close to and interacting with existing populations.

Another major vector was the evangelisation of the Pacific, beginning with the arrival of the London Missionary Society clergy in Tahiti in 1797. The Christian message spread rapidly westward, reaching Island Melanesia in 1839. In addition to the European missionaries, Polynesian pastors or "teachers" played an important role in the islands of Melanesia.

Finally, and perhaps of greatest impact, was the colonisation process, whereby European powers, following the Christian missionaries, gradually annexed and colonised the islands of the Pacific, introducing major world languages, such as English, French, German and Spanish.

Pre-Contact Encounters and Linguistic Responses

Prior to the arrival of the European explorers in the Pacific, and independently of this, even in the colonial period, Pacific Islanders speaking different languages were in frequent contact, often in the context of trade and exchange but also in the process of colonisation and settlement or re-settlement. The major contact here was between Austronesian speakers and already long-established populations of Papuan speakers, whose arrival predated that of the Austronesians by many millennia. Indeed, it is to this very contact that the great linguistic diversity, even within Austronesian languages, is attributed in Melanesia today.

Some of the languages have interacted to such an extent that it is sometimes difficult to determine whether one is dealing with an Austronesian or a Papuan language. Such is the case with Maisin, in the Northern Province of Papua New Guinea, for example, or indeed with Äiwoo (Reefs) and Nendö (Santa Cruz) in the Te Motu Province of the Solomon Islands.[2] Another well-known example is Hiri Motu, the pidgin variety of Motu, an Austronesian language spoken around Port Moresby, Papua New Guinea. This language evolved as a result of trading voyages between the Port Moresby area and the Gulf of Papua, where Austronesian pottery was exchanged for sago and other food products. Pidgin languages, of which there are some 140 in the world, are born of necessity to communicate, usually in a trading context. Even among Austronesian languages, trade languages were born, such as that used in the famous *kula* ring in the Papuan Tip area of Papua New Guinea.

The most striking linguistic changes are a direct result of contact between Melanesian and Polynesian language communities. There are some sixteen Polynesian Outlier languages, Polynesian languages located in Melanesia (with a few in Micronesia) as a result of back migrations some 500–800 years ago (see figure 2.3). These Polynesian languages, a readily identifiable subgroup of Oceanic Austronesian, have interacted with many Melanesian languages, resulting in significant morpho-syntactic and lexical changes to both the Melanesian and Polynesian languages. One example is the Mele-Ifira language of Vanuatu, a Polynesian Outlier language contiguous to a Melanesian language, South Efatese. As a result of prolonged contact and evident bilingualism, among other features, the Polynesian language has partially adopted the Melanesian inalienable possession system. Thus, instead of the expected *To-ku tama* "my father," we have *Tama-ku* "my father."

Figure 2.3. "Languages of the Eastern Outer Islands."

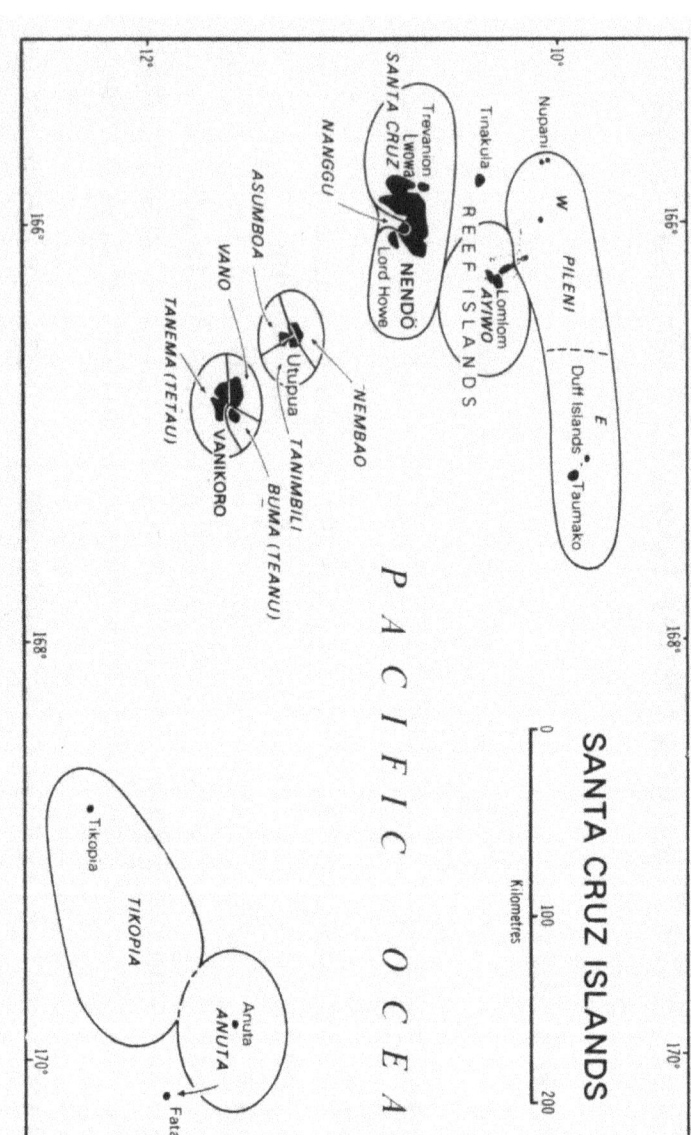

Source: Darrell T. Tryon, "Language contact and contact-induced language change in the Eastern Outer Islands, Solomon Islands", in Tom Dutton and Darrell T. Tryon eds., *Language Contact and Change in the Austronesian World*. Berlin & New York: Mouton de Gruyter, 1994, 612. Reproduced with permission of Mouton de Gruyter.

Figure 2.4. "Trade networks in the Santa Cruz Island Group."

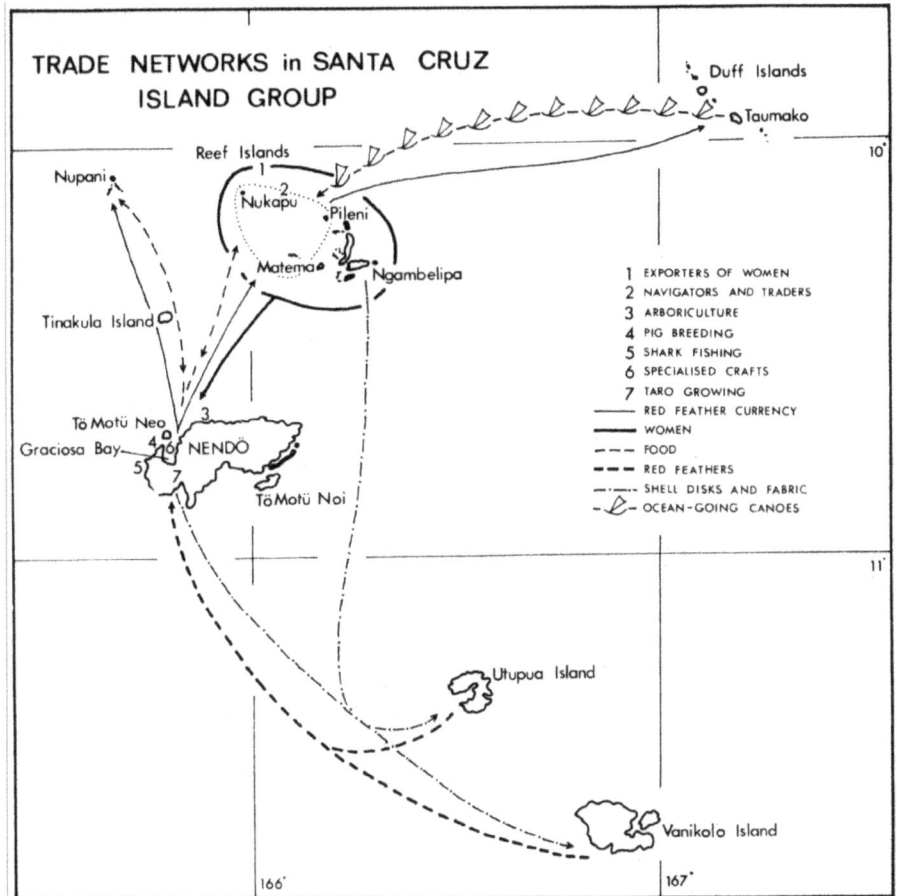

Source: R.C. Green & M.M. Cresswell eds., *Southeast Solomon Islands Cultural History*. Wellington, New Zealand: The Royal Society of New Zealand, 1976, 16. Reproduced with permission of The Royal Society of New Zealand.

Even more striking is the result of language contact between Melanesian, Polynesian and so-called Papuan languages in the Santa Cruz archipelago of the Solomon Islands (Tryon 1994) (see figure 2.4). There are eleven languages spoken in the Santa Cruz group (Tryon and Hackman 1983). They are:

Table 2.2. Eleven languages of the Santa Cruz Group.

1	Nendö (Santa Cruz)	spoken on the island of Nendö, Tö Motu Neo, and Tö Motu Noi	3,000 speakers
2	Nanggu	spoken in southern Nendö	200 speakers
3	Äiwoo (Reefs)	spoken on the Main Reef Islands	4,000 speakers
4	Pileni	spoken on the islands of Pileni, Nupani, Nukapu, and Matema, in the Main Reef Islands; also in the Duff Islands (Taumako)	1,000 speakers
5	Tikopian-Anutan	spoken on Tikopia and Anuta; two distinct dialects	2,000 speakers
6	Nembao (Amba)	spoken in Ahme and Mbao villages, Utupua	150 speakers
7	Asumboa	spoken in a single village of the same name, Utupua	50 speakers
8	Tanimbili	spoken in eastern Utupua	50 speakers
9	Buma (Teanu)[3]	spoken in Teanu village, Vanikoro	200 speakers
10	Vano (Vana)	spoken in Vano village, Vanikoro	5 speakers
11	Tanema (Tanima)	spoken in Tanema village, Vanikoro	3 speakers

Of the eleven languages of the Santa Cruz archipelago, three have been classified as Papuan (non-Austronesian) and eight as Austronesian, of which two are Polynesian Outlier languages. The "Papuan" languages are Äiwoo (Reefs), Nendö (Santa Cruz), Nanggu. The Austronesian languages are: Nembao, Asumboa, Tanimbili, Buma, Vano, Tanema, Pileni and Tikopian-Anutan. The two last named, Pileni and Tikopian-Anutan, are Polynesian Outlier languages.

In this clearly defined geographical area, none of the languages became pre-eminent or took on the role of regional trade language. Rather, each group spoke its own language with its trading partner or partners. Prolonged contact resulted in some striking linguistic change.

For example, the "Papuan" languages Nendö and Äiwoo adopted the four possessive noun classes (body parts/kinship terms, edibles, drinkables, general possession) which characterise Austronesian languages outside Papua New Guinea in Island Melanesia. (The Austronesian languages of Papua New Guinea did not develop the edible/drinkable noun class distinction). Thus:

Table 2.3. Example possessive noun classes for "Papuan" languages Nendö and Äiwoo.

mü-nga	"my arm"
mü-mü	"your arm"
apla-sa-nga	"my stone"
mü-nga lue	"my water"
na-nga mbia	"my breadfruit"

However, the verb morphology is typically Papuan, the verb stem being followed by a complicated set of suffixes indicating actor, tense, negation and a sometimes bewildering array of other information.

Äiwoo, the "Papuan" language of the Reef Islands, provides an even more striking case of contact-induced language change, for in that language, apart from the adoption of an Austronesian possessive system, there has been a unique development in terms of the verb phrase. For intransitive verbs take subject prefixes, a basic Austronesian feature in Island Melanesia, while transitive verbs have their subject markers suffixed to the verb stem, following the Papuan model.

Examples:

dyi-ki-engi "we cry"

dyi-ku-numbo "we die"

dyi-ki-ebu "we fall down"

(In the above examples, the *realis*/factual aspect is indicated by the verbal prefix *-k-*). Contrast the intransitive examples above with the following transitive clauses:

nyenaa ki-bwaki-dyi
stick fact-break we pl.inc.
"We broke the stick"

nyiiva ki-gidamii-dyi
stone fact-move-we pl.inc.
"We moved the stone"

Apart from the Austronesian/Papuan symbiosis noted for these languages, a sample of Polynesian borrowings into the non-Polynesian languages of the Santa Cruz group includes the following:

Table 2.4. Sample of Polynesian borrowings into the non-Polynesian languages of the Santa Cruz Group.

1.	"rain"	Äiwoo, Santa Cruz *tewa* < Pileni, Tikopia, Anuta *ua*
2.	"shark"	Vano *tepakio*, < Pileni *pakeo*
3.	"betelnut"	Santa Cruz *kalva* < Tikopia *haula*, Anuta *kaura*
4.	"eel"	Santa Cruz *tuna* < Pileni, Tikopia *tuna*
5.	"dog"	Äiwoo, Santa Cruz, Nembao, Asumboa, Tanimbili, Buma, Vano, Tanema *kuli*, Pileni *kuli*, Tikopia, Anuta *kuri*
6.	"flying fox"	Äiwoo *tepaka* < Pileni, Tikopia, Anuta *peka*
7.	"louse"	Santa Cruz *tökutu* < Pileni, Tikopia *kutu*
8.	"turtle"	Äiwoo *toponu* < Anuta *ponu*
9.	"breadfruit"	Nanggu *toklu* < Pileni *kulu*
10.	"chief"	Buma *teliki*, Vano *lamuka teliki*, Tanema *talinggi* < Pileni *aliki*, Tikopia, Anuta *ariki*

At the same time, the Polynesian Outlier languages, especially Pileni, in close geographical proximity to Äiwoo and Santa Cruz, borrow from the non-Polynesian languages, for example:

Pileni nöla < Äiwoo nula, Santa Cruz nöla "branch"

Where the Polynesian article *te* often marks lexical borrowings into Äiwoo and Santa Cruz and the Austronesian languages of Utupua and Vanikoro, the Oceanic article *na* signals loans into the Outlier languages.

While the loans just listed from and into the Polynesian languages are relatively recent, the irregularity of sound correspondences (see Tryon 1994, 638–44) points to considerable lexical borrowing right around the Santa Cruz group over a long period. This is not at all surprising when one considers the trade voyages (see figure 2.4), which are well documented throughout the archipelago. Indeed, there is even evidence of Tongan borrowings in Anutan, via East Uvean (Biggs 1980).

The overall picture in the Santa Cruz archipelago of the Solomon Islands is one of constant and intensive contact and interaction. While this has produced a largely predictable result in terms of borrowings, its extent and nature in Äiwoo and Nendö is quite remarkable, so extensive in fact that the status of these languages as Austronesian or Papuan has never been completely determined.

Post-Contact Encounters and Linguistic Responses

European and other foreign contacts with the Pacific Islands provided the conditions for the development of a number of lingua francas, languages of intercultural communication. As mentioned above, even in pre-contact days, in Fiji there developed a "foreigner talk," a simplified register of Fijian used when trading and interacting with their Tongan neighbours to the east (Geraghty 1983).

During the plantation era, again in Fiji, in the last decades of the nineteenth century, there developed a Pidgin Fijian, used for communication with Melanesian plantation workers recruited mainly from Vanuatu, the Solomon Islands and Kiribati. For Pidgin English was not much used in Fiji. At the same time, the arrival of Indian indentured labour in Fiji around 1880 gave rise to the development of a simplified Hindi, known as Fiji Hindi, used for communication between Fijians and the Fiji-Indian population.

In New Caledonia, as a result of the displacement of Kanak populations from the north of the island and the relocation of some of these people, speaking different mother tongues, in a single community in the St. Louis/La Conception area in the late nineteenth century, a pidgin French, known as Tayo, has developed and is still in daily use.

One of the most important vectors for Pacific Islander–European contact, especially in the last two decades of the eighteenth century and the whole of the nineteenth century, was the huge influx of foreigners into the Pacific (see figure 2.2 for a diagrammatic representation of Pacific voyaging between 1788 and 1840). This involved whalers, sealers, beche-de-mer traders, sandalwood traders and labour recruiters, to say nothing of Christian evangelists.

However, by far the greatest bringing-together of Pacific Islanders from all over Melanesia took place between 1863 and approximately 1906, commonly referred to as the "plantation" or the "blackbirding" period. As discussed above, during this period more than 100,000 Pacific Islanders worked overseas, mainly in Queensland and Fiji (see table 2.5). The Papua New Guineans were not deployed to the same destinations as the other recruits. Nearly all of them worked first on plantations in German New Guinea, on New Britain and New Ireland, and were then engaged in German Samoa from about 1885. Other Papua New Guineans, mainly from the islands around the Papuan tip, outside the German sphere of influence, worked in Queensland, but only for two years: 1884–85.

One of the results of this mixing of Melanesians of diverse mother-tongue backgrounds was the development of what became known as Melanesian Pidgin English, itself a development of the earlier South Seas English and Sandalwood English (see Tryon and Charpentier 2004). By the turn of the nineteenth century there was a generalised Pacific Pidgin spoken in Queensland and in the islands of Melanesia, promoted by returned recruits. It was in the twentieth century, with the establishment of plantations in the new colonies of British and German New Guinea, the Solomon Islands and the New Hebrides (Vanuatu), that the generalised Pidgin English developed into the three pidgins spoken in these states today, Tok Pisin, Solomon Pijin and Bislama.

> A pidgin language—and there are more than a hundred of them in the world today—is a language that has developed as a result of contact between two groups speaking different mother tongues. This contact occurs in a restricted environment, usually for purposes of trade or commerce, or on ships or in plantation situations where speakers of many languages live and work together. A pidgin language is not the first language of either group, but is born of necessity (Tryon 2001, 198).

Pidgin languages are characterised by a simplified grammar and sound system, and a reduced vocabulary. In most cases, especially in colonial and postcolonial situations, almost all of the vocabulary is drawn from the language of the colonisers. On the other hand, the grammar is commonly based on the language or languages of the colonised people.

Table 2.5. Queensland plantation labour 1863–1906.

Year	Loyalties	Vanuatu	Solomons	PNG	Kiribati	Other
1863	–	67	–			
1864	–	134	–			
1865	–	148	–			
1866	36	141	–			
1867	329	874	–			34
1868	280	625	–			33
1869	–	313	–			
1870	27	607	–			9
1871	292	978	82			
1872	44	416	–			
1873	7	987	–			
1874	47	1332	124			
1875	5	1931	728			17
1876	–	1575	74			39
1877	–	1986	–			
1878	–	1218	240			5
1879	–	1821	354			7
1880	–	1934	61			
1881	–	1976	641			26
1882	–	2699	440			
1883	–	2877	1127	1269		
1884	–	1010	714	1540		
1885	–	1379	533			4
1886	–	1148	444			3
1887	–	1431	553			4
1888	–	1125	1143			23
1889	–	1412	620			
1890	–	1294	1165			
1891	–	534	516			
1892	–	229	235			
1893	–	714	416			
1894	–	806	945			
1895	–	519	577			
1896	–	359	423			
1897	–	201	733			
1898	–	455	721			
1899	–	674	848			
1900	–	859	884			
1901	–	530	1151			
1902	–	264	875			
1903	–	374	663			
1904	–	19	59			
1905	–	–				
1906	–	–				
Total	1067	39975	18217	2809	191	204

Source: Darrell T. Tryon and Jean-Michel Charpentier, *Pacific Pidgins and Creoles: Origins, Growth and Development*. Berlin and New York: Mouton de Gruyter, 2004, 177–8. Reproduced with permission of Mouton de Gruyter.

Apart from Melanesian Pidgin English, there are a number of other pidgin languages spoken in various parts of the Pacific, the reasons for their existence being outlined above. So, for example, there is Parau Tinito, a simplified Tahitian, spoken in French Polynesia between Tahitians and Chinese storekeepers. There is also what has been described as a "cant," the English variety spoken on Pitcairn and Norfolk Islands, heavily influenced by Tahitian, dating back to the mutiny on the *Bounty* in 1789. And in the second half of the nineteenth century there was for a time a variety of Pidgin French spoken in New Caledonia. There were more, such as Palmerston English and a Nauruan Chinese-English Pidgin. However, by far the most important linguistic development from these Pacific-European encounters in the nineteenth century, numerically at least, was the development of Melanesian Pidgin English in its various guises.

One of the other results of European encounters with Pacific populations was due to the activities of Christian missionaries, dating to the arrival of the first representatives of the London Missionary Society in Tahiti in 1797. The missionaries soon learned the languages of eastern Polynesia and reduced them to writing in a relatively short time. In their Bible translations they introduced many loan words from European languages, especially the classical languages, Greek and Latin. These loans, first introduced into Polynesian languages, soon found their way into some of the languages of Melanesia in translations of the Scriptures. Thus one has, for example, such oddities as *peritomon* "circumcise" in Drehu (Loyalty Islands), New Caledonia. Other Polynesian words, such as Samoan *lotu* and *tapu*, were almost universally adopted in Island Melanesia.

Another consequence of mission activity was the establishment of "mission languages," whereby the Christian missions selected a single regional language as the language of the church, so extending its range and role. Examples of this are the Anglican Church's choice of Mota, the language of the island of the same name in the Banks Islands, Vanuatu, as the church language for all of the south-east Solomons and north-eastern Vanuatu. There are many other cases, such as the liturgical use of Motu and Yabem in Papua New Guinea, Ghari and Roviana in the Solomons and Wailu in New Caledonia.

The most obvious linguistic outcome of the European colonisation of the Pacific has been the introduction of the major world languages: English, the European language most widely used by far; French (in French Polynesia, New Caledonia, Wallis and Futuna, and partially in Vanuatu); Spanish in Easter Island, and for a short period in Micronesia at the end of the nineteenth century; German (in German New Guinea, Micronesia and German Samoa), until 1914; and Japanese in Micronesia until World War II. These languages all became national or official languages and the languages of education. Even though nearly all Pacific territories today are independent states, they have all maintained their former coloniser's language as their international language, often along with the local vernacular, especially in the case of Polynesia and Micronesia. In linguistically diverse Melanesia, local languages have too small a coverage to become national or even regional languages, except as church languages as discussed above. It should perhaps also be observed that English was more prominent than French in what became French Polynesia, especially in the pre-1880 period, resulting in a considerable number of English loan words in Tahitian. We have, for example, *tavana* "governor" and *puta* "book," Tahitian replacing English [k] with [t], and [b] with [p].

Naturally, even the English and French spoken in the Pacific is affected by the local vernaculars, with numerous borrowings from, for example, New Zealand Maori into New Zealand English, and Tahitian into French Polynesian French. This is an inevitable consequence of the original encounters between coloniser and colonised populations. Even New Caledonian French has numerous loan words reflecting earlier settlements from Reunion and from Indonesia. Such cases can be repeated throughout the Pacific.

Globalisation and the Modern World

The Pacific is now well and truly involved in daily encounters with countries, people and states all around the world. There are linguistic consequences of such encounters, often in the shape of threats to the very existence of many small languages, especially as the Pacific becomes increasingly urbanised. In Melanesia, for example, Melanesian Pidgin English varieties are having a considerable impact on local vernaculars, at both the lexical and grammatical levels.

The modern phenomenon of Polynesian and Micronesian diaspora, where there are often more speakers of a given language living outside the homeland than at home, is resulting not only in language change in the new country of residence but also serious language endangerment. Thus, there is now a Samoan dictionary produced for Samoans living in New Zealand, as the Samoan language in New Zealand undergoes different influences than the variety spoken at home in Samoa. Niuean is almost an endangered language, as there are fewer than 2,000 Niueans living on Niue, with roughly 16,000 in New Zealand, many of whom are young Niueans incapable of speaking anything but English.

This melding of Pacific people in the metropolitan areas of Pacific Rim countries such as Australia, New Zealand, Hawai`i and California is not without linguistic consequences for metropolitan languages too, as regional varieties of English (and to a lesser extent French) emerge both in these countries and at home, as globalisation increasingly impacts through electronic media.

References

Biggs, Bruce

1980 The position of East `Uvean and Anutan in the Polynesian language family. *Te Reo* 23: 115–34.

Geraghty, Paul

1983 *The History of the Fijian Languages*. Oceanic Linguistics Special Publication 19. Honolulu: University of Hawai`i.

Green, Roger, and M.M. Cresswell, eds

1976 *Southeast Solomon Islands Cultural History: A Preliminary Survey*. Bulletin 11. Wellington: Royal Society of New Zealand.

Hezel, Francis Xavier

1979 *Foreign Ships in Micronesia*. Saipan, Mariana Is.: Trust Territory Historic Preservation Office and US Heritage Conservation & Recreation Service.

Lincoln, Peter

1978 Reef-Santa Cruz as Austronesian. In *Second International Conference on Austronesian Linguistics Proceedings,* eds Stephen A. Wurm and Lois Carrington. Canberra: Pacific Linguistics C-61. 92967.

Lynch, John

1981 Melanesian diversity and Polynesian homogeneity: The other side of the coin. *Oceanic Linguistics* 20 (2): 95–129.

Moore, Clive

1985 *Kanaka: A History of Melanesian Mackay*. Port Moresby: University of Papua New Guinea.

Pawley, Andrew

1981 Melanesian diversity and Polynesian homogeneity: A unified explanation for language. In *Studies in Pacific Languages and Cultures, in Honour of Bruce Biggs*, eds Jim [K.J.] Hollyman and Andrew Pawley, 269–309. Auckland: Linguistic Society of New Zealand.

1998 The Trans New Guinea Phylum Hypothesis: A reassessment. In *Perspectives on the Bird's Head of Irian Jaya, Indonesia,* ed. Jelle Miedema, Cecilia Odé, and Rien A.C. Dams, 655–90. Amsterdam and Atlanta: Rodopi.

Ross, Malcolm

1995 Some current issues in Austronesian linguistics. In *Comparative Austronesian Dictionary*, ed. Darrell Tryon, 45–120. Berlin: Mouton de Gruyter.

Ross, Malcolm and Åshild Næss

2007 An Oceanic origin for Äiwoo, the language of the Reef Islands? *Oceanic Linguistics* 46: 456–98.

Shineberg, Dorothy

1967 *They Came for Sandalwood: A Study of the Sandalwood Trade in the South-West Pacific, 1830–1865*. Melbourne: Melbourne University Press.

1999 *The People Trade: Pacific Island Laborers and New Caledonia, 1865–1930*. Honolulu, HI: University of Hawai`i Press.

Solomon Islands Government (SIG)

2000 Report on 1999 Population & Housing Census. Honiara: Statistics Office.

Spriggs, Matthew

1997 *The Island Melanesians*. Oxford: Blackwell.

Tryon, Darrell

1994 Language contact and contact-induced language change in the Eastern Outer Islands, Solomon Islands. In *Language Contact and Change in the Austronesian World*, eds Tom Dutton and Darrell Tryon, 611–48. Berlin: Mouton de Gruyter.

1995 ed., *Comparative Austronesian Dictionary*. Berlin: Mouton de Gruyter.

2001 Pacific Pidgin Englishes: The Australian connection. In *Who's Centric Now: The Present State of Post-Colonial Englishes*, ed. Bruce Moore, 198–218. Melbourne: Oxford University Press.

Tryon, Darrell, and Jean-Michel Charpentier

2004 *Pacific Pidgins and Creoles: Origins, Growth and Development*. Berlin: Mouton de Gruyter.

Tryon, Darrell, and Tom Dutton, eds

1994 *Language Contact and Change in the Austronesian World*. Berlin: Mouton de Gruyter.

Tryon, Darrell, and Brian Hackman

1983 *Solomon Islands Languages: An Internal Classification*. Pacific Linguistics Series C, no. 72. Canberra: Department of Linguistics, The Australian National University.

Wurm, Stephen

1978 Reefs-Santa Cruz: Austronesian, but...! In *Second International Conference on Austronesian Linguistics Proceedings,* eds Stephen A. Wurm and Lois Carrington. Canberra: Pacific Linguistics C-61. 637–74.

Notes

[1] The status of some of these languages is controversial. See further discussion below.

[2] The status of Äiwoo and Nendö as Papuan languages has been under challenge for some time (Lincoln 1978; Wurm 1978; more recently Ross and Næss 2007).

[3] While Vanikoro has a population of more than 800 (SIG Census 2000), the majority are immigrants, from Tikopia and other islands. Fluent Buma (Teanu) speakers are in fact many fewer than the 200 speakers listed here.

Chapter 3

The Sediment of Voyages: Re-membering Quirós, Bougainville and Cook in Vanuatu

Margaret Jolly

Introduction: An Archipelago of Names

This chapter juxtaposes the voyages of Quirós in 1606 and those eighteenth-century explorations of Bougainville and Cook in the archipelago we now call Vanuatu.[1] In an early and influential work Johannes Fabian (1983) suggested that, during the period which separates these voyages, European constructions of the "other" underwent a profound transformation. How far do the materials of these voyages support such a view? Here I consider the traces of these journeys through the lens of this vaunted transformation and in relation to local sedimentations (and vaporisations) of memory.

Vanuatu is the name of this archipelago of islands declared at independence in 1980 – *vanua* "land" and *tu* "to stand up, endure; be independent" (see figure 3.1). Both words are drawn from one of the 110 vernacular languages still spoken in the group. But, alongside this indigenous name, there are many foreign place names, the perduring traces of the movement of early European voyagers: Espiritu Santo – the contraction of *Terra Austrialia del Espiritu Santo*, the name given by Quirós in 1606;[2] Pentecost – the Anglicisation of *Île de Pentecôte*, conferred by Bougainville, who sighted this island on Whitsunday, 22 May 1768; Malakula, Erromango and Tanna – the contemporary spellings of the Mallicollo, Erromanga and Tanna conferred by Cook who named the archipelago the New Hebrides in 1774, a name which, for foreigners at least, lasted from that date till 1980.[3] Fortunately, some of these foreign names proved more ephemeral: the island we now know as Ambae, Bougainville called *Île des Lepreux* (Isle of Lepers), apparently because he mistook the pandemic skin conditions of *tinea imbricata* or leucodermia for signs of leprosy. This sedimentation of names thus inscribes on this Pacific place the memories of what were evanescent but ultimately consequential encounters with Europeans. In this chapter I consider some of the materials – primarily texts[4] – from these three voyages: Quirós (1606), Bougainville (1768) and Cook (1774). But I also ponder how these voyages have sedimented or, more often, evaporated in the place of Vanuatu and the memory of its people.

Figure 3.1. Map of Vanuatu.

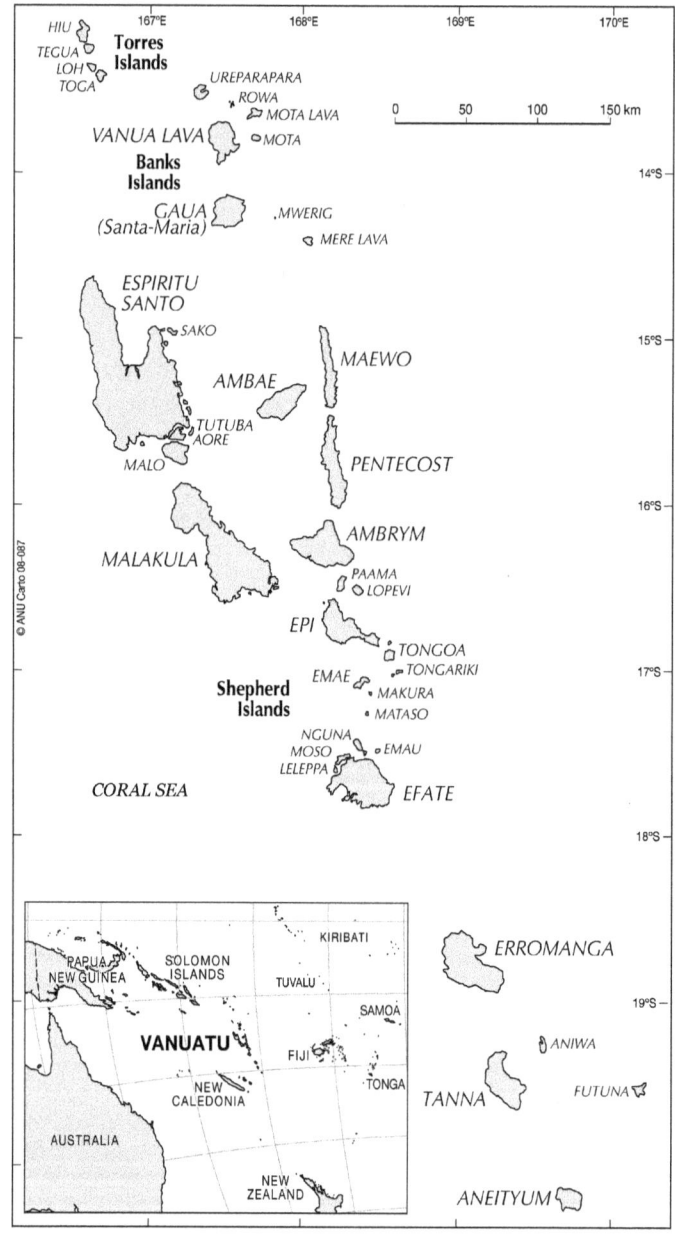

Map courtesy ANU Cartographic Services, RSPAS, ANU, Canberra.

First Contact and the Beach: The Limen of Colonialism

In revisioning these voyages I critically consider the trope of "first contact" and the associated idea of "the beach" in the historical anthropology of the Pacific (Dening 1998; 2004). This stress on the limen of the encounter between indigenes and foreigners, between Pacific peoples and Europeans, between Islanders and Outlanders,[5] still pervades much of the writing about the historical anthropology of the Pacific. Unlike the celebrated "first contacts" of the Highlands of Papua New Guinea (memorialised in the films and writings of Bob Connolly and Robin Anderson (1987), for example) for which we have textual, photographic and cinematic representations, eyewitness accounts of living (or recently dead) Australians and Papua New Guineans, and the accumulations of later oral histories, for these much earlier voyages we have only European documents, images, collected objects and a few traces in the ground of Vanuatu and the memories of its peoples. These voyages, the visits of Quirós, Bougainville and Cook, are not the preferred subjects of indigenous history. Unlike later encounters with labour traders and Christian missionaries, their voyages have left few sedimentations in ni-Vanuatu memory beyond the mnemonic names dispersed among the several islands (but see Taylor 2008; Lindstrom 2009).[6]

In critically considering the trope of "first contact," I isolate three major problems. Firstly, there is that very presumption of the "first", the privileging of that originary moment of corporeal touch, the transcendental brush of the encounter which erupts in the flow of time, and which relegates foregoing moments to a kind of cross-cultural zero. This very idea of first-ness, of precedence, tends to occlude all the contacts, both imaginary and corporeal, that came before. On both sides of such encounters there were categorical anticipations and discursive expectations about strangers – from monstrous beings to divine gods. This has been far more thoroughly investigated for Europeans, with debates about how images of non-Western "others" changed from the Medieval or Renaissance periods to the Enlightenment (Fabian 1983; McGrane 1989; Pagden 1982; Salmond 1991) or from the eighteenth to the nineteenth century (see Smith 1984, 1985, 1988, 1992; Jolly 1992; Douglas 1999, 2006, 2008). But there have also been important discussions about the anticipations and expectations of Islanders and of Highlanders in questions about how far Captain Cook was perceived as a manifestation of Lono (Sahlins 1981, 1982, 1985, 1989, 1995; Obeyesekere 1992; Salmond 2003; Thomas 2003), and also, in the continuing controversies about whether and for how long New Guinea peoples saw Europeans as spirits or returning ancestors (Ballard 2003 [1992]; Schieffelin and Crittenden 1991).

Secondly, as well as these generalised questions about prevailing preconceptions – of others as similar and/or different – there are questions of changing perceptions more intimately grounded in the events of encounters. It has often been asked how European voyagers' perceptions and reactions were dynamically influenced by the unfolding events of which they were part (see Smith 1985; Jolly 1992; Douglas, this volume). Thus, Smith (1985, vii) long ago stressed that his concern was not simply with preconceptions imposed on experience, but how the embodied experience of Pacific places and peoples transformed European visions. For Pacific peoples too, the events of encounters challenged and transformed their perceptions of the "strangers" along an alleged spectrum from divinity to humanity.[7]

But, finally, I want to link the conventional idea of "first contact" to Dening's far more powerful concept of "the beach" (Dening 1998, 2004). Much more than a physical space, Dening's beach is a limen, a place in-between (see Jolly 2009). Throughout his magisterial corpus and especially in *Beach Crossings* (2004), Dening consummately explores such crossings, in which the horizons of conventional meaning, on both sides of an encounter, are displaced, expanded and put at risk: "On the beach edginess rules (hardcopy book-jacket)." But, as in this chapter, the paths of entrance and exit to the beach are typically retraced through the stories of early European visitors, "to reveal what their unseeing eyes were seeing, life on the other side of the beach as the islanders actually lived it" (2004, book jacket). Thus, the privileged crossings for Dening are those canonical cross-cultural encounters *between* Europeans and Islanders. This tends to suppress parallel histories, other crossings, other cross-cultural encounters *between* Islanders. And, moreover, such a stress on the encounters of Europeans and Islanders often reinscribes these past "beach crossings" from the expanded horizons of an optimistic post-colonialism, the promise of living together in new-found equality and reconciliation. And so we should consider how our stories of "first contacts" and "beach crossings" reverberate in the "echo chamber of the present"[8] (Luker n.d.).

Pedro Fernández de Quirós, 1606: Salvation, Treasure and Phantasmagoria?

> The history of the New Jerusalem was a phantasmagoria: Quirós was now in the grip of a religious mania (Spate 1979, 136).

Accounts of Quirós' voyage of 1605–06 are usually structured not just by the limen of cross-cultural encounter but the limen of hallucination.[9] The pervasively Christian imaginaries of this period are often endowed with a kind of madness by some twentieth-century historians, like Oskar Spate whom I quote above, and by many witnesses on the eighteenth-century voyages, who regularly dispute Quirós' views of the archipelago on the basis of their own experience of "being there."[10] Quirós, like many Iberian navigators from the fifteenth to the seventeenth centuries, is typically portrayed in Anglophone accounts through the figure of the conquistador, as spiritually and materially driven, in dual pursuit of souls and gold. This perduring portrait of Quirós in Oceania has been recently challenged by two scholars (Luque and Mondragón 2005), who combine a meticulous rereading of the Hispanic archives with an ethnographic appreciation of indigenous perceptions and agency.[11]

Earlier understandings of this voyage have been heavily reliant on poor and partial English translations of the several voyage texts and subsequent reports (e.g. Markham 1967 [1904])[12] and often lack the cultural contextualisation needed for insightful interpretation. So let me first explore the Iberian context of this voyage and of Quirós in particular, on the basis of Luque and Mondragón's (2005) reconstruction. As they point out, Quirós' voyage of 1606 occurred at a time of "imperial climax and crisis" (2005, 135): the Iberian peninsular was politically united since the Portuguese were yoked to the Spanish imperium, but undue global expansion had also generated insolvency. Quirós, himself of Portuguese ancestry, was an ambiguous product of that epoch of Iberian union and Castilian imperial expansion.

The Pacific Ocean had become a "Castilian Lake," with colonies stretching from Peru to the Philippines.[13] Quirós was doubtless inspired by the prevailing quest for that great south land, *Terra Australis nondum cognita*, of ancient Ptolemaic and Renaissance cartography (see figure 1.1, Introduction). He perceived the few Pacific Islands "discovered" in the 1590s as insular outliers of that continent and was eager to be the first to chart its coastline. Other motivations for his quest have also been imputed: to find a place for settlement as desirable as the Americas and a fervent desire to save the souls of "Indians."[14]

Some scholars have derived his "religious mania" not just from the prevailing ethos of the time but from his previous encounters in the Pacific. When Quirós was the pilot on Mendaña's voyage in 1595–96, Spate (1979) and Jack-Hinton (1969) suggest he experienced a kind of Oceanic epiphany. I quote the latter's citation of Quirós–Bermúdez' account of that moment near the Marquesas when a 10-year-old boy approached the ship in a canoe:

> His eyes were fixed on the ship, his countenance angelic, with an aspect and vigour that promised much, of a good colour, not fair but white, his locks like those of a lady who prized them greatly. He was everything that I am able to say with reason about him, so that I never felt in my life such anguish as when I thought that so beautiful a creature should be left to go to perdition (from the Quirós–Bermúdez *relacion*, cited in Jack-Hinton 1969, 134).[15]

The profoundly spiritual character of his quest has also been witnessed in the fact that, before he sought the support of the Spanish monarchy for his voyage, Quirós made an extended visit to Rome as a pilgrim in the Holy Jubilee Year 1600 and secured the support of Pope Clement VIII through a persuasive personal audience. He was also backed by the Spanish Ambassador to the Holy See, with whom he stayed for eighteen months, and leading mathematicians and cosmographers in Rome, who were impressed by his navigational skills.[16]

But, as Luque and Mondragón (2005, 138–40) attest, Quirós' religiosity and millennial evangelism also had a more particular origin in the town of his birth, Évora, in the Portuguese province of Piedad. His family, though wealthy, was not noble. This place was pervaded by a "frontier mentality," forged in the reconquest of regions dominated by the Moors and was strongly influenced by radical Franciscans. The latter were dedicated to an emotional spiritual life, modelled on the life of Jesus and in full anticipation of a Paradise on Earth. Their millennial vision was mingled with a proto-nationalism that advocated the liberation of Portugal from Spanish control. Quirós was thus culturally predisposed to an ongoing commitment to the Franciscan Order (he personally recruited Franciscan friars for the voyage of 1606) but an uncertain loyalty to the Spanish Crown. Yet, Spanish support was crucial to his voyage.

In 1603 he obtained authorisation from the Spanish monarch, Philip III, despite opposition from the widow of Mendaña, Doña Isabel Barreto, and her new husband (who fancied himself governor of the Solomons in succession to Mendaña). Spate notes that the king's instructions to the Viceroy of Peru were "couched in unusually strong terms" (1979, 133).[17] The voyage was equipped with two sailing ships: the *San Pedro y San Pablo* as flagship and *San Pedro* as *almiranta* with a *zabra*, or launch, for inshore sailing. The expedition involved between 250 and 300 people (including six Franciscan friars) and had provisions for a year, and seeds and animals for a new settlement. But, as all commentators observe, the seaborne hierarchy was designed to be problematic. There was prejudice from the predominant Spanish contingent against Quirós as a Portuguese; Luis Vaez de Torres, his *almirante* (second-in-command and chief navigator), though superficially loyal, had little respect for Quirós, while the chief pilot Bilboa was reluctant to go at all. Both had major disputes with Quirós from early in the voyage about the best course for navigation.[18] The Spanish aristocrat Don Diego de Prado y Tovar was a volunteer and probably hoped to eclipse Quirós' authority. In Spate's view he convicts himself of "malice, disloyalty, and an unscrupulous determination to exploit his ambiguous status" (133). The rivalrous and rebellious relations between the leading members of this expedition are palpable not just in the contested itineraries but also in the disparities between the several accounts of the voyage.[19]

Figure 3.2. Detail from "New Hebrides, Banks and Duff Groups, showing Discoveries of Quiros in 1606".

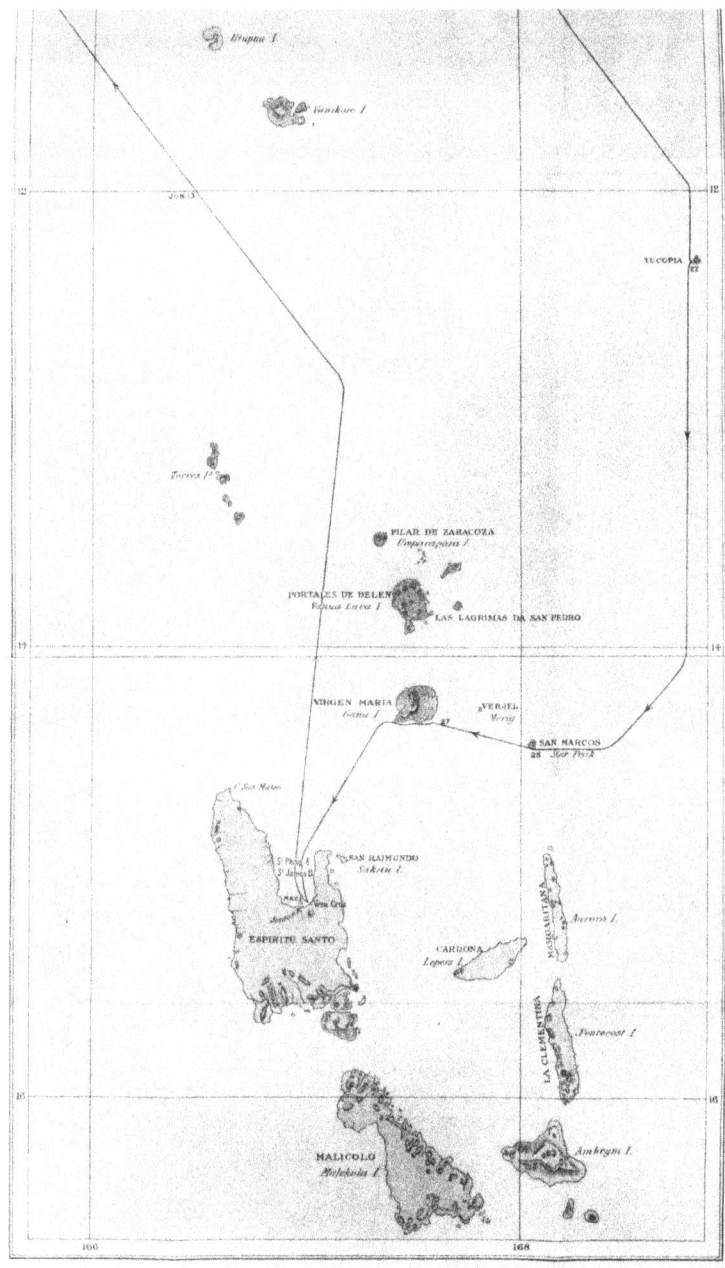

Source: Pedro Fernandez de Quiros, *The Voyages of Pedro Fernandez De Quiros, 1595 to 1606*. Translated and edited by Sir Clements Markham. Works issued by The Hakluyt Society, second series No. XIV, Vol.1.

As we can see from figure 3.2, the voyage passed by the islands of Tikopia and Taumako in the Santa Cruz group before reaching the northern islands of what we now call Vanuatu, where we join the voyage. In the several accounts, the spiritual conception of the journey is obvious. When the Spanish navigators first sighted the far northern islands of what we now call the Banks and Torres, they gave them saints' names usually appropriate to the day of their sighting: Mere Lava was San Marcos, Mota was Las Lagrimas de San Pedro, Vanua Lava was Los Portales de Belen, Gaua was Santa Maria or La Virgen Maria. As soon as they came ashore their actions revealed two classic movements of incorporation: the extension of the sacred core of Christendom to this outer periphery through these acts of naming, and precipitate and forcible attempts at salvation.

Their initial contacts were with people on the island of Gaua, a high island with "many palm trees, plantains, verdure, abundant water and thickly inhabited" (Markham 1967 [1904], 236). At first the local inhabitants seemed more enthusiastic for contact than the Spaniards, since "four canoes with unarmed natives" (i.e. men; Markham 1967 [1904], 236) came and offered to take them into shore. When the strangers declined, they presented them with coconuts and other fruits. Later, while the launch was surveying the coast in search of a safe anchorage, a man on the shore jumped into it. Judging from the sign language he used, the Spanish concluded that he asked them as to their origins and purpose. An unnamed Spaniard replied "*Venimos de oriente, somos cristianos, a vos buscamos, y queremos que lo seáis*" – "We come from the east, we are seeking you and we want you to be [Christians]" (Pérez 2000, 245–6).[20]

The man from Gaua no doubt failed to understand these words, but the actions of the Spaniards were self-explanatory: they seized him and took him on board. They then captured another man and placed him in heavy chains, secured with a padlock. After he almost drowned in an attempt to escape, they took him on board too. Both were treated to a Spanish supper with wine, but in case such delicacies of Christendom proved insufficient enticement, they were placed in stocks overnight.[21] On board the next morning the captain then

> ordered the barber to shave off their beards and hair, except one tuft on the side of their heads. He also ordered their finger-nails and toe-nails to be cut with scissors, the uses of which they admired. He caused them to be dressed in silks of divers colours, gave them hats with plumes, tinsel, and other ornaments, knives and a mirror, into which they looked with great caution (Markham 1967 [1904], 238).

So attired, they were taken back to shore, where they were received by many people, including "a woman with a child in her arms who received the two with great joy" (Markham 1967 [1904], 239). Quirós speculated that she must have been the wife of the first man they captured and that this man was a chief "for all respected and obeyed his orders" (Markham 1967 [1904], 239). He also claimed that such a good understanding was established that the woman allowed her baby to be held and embraced by the Europeans. The pen portrait of her in the Quirós–Bermúdez account is rapturous; she is painted as a Black Madonna. But this good understanding proved fragile and ephemeral. As they were preparing to depart, those they had befriended gave them plantains, coconuts, sugarcanes, fruit, water and a pig. But some neighbouring people (the Quirós–Bermúdez account speculates, either "envious or angry" because the Spaniards failed to stop and talk with them) attacked with bows and arrows. The Spaniards responded with aquebuses.

After leaving Gaua, they passed the islands of Pentecost, Maewo and Ambae, and then on the coast of Santo they saw "many tawny men very tall with bows in their hands" (Markham 1967 [1904], 241). These men, too, tried to entice them ashore first by throwing fowls' feathers into the sea and then by sending boys as envoys, swimming out to the ships.[22] When the sailing ships passed them by, they fired arrows. Finally, on 1 May 1606 they found a safe anchorage in a large and deep bay on the north of this island (the present Big Bay of Santo). Some canoes approached, this time with armed men: the Spaniards fired on them and they retreated. Two days later the two vessels found anchor in this bay, but the tactics which worked on Gaua, namely, to entice or capture, take them on board and send them back "clothed and kindly treated," did not work here.

When a party landed in the launch the next morning, Quirós' desires to "establish peace and friendship based on the good work we intend to do for them" (Markham 1967 [1904], 242) were quickly dashed when a soldier killed a Santo man, cut off his head and foot and hung the severed parts in a tree. Quirós, as usual, dissociated himself from this cruel monstrosity, claiming it was the rash actions of a Moor underling (but thereby also admitting his own lack of authority). The local people were aghast and their "great sorrow" soon turned to revenge, as they attacked the landing party with arrows, darts and stones. They were quickly overcome by guns and cannon fire from the ships and retreated. In a subsequent skirmish an old man, whom the Spaniards took to be a chief, was killed. Thus, proclaims the Quirós–Bermúdez account, was "peace turned into war."

The Spaniards remained at anchor in this bay for some weeks and, despite continuing hostilities with local people, were resolved to transform this heathen place into a site of Christendom and to save some souls by taking them back to Spain. The site of their settlement they called *La Nueba Hierusalem* (New Jerusalem); the large rivers that flowed into the bay: Jordan and San Salvador; the bay itself: the Bay of San Felipe y Santiago (St. Philip and St. James; see figure 3.3). The island was named Austrialia del Espiritu Santo. They took possession of the place not just in the name of the King of Spain but pre-eminently

Oceanic Encounters

the Catholic Church and the Holy Trinity.[23] As Luque and Mondragón attest, Quirós was "well acquainted with the judicial formulae associated with claims on new territories" and "organised a series of founding acts rich in symbolism and purport" and "mirroring a widespread inclination for the baroque theatrics of his age" (2005, 142).

Figure 3.3. The Site of La Nueba Hierusalem and the Bay of San Felipe y Santiago.

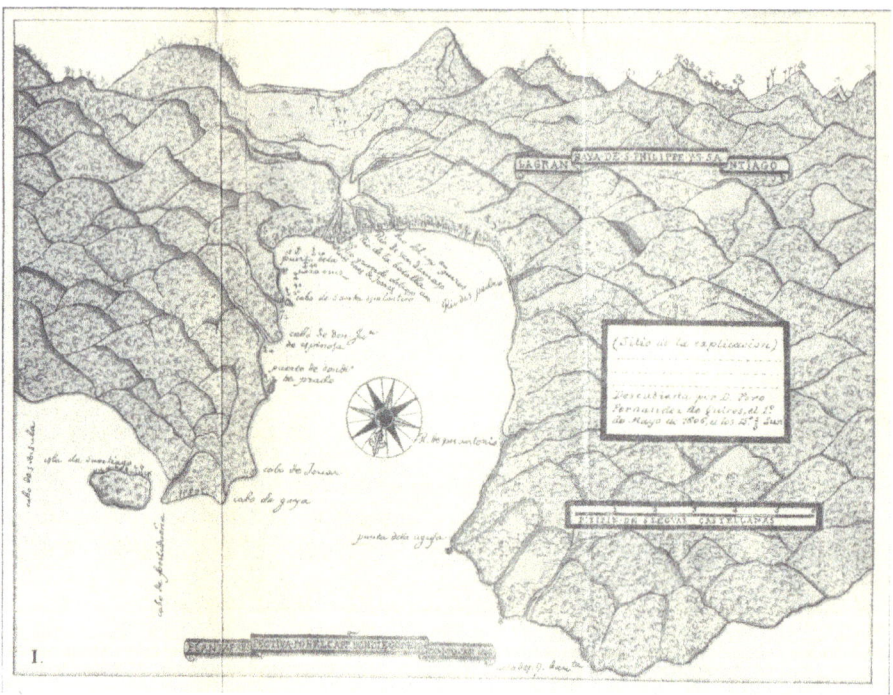

Detail from "*Planos de las Bahías descubiertas el año de 1606, en las islas del Espíritu Santo y de Nueva Guinea y Dibujadas por D. Diego de Prado y Tovar en Igual Fecha*" (Soc. Georgr. De Madrid, 1878).
Source: Pedro Fernandez de Quirós, *The Voyages of Pedro Fernandez De Quiros, 1595 to 1606*. Translated and edited by Sir Clements Markham. Works issued by The Hakluyt Society, second series No. XIV, Vol.1.

Within a day of their arrival, they constructed a church with a small altar under a canopy of leaves with a cross hewn from local orange wood. Then followed the enactment of Christian rituals: mass was regularly celebrated and the rituals of Pentecost (on May 14) and Corpus Christi (on May 25) were performed with extraordinary zeal, with music, dancing, feasting and fireworks. Startled local people retreated further into the bush, unaware that these rites were intended as divine spectacles for them as well as the believers. Quirós described how in the midst of Corpus Christi, on May 25,

> [t]he native who was taken from Taumaco[24] and was afterwards named Pedro, went about dressed in silk with a cross on his breast, and bows and arrows, so astonished and pleased at all he saw, and at his cross, that

he looked about and showed it, putting his hand on it, and named it many times. It is a thing worthy of note that the cross elevated the mind, even of a barbarian who did not know its significance (Markham 1967 [1904], 261).

As well as encouraging their hostages to take part in such rituals, Quirós set up a complicated machinery of municipal government: magistrates, justices of the peace, a chief constable, a treasurer, a storekeeper, a minister of war and a registrar of mines (Markham 1967 [1904], 254).[25] The aggressive and extractive portents of these last titles were soon realised in excursions the strangers made into the interior. They carried off live pigs and chickens, they took roast pigs and tubers from earth ovens deserted by local villagers who had fled. They caught fish, foraged for roots and planted their own crops – maize, cotton, onions, melons, pumpkins, beans and pulses – in a "native farm" close to the shore. And, in addition to making "free use" of the land in this way, they also kidnapped three boys, to save their souls. This was the subject of disputes with the crew: Quirós–Bermúdez reported one sailor declaring "thirty pigs would be better eating than three boys" (Markham 1967 [1904], 256). But Quirós prevailed over this "rude voice" (with its threat of a European cannibal appetite),[26] affirming that spiritual incorporation was more gratifying than corporeal gluttony. Relations with local people swiftly deteriorated with these plunderings and kidnappings: they attacked watering parties and attempted to destroy the church. Quirós suspected that several more local people were killed in "encounters with the natives," but his crew denied this. The capture of the boys clearly distressed and enraged local people and they made several vain attempts to retrieve them, offering pigs and other produce in their stead. But the Spanish were ever wary of ambush and attack, and on one occasion cruelly deceived them by suggesting that they were about to be returned by leaving goats on the shore, but then departed with both goats and boys.

Because of these continuing hostilities and dissent within his own camp, Quirós resolved to leave the bay on the evening of Corpus Christi, May 25, but acceded to the request of his rival Torres that they remain for a day or so in order to catch more fish. This unfortunate fishing expedition got a haul of *pargos* (Markham 1967 [1904], 390, 477). This was probably Red Bass or Red Sea Bream, which proved poisonous, inducing nausea, vomiting and fever in many of the afflicted sailors, who were sick for a week.[27] This misfortune fuelled ongoing disputes about the future course of the voyage. They sailed again on June 8, but encountered strong southeasterly winds. Quirós decided to return and build a fort and a brigantine and wait until the seasonal patterns of the winds were clearer. But the pilots could not work up the bay in the prevailing winds (or so they claimed). In the ensuing confusion the two boats were separated. Prado claims there was a mutiny on Quirós' ship. This may be wishful thinking on his part, but Quirós at this point had patently lost control and was left to contemplate the perils of insubordination on the long journey home (see Spate 1979, 137–8). Quirós returned to Spain via Mexico, while Torres continued on to Manila, charting his famous course between Australia and New Guinea.

Despite this violent history of kidnap and killing and the internecine strife, both in his account of the voyage (authored by Bermúdez) and in his incessant later memoranda to Philip III, Quirós presented a positive, even idyllic, picture of Vanuatu. This was in part self-justifying suppression of awkward or unfavourable facts and is hotly contested in de Leza's reports. But even allowing for this, the portraits of place and people are rapturous. By this report, the waters of the rivers were "sweet, pleasant and fresh" (Markham 1967 [1904], 264), the earth black and rich, and so fertile as to yield an abundance of food, much of which Quirós named and described (266ff.). In one of his later reports to the court he gave a lyrical evocation of the environment on Espiritu Santo:

> For from break of day there is heard from the neighbouring woods a great harmony of myriads of different birds, some appearing to be nightingales, thrushes, buntings, linnets and an infinite number of swallows, paroquets and many other kinds of birds ... The mornings and afternoons were enjoyable, owing to the pleasant odours sent out by so many kinds of flowers, including the orange flower and the sweet basil. From all this I judge the climate to be clement, and that it maintains its natural order (Markham 1967 [1904], 489).

He wrote (incorrectly) there were no mosquitoes or ants and (correctly) that there were no alligators or poisonous spiders or snakes. He did not mention the poisonous *pargos*. He claimed he saw potential quarries of marble – probably the limestone cliffs prominent on the western spur of Big Bay (Luque and Mondragón 2005) – as well as ebony and jasper. He suggested that Big Bay would make a better harbour than any other he had seen in the Pacific or South America. Although, in his view, such an abundant country made the people indolent, he also thought the health of the climate was obvious from the vigour and size of the natives (Markham 1967 [1904], 270) and the fact that they were corpulent and clean. He also thought them "courageous and sociable" and, as is clear from the taking of hostages, eminently capable of salvation. This is apparent in descriptions of one of the boys they captured from Santo, Pablo. Despite the kidnappings and the killings, and their own state of embattlement on Santo, Quirós' hopes for peace coupled with conquest never foundered.

This ecstatic optimism has been seen by Spate (1979) as evidence of his phantasmagoria, his religious hallucination. But as Luque and Mondragón (2005) attest, his religious zeal was not so extraordinary for the period and, indeed, has probably been exaggerated, not least by Quirós himself. His religiosity had its origins not just in the prevailing Catholic worldview of the period but in the particular millennial vision of the Franciscans, characteristic of his Portuguese home province of Piedad and in the more generalised utopian influences of Ioachim di Fiore and Sir Thomas More. He deployed this utopianism in strategic ways to gain crucial support from Philip III and others. His contemporaneous Spanish critics shared his religious worldview; they did not satirise from the same perspective as modern scholars, often writing from an avowedly secular stance. The dissent of his contemporaries was rather about power relations on the voyage and against Quirós' presumption of total authority. The hyperbole of his later memoranda and reports to Philip III can be read as the desperation of a man whose voyage had failed in crucial ways, who was castigating his rivals' reports, and whose evocations of an idyllic continent were intended not just to interest the Spanish monarchy in creating another colony[28] but to rescue himself from the state of dire poverty to which he was reduced in later life.

A more pessimistic and critical interpretation is offered not only by later navigators like Georg Forster on Cook's second voyage (see below) but also by Quirós' contemporaries. The rival reports of Munilla, Torres and Prado y Tovar not only challenge his claims about precious minerals but also offer a far less favourable view of indigenous people as warlike, treacherous and cunning (Kelly 1966, 87). Indeed, Prado y Tovar attacked Quirós thus:

> You would give us so much gold and silver that we could not carry it, and the pearls should be measured by hatfuls ... We have found only the black devils with poisoned arrows; what has become of the riches ... all your affairs are imaginary and have gone off in the wind (cited in Spate 1979, 137).

Yet, despite such devastating contemporary critiques of Quirós, both in their distilled later reports and in their journals of ongoing encounters, *all* the Spanish treat both the place and people of Vanuatu as instantly available for incorporation within Christendom: foreign islands are christened with the names of saints; the cross is displayed to heathens, who thereby have the chance of redemption; and if they prove unwilling in their salvation, they can be taken hostage to save their souls.[29]

But what can the texts of de Quirós' voyage tell us about ni-Vanuatu? Not much, and certainly not nearly so much as the texts and images of eighteenth-century voyagers. These Iberian navigators seem singularly uninterested in the language or the culture of those whose souls they might save. The language of signs suffices, there is no attempt to ask what pre-existing names places or people had – the island we now call Mota is peremptorily called Las Lagrimas da San Pedro (the tears of San Pedro); the man from Taumako becomes Pedro; the eldest boy from Santo, Pablo. Indigenous clothes are not described before they are summarily replaced by silks of diverse colours and plumed hats; local hairstyles are not depicted before men are taken hostage and subject to Spanish coiffure. There are few depictions of houses and gardens, although the Quirós–Bermúdez account offers detailed descriptions of food. There is almost no attempt to portray indigenous polity and religion, apart from the speculations that the Gaua woman is the wife of a "chief" and suggestions of emnity between neighbouring groups being fuelled by envy about contact with the foreigners.[30]

The texts of Quirós' voyage are relatively impervious to "reading against the grain" or of finding traces of indigenous agency. But there are a few glimpses. First, the initial responses of those on Gaua in the Banks were not just welcoming but enthusiastic for contact and exchange. It was exclusively men who came out in canoes, but they came unarmed and with gifts of coconuts and fruits. They were hardly Prado's "black devils with poisoned arrows" (cited in Spate 1979, 137). Even after the violence of hostage-taking and coerced coiffure, the men of Gaua again offered abundant food – plantains, coconuts, sugarcanes, fruit, water and a live pig – perhaps attempting to placate these forceful strangers. Both on Gaua and on Espiritu Santo, the Spaniards were rather attacked when they passed people by. It was when the Spaniards sailed past, failing to respond to their enticements, entreaties and the young boys sent out, likely as swimming envoys, that the Spaniards were first attacked with bows and arrows. So, we witness an openness for exchange and indeed a strong desire for engagement with the strangers (as against many late eighteenth-century constructions of ni-Vanuatu as insular and bellicose). And, it seems that pre-existing divisions between groups were exacerbated by differential access to the Spaniards: those who were not party to these exchanges were, if we are to believe the Quirós–Bermúdez account, "envious and angry." But, as the strangers' actions become more invasive and exploitative – stealing food, water and wood and taking hostages – the islanders' initial welcome turns to hostile resistance.

The northern islands of the Banks were likely too far distant geographically, linguistically and culturally for news of the strangers to have travelled on canoes in advance of the sailing ships, and so the rather different interactions on Santo were unlikely to have been influenced by the unfolding of events on Gaua. The continuing battles which the Spaniards had around Big Bay derived, in Quirós' own view, not from the inherent bellicosity of local men, but from their understandable response to the violence of the initial landing, when a Santo man was not only killed but dismembered and his severed parts displayed. This monstrous cruelty, together with the kidnap of the three boys and perhaps the threat of a longer settlement and continuing depredations of gardens and pig herds no doubt all contributed to the ongoing attacks on the Spaniards, which together with the internecine strife resulted in their abandonment of New Jerusalem in late May and June 1606.

In their reappraisal of Quirós' voyage of 1606 Luque and Mondragón conclude that:

> the convoluted procedures and overall behaviour of the Spanish men in Big Bay were neither the result of one man's extravagant religiosity nor simply of Spanish arrogance, but encompass overlapping medieval, renaissance and (to a lesser degree) baroque legal and cultural canons which have hitherto been glossed over in scholarly analyses of the earliest European explorations of Oceania (2005, 134).

I concur but stress how Quirós and his Spanish compatriots alike exhibited a particular relation to indigenous people, characterised by a staunch sense of superior spiritual and temporal potency, and an unflagging presumption to hastily incorporate foreign places and peoples into their expanding imperial congregation.[31]

This conforms to how both Fabian (1983) and McGrane (1989) suggest the "other" is represented in Renaissance theology and cosmography. Fabian plots an image that, he claims, dominates the perceived relation of the known Christian and the unknown pagan worlds: a series of concentric circles spreading out from the sacred core of Rome and Jerusalem through the world of the Circum-Mediterranean to the outer periphery of paganism. By the logic of incorporation people are moved from the one to the other by the process of saving souls, or else the space of the sacred core is moved to this outer realm by a process of Christian expansion. Clearly both these movements are abundantly illustrated by the accounts of Quirós' voyage: the place and person of the foreign is rendered rapidly proximate, precipitately incorporated as familiar. Fabian (1983) makes a strong contrast between this pre-modern and modern spatio-temporal logic, evinced in the more secular Enlightenment anthropology (see figure 3.4). He finds the rupture not just in the shift from a pervasively religious to a secular frame but in a shift from incorporation to distantiation: Enlightenment and evolutionary anthropologies by contrast deny the coeval presence of the "savage" or the "primitive" in the time and place of the European self. I will now critically consider this proposition in the later voyages of Bougainville and Cook, but first let me telegraphically situate their voyages in that late eighteenth-century moment in which both imperial power and Enlightenment knowledge expanded.

Figure 3.4. "Modern time/space: distancing" – Fabian's Plotting of the Other in the Pre-Modern and Modern Periods.

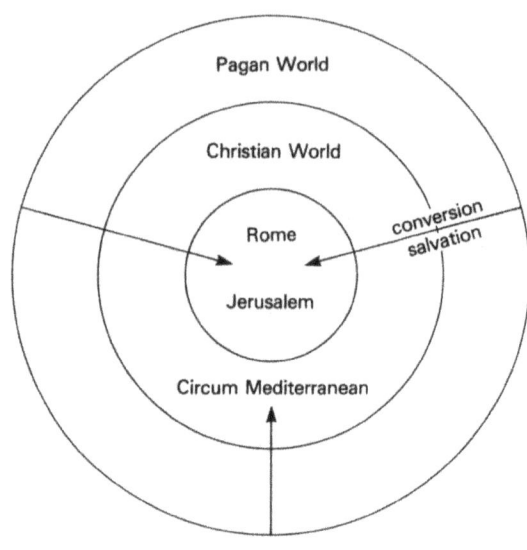

Figure 1.1. Premodern time/space: incorporation

Figure 1.2. Modern time/space: distancing

Source: Johannes Fabian, *Time and the Other: How Anthropology Makes its Object*. Second Edition. With an Introduction by Matti Bunzl. New York: Columbia University Press, 1983, 27. Reproduced with permission of Johannes Fabian.

The "Season of Observing": Nature, Enlightened Explorations and Imperial Power

Despite the celebrated differences between France and Britain in this period, the cultural and historical background of both voyages is similar and indeed mutually constitutive. France and Britain were rivals in these late eighteenth-century navigations in the Pacific, which combined the new Enlightenment quest for knowledge of nature with imperial projects (Bloch and Bloch 1980; Jordanova 1980, 1989). The relation between that knowledge and that power has been hotly contested from the moment of these voyages to the present (see Smith 1985; Thomas 2003). Whereas Quirós' voyage of 1606 occurred at the time of Spain's "imperial climax and crisis," the voyages of Bougainville and Cook occurred, rather, when the French and British empires were on an upward trajectory of expansion.

Doubtless the evidence of texts, images and objects from these voyages accords with the view that this was the "season of observing" (Dening 1998; cf. Merle this volume) and, indeed, the "season of collecting" (Thomas 1997, 93–132). The vast knowledge of Pacific peoples and places accumulated in this period was legitimated not just by the experience of "being there" but by scrupulous observation and by dedicated recordings of those observations in texts and images and in collecting of objects, flora and fauna, and on occasion Pacific people, like Omai and Tupai`a (see Hetherington 2001; Dening 2004; Jolly 2009). As Smith (1985) has shown, scientific fidelity in observing and recording nature became a predominant value in the drawing and painting of island views, landscapes, flora and fauna and portraits of people.[32] This has been much discussed by Smith and many other art historians for Australia and New Zealand (e.g. the botanical drawings of Australian plants by Sydney Parkinson or the portraits of Maori by William Hodges). Textual accounts are no less obsessed with the visual, and with the faithful recording of the look of people and places and the events of embodied encounters.

This stress on observing, recording and collecting is palpable in the materials from both Bougainville's and Cook's voyages in the archipelago we now call Vanuatu. But how far did this stress on the faithful representation of the experience of "being there" also entail a tendency to distantiate Pacific peoples as the objects of an Enlightenment gaze? There was a persistent recognition of the shared humanity between observers and observed, but that was increasingly vitiated by a language of difference, of place and race, which kept indigenous people at a distance (see Jolly 1992). And perhaps, as Fabian (1983) has suggested, that entailed not just the denial of shared and coeval presence in the time and place of embodied encounters but a claim that these people inhabited a place and time which Europeans had moved *from*. These late eighteenth-century voyagers were influenced by and in dialogue with philosophers of both the

French and Scottish Enlightenments (see Tcherkézoff 2004a, 2004b, and this volume, on the complex links between Bougainville's narratives and Diderot's theoretical arguments; and Harris 1968 and Thomas 1997, 86–7, on Millar and others of the Scottish Enlightenment). Though divergent in details, most were developing stadial theories of human society, which paralleled the ontogeny of an individual's life from infancy through childhood to maturity (and on occasion civilised senility!). Although these late eighteenth-century plots were distinctive and should not be conflated with narratives of nineteenth-century evolutionism, they shared a common spatio-temporal arc: "others" were relegated to the infancy of savagery or the childhood of barbarism, an anterior time, a more primitive place, and, increasingly, a more bestial race, which Europeans had progressed beyond and eclipsed.

Louis de Bougainville, *A Voyage Round The World*, 1768: "Such an Abuse of the Superiority of our Power"

On his "voyage round the world" from 1766 to 1769 in the frigate *La Boudeuse* and the storeship *L'Etoile*, Bougainville sailed into what he called *Archipel des grandes Cyclades* (see figure 3.5). Here I focus primarily on the English translation of Bougainville by Johann Reinhold Forster, published in 1772. Bougainville sighted and renamed several of the northern islands: *Pentecôte* (Pentecost, named for Whitsuntide); *Île des Lepreux* (Isle of Lepers; as noted above, now Ambae) and *Aurore* (Aurora, because it was sighted at dawn; now Maewo). He also sighted the tiny peak *Pic de l'Etoile* (this was probably named for their storeship rather than its shape, which was rather like a "sugar-loaf" (Bougainville 1967 [1772], 287). On the island of Aurora, as well as the steep shores and dense woods, they observed several natives, all of them men in canoes. Though these canoes followed them along the coast, in contrast to Quirós' experience in the Banks, "none seemed desirous to come near us" (288). Finally, they found a good anchorage on the coast of Ambae, but saw men lined up on the shore with bows and arrows. Despite this forbidding aspect the French decided to land in order to get refreshments (especially for those who were sick with scurvy and "the venereal") and to gain "intelligence concerning the country" (288). Three armed boats preceded the main landing party and, despite initial signs of resistance, they landed unopposed: "in proportion as our people advanced, the savages retired" (289). When Bougainville landed, the advance party was already cutting wood and local men were helping them carry it to the boats.

At first these Ambae men kept their distance with arrows and stones poised, but when the Prince of Nassau (an aristocrat who was travelling with the voyage) advanced alone and proffered gifts of red cloth, the men accepted these and this occasioned "a kind of confidence between them" (Bougainville 1967 [1772], 289). This confidence may have originated in the affinities perceived between such red cloth and valued local textiles, plaited from pandanus, often dyed red, and used as both male and female clothing and ceremonial valuables (see Bolton 2003; and figure 3.6).[33] Significantly, the Ambae men were completely uninterested in nails and iron (in dramatic contrast to Tahiti) and were loathe to part with their bows and arrows. They gave only a few arrows in return for the red cloth. Once he had laden the boats with fruits, water and wood, Bougainville peremptorily took possession of the islands by burying an engraved sign on an oak plank at the foot of a tree and made a hasty departure. As with Quirós on Gaua, it was at this point that men attacked them, using bows and arrows, ironwood clubs and stones, one of which slightly wounded a French sailor. The French responded with musket fire, at first in the air and then "better directed" (290). Bougainville does not report as to whether anyone was hurt, only that "they fled to the woods with great cries" (290).[34]

Figure 3.5. Bougainville's Tracks in 1768.

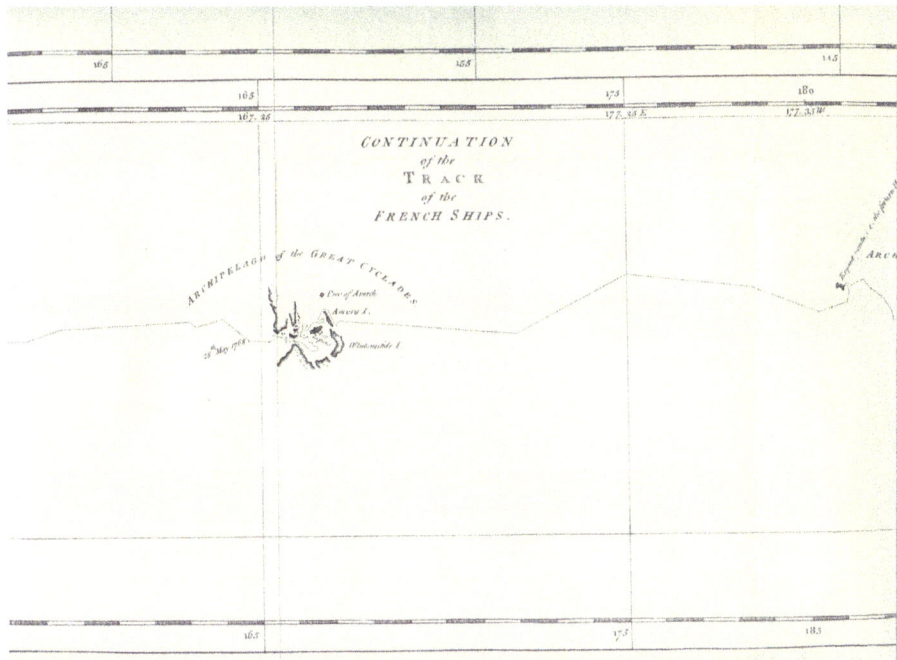

("Chart of the Discoveries in the South Pacific Ocean made by M. de Bougainville in 1768: Continuation of the Track of the French Ships").
Source: Bougainville, Louise de 1967 [1772] *A Voyage Round the World*. Translated from the French by John Reinhold Forster, Amsterdam. N. Israel: New York, Da Capo Press 1961, faces p.205. Reproduced with permission of ASHER Rare Books, Ijmuiden and the Perseus Books Group.

Bougainville found ni-Vanuatu men bellicose. Moreover, their propensity for war was for him a sign of their state of savagery, though presumably the state of armament of the French party did not condemn them to a similar status. Observing that the first group they met on Ambae appeared to be at war with another group from the western part of the island, he declared, "I believe they are very wretched, on account of the internecine war, of which we were witnesses, and which brings great hardships upon them" (Bougainville 1967 [1772], 292).

Inter-tribal war was likely a condition of life in pre-colonial Vanuatu, but Bougainville overemphasises the warlike state of the indigenes, as he underemphasises that of the French. He took the rhythms of slit gongs as signs for rallying to battle, whereas slit gongs were used to communicate a wide variety of messages in rituals of rank and in daily life (likely including the unexpected arrival of strangers on curious ships with many sails). Slit gongs were not just "war drums" (see Layard 1942, 310ff). Similarly, Bougainville thought enclosed pallisades might be entrenchments, when they were more likely routine enclosures that kept pigs out of gardens and settlements.[35] Moreover, he did not recognise – as Quirós had done – that his own presence and the differential access to exchanges with foreigners probably precipitated greater preparedness for war and aggravated pre-existing differences or hostilities between ni-Vanuatu. In any case, his anxiety about the warlike state of the locals inhibited Bougainville from making another landfall in the group.

As on Quirós' voyage, most of the natives seen were men, standing armed on the shores of islands or sailing canoes tracking the foreigners along the coast. Women were seen but at a distance and were not party to the exchanges of goods or of violence. Unlike Quirós' experience on Guau however, Ambae men were wary rather than enticing and keenly enthusiastic to exchange goods. Interactions on Ambae, at first peaceful, quickly turned violent. The male activity of war thus becomes diacritical in Bougainville's labelling the natives "wretched" or "savage." Their debasement, compared to the noble Tahitians, was apparent to Bougainville in the crudeness of their houses, "into which one could not enter otherwise than creeping on all-fours" (Bougainville 1967 [1772], 292), in the character of their clothes, and especially in their bodies.

> These islanders are of two colours, black and mulattoes. Their lips are thick, their hair woolly, and sometimes of a yellowish colour. They are short, ugly, ill-proportioned, and most of them infected with leprosy; a circumstance from which we call the island they inhabit, Isle of Lepers [*Ile des Lepreux*]. There appeared but few women; and they were no less disagreeable than the men; the latter are naked, and hardly cover their natural parts; the women wear some bandages to carry their children on their backs; we saw some of the cloths, of which they are made, on which were very pretty drawings, made with a fine crimson colour (Bougainville 1967 [1772], 290–1).

Figure 3.6. Pandanus red textile from Ambae, plaited and dyed by women but worn by men ("Men's mat *singo tuvegi,* Ambae, Vanuatu")

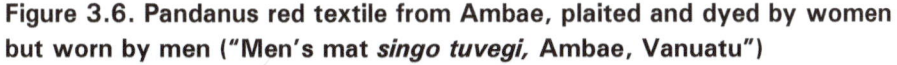

Collection: Museum der Kulturen, Basel, Vb 4486. Photo: Peter Horner. Reproduced with permission of the Museum der Kulturen, Basel.

So, apart from finding the pandanus textiles of Ambae women fine (see figure 3.6), Bougainville's pen portrait of the people of Ambae and their accoutrements is resoundingly negative.[36] They are ugly and unhealthy savages, far removed from Quirós' rosy portraits of clean and corpulent pagans. Moreover, as this quote suggests, there is another rupture here, for in the emergent language of race the people of Ambae are portrayed in a language that distantiates them, and as "wretched savages" they are more removed from the Europeans than the Tahitians. As if to clinch this adjudication, Bougainville quotes from Aotourou, their Tahitian guide and interpreter: "Our Taiti-man, who desired to go on shore with us, seemed to think this set of men very ugly; he did not understand a single word of their language" (Bougainville 1967 [1772], 292).

Bougainville's short stay on Ambae was the only landfall. After this, both ships were often becalmed in the waters of the archipelago, "shut up in a great gulph" (Bougainville, 293). They saw canoes crossing from island to island and saw (on what proved to be Santo) fertile ground, great plantations and a red colour in the mountains, which indicated minerals (probably ferric soils rather than Quirós' imagined treasures). Again men approached in canoes but as soon as they were within musket shot would come no closer. Perhaps word about the strangers had spread to nearby islands in the archipelago on the canoe crossings that were part of indigenous exchange circuits. Then, off the west coast of Santo, musket shot was heard from a boat that had come close to the shore and was dangerously proximate to three canoes, from which men were shooting arrows. The boat got free of these canoes. But Bougainville writes:

> The negroes howled excessively in the woods, whither they had all retired, and where we could hear their drum beating. I immediately made signal to the boat to come on board, and I took my measures to prevent our being dishonoured for the future, by such an abuse of the superiority of our power (Bougainville 1967 [1772], 296).

They were in dire need of wood, water and fresh food. Bougainville thus sought a deeper anchorage on Santo, and one safe enough to protect his landing craft from attack, but found none. To have landed in such circumstances, he adjudged:

> [W]e would have been obliged to have our arms in hand, in order to cover the workmen against surprises. We could not flatter ourselves that the natives should forget the bad treatment they had just received and should content to exchange refreshments (Bougainville 1967 [1772], 296–7).

Summarily leaving Santo and the consequences of these violent exchanges, Bougainville concluded that the inhabitants were of the "same species" as Ambae, "black, naked, except their nudities, wearing the same ornaments of collars, and bracelets, and using the same weapons" (Bougainville 1967 [1772], 297). He takes a final passing shot at Quirós – Espiritu Santo was no great southern continent but just a larger island in a sea of islands.[37]

Captain James Cook, 1774 – Distantiation or Incorporation of the "Other"?

On Cook's second voyage, the *Resolution* and *Adventure* moved through the archipelago for six weeks between 18 July and 1 September 1774 (figure 3.7). As can be seen from the map, the longest contacts were on the islands of Malakula (at a place he named Port Sandwich, July 21–23) and Tanna (at a bay he named Port Resolution after one of the boats, August 5–20). In between there was a brief but violent encounter on Erromango.

This voyage is far more interesting and consequential not just because it was longer and entailed far more interactions with local people but also because we have several excellent sources and much more critical debate around these sources, texts and images. I have already written about the second voyage in Vanuatu: about the tensions between the several accounts, the gap between accounts of events and summarising distillations, the dissonance between texts and images (Jolly 1992) and especially about how women were perceived and related to (in contrast to Hawai`i, Tahiti and Aotearoa New Zealand, see Jolly 1993, 1996b, 1997). I first briefly summarise some of my earlier arguments about European perceptions, in relation to Fabian's claims about the character of Enlightenment visions of "the other." I then focus more closely on how we might reconstruct ni-Vanuatu perceptions of Europeans and how such visions might have been transformed by the exchange of words, gestures, goods and especially violence with the strangers.

Fabian (1983) claimed that there was a shift from the language of incorporation to distantiation in Enlightenment anthropology, through a denial of coeval presence. The discourses of secular science and an emergent evolutionism generated an image of the "other" that was more separated from the "us" of civilised Europe, as the space between them was reconfigured as a distance in time or epoch. There was a novel equation drawn between contemporaneous living peoples and the past from which Europe had supposedly progressed, and societies were arranged along a continuum from savagery to barbarism to civilisation (Fabian 1983, 27; see figure 3.4). An emergent language of race seemingly reinscribed that sense of difference and distance. Yet, as I argued earlier (Jolly 1992), it is wrong to conflate the inchoate fluidity of the perceptions of late eighteenth-century voyagers with the more rigid racialist science and evolutionism of many nineteenth-century thinkers.[38] And so I juxtaposed the oft-quoted adjudications of Cook himself apropos Malukulans as an "Apish nation" with other voices on that voyage, most notably Georg Forster, who rather asked "who are we to make such ill-natured comparisons between men and monkeys?"[39]

Oceanic Encounters

Figure 3.7. The tracks of the Resolution and Adventure on Cook's second voyage, 1774. ("Vanuatu/New Hebrides Islands, showing Cook's track in 1774").

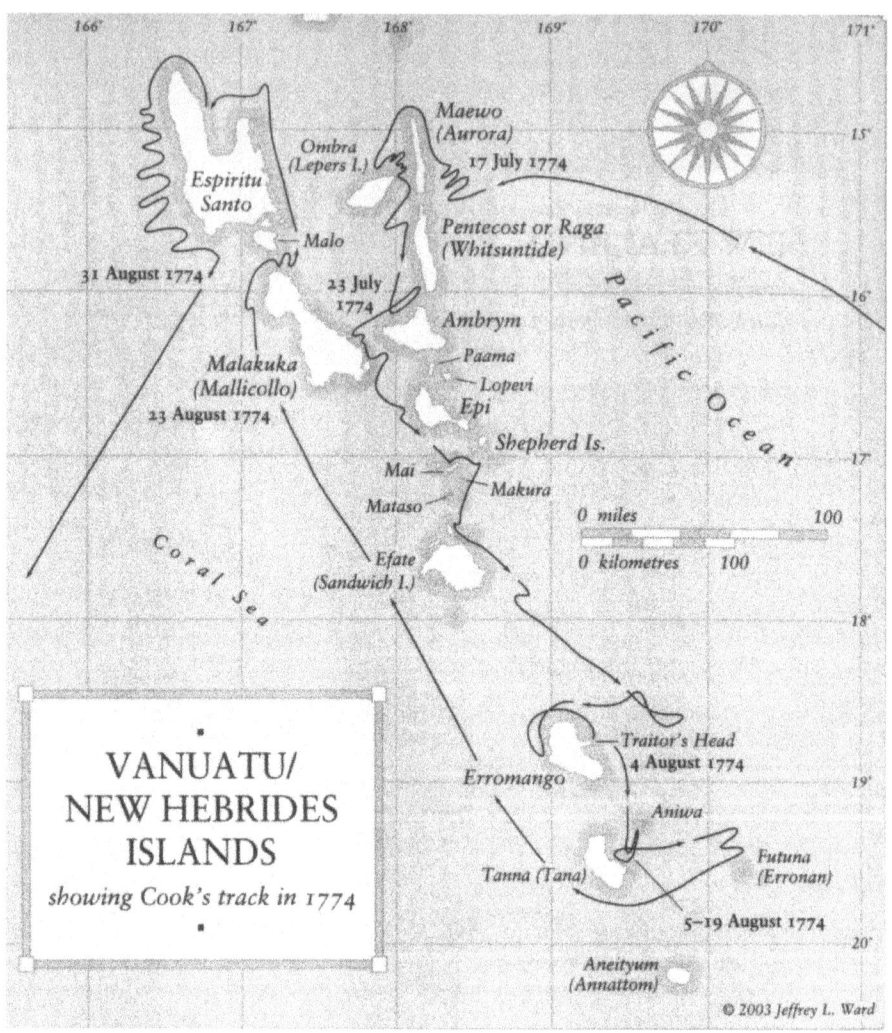

Source: Nicholas Thomas, *Discoveries: The Voyages of Captain Cook*. London: Allen Lane, 2003, 424. Map © 2003 Jeffrey L. Ward. Used by permission.

A close reading of the several voyage narratives and the magnum opus by Johann Reinhold Forster, *Observations Made During a Voyage Round the World* (1996 [1778]), suggested that, rather than implicating an immutable biology witnessed in the colour of skin, the shape of faces and the texture of hair, far more fluid and contested notions of human difference prevailed in contemporary concepts of "race," "nation" and "species" and that the value of shared humanity co-existed with such a radical stress on difference (see Douglas 2006). Moreover, the effects of climate and distance from cultural origins were seen to be equally crucial in determining differences between Pacific peoples. The language of progressive evolutionism jostled with a language of devolution and degeneration so that, for example, the Maori were described by Johann Reinhold Forster as "slipping down" because of their isolation, their need to cultivate new crops and the rigours of a cold climate (see Jolly 1993).

I also argued that the pen portraits of the several texts need to be compared with the rather different views suggested by the drawings and paintings of William Hodges and the engravings based on these. In particular the engravings based on the finished version of Hodges' *Man of the Island of Mallicollo* and *Woman of the Island of Tanna* represent views of ni-Vanuatu men and women which were ennobling and rather flattering, in contrast to the textual laments about ugly, ill-proportioned and disagreeable bodies (see figure 1.3, Introduction, and figure 3.8). Still, there was at least an aesthetic evolutionism (see Thomas 1996, xxviii–xxxv) which typically denigrated the unfortunate Malakulans at the expense of the felicitous Tahitians (see figure 3.9). Since I have elsewhere written much about how perceptions of, and relations with, women were foundational to such views, I here focus on ni-Vanuatu men in four crucial aspects of embodied exchange: words, gestures, goods and violence. I speculate about how ni-Vanuatu perceived the strangers and how the events of encounters unfolding on Malakula, Erromango and Tanna might have shaped the reciprocal perceptions of Europeans and ni-Vanuatu. Let me first situate this in relation to some interpretations by Anne Salmond (2003).

Figure 3.8. "Woman of the Island of Tanna. Drawn from Nature by William Hodges, engraved by James Basire" (likely William Blake in Basire's studio).

Source: James Cook, *A Voyage Towards the South Pole, and Round the World*. London: Wm. Strahan & Thos. Cadell, 1777. Plate No XLV. Reproduced with permission of the National Library of Australia, nla.aus-nk5677-2-s12x.

Figure 3.9. "Omai. Drawn from Nature by William Hodges, engraved by James Caldwall."

Source: James Cook, *A Voyage Towards the South Pole, and Round the World*. London: Wm. Strahan & Thos. Cadell, 1777. Plate No LVII. Reproduced with permission of the National Library of Australia, nla.pic-an7682836.

"Monboddo's Monkeys" and the "Ghosts of their Forebears"

In her most recent magnum opus Anne Salmond (2003) has offered a superb distillation of the three voyages of Captain Cook in the South Seas. There is no doubt that her scholarship, like that of Marshall Sahlins, consummately infuses a dedicated reading of the voyage sources (and a few select secondary sources) with an anthropological sensibility about Pacific cultures. This book, like another text published in the same year by Nicholas Thomas (2003), is designed to be accessible to the general reader and eschews that scholarly style of history writing, "with a protective bristle of footnotes hanging off every page" (Clendinnen 2003, 4). The day-by-day narrative style which Salmond deploys, perforce, tends to smooth over some of the differences emergent between the several sources, in the interests of a more comprehensible and congenial account of experience. The narrative arc of her story is ultimately an epic, which highlights not the conquest and colonialism which ensued in the wake of Cook's voyages, but the "dreamlike quality" of these extraordinary encounters in which "two worlds" collided. Though acknowledging the violence of this collision, especially on Cook's third voyage, she argues for the cross-cultural depth of the encounter and the mutual transformation it effected. So she casts Cook as neither hero nor villain in an imperialist imaginary, but as a man who became more and more Polynesian, not just in the eyes of Pacific people, "our ancestor Kuki," but in his own self-perception. Thus, in lieu of Fabian's contention about the Enlightenment tendency to distance the other from the European self, here the "great navigator" is rather seen as incorporating the "other" as part of himself.

Like the voyages themselves, the book does not drop anchor long in the islands of the western Pacific: a mere twenty pages of chapter 13 are devoted to a depiction of encounters in Vanuatu. That chapter bears the startling title "Monboddo's Monkeys."[40] Here Salmond offers an elegant summary of the several primary sources and the insights of later commentators. But, like Beaglehole and others before her, Salmond is inclined to be too categorical in imputing meanings and motivations to indigenous people and at times unduly confident about the ethnographic authority of her later sources. Apropos the first encounters off Malakula she says, "These people spoke a language unlike any they had previously encountered, constantly using the word '*Tomarr*', meaning 'ancestors.' According to later accounts, they understood the Europeans to be the ghosts of their forebears and approached them with caution, for such spirits could be malevolent" (Salmond 2003, 265). Later, after an account of the violence between Erromangan men and Cook's crews, which prevented them from landing, she says, "Now that these 'ghosts' had shown themselves to be hostile, they wanted to drive them away, and they succeeded" (268). Finally, on the island of Tanna, she interprets the offerings of food to the strangers in ritual terms, "Paowang and two other elders piled up some bunches of plantains, a yam and two taro roots marked by four small reeds as an offering to the white-skinned 'ghosts'" (270). So, the original translation of *Tomarr* as ancestors, ghosts or malevolent spirits has migrated with Cook from Malakula to Erromango, to Tanna.

Yet, as Salmond herself acknowledges, the communication of words and gestures in these early encounters was inflected with great uncertainty, doubt and sometimes outright misrecognition. Their Tahitian guide and interpreter, Tupaia, who had been so helpful in many other islands of the Pacific where cognate Polynesian languages were spoken, was little use as a translator of these very different languages of Vanuatu (see Jolly 2009). Moreover, the languages spoken on these three islands were not mutually intelligible and on each island several different languages (not dialects) were spoken. So, despite the valiant efforts of Johann Reinhold Forster to record vocabulary, there were often mistranslations, misrecognitions and perhaps even wilful deceptions in this faltering communication of words. So, the very name of the island Tanna derives from an early mistranslation. In asking what the island was called, Johann Reinhold Forster pointed to the ground, and his Tannese interlocutors replied with the word *tanna*, which means land or ground in one of the Tannese languages (see Introduction, this volume). Later, a rather more egregious example of the consequences of mistranslation on Tanna is reported. I quote from Salmond's own depiction of this incident:

> On 15 August when Johann Forster was in the forest collecting plants, he came across a nutmeg tree where some pigeons were feeding. He asked his guide the local name of this tree, and thinking that Johann was pointing at the birds, the man told him '*guanattan*' (*yawinatuan* or 'green pigeon' in his dialect). Upon returning to the landing place, Johann showed the leaves from this tree to another group of people, who gave it another name altogether. When Johann testily insisted that this was a '*guanattan*,' the guide tried to get his fellow islanders to agree, in an effort to placate the stranger. As soon as Johann realised what was going on, he flew into a rage, yelled that he was being cheated, and according to William Wales, shoved the guide with his foot and spat in his face for giving him false information (Salmond 2003, 274).[41]

This incident precipitated a violent quarrel between Johann Forster and Captain Clerke, which I cannot detail here (but see Salmond 2003, 274–5). Yet, this surely suggests that the translation of words and signs was not an exact science and so I am less confident than Salmond that we can unequivocally suggest that Malakulans, Erromangans and Tannese all perceived the Europeans as the "ghosts" of their forebears, returning especially in their malevolent aspect. Let us consider the way in which this word is recorded in the context of the first encounters on Malakula, using primarily the sources of Sparrman (1953), Marra

(1967 [1775]) and *The Resolution Journal of Johann Reinhold Forster, 1772–1775* (Forster 1982).

Green Boughs, Salt Water and *Tumora, Towmarro*

On 21 July 1774, as the ships approached the island of Malakula, men waded out into the sea with clubs, bows and arrows in their hands but also waving green branches. After exploring the coast, Cook found a bay that was sheltered by a coral reef and there anchored (at a place he called Port Sandwich; again, after Lord Sandwich). They were approached by several men in canoes waving green branches, dipping their hands in the sea and pouring water over their heads and faces. Here are some excerpts from Marra's account:

> The ship was scarce moored before the natives came off in their canoes from the East side of the bay, and many swam from the West side; the distance not above a quarter of a mile. They were of the negroe kind, quite black and woolly headed, poor mean despicable looking wretches, but armed with bows and poisoned arrows, with every one a club made of hard wood flung over his shoulders. ... As soon as they approached the ship, or came near any of the crew, they sprinkled water over their heads, patted their heads with their open hands, crying Towmarro, Towmarro; but offering no kind of rudeness nor misbehaviour of any kind. They kept about the ship, with lights, after it was dark, and when they had sufficiently gratified their curiosity, they went quietly away (1967 [1775], 260–2).[42]

Sparrman's account offers more on the language of words and signs:

> They were remarkable for their cleverness and quick-wittedness, and they could at once grasp and repeat clearly whatever English or any words I spoke. We, on the other hand, had far more difficulty in imitating even a few of their words, which were rich in consonants, and expressed with noise and puffing, as, for instance, Assumbrassum, Bruhmmbrhum and Psoh, the latter being pronounced with an explosion and a shooting forward of the head, not unlike the grimace of an ape. Sometimes they used a hissing sound like that of geese. One of them said he was called Mambrum, another Bonombrooai. I remember that they often uttered a word rich in vowels – *tumora* (1953, 135).

And later:

> As a sign of friendship and peace, they poured water on their heads with their hands, and seemed very satisfied when anyone replied to them with the same ceremony. Do these savages worship the watery element, as the Persians worship its opposite, fire? Have they perhaps some conception of water as an emblem of cleansing, purity, and truth for

body and soul or morals, as among the Egyptians and Jews? Or was their self-baptism reminiscent of an ancient rite which was performed and preached far and wide by the disciples of John and Christ for reform and chastity? (1953, 136).

Sparrman's series of rhetorical questions spirals into a sort of ethnographic vertigo. But he is not alone in his sense of puzzlement. And this perplexity and wonder at the strangeness of the strangers was shared by ni-Vanuatu. Alongside that word frequently recorded among the Malakulans (*tomarr*), later in Tanna, many of the voyage sources report another prevalent word – transcribed variously as *hibao* or *hebow*. Says Marra, "When these people make a wonder at any thing, they cry Hebow, and shake their right hand" (1967 [1775], 275). Sparrman describes an early incident on Tanna, when Cook gave an old man in a canoe a mirror, in which he looked many times with astonishment as he fitfully paddled his canoe to shore. There he was surrounded by many other men,

> and while they were looking at themselves in the mirror, there were thousands of shrill outcries of '*hibao*', for with this the Tannese announced their wonderment over anything strange that they noticed among us, such as our white faces, clothing, weapons (Sparrman 1953, 143).[43]

There are many self-conscious reflections by writers on this voyage as to how ni-Vanuatu saw them. So, Marra speculates:

> Here we cannot help remarking, that, by the savages bringing every where, upon the approach of the ship, cocoa-nuts, and other fruits, it should seem that they imagined the strangers to be a people like themselves, come from some distant island to visit them; and that therefore, it being usual for such visitors to be in want of such refreshments, it might be the custom for the inhabitants upon their first coming, to supply them; but that when they saw a people totally unlike themselves, and in a vessel too different from any they had ever before seen, it was but natural for them to retreat, not knowing their errand, and dreading perhaps an invasion, or some mischief to befall their country. Something of this kind must certainly have been the case, otherwise it is not easy to account for their coming off in their canoes loaded with fruit, and then retiring back without daring to go near the people they intended to supply (1967 [1775], 269–70).

And so we have the question: were these foods left warily for the strangers as supplications to those who were obviously hungry "white-skinned ghosts" (as Salmond suggests) or were they the offerings of hospitality to visiting human neighbours, whose arrival might presage conflict as well as an exchange of goods? This is not a question that the sources allow us categorically to answer, and indeed both interpretations might have been simultaneously sustained by ni-Vanuatu as they tried to work out how to respond to the strangers. The strangers were a people "like themselves" but also a "people totally unlike themselves". I am not dismissing the argument that the strangers *might* have been seen as returning ancestors or ghosts. Indeed, there is much evidence from later oral histories of ni-Vanuatu that, from early European contacts through to the experience of Americans in World War II, powerful strangers are often linked to the category of departed primordial gods or ancestral spirits (White and Lindstrom 1989, 404ff; Jolly 2003).

Certainly, the ways in which both Malakulans and Tannese handled their embodied encounters with the strangers suggests that there was a spiritual as much as a corporeal threat. Indeed, given indigenous aetiologies, corporeal and spiritual danger to the person could hardly be separated. So, as well as the wariness of food being left on the beaches for collection, we also have frequent reports that whenever objects were received, ni-Vanuatu men wrapped them in green leaves and that whenever the strangers touched their bodies, they wiped their skin with these same leaves.[44] Says Marra:

> It is not a little remarkable, that the natives of this island were more scrupulous in taking any thing from the sailors than those of any other nation, and never would touch with their bare hands what was given them, but always received it between green leaves, which they afterwards tied up, and carried upon the ends of their clubs; and if ever any of the sailors touched their skin, they always rubbed the part with the like green leaf (1967 [1775], 275).[45]

This may have been because the strangers were seen as powerful ghosts, but it might also be that exchanges with strangers threatened their own sacred power (and the wrapping was thus a sheath that protected such a loss) or it might be that they were wary that the strangers might attempt to ensorcell them with the residues of their own bodies, through the exchange of sweat or the touch of skin.[46]

Similarly, the "self-baptism" with salt water, which Sparrman describes above, is an act which allows no definitive ethnographic translation. To this day ni-Vanuatu use the medium of salt water not so much for purification as for sacralisation and desacralisation in ritual moments when powerful sacred forces endanger the living. So in some ceremonies after childbirth, for example, infants are taken for baths in the ocean at five-day intervals to strengthen them and to bring them from a state of liminality and danger into the world of the living (see Jolly 1994, 146; Layard 1942, 179). The head is the most sacred part of a person, through which the power of ancestors is transmitted to the living, and thus requires special attention. Salt water is also used as a medium in the transfer of malevolent spirits out the body of a person possessed, in which case the spirit once exorcised is trapped in a bamboo tube containing salt water (see Jolly 1994, 168–70). Anointing one's own head with salt water can be seen to strengthen or protect the spiritual state of the person, in a situation of danger, but it does not necessarily tell us that the person was being threatened by a "ghost."

What, then, of the seemingly definitive evidence that Malakulans called Europeans *tomarr*, a word which Salmond translates as ancestor or ghost? Contemporary linguistic studies of the languages of the peoples of Port Sandwich in Malakula rather record the word *ramač* as the word for ghost or devil and the word *na-tamat* for those islands off the south-east coast of Malakula (Charpentier 1979, 1995). This latter word is very close to the word for "peace" in many of the languages of North Vanuatu, variously *tamwate, tamwata, tagwata, tamate* (see also Deacon 1934, 750, *ni-tamate* "prayer, peace"), while in the Port Sandwich language it becomes *ramar*, which also means "neutral place".[47] Is it possible that the Malakulans who apprehensively approached the sailing boats in their canoes were rather uttering this word, invoking peace? This seems implied in Georg Forster's observation that they were "repeating the word Tomarr or Tomarro continually, which seemed to be an expression equivalent to the Taheitan Tayo (friend)" (Forster 2000 [1777] 2: 480). I am not arguing this contrary case, but rather suggesting that the sources, including the seemingly definitive verdicts of later ethnographers, allow for more uncertainty than Salmond admits.

There are other gestures that the strangers took unambiguously as signs of greeting or peace-making – namely, the waving of green boughs (cf. Tcherkézoff, this volume). Johann Reinhold Forster says this of the Malakulans:

> Several a shore & in the boats presented green bows of plants especially the *Croton variegatum* and *Dracæna terminalis* Linn: & waved with them towards us: nevertheless the greater part of the people were armed with bows & arrows, & some few with Spears (1982, 565).

Cook reciprocated with the waving of green boughs in return, which seemed to gratify the Malakulans (although whether he chose these precise species is unclear). This mutual exchange of waving green boughs is represented in the engraving of the landing at Malakula as a sign of peaceful greeting and civility. And most of the contemporary commentators were persuaded that this was its meaning. So, Marra describes Erromangans making "signs for the voyagers to land, by waving green boughs, the emblems of peace" (1967 [1775], 266). But the use of the two species of plants named by Forster is suggestive, for both croton and dracaenas are plants used in many islands of the archipelago to mark sacred states (e.g. they are planted in the rites of rank-taking in the *magi*, or graded society, of Malakula) and to cordon off sacred areas (see Jolly 1994, 189ff; Layard 1942, 709). Despite the initial hopes of peace expressed in Malakula, Erromango and Tanna, encounters on all these islands culminated in violent exchanges. And in these unfolding events it was not just the alleged bellicosity of indigenous men that was to blame but a tendency to violent overreaction on the part of both Cook and his men, vastly at odds with his desire for moderation and "gentle civility" with the natives. I will describe three successive incidents, on Malakula, Erromango and Tanna.

Pacifying Exchanges and "The Power of our *Jus Canonicum*"

On Malakula the ships were at first regularly visited by men in the early dawn, coming aboard unarmed and "swarming up the masts with the greatest readiness and confidence" (Sparrman 1953, 137). When the numbers became too great, orders were given to the boatwatch to restrict the visitors. "One Indian who was motioned away however took the sign in an unfriendly manner" (137). One of the sailors pushed his canoe off with a boat hook and the man shoved back with a bamboo cane. The "Indian" took an arrow from his quiver and was about to shoot with his bow when one of his compatriots already on board leapt out of the cabin window to try to stop him. In the ensuing struggle Captain Cook was called on deck and aimed his gun at the man, who then turned around and aimed at Cook instead. At this point Cook shot him in the head with smallshot:

> [B]ut after the wounded man had merely rubbed the wounds on his face a little, he soon plucked up courage again for revenge with a choice poisoned arrow, which he placed in his bow, but was frustrated again with a larger charge of shot [this time from Pickersgill, not Cook] so that his comrades had to paddle away with him (Sparrman 1953, 137).

Another man who fired an arrow at Cook was shot with a musket ball (which missed) and then a cannon was fired, which caused all the Malakulan men to paddle back to shore. Marra claims that one of the men in departing discharged an arrow at an officer and "paid for his audacity with his life" (1967 [1775], 262).

Cook tried to undo the effects of this spiralling violence later that day by landing alone and unarmed and carrying a green branch. The man who seemed to be leader of the Malakulans likewise disarmed and offered Cook a green branch and a pig. From this point onward there was an extended exchange of goods, by which the Europeans hoped to show their willingness to be friends. The Malakulans "did not show any enthusiasm over our iron ware" (Sparrman 1953, 138; and certainly did not try to steal nails like the Tahitians). They showed far more interest in red cloth, marble paper and barkcloth from Tahiti. In exchange for these "few trifles," the Malakulans offered weapons, but, according to Marra, were deaf to Cook's entreaties for water and more food. "None of these people brought either flesh or fruit to dispose of; nor could the captain procure more than one lean hog, though there were many within sight" (Marra 1967 [1775], 263).

Although Cook and the Forsters were allowed to do some sightseeing that afternoon around a village where they saw lots of alluring fresh food – piles of yams and many pigs and chickens – they were not offered any (which rather subverts the image of abundant supplicatory offerings to returning ancestral spirits). They were eventually allowed to cut wood, but penetration further inland was refused:

> However, we botanists sometimes managed to creep three or four paces inside the edge of the woods from the bare coral beach, and succeeded in hastily gathering a few plants, much as people pull firebrands out of the fire; but soon they motioned us back to the beach, as being impertinent, unjustified, and thrusting violators of their prohibition (Sparrman 1953, 138).

The strangers were vulnerable not just because of their need of wood, water and fresh food but also because of their scientific curiosity. It is unclear what the Malakulans made of their strong desire to collect leaves, but their prohibition on the strangers' movement seems to accord more with resistance to unwanted invasion, or perhaps suspicion of motives of sorcery, than the way in which dangerous ancestral spirits might be treated (see also Mosko this volume).

Later cycles of violence on Erromango and Tanna might again have induced ni-Vanuatu to see these strangers as unwanted and bellicose invaders rather than returning ghosts who had to be supplicated.[48] In early August, Cook anchored off the east coast of Erromango, taking two armed boats ashore in search of a safe harbour. He disembarked in a bay, carrying only a green branch, and was surrounded by a large crowd of armed warriors. He exchanged a few trinkets for a bamboo tube filled with water, some coconuts and a yam with a man who seemed a leader. But then, when Cook climbed back on board one of the boats, some of the armed warriors grabbed the gangplank while others seized the oars. Cook pointed his musket at the leader, who he thought had betrayed him, but his musket misfired and in the ensuing rain of arrows and spears discharged by the warriors, Cook ordered his men to open fire. Despite the unreliability of the British flints, at least four Erromangan men appeared to have been killed by musket fire,[49] while only two of the sailors were slightly wounded. Although a "few Indians returned with the captured oars" (Sparrman 1953, 142), it was

> considered expedient to teach them to realise the power of our *jus canonicum*, of which they had only heard explosions; therefore a four-pound ball was loosed off at them which, though it fell short of the beach, frightened them so much that not one was seen again. We saw the oars standing against a bush, but with the good breeze that sprang up we preferred to make sail and find some better place (Sparrman 1953, 142).

Finally I want to return again to a violent incident on Tanna that I have discussed earlier (Jolly 1992), especially in relation to the reflexive character of the voyage narrative by Georg Forster (2000 [1777], 1968). In general the stay on Tanna was far more pacific. Cook developed strong relationships with the leader Paowang,[50] and the procurement of wood, shale ballast and water and the collection of natural specimens, vocabularies and cultural knowledge proceeded in a less inhibited way than on Malakula or Erromango.[51] But a violent incident marred their last days on Tanna. I have earlier observed (Jolly 1992) how Georg Forster's construction of this incident in his narrative reinforced a sense of irony and self-criticism, and I here repeat some of that earlier analysis. It occurred while he and Sparrman were abroad in the interior, on their habitual naturalistic treks, although this time on separate tracks. While strolling through the Tannese countryside observing the varied landscape of field and forest and enjoying the calm of human cultivation Forster is led to reflect on how the Tannese had gradually come to trust them: "Our cool deliberate conduct, our moderation and the constant uniformity in all our proceedings, had conquered their jealous fears" (Forster 2000 [1777], 2: 549. Rather than viewing the Europeans as a base and treacherous enemy, the Tannese now saw them as fellow creatures. Forster then enters into a rapturous reverie about the intimacy they had been accorded:

> They permitted us to visit them in their shady recesses, and we sat down in their domestic circles with that harmony which befits the members of one great family. In a few days they began to feel a pleasure in our conversation, and a new disinterested sentiment, of more than earthly mould, even friendship, filled their heart. This retrospect was honourable to human nature, as it made us the benefactors of a numerous race (Forster 2000 [1777], 2: 549).

But coming from the interior on that day they met a woman trembling with fear and then some men, who motioned for them to return to the beach. There they saw two Tannese men holding another who was dead – a musket ball had penetrated his arm and his ribs. This had been fired by a sentry who was guarding the sailors while they were felling wood. A Tannese man had deliberately crossed the boundary line which, as usual, had been drawn to prevent local people coming too close. This man disregarded several warnings, crossed and recrossed and then took aim with a bow and arrow at the sentry who returned the lethal shot (Forster 2000 [1777], 2: 550). Cook attempted to appease the Tannese by putting the culprit in irons (although this act was later undone by Edgecombe, the lieutenant of Marines; cf. Adams 1984, 29–30).

In his description of this violent incident Forster's sympathy for the dead man is clear. He was trespassing across the boundary "perhaps with no other motive at present than that of asserting his liberty of walking where he pleased" (Forster 2000 [1777], 2: 550). Forster thought the Tannese would be justified in thinking of them as a "cruel and treacherous people who had polluted their island" (550) and was amazed that they took no retribution for the death of this man. He and Sparrman were

> struck with the moderation of the people, who had suffered us to pass by them unmolested, when they might easily have taken a severe revenge for the murder of their countryman (Forster 2000 [1777], 2: 550).[52]

Forster concluded blackly that "one dark and detestable action effaced all the hopes with which I had flattered myself" (Forster 2000 [1777], 2: 551). He then generalised this incident on Tanna to an overall appraisal of the voyage, lamenting the "many rash acts which we had perpetrated at almost every island in our course" (551). Although eager to collect knowledge about all these islands, he thought that this should never be pursued if violence was a likely result. Thus, on Tanna they had to give up all hopes of approaching the summit of the volcano, where "new observations" would have been possible "if the jealousy of the natives had not continually prevented our examining it" (552). Tannese resistance he construed as possessiveness or mistrust, rather than malevolence. Similarly on Erromango, he was not persuaded that people had had hostile intentions in detaining their boat, but thought rather that by levelling a musket at their chief, they had provoked the attack (505). While generally adhering to the opinion that contact with Europeans should be beneficial and improving he concluded that "it is much to be lamented that the voyages of Europeans cannot be performed without being fatal to the nations whom they visit" (505). He was not alone in his critique of the violence on Tanna. "It was most deplorable that, after fourteen days' sojourn here, on the day arranged for our departure we were compelled to stain the hospitable shore with the blood of a native" (Sparrman 1953, 150–1).

On the Beach, Unsettled Colonies and "Dancing With Strangers"

In Cook's journal entry for 20 July 1774, he observes that "Off the North end of the latter Island lies a rock above water not far from the Shore" (Cook 1969, 459). The island he depicts here is Pentecost and the rock probably Vathubwe, a place known in Sia Raga cosmography as the island's "stepping stone," the ancestral starting point of all humans who arrived on the island and the place where spirits jump off and leave after death. Says John Taylor, "Cook could not have known that his northerly approach, like that of Bougainville before him, enacted the retracing of more primordial itineraries" (2008, 51). According to the voyage narratives, Cook observed Pentecost (Whitsuntide) only from afar, but William Wales imaginatively reconfigured the intensive cultivation of its taro gardens into something more familiar: "imagining one's self in sight of England, with an extensive View of enclosed Fields before one" (Cook 1969,

459). Despite this prospect of a land available for civilised cultivation, Cook never set foot on the beach or in these "Fields."

But today on the beach at Aroa there is a local testament to Cook's arrival, in words carved in stone. Sand has swept over these rocks, the inscriptions are no longer clear, but some Sia Raga insist that Cook himself inscribed them. There are three different accounts of what is written there: "New Hebrides discovered by James Cook–Moon," "Sun–Moon" or "Captain Cook 1887" (Taylor 2008, 51). One of Taylor's Sia Raga interlocutors says there is "a picture of a crescent moon," traces of Cook's footprints and "a mark from his walking stick" (Taylor, pers. comm., July 2005):

> Just as the founding ancestor Bwatmahana and his nemesis Tagaro in their primordial journeys across the island created features in the landscape as signs of their power and passing, so too did Captain Cook leave his mark, appropriately on one of those Pacific beaches crucially situated as a boundary (Taylor 2008, 52).

Despite the contest about the inscription, the fact that the date engraved on the rock is more than a century after our received histories of Cook's voyage in Vanuatu, and that none of the primary sources suggest Cook made landfall on North Pentecost, this rock is for Sia Raga *dovonana* "memorial and proof" of his arrival. It seems, then, that for some descendants of those who had *no* such embodied contact with Cook, the idea of assimilating the voyages of Cook to the itineraries of their ancestors is compelling.[53] There is no such memorial of Quirós or Bougainville in stone or the flesh of memory.[54] But intriguingly in Sia Raga history Captain Cook is generally thought to have arrived *after* Jimmy, another white man (whose persona seems, rather, to derive from the era of the labour trade).[55] He was kidnapped, adopted and he assumed the clothes and customs of Sia Raga for many years, before he departed with some later visiting Europeans. The narrative arc of both the story of Cook and the story of Jimmy not only *re*-members the voyages of Europeans through the itineraries of indigenous gods or ancestors but also reflects on much *later* entanglements between ni-Vanuatu and Europeans, which were a part of their shared history of colonialism. In Sia Raga idiom, the ways of the place (*alenan vanua*) and those of Europeans (*alenan tuturani*) are *wasi*. As John Taylor has argued in his superb recent book (2008), the same idiom is used to depict the relation of the two moieties, the two sides of a house, or the two halves of a pandanus textile plaited together; they are necessarily imbricated or "stuck, entangled." They are locked in the tense embrace of both attraction and repulsion. Re-membering Cook in contemporary North Pentecost Vanuatu is an act of memory saturated with moral and political portent for the present, as Deborah Bird Rose has argued (1984, 2000) for similar stories about Captain Cook arriving in places far from his known landfalls in Australia.

Figure 3.10. The late Bong or Bumangari Kaon of Bunlap in the 1970s

Photograph: Margaret Jolly, taken August 1977. Previously published in Margaret Jolly, *Women of the Place: Kastom, colonialism and gender in Vanuatu*. Chur, Switzerland; Philadelphia: Harwood Academic Publishers, 1994, 4 (Plate 2). Reproduced with permission of Harwood Academic Publishers/Taylor & Francis Books UK.

In my view the memorialisation of Cook as akin to indigenous gods and ancestors is likely not a perpetuation of an indigenous oral history created at the moment of the embodied encounters of 1774 and generalised throughout the archipelago. More probably it is an oral historical reflection on the later centuries of colonial encounters and the way in which Europeans and ni-Vanuatu became "stuck together," entangled in a shared history. To claim Cook as akin to indigenous gods or ancestors is also to incorporate his power and in a way to domesticate it by making it indigenous. It has, I suggest, the same moral and political portent as the claim made by the late Bumangari Kaon, my interlocutor in South Pentecost in the early 1970s (see figure 3.10) that Europeans are like flighty birds, while ni-Vanuatu are like strong-rooted banyans, precedent and powerful as the "people of the place" (Jolly 1982, 1994). But, whereas Bumangari Kaon stressed the difference and distance between the ways of the place, *kastom* and European ways, Kolombas Todali and the Christian Sia Raga, with whom John Taylor lived thirty years later, embraced that difference within a logic of complementary opposites, which are like the sides of a house or a red pandanus textile, "stuck together," attracted and repulsed, similar and different.

Thus, we might re-member Fabian's propositions about the shifting language of sameness and difference, of incorporation and distantiation of others, in European visions from many centuries ago, by looking at how ni-Vanuatu too deploy such languages of shared humanity with, and ethnic and cultural difference from, Europeans. These shifting adjudications are situated in space and time, not just in the sense that they are contextually or historically fluid, but that present or proximate relations can be projected onto a past time or a more distant place. By re-membering Captain Cook as a later figure in a "beach crossing," Sia Raga affirm his sameness and his difference. But simultaneously, they proclaim their own precedence as the first people of the place and the powerful custodians of an independent future, in defiance of the compelling power of development and globalisation, arguably the discourses of teleological evolutionism in the twenty-first century.

But, we might ask, are the ways of Europeans and indigenes "stuck together" in quite the same way in places like Vanuatu and Australia, or Aotearoa New Zealand, or Hawai`i? There is perhaps a rather different resonance in the recirculation of stories of beach crossings in those places where settler colonialism still prevails and where the narratives of exploration are foundational stories in the continuing narrative justification of white settlement. For authors like Anne Salmond (2003) concerned to redress the consequences of colonialism and to push for the values of biculturalism in the present, in her own country of Aotearoa New Zealand, there is surely a desire to move beyond the logic of "two worlds" and "between worlds" to the position where Kuki might become an ancestor of Pacific peoples too. This is a noble aim, but we need to acknowledge how our contemporary political projects might structure our historical and anthropological imaginations in large and small ways. Perhaps one consequence of the stress on the bicultural agenda, in reconciling Maori and Pakeha in Aotearoa New Zealand, has been a tendency to occlude some of the deeper ancestry between Maori and other Pacific peoples – when they are constructed divergently as "natives" and "migrants". In such ways, their relationships to each other are defined not through their shared history of ancestral voyages or contemporary connections, but through the narrative of the bicultural nation-state. Their relation to each other is thus mediated by their respective relations to Pakeha (Jolly 2001; Teaiwa and Mallon 2006).[56] The privileged "beach crossing" is again that of European and Islander (see Jolly 2009).

Recirculating stories of first contact and especially of Captain Cook surely assume a particular local inflection in the context of Hawai`i and Australia too. The titanic contest between Sahlins and Obeyesekere as to whether Cook was perceived as a manifestation of Lono by eighteenth-century Hawaiians was not just a scholarly debate but echoed in the politics of the sovereignty struggle of twentieth-century Hawaiians in relation to foreign interests and the culture of "militourism" consequent on becoming the fiftieth state of the United States of America (see Teaiwa 1992). At the time of the Sahlins–Obeyesekere debate, a Sydney tabloid ran a banner headline: "Captain Cook Hero or Villain", and in a review of the latest flurry of Cook books a reviewer in *The Canberra Times* asks "James Cook: benign explorer or invader?" (Fuller 2008). As Nicholas Thomas has observed, scholarly works like popular appraisals "tend to lurch between the celebration of the discoverers and their demonization" as "evil harbingers of colonialism" (Forster 2000, xiv; cf. Williams 2008, 3–4). But, if we are to get beyond this tendency to lurch, we need to acknowledge that moral and political concerns pervade not just the contemporary oral histories of Pacific Islanders but the contemporary textual constructions of scholars. Stories of past Oceanic encounters are remembered in the moral and political relations we construct between those pasts and our presents.

References

Adams, Ron

1984 *In the Land of Strangers: A Century of European Contact with Tanna, 1774–1874*. Pacific Research Monograph No. 9. Canberra: The Australian National University.

Angleviel, Frédéric, ed.

2007 *Pedro Fernández de Quirós et le Vanuatu: Découverte mutuelle et historiographie d'un acte fondateur 1606*. Port Vila: Groupe de Recherche sur l'Histoire Océanienne Contemporaine / Délégation de la Commission Européenne au Vanuatu / Sun Productions.

Baert, Annie

2007 La découverte du Vanuatu par Pedro Fernadez de Quirós. In *Pedro Fernández de Quirós et le Vanuatu: Découverte mutuelle et historiographie d'un acte fondateur 1606,* ed. Frédéric Angleviel, 31–56. Port Vila: Groupe de Recherche sur l'Histoire Océanienne Contemporaine / Délégation de la Commission Européenne au Vanuatu / Sun Productions.

Ballard, Chris

2003 [1992] First contact as non-event. Invited paper prepared for session "Early Contact in Melanesia" at the 91st Annual Meeting of the American Anthropological Association, San Francisco, 2–6 December 1992. Published in French as "La fabrique de l'histoire: événement, mémoire et récit dans les Hautes Terres de Nouvelle-Guinée [Making history: Event, memory and narrative in the New Guinea Highlands]." In *Les rivages du temps: Histoire et anthropologie du Pacifique*, eds Isabelle Merle and Michel Naepels, 111–34. Cahiers du Pacifique Sud Contemporain no. 3. Paris: L'Harmattan.

Bloch, Maurice, and Jean H. Bloch

1980 Women and the dialectics of nature in eighteenth-century French thought. In *Nature, Culture and Gender*, eds Carol P. MacCormack and Marilyn Strathern, 25–41. Cambridge: Cambridge University Press.

Bolton, Lissant

2003 *Unfolding the Moon: Enacting Women's Kastom in Vanuatu.* Honolulu: University of Hawai`i Press.

Borofsky, Robert, ed.

2000 *Remembrance of Pacific Pasts: An Invitation to Remake History.* Honolulu: University of Hawai`i Press.

Bougainville, Louis de

1967 [1772] *A Voyage Round the World*, trans. from the French by John Reinhold Forster. London: Fascimile eds in Bibliotheca Australiana Series, vol. 12. Amsterdam and New York: Nico Israel and Da Capo Press.

Camino, Mercedes

2007 Cross-Cultural Engagements in the South Pacific: Quirós' Austrialia 1606. In *Pedro Fernández de Quirós et le Vanuatu: Découverte mutuelle et historiographie d'un acte fondateur 1606,* ed. Frédéric Angleviel, 57–83. Port Vila: Groupe de Recherche sur l'Histoire Océanienne Contemporaine / Délégation de la Commission Européenne au Vanuatu / Sun Productions.

Charpentier, Jean-Michel

1979 *La langue de Port-Sandwich (Nouvelles-Hébrides): Introduction phonologique et grammaire*. Paris: SELAF.

1995 Port Sandwich. In *Comparative Austronesian Dictionary: An Introduction to Austronesian Studies*, ed. Darrell T. Tryon, pt 1, fasc. 2, 829–36. Berlin: Mouton de Gruyter.

Cheesman, Evelyn

1949 *Camping Adventures on Cannibal Islands*. London: George C. Harrap and Co. Ltd.

Connolly, Bob, and Robin Anderson

1987 *First Contact: New Guinea's Highlanders Encounter the Outside World*. New York: Viking.

Clendinnen, Inga

2003 *Dancing with Strangers*. Melbourne: Text Publishing.

Cook, James

1777 *A Voyage towards the South Pole, and round the World, Performed in His Majesty's Ships, The Resolution and Adventure, in the Years 1772, 1773, 1774, and 1775*. London: W. Strathan and T. Caddell.

1969 *The Journals of Captain James Cook On His Voyages of Discovery, Vol 2. The Voyage of the Resolution and Adventure, 1772–1775*, ed. John C. Beaglehole. Cambridge: Cambridge University Press for the Hakluyt Society.

Deacon, Arthur Bernard

1934 *Malekula: A Vanishing People in the New Hebrides*, ed. Camilla H. Wedgwood. London: G. Routledge.

Dening, Greg

1998 *Readings/Writings*. Carlton, Vic.: Melbourne University Press.

2004 *Beach Crossings: Voyaging across Times, Cultures and Self*. Carlton, Vic.: Miegunya Press/Melbourne University Publishing.

Douglas, Bronwen

1999 Science and the art of representing "savages": Reading "race" in text and image in South Seas voyage literature. *History and Anthropology* 11: 157–201.

2006 Slippery Word, Ambiguous Praxis: "Race" and Late-18th-Century Voyagers in Oceania. *The Journal of Pacific History*. Vol 41: 1–29

2008 Climate to Crania: science and the racialization of human difference (33–96), and 'Novus Orbis Australis': Oceania in the science of race, 1750-1850 (99–155). In *Foreign Bodies: Oceania and the Science of Race 1750–1940* eds Bronwen Douglas and Chris Ballard. Canberra: ANU E-Press. http://epress.anu.edu.au/foreign_bodies_citation.html

Douglas, Bronwen, and Chris Ballard, eds

2008 *Foreign Bodies: Oceania and the Science of Race 1750–1940*. Canberra: ANU E-Press. http://epress.anu.edu.au/foreign_bodies_citation.html

Fabian, Johannes

1983 *Time and the Other: How Anthropology Makes its Object*. New York: Columbia University Press.

Forster, Georg

1777 *A Voyage Round the World in His Britannic Majesty's Sloop* Resolution, *commanded by Capt. James Cook, during the Years 1772, 3, 4 and 5*. London: B. White.

1968 [1777] *Georg Forsters Werke* [*A Voyage Round the World in His Britannic Majesty's Sloop* Resolution], vol. 1, ed. Robert L. Kahn. Berlin: Akademie-Verlag.

2000 [1777] *A Voyage Round the World by George Forster,* eds Nicholas Thomas and Oliver Berghof. 2 vols. Honolulu: University of Hawai`i Press.

Forster, Johann Reinhold

1778 *Observations Made during a Voyage round the World, on Physical Geography, Natural History, and Ethic Philosophy*. London: Printed for G. Robinson.

1982 *The Resolution Journal of Johann Reinhold Forster, 1772–1775*, vol. 4, ed. Michael E. Hoare. London: Hakluyt Society.

1996 *Observations Made during a Voyage Round the World*. New edition, eds Nicholas Thomas, Harriet Guest, and Michael Dettelbach; with a linguistic appendix by Karl H. Rensch. Honolulu: University of Hawai`i Press.

Fuller, Peter

2008 James Cook: benign explorer or invader? *The Canberra Times – Panorama*, 4 October, 2008, 14–15.

Harris, Marvin

1968 *The Rise of Anthropological Theory: A History of Theories of Culture*. New York: Crowell.

Hetherington, Michelle, ed.

2001 *Cook and Omai: The Cult of the South Seas*. Parkes, ACT: National Library of Australia.

Jack-Hinton, Colin

1969 *The Search for the Islands of Solomon 1567–1838*. Oxford: Clarendon Press.

Jolly, Margaret

1982 Birds and banyans of South Pentecost: *Kastom* in anti-colonial struggle. In *Reinventing Traditional Culture: The Politics of* Kastom *in Island Melanesia*, eds R.M. Keesing and R. Tonkinson. *Mankind* 13 (4): 338–56. Special issue.

1992 "Ill-natured comparisons": Racism and relativism in European representations of ni-Vanuatu from Cook's second voyage. In *Colonialism and Culture*, ed. Nicholas Thomas. *History and Anthropology* 5 (3–4): 331–64. Special issue.

1993 Lascivious ladies, beasts of burden and voyaging voyeurs: Representations of women from Cook's voyages in the Pacific. Paper presented to 9th David Nichol Smith Memorial Seminar, "Voyages and Beaches, Discovery and the Pacific 1700–1840", University of Auckland, New Zealand, August 24–28.

1994 *Women of the Place: Kastom, Colonialism, and Gender in Vanuatu*. Chur, Switzerland; Philadelphia: Harwood Academic Publishers.

1996a Devils, holy spirits, and the swollen god: Translation, conversion and colonial power in the Marist mission, Vanuatu, 1887–1934. In *Conversion to Modernities: The Globalization of Christianity*, ed. Peter van der Veer, 231–62. New York and London: Routledge.

1996b Desire, difference and disease: Sexual and venereal exchanges on Cook's voyages in the Pacific. In *Exchanges: Cross-cultural Encounters in Australia and the Pacific*, ed. Ross Gibson, 187–217. Sydney: Museum of Sydney/Historic Houses Trust of New South Wales.

1997 From Point Venus to Bali Ha`i: Eroticism and exoticism in representations of the Pacific. In *Sites of Desire, Economies of Pleasure: Sexualities in Asia and the Pacific*, eds Lenore Manderson and Margaret Jolly, 99–122, 303–6. Chicago: University of Chicago Press.

2001 On the edge: Deserts, oceans, islands. In *Native Cultural Studies in the Pacific*, eds Vicente Diaz and J. Kehaulani Kauanui. *The Contemporary Pacific* 13(2): 417–66. Special issue.

2003 Spouses and Siblings in Sa Stories. *The Australian Journal of Anthropology* 14 (2): 188–208.

2007 Unsettling memories: Commemorating "Discoverers" in Australia and Vanuatu in 2006. La découverte du Vanuatu par Pedro Fernadez de Quirós. In *Pedro Fernández de Quirós et le Vanuatu: Découverte mutuelle et historiographie d'un acte fondateur 1606,* ed. Frédéric Angleviel, 197–219. Port Vila: Groupe de Recherche sur l'Histoire Océanienne Contemporaine / Délégation de la Commission Européenne au Vanuatu / Sun Productions.

2008 Moving Objects: Reflections on Oceanic Collections. Distinguished Lecture presented to European Society of Oceanists, Verona, Italy, 10-12 July 2008.

2009 Beyond the beach: The limen of Oceanic pasts, presents and futures. In *Changing Contexts, Shifting Meanings,* ed. Elfriede Hermann. Honolulu: University of Hawai`i Press and Honolulu Academy of Arts.

n.d. *An Ocean of Difference: Revisioning Gender and Sexuality on Cook's Voyages in the Pacific.* Ms in preparation

Jordanova, Ludmilla J.

1980 Natural facts: A historical perspective on science and sexuality. In *Nature, Culture and Gender*, eds Carol MacCormack and Marilyn Strathern, 42–69. Cambridge: Cambridge University Press.

1989 *Sexual Visions: Images of Gender in Science and Medicine between the Eighteenth and Twentieth Centuries.* New York: Harvester Wheatsheaf.

Kelly, Celsus, ed.

1966 *La Austrialia del Espiritu Santo: The journal of Fray Martin de Munilla O.F.M. and other documents relating to the voyage of Pedro Fernandez de Quiros to the South Sea (1606–1606) and the Franciscan Missionary Plan (1617–1627),* trans. and ed. Celsus Kelly. 2 vols. Cambridge: Cambridge University Press.

Layard, John

1942 *Stone Men of Malekula: The Small Island of Vao.* London: Chatto and Windus.

Lightner, Sara, and Anna Naupa

2005 *Histri Bilong Yumi Long Vanuatu: An Educational Resource.* 4 vols. Port Vila: Vanuatu Cultural Centre.

Lindstrom, Lamont

2009 Naming and memory on Tanna, Vanuatu. In *Changing Contexts, Shifting Meanings,* ed. Elfriede Hermann. Honolulu: University of Hawai`i Press and Honolulu Academy of Arts. Forthcoming.

Luker, Vicki

n.d. Introduction. In *Engendering Health in the Pacific*. (m.s.), eds Vicki Luker and Margaret Jolly.

Luque, Miguel and Carlos Mondragón

2005 Faith, fidelity and fantasy: Don Pedro Fernández de Quirós and the "foundation, government and sustenance" of *La Nueba Hierusalem* in 1606. *The Journal of Pacific History* 40 (2): 133–48.

Markham, Clements

1967 [1904] *The Voyages of Pedro Fernandez de Quiros 1595 to 1606*, vol. 1. Nendeln/Liechtenstein. London: Hakluyt Society.

Marra, John

1967 [1775] *Journal of the Resolution's Voyage in 1771–1775*. Fascimile eds in Bibliotheca Australiana Series, vol. 15, ed. David Henry. Amsterdam: Nico Israel.

McGrane, Bernard

1989 *Beyond Anthropology: Society and the Other.* New York: Columbia University Press.

Mondragón, Carlos

2006 Remembering 1606 in Vanuatu: Memory, manipulation and the unequal representation of the past in Oceania. Paper presented to Pacific and Asian History seminar series, The Australian National University, Canberra, 16th June 2006.

2007 Ethnological Origins of the ni-Vanuatu "Other": Quirós and the early Spanish historiography of Asia and the Pacific. In *Pedro Fernández de Quirós et le Vanuatu: Découverte mutuelle et historiographie d'un acte fondateur 1606,* ed. Frédéric Angleviel, 145–67. Port Vila: Groupe de Recherche sur l'Histoire Océanienne Contemporaine / Délégation de la Commission Européenne au Vanuatu / Sun Productions.

Obeyesekere, Gananath

1992 *The Apotheosis of Captain Cook: European Mythmaking in the Pacific.* Princeton, NJ: Princeton University Press.

Pagden, Anthony

1982 *The fall of natural man: the American Indian and the origins of comparative ethnology.* Cambridge and New York: Cambridge University Press.

Pérez, Roberto Ferrando, ed.

2000 *Descubrimiento de las regiones austriales.* 3d ed., rev. Madrid: Dastin.

Perez, Michel

2007 Spain in the Pacific: A Re-Reading of Colonial History. Quirós against the background of colonial rivalries. In *Pedro Fernández de Quirós et le Vanuatu: Découverte mutuelle et historiographie d'un acte fondateur 1606*, ed. Frédéric Angleviel, 169–96. Port Vila: Groupe de Recherche sur l'Histoire Océanienne Contemporaine / Délégation de la Commission Européenne au Vanuatu / Sun Productions.

Rose, Deborah Bird

1984 The saga of Captain Cook: Morality in Aboriginal and European law. *Australian Aboriginal Studies* 2: 24–39.

2000 *Dingo Makes us Human: Life and Land in an Australian Aboriginal Culture*. Cambridge: Cambridge University Press.

Sahlins, Marshall

1981 *Historical Metaphors and Mythical Realities: Structure in the Early History of the Sandwich Islands Kingdom*. ASAO Special Publications Series, vol. 1. Ann Arbor: University of Michigan Press.

1982 The apotheosis of Captain Cook. In *Between Belief and Transgression: Structuralist Essays in Religion, History, and Myth*, eds Michel Izard and Pierre Smith. Chicago: University of Chicago Press.

1985 *Islands of History*. Chicago: University of Chicago Press.

1989 Captain Cook in Hawaii. *Journal of the Polynesian Society* 98 (4): 371–423.

1995 *How "Natives" Think: About Captain Cook, for Example*. Chicago and London: University of Chicago Press.

Salmond, Anne

1991 *Two Worlds: First Meetings between Maori and Europeans 1642–1772*. Auckland: Viking.

2003 *The Trial of the Cannibal Dog: Captain Cook in the South Seas*. London: Allen Lane, Penguin Books.

Schieffelin, Edward L., and Robert Crittenden

1991 *Like People You See in a Dream: First Contact in Six Papuan Societies*. Stanford: Stanford University Press.

Smith, Bernard

1984 Captain Cook's artists and the portrayal of Pacific peoples. *Art History* 7 (3): 295–312.

1985 [1960] *European Vision and the South Pacific, 1768–1850*. 2nd ed. Sydney: Harper & Row.

1988 *Style, Information and Image in the Art of Cook's Voyages*. Christchurch, NZ: School of Fine Arts, University of Canterbury.

1992 *Imagining the Pacific: In the Wake of the Cook Voyages*. Carlton, Vic.: Miegunyah Press/Melbourne University Publishing.

Sparrman, Anders

1953 *A Voyage Round the World With Captain James Cook in H.M.S. Resolution*. London: Robert Hale.

Spate, O.H.K.

1979 *The Spanish Lake: The Pacific Since Magellan*, vol. 1. London: Croom Helm. Online version by ANU E Press (The Australian National University, Canberra), http://epress.anu.edu.au/spanish_lake_citation.html

Taylor, John Patrick

2008 *The Other Side: Ways of Being and Place in Vanuatu*. Pacific Islands Monograph Series 22. Honolulu: University of Hawai`i Press.

Tcherkézoff, Serge

2004a *Tahiti 1768—Jeunes filles en pleurs: La face cachée des premiers contacts et la naissance du mythe occidental*. Papeete: Au Vent des Îles.

2004b *"First Contacts" in Polynesia: The Samoan Case (1722–1848). Western Misunderstandings about Sexuality and Divinity*. Christchurch and Canberra: Macmillan Brown Centre for Pacific Studies, New Zealand, and *Journal of Pacific History*.

Teaiwa, Teresia K.

1992 Bikinis and other s/pacific n/oceans. *The Contemporary Pacific* 6 (1): 87–109.

Teaiwa, Teresia and Sean Mallon

2006 Ambivalent Kinships? Pacific People in New Zealand. In *New Zealand Identities, Departures and Destinations*, eds James Liu, Tim Mc Creanor, Tracy Macintosh and Teresia Teaiwa, 207–99. Wellington: Victoria University Press.

Thomas, Nicholas

1996 On the varieties of the human species: Forster's comparative ethnology. In *Observations Made During a Voyage Round the World, on Physical Geography, Natural History and Ethic Philosophy*, by Johann Reinhold Forster. New edition, eds Nicholas Thomas, Harriet Guest, and Michael Dettelbach, xxiii–xl. Honolulu: University of Hawai`i Press.

1997 Objects of knowledge: Oceanic artifacts in European engravings. In *In Oceania: Visions, Artifacts, Histories*, Nicholas Thomas, 93–132. Durham and London: Duke University Press.

2003 *Discoveries: The Voyages of Captain Cook*. London: Allen Lane, Penguin Books.

Williams, Glyn

2008 *The Death of Captain Cook: A Hero Made and Unmade*. London: Profile Books.

White, Geoffrey M. White and Lamont Lindstrom

1989 *The Pacific Theater: Island Representations of World War II*, Pacific Islands Monograph Series, No 8. Honolulu: University of Hawai`i Press.

Notes

[1] I have benefited from close readings and insightful comments from Chris Ballard, Lamont Lindstrom, Mark Mosko, Serge Tcherkézoff and John Taylor, and two anonymous reviewers to all of whom I offer warm thanks. My heartfelt thanks also to Annegret Schemberg for her copyediting and proofreading (just prior to her retirement), to Lia Szokalski for her work on the entire manuscript and to Michelle Antoinette for meticulous editing and for consummately shepherding the final version to the press. All errors and misinterpretations are, of course, my own.

Vanuatu is, of course, an anachronism in that during the three voyages considered in this chapter, the names of the several islands and the archipelago changed from Terra Australis del Espiritu Santo to Archipel des grandes Cyclades, to New Hebrides/Nouvelles-Hébrides. There was no indigenous name for the entire archipelago and no indigenous sense of its unity until the mid-twentieth century in the colonial and postcolonial periods. Although I use Vanuatu as a transhistorical label and even call the people of the place ni-Vanuatu, I prefer this anachronism to the shifting foreign appellations of earlier periods.

[2] There is some contention about the spelling of this name. As Jack-Hinton (1969) notes, Quirós claimed he had changed the traditional spelling Austral to Austrial in recognition of the royal connection between Austria and the king of Spain. It is possible that on the voyage he actually named the island La Australia del Espiritu Santo, since this name appears in a manuscript which predates the Quirós– Bermúdez *relacion*. In two later reports he writes of *Las Tierras Australes* and *La Australia*. It was given various names by the different members of the expedition, de Prado called it *La Grande Australia del Spiritu Santo*, de Leza *La Parte Austral del Espiritu Santo*, and Torres *Espiritu Santo*, the name it bears today. Luque and Mondragón (2005, 142) are categorical: Quirós baptised the island *Austrialia del Espiritu Santo*, not Australia, in honour of the Spanish monarch's link to the royal house of Austria.

[3] Cook, in this naming, evoked the Old Hebrides Islands off Scotland, just as his naming of New South Wales also evoked the more familiar coastline of his home island.

[4] As well as texts there were, on Cook's voyage, also many images created and many objects collected. I cannot consider these here (but see Jolly 1992 and Jolly 2008, n.d.).

[5] I owe this witty locution to Borofsky (2000), who deploys it in the introduction to a collected volume of essays on Pacific history.

[6] The relation between ni-Vanuatu memories and European projects to celebrate the anniversaries of these early navigators is interesting and important. This was made clear in the process of the celebration of the 400th anniversary in May 2006 in Port Vila, Luganville and Matantas, Espiritu Santo, organised by the Delegation of the European Commission and the Embassies of Spain (in Australia) France and Germany (in Vanuatu). Prior to this event Quirós seems to have been unimportant in indigenous oral histories (Ralph Regenvanu, pers. comm., February 2006). But the processes leading up to this celebration occasioned some local leaders and indeed the government of Sanama Province to revive his memory and, despite abundant evidence of the violence of his sojourn on Espiritu Santo, to recuperate him as the man who first brought Christianity to Vanuatu (see Mondragón 2006; Jolly 2007). As can be seen in the commemorative stamp (reproduced in Jolly 2007, 207), the privileged theme at these events was exchange: the meeting of two cultures, or in Bislama *"tufala kaljai mitim tufala"*. For a critical appraisal of these events see Mondragón (2006) and Jolly (2007).

[7] Both in the debates about the Hawaiians' perception of Cook as Lono and Papua New Guinea Highlanders' changing perceptions of whites there is a tendency to make a categorical distinction

between gods or spirit beings and humans, which – as Dening (2004), Tcherkézoff (2004b) and Salmond (2003) suggest – is at odds with Pacific perceptions. Living humans could be seen as instantations of the gods, as in the Polynesian perceptions of high-ranking people as embodying *akua*. And even in less hierarchical polities and pantheons, such as the Papua New Guinea Highlands or Vanuatu, living humans were often endowed with a spiritual aspect which connected them with ancestors, and which at death transformed them into "ghosts" or spiritual presences. For a further discussion of this problem see the introduction to this volume.

[8] Although at risk of mixing metaphors here, I owe this powerful phrase to Vicki Luker, who uses it in her introduction to our co-edited volume *Engendering Health in the Pacific* (Luker and Jolly n.d.).

[9] There has been some recent work on Quirós' voyage by both archaeologists (Matthew Spriggs et al.) and anthropologists and historians (Carlos Mondragón and Miguel Luque), to which I am heavily indebted, see below. There are also some excellent essays in the recent book edited by Angleviel (2007); see especially Michel Perez (2007, 169–96) on "Anglo-Saxon double standards" and the neglect of Spain in broader historiographies of the Pacific; Annie Baert (2007, 31–56) on the Iberian expansion and the "clearer zones" and "darker aspects" of events in Vanuatu; and Baert (2007, 31–56) and Mercedes Camino (2007, 57–83) on the construction of an earthly paradise in the context of cross-cultural exchange.

[10] Captain Clerke, of Cook's voyage of 1774, said: "He has given a most pompous description of this Country in his Memorials to the King of Spain, wherein he solicits the settlement of these Isles, however I firmly believe Mr Quiros's Zeal and warmth for his own favourite projects has carried him too far in the qualities he has ascribed to this Country" (Cook 1969, 516–7). Georg Forster, also on Cook's second voyage in 1774, proclaimed a slightly more rational motivation for Quirós' claims of having found treasure on Espiritu Santo: "I will not pretend to say that they would find great riches of silver and pearls, which Quiros was forced to speak of, in order to engage an interested, avaricious court, to support his great and spirited undertakings. These incitements are not necessary now a-days, when several monarchs in Europe have convinced the world that they can institute voyages of discovery, with no other view than the increase of human knowledge, and the improvement of mankind" (2000 [1777], 2: 561).

[11] Luque and Mondragón (2005) are dedicated to explaining the cultural logic of these encounters from the Hispanic side, while forthcoming papers explore them from an indigenous perspective, grounded in recent ethnography and oral history, in both Big Bay and Taumako. Luque and Mondragón (2005, 134) discern the Anglophone stereotype of Quirós not just in specialist texts but in general histories of the Pacific.

[12] To some extent I am still dependent on such partial texts, since I do not have the same access to the definitive documents "which lie scattered across diverse Iberian and American archives" (Luque and Mondragón 2005, 134). Many key Iberian sources long ago translated into English or French suffered from bad translation or inadequate contextualisation. So, Markham's text (1967 [1904]) uses a nineteenth-century compilation by Zaragoza, which relies on incomplete manuscript sources (Luque and Mondragón 2005, 135). Luque and Mondragón rather rely on a new and definitive Spanish edition (Pérez 2000), based on fuller manuscripts held at the Biblioteca Nacional and Museo Naval in Madrid. Since I have neither the linguistic nor cultural capacity to read these sources, unlike Luque and Mondragón, I am heavily dependent on their reinterpretations and can only partially redress the problems with the English-language sources I cite here.

[13] This is clearly a critical reference to the title of the influential work by Spate (1979): rather than a "Spanish Lake," they suggest it was a "Castilian Lake," since the Spanish monarch was based in the Kingdom of Castile.

[14] Says Colin Jack-Hinton: "It was during his voyage to Santa Cruz as Mendaña's Chief Pilot that Quirós became obsessed with the idea which was to dominate the remainder of his life; the discovery of the antipodean continent, or *Nuevo Mundo* as he was later to call it, which he believed must occupy a quarter of the globe, and to the supposed inhabitants of which he wished to offer the means for the salvation of their immortal souls. Of Quirós it surely can be said, with little reservation or qualification, that his motives were religious, his interests those of a curious, enquiring, Renaissance cosmographer and explorer" (1969, 133).

[15] Serge Tcherkézoff (pers. comm., November 2002) suggests that this was more likely a girl than a boy, but, although this is clearly consequential, I cannot elaborate on the importance of gender misrecognition here.

[16] Spate comments: "His holy design may have been implanted in his mind by the unforgettable sight of the young Marquesan, so beautiful and yet damned; but if he arrived in Rome as a man with a mission, it was here that he became a man possessed, and his possession held him through humiliating failure,

grinding poverty, and the sickness of hope ever deferred, until death 'saved him from further frustration and humiliation and the Spanish authorities from further inconvenience'" (1979, 133).

[17] Luque and Mondragón (2005, 141) concur that he obtained an unprecedented authority from the "inexperienced but pious Philip III," who had been persuaded both by the prior support given by Pope Clement VIII and Quirós' persuasive rhetoric about the need to take Christianity to the heathen peoples of Terra Australis. But they see this rhetoric of religious zeal as motivated by the desire to oppose Mendaña's widow, Doña Isabel Barreto, and to underwrite an ambitious navigation in a period of stringent financial constraints. He succeeded in gaining personal authority from Philip III and in circumventing approval from the Council of the Indies, being directly financed by the Council of State (2005, 140).

[18] As Luque and Mondragón (2005, 138) recount, Quirós intended to sail straight south-west from Peru, but Torres and Bilboa overrode his instructions and headed north by north-west, a route in which he had to acquiesce given that the prevailing winds were west/north-west. Eventually Quirós directed a due west course toward the Santa Cruz group, known from the Mendaña expedition, where they encountered the outlier of Taumako.

[19] There are seven accounts of the voyage, of which only those of Gasper Gonzales De Leza, the pilot, and Fray Martin de Munilla, the Franciscan commissary, are journals. The other accounts are those of Quirós (actually written by Luis de Belmonte Bermúdez, his personal scribe, cited as Quirós–Bermúdez herein), the narrative of Fray Juan de Torquemada, and brief summaries by the accountant Juan de Iturbe; de Torres and Don Deigo de Prado y Tovar (see Kelly 1966, 1: 6–7).

[20] Note the difference between this correct Spanish translation and that offered by Markham: "We come from the east, we are Christians, we seek you and we want you to be ours" (Markham 1967 [1904], 237). I am grateful to Carlos Mondragón for this correction (pers. comm., August 2008).

[21] There is some doubt as to whether Quirós knew in advance of their being put in stocks; if so, he could not admit it publicly, since this was against the instructions of the court. There is also some doubt about who ordered the barbering.

[22] Their status as envoys is implied in this source, but the boys may have been equally inspired by playful curiosity as much as the collective desire for engagement and exchange (John Taylor, pers. comm. by email, July 2005).

[23] Luque and Mondragón (2005, 141–2) observe how Quirós' creation of the Chivalric Order of the Holy Ghost has been most ridiculed, but finds the most likely rationale for this celebration of the Holy Trinity in his devotion to the Franciscan order and in the alluring model of the chivalric knight or paladin, who dominated many popular tales of the time. They also observe that in the first act of formal possession on May 14, as recounted by Quirós– Bermúdez, the land is claimed first in the name of Jesus, God, Mary and then, last, the king of Spain. This was apparently challenged by the Spanish aristocrat Diego Prado y Tovar, who interrupted the scribe and proclaimed in the name of the king. Quirós rebuffed him, thus manifesting what Luque and Mondragón perceive as his divided political and religious loyalties. By naming God and his temporal envoy the pope as precedent in power, Quirós was perhaps deviously securing the potential of a future claim by a sovereign Portugal over Terra Australis, the pope willing (Luque and Mondragón 2005, 144).

[24] This is the spelling of Taumako, an outlier of the Santa Cruz group used in this source and it suggests that despite the lack of interest in language and the names of people and places, the Hispanic navigators recorded at least one indigenous name.

[25] This ponderous machinery of government has been much satirised, even by his contemporaries. Fray Martin satirised the diversity of knights: "negro-knights and Indian-knights and knights who were knight-knights" (cited in Spate 1979, 137). Spate defends Quirós, suggesting that he was only setting up the usual machinery of a Spanish municipality. Quirós did surely go further than this by instituting a new Chivalric Order of the Holy Ghost, and requiring all to wear the insignia of blue taffeta crosses. Fray Martin wisely declined, but "even two negro cooks were rewarded by their largesse … for their gallantry and courage. Besides, on that day he granted them their liberty, though they did not belong to him, and what is more they afterwards continued in the self-same state of slavery" (cited in Spate 1979, 136–7). However, as Luque and Mondragón suggest, these contemporary Spanish critics were *not* criticising these rituals from a modern secular viewpoint as "deranged theatrics" (2005, 142), but were, rather, expressing their contempt for the authoritarian ineptitude of a presumptuous Portuguese. Moreover, they suggest that the organisation of the secular authority adhered strictly to the requirements of the Common Law of the period and prevailed in the Indies.

[26] See Obeyesekere (1992, 17–8, 139).

[27] This fish, which the Spanish called *pargos*, was probably Red Sea Bream (*Sparus erythrinus*) and like many fish in tropical waters is not so much poisonous in itself but seasonally poisonous, if it has been eating plankton, mangrove fruits or has been affected by degraded coral (see Kelly 1966, 1: 233). There is a large literature on this kind of fish poisoning, or as it is now called *cigarateria*. The several accounts of Cook's voyages also report the consumption of poisonous fish in a similar season, on 23 July 1774. This led to acute headache, vomiting, diarrhoea, numbness, swelling and profuse salivation. By a series of experiments with unfortunate dogs, the scientists on Cook's second voyage established that it was the diet rather than the fish that was responsible. Georg Forster observed that the fish acquired this quality through feeding on poisonous vegetables, since the most venomous portion was the intestine. He noted not only that men but also that "hogs, dogs and even the parroquet from the Friendly Isles who dined on it took ill and some died" (2000: 2, 496). A day later he observed that the ship was still like a hospital. Later on in that voyage, whilst fishing off Tanna, they ate the same fish without ill effect.

[28] In one of his many later reports, the Memorial 40, he envisaged the New Jerusalem as a city with five large plazas, shaped in the form of a large cross, and of two other great cities: one facing west toward the Philippines, the other east toward Peru. The New Jerusalem was thus envisaged as in the middle of the Castilian Lake (Luque and Mondragón 2005, 146). As Luque and Mondragón (148) attest, this was not the only New Jerusalem of the epoch: Florence and Münster in Europe and several Asian cities were also so proclaimed.

[29] Quirós kidnapped four young men from Taumako, but three escaped in the waters off Tikopia, leaving the fourth, whom we know as Pedro, to continue on the voyage (Spate 1979, 135). Of the three boys taken from Santo, Pablo was the eldest. Both he and Pedro died in Mexico in 1607 (Kelly 1966, 1: 265). We do not know the fate of the other two boys.

[30] In a recent paper presented at the conference to mark the 400th anniversary of Quirós in Vanuatu, Mondragón notes the paucity of ethnographic depiction and speculation about the peoples of north Vanuatu (2007, 166–7). He notes the contrastive way in which Quirós–Bermúdez and Diego de Prado y Tovar spoke of skin colour, the former were more subtle, the latter vituperatively negative "a very black and ugly people" (Mondragon 2007, 164). Quirós–Bermúdez and others also reported on clothing, weapons, tools and especially pottery as markers of relative cultural sophistication but little about indigenous government, not at all in Big Bay and only briefly on Gaua. But the stress in my reading is less on plotting a cultural or racial hierarchy of peoples and more on plotting a spatial cosmography of Hispanic imperial influence in which Asia and the Pacific were seen primarily in relation to the peoples of the Hispanic colonies in the New World and the Philippines, and typically understood in terms of a providentialist framework that stressed the unity of humanity and the universal potential for salvation through the work of messianic missionaries (Mondragón 2006a, 6–11).

[31] See the statement by Diego de Prado y Tovar, apropos the people of Big Bay, that "with barbarians such as these you cannot use reason, and we needed to teach them not to be impertinent to the Spanish people, who are the most respected of all the nations on earth" (quoted by Mondragón 2006a, 15).

[32] Smith does not thereby suggest a naive naturalism, but a tendency to mediate neo-classical theories of art with "empirical habits of vision" (1985, 3).

[33] I thank John Taylor for reminding me of this possibility.

[34] Says Bougainville: "This early departure, doubtless, ruined the project of the islanders to attack us, because they had not yet disposed everything to that purpose; at least we were inclined to think so, by seeing them advance to the sea-shore, and send a shower of stones and arrows after us. Some muskets fired off into the air, were not sufficient to rid us of them; many advanced into the water, in order to attack us with more advantage; another discharge of muskets, better directed, immediately abated their ardour, and they fled to the woods with great cries. One of our sailors was slightly wounded by a stone" (1967 [1772], 290).

[35] To be fair, Bougainville does acknowledge that they could not determine whether these three-foot-high pallisades were "intrenchments, or merely limits of different possessions" (1967 [1772], 292).

[36] His depictions of men's jewellery – nose ornaments, ivory and pigs' tusks bracelets and tortoise-shell necklets – are presented as curious, and their weapons – bows and arrows (some pointed with bone or barbed), ironwood clubs and stones – are described indifferently. The light and shallow soil of Ambae was thought responsible for the fact that fruits of the same species of Tahiti "are not so fine and not so good here" (Bougainville 1967 [1772], 292).

[37] So, Bougainville comments: "I called the lands we have now discovered, Archipelago of the great Cyclades [*Archipel des grandes Cyclades*]. To judge of this Archipelago by what we have gone through, and by what we have seen of it at a distance, it contains at least three degrees of latitude and five of longitude. … As for ourselves, when we fell in with it, every thing conspired to persuade us that it

was the *Tierra Austral del Espiritu Santo*. Appearances seemed to conform to Quiros's account, and what we daily discovered, encouraged our researches. It is singular enough, that exactly in the same latitude and longitude where Quiros places his bay of St. Philip and St. Jago, on a coast which at first seemed to be that of a continent, we should find a passage exactly of the same breadth which he assigns to the entrance of his bay. Has this Spanish navigator seen things in a wrong light? Or, has he been willing to disguise his discoveries? Was it by guess that the geographers made this Tierra del Espiritu Santo the same continent with New Guinea? To resolve this problem, it was necessary to keep in the same latitude for the space of three hundred and fifty leagues further. I resolved to do it, though the condition and the quantity of our provisions seemed to give us reason to make the best of our way to some European settlement. The event has shewn that little was wanting to make us the victims of our own perseverance" (1967 [1772], 298–9).

[38] Arguments such as these have been both echoed and complicated in later writings by others, most notably in the volume *Foreign Bodies*, edited by Bronwen Douglas and Chris Ballard (2008). See also Douglas 2006.

[39] It is probably worthwhile reproducing these quotes in full. Cook said that the Malakulans were an: "Apish nation, for take them in gener[a]l they are the most ugly and ill proportioned people I ever saw and in every respect different from any we have yet seen in this sea. They are rather a Diminutive Race and almost as dark as Negros, which they in some degree resemble in thier [sic] countenances, but they have not such fine features" (Cook 1969, 466). Of Malakulan women he said, "We saw but few Women and they were full as disagreeable as the Men" (Cook 1969, 465), and of Erromangan women, "I saw some few Women which I thought ugly" (Cook 1969, 480).

[40] This is a reference to the theory of Lord Monboddo who embraced orang-utans in his conception of humanity, although he saw them as degenerated humans who had lost the power of speech. Both Johann and Georg Forster were disputing this theory in the context of adjudications about Malakulans.

[41] According to Lamont Lindstrom, Salmond has misinterpreted these events since *guanattan* does in fact mean nutmeg in Kwamera language spoken around Port Resolution (its contemporary transcription is *kwanetan*). As Lindstrom reminds me, "George has the story as Johann cutting open a pigeon, finding a nutmeg in its craw, and asking a Tannese guide to lead him to a nutmeg tree in return for a mother of pearl shell. The Tannese guy led Johann to a small tree about half a mile away, but apparently this was *not* a kwanetan tree" (Lindstrom, pers. comm. by email, 10 March 2006).

[42] I have elsewhere (Jolly 1992) used this source to suggest how bodies were perceived in relation to debates about the emergent language of race.

[43] Lamont Lindstrom notes that *hibao/hebow* (or in contemporary transcription *epo*) is an interjection still used by Tannese, expressing not so much astonishment, but affirmation to a self-evident statement (Lindstrom, pers. comm. by email, 10 March 2006).

[44] In a recent paper Lindstrom notes that "A week after Cook's arrival, people were still using leaves to pick up small gifts the English had left on the beach. This was a prophylactic response to alien danger whether or not the Tannese by then took Cook and his crew to be human or spirit" (Lindstrom 2009 forthcoming). Given that the Tannese blocked the strangers' route to the volcano it seems unlikely Cook and his crew *were* seen as ancestral spirits or gods, since Yasur, the volcano, was their abode.

[45] I cannot resist the continuation of this quote: "Our journalist observes, that, notwithstanding this false delicacy, they gave the sailors to understand, that they eat one another; and one day when the inhabitants about the bay were in motion and many of them marched forth armed to some distant part of the island, those that remained invited the gentleman to feast upon a man that they had barbiqued; which they refused with the utmost disgust" (Marra 1967 [1775], 275).

[46] Mosko (this volume) suggests that Europeans who were collecting flora and fauna might readily be seen to be collecting material for sorcery. The same speculation might have been made by ni-Vanuatu about naturalists, like the Forsters. Sorcery material often include the detritus of the body of the person to be ensorcelled, together with powerful leaves drawn from particular plants.

[47] Of course, we cannot rule out the possibility of linguistic change and of the movement of peoples. But if the same people as those resident in Port Sandwich were there two hundred years ago, it is unlikely that there would have been a shift from *ramač* to *tomarro* (Tryon, pers. comm., November 2003). Let me also reflect on the difficulties of such decontextualised translations of single words, especially in the context of a contemporary cosmology dramatically influenced by Christianity. In Sa, the language I learnt in South Pentecost in the 1970s, *tegar* denotes an ancestral spirit in its malevolent aspect (for which the word *adumwat ensanga* is also used). Such spirits, however, are particularly associated with the spirits of the recently deceased and distinguished from the *adumwat* of earlier generations, one's forebears and the more primordial ancestral creator beings, which are more often

⁴⁸ Salmond says that according to the descendants of these "armed warriors", they "also took Cook and his men to be ancestor spirits" (2003, 267). Her ethnographic authority for this is oral histories told to the twentieth-century naturalist Evelyn Cheesman and recorded in *Camping Adventures on Cannibal Islands* (1949); (see Salmond 2003, 474, n. 9). Curiously she does not refer to any works on Vanuatu by anthropologists, foreign or indigenous, published in the twentieth and twenty-first centuries. But her use of this singular source poses the crucial question of the relation between eighteenth-century perceptions of Cook and the constructions of later generations of ni-Vanuatu.

⁴⁹ Although Sparrman claims that two of them were not killed and crept out of the way among the bushes. He also elaborates that one sailor was wounded by a blunt pointed spear that pierced through the upper lip, while the second, Master Gilbert, was hit by an arrow in his chest, which "scarcely penetrated the skin" (Sparrman 1953, 142).

⁵⁰ As Lindstrom notes in a recent paper, many of the names for men recorded by Cook and the Forsters are still current, though differently transcribed: Paowang (Paw-yangom), Georgy or Yogai (Iokai) and Yatta (Iata). He also notes that some of the names suggest men came in from Futuna, e.g. Fannokko (Fanoko) and the White Sands area. The word lists collected by the Forsters are from three different languages: Kwamera from around Port Resolution, White Sands language and Futunese (Lindstrom 2009 forthcoming).

⁵¹ They had more difficulty in obtaining food, since, as Lindstrom notes, in August people would have been busy clearing and burning fields to plant new yams and their previous yam harvest would have been almost exhausted, except for seed yams. Cook did receive a small pig (Lindstrom 2009 forthcoming), and several sources suggest plantains and some yams were received.

⁵² Lindstrom has raised the question as to whether such moderation might be explained by the fact that this man was perhaps a visitor from the White Sands area or from Futuna, and therefore not seen as their "countrymen" (Lindstrom, pers. comm. by email, 10 March 2006). Still, as the sources suggest, two Tannese men did cradle the dead man.

⁵³ In his superb discussion of landscape and memory on Tanna, Lindstrom notes how Tannese conflate the name of Cape Cook and Captain Cook and suggests "Captain Cook for example is not some distant or forgotten historical personage. Instead he has become a Port Resolution rocky projection who has always already been recalled in this landscape of memory" (Lindstrom 2009 forthcoming).

⁵⁴ But subsequent to my original writing of this sentence a very large memorial to Quirós was erected at Big Bay on Espiritu Santo, by Europeans, with generous funding from several European governments and the European Commission, in May 2006 on the occasion of the 400th anniversary of his voyage (see Mondragón 2006; Jolly 2007). Whether Quirós will be re-membered in ni-Vanuatu memories over generations is moot.

⁵⁵ But, as John Taylor suggests (pers. comm., July 2005) these views are likely to change with the imminent introduction of new history curricula in the schools of Vanuatu (Lightner and Naupa 2005).

⁵⁶ Note the critique which I advanced of Te Papa Tongareva (Jolly 2001) is no longer appropriate to the refurbished Pacific Islander halls, as described by curator Sean Mallon at recent conferences in Canberra ("Pacific Cultural Heritage in Australian Museums and Galleries: A Regional Dialogue", 22–23 November 2007) and Paris ("Exhibiting Polynesia: Past, present, future," Musée du quai Branly, 17–18 June 2008).

Chapter 4

A Reconsideration of the Role of Polynesian Women in Early Encounters with Europeans: Supplement to Marshall Sahlins' Voyage around the Islands of History

Serge Tcherkézoff

Europeans have been losing their way in the Pacific from the beginning when early explorers made up for navigational errors by claiming inhabited islands as new discoveries. Never mind that the islanders had simultaneously discovered the explorers, no doubt with a fair bit of despair and surprise, but since it took years for islanders to learn the tiny scratches that the visitors called writing, the European claims had a head start in the history books.

(Aiavao 1994)

Je n'ai jamais pu concevoir comment et de quel droit une nation policée pouvait s'emparer d'une terre habitée sans consentement de ses habitants.

(Marchand 1961, 253)

Ethnohistorical work on first and subsequent early encounters between Polynesians and Europeans remained focused on particular archipelagoes, which has meant that comparative hypotheses spanning the entire Polynesian region have not emerged. Moreover, it has been conducted mainly in eastern Polynesia (including Aotearoa), thus leaving aside the western part of the region.[1] In this chapter I examine early encounters in Samoa, from western Polynesia, and also reconsider the Tahitian case, from eastern Polynesia, thus building a comparison of the nature of these early encounters across the region.

The focus of the chapter is the apparent sexual offers that women made to the newcomers. If we go back to a number of journals written during the early voyages which have still not been studied in as much detail as they deserve, namely La Pérouse's journal and, for Bougainville's expedition, those of Nassau and Fesche,[2] we can see that a crucial aspect of these apparent sexual offers –

the "girls' very young" age and their "weeping" – has been overlooked. We shall see that it was not a matter of women "offering their favours" but a forced presentation and, indeed, that those who were being presented to the French visitors were not "women" but girls.

In order to further ethnohistorical knowledge of the so-called "first contacts" in this part of the Pacific, we must first of all deconstruct the Western hegemonic view of Polynesian society, based on the official narratives of voyages and encounters. This pervasive discourse has meant that for more than two centuries the Polynesian perspective on such experiences – how Polynesians endured relations with Europeans and their own interpretations of the encounters – was occluded. Moreover, the exclusively masculinist vision of these episodes, the collective narrative voice of the captains and naturalists, had effectively silenced the visions and voices of Polynesian women.

This chapter will address this issue through a specific dimension of such encounters. It will attempt to recover and reveal the painful process of coercion that some Polynesian young girls had to endure when meeting Europeans for the first time. Fesche wrote in 1768 that this was an "operation." It was, in fact, the same "ordeal" that was customary in Samoa when young girls were married to high chiefs (Pritchard 1866). But in their forced presentation to the Europeans the girls were apparently overwhelmed with the fear that the newcomers inspired. It was pain and fear that made the girls weep. This occurred in 1768 in Tahiti, in 1787 in Samoa and, elsewhere as well, even if the evidence is much more scanty, in Aotearoa in 1772, and in Tonga and the Marquesas in 1791.

In a lecture given in Paris in 1981, Sahlins started peeling back the layers of Eurocentrism covering Hawaiian history. He hypothesised that, contrary to what these early voyagers had thought, it was not "sexual hospitality" offered to male travellers. Rather, said Sahlins, it was a transposition of a mythical and social schema: "theogamy" (marriage with the gods) and hypergamy (marrying-up with a chief). The aim was to procreate powerful children and to secure new kinds of powers. Sahlins had found in Diderot's (1964 [1796]) text, entitled *Supplement to Bougainville's Voyage*, a first expression of that hypothesis,[3] and he thus entitled his lecture "Supplement to Captain Cook's Voyage," published later as chapter 1 of his *Islands of History* (Sahlins 1985).[4]

A further dimension to this mythical and social scheme now needs to be examined for other parts of Polynesia. Why, in Samoa and in Tahiti, did the females who were presented to the first European male visitors have to be so young? Why were they weeping? The aim of this chapter is to consider these questions about early sexual encounters through a critical rereading of the journals kept during the Polynesian visits of the European voyages and of the official accounts in light of more recent ethnographic knowledge about Polynesian cosmology. Evidence of the "very young age" of all the "women" presented is assembled and discussed in this chapter. Overlooked passages in some of the journals clearly show that the girls must have been virgins. The fact that the Samoan and Tahitian girls were very young and were virgins raises the possibility that this was the case everywhere: similar scenes, briefly noted by voyagers, which occurred in Tonga and the Marquesas tend to confirm this. In the last section of the chapter, hypotheses will be considered as to why Polynesian chiefs and elders chose to present their very young and apparently virgin daughters to Europeans. A plausible explanation involves the Polynesian ideology of the process of procreation, shared by men and women, which attributed a more certain intensity to the sacredness of the first child, conceived by a female of high rank where the union was theogamous or hypergamous.

We shall see that the girls were obviously not eager to play their role in this scheme, enforced by the chiefs. Indeed the girls presented to the Europeans sometimes had to be dragged forcibly and held firmly by adults. Some of the Europeans observed this and wrote about it in their journals. But no mention of their reluctance made its way into the official voyage narratives that were published first in Paris and then in London (Bougainville 1771, 1772; Cook 1773). These accounts immediately established an official, and ultimately unquestioned, view of the encounters with Polynesians: one saturated by images of peace and love, of happiness and plenty.

The new evidence that will be presented here suggests that the Western construct of Polynesian societies as island paradises, where sexual freedom was the norm in adolescence and where young girls and young women were sexually accommodating, must be radically revised. This is a construct largely built, as we shall see, on the male fantasies and Eurocentric misreadings of early French visitors to the region, and then revisited and recycled from the same masculine, Eurocentric perspective in centuries to come.

Western "Knowledge" About Pre-Christian Samoan and Tahitian "Customs" Relating to Adolescence and Marriage

Samoa

The very first Europeans to set foot on Samoan soil were French, the officers and crew of La Pérouse's expedition. The date was December 1787. "Observations" were made over two days (December 10 and 11) by various officers, and La Pérouse put these together in his journal. Apart from many notes about material culture, the report describing the behaviour of the inhabitants insisted on two aspects. The Samoan men were "ferocious barbarians" because, on the second day, they "massacred" a dozen French men who wanted only to "peacefully barter" some goods and to fill up casks with fresh water. The women, on the other hand, gained the admiring approval of the French visitors. Even after the "massacre," La Pérouse noted:

> Among a fairly large number of women I noticed two or three who were very pretty and who [one] could have thought had served as a model for the charming drawing of the Present Bearer of Cook's third voyage,[5] their hair was adorned with flowers ... their eyes, their features, their movement spoke of gentleness whereas those of the men depicted ferocity and surprise. In any one sculptor['s] study the latter would have been taken for Hercules and the young women for Diana, or her nymphs (La Pérouse 1995, 412–3).

La Pérouse's bias in favour of the women is explained by the sexual encounters that occurred during the stay and to which the French captain refers in his conclusion on the "customs" of the Samoans:

> Whatever navigators who preceded us might say, I am convinced that at least in the Navigators Islands girls are mistresses of their own favours before marriage, their complaisance casts no dishonour on them, and it is more likely that when they marry they are under no obligation to account for their past behaviour. But I have no doubt that they are required to show more restraint when they are married (1995, 420).

After a mere two days of encounters on land – and only a day in which peaceful encounters were possible – La Pérouse, without being able to understand a single word of the local language, had formed an opinion about the Samoan customs governing adolescence and marriage! Of course, he had already certain preconceptions of the ways of the "Indians" in that part of the Pacific through his reading of Bougainville's and Cook's accounts of Tahiti and neighbouring islands.

A careful reading of the succession of events described in La Pérouse's journal (Tcherkézoff 2004a, 28–67) reveals the only scenes that La Pérouse and/or his officers could have seen and participated in. The first occasion was when a Samoan crowd gathered on the shore, and from which the French soldiers tried to keep at a distance while the seamen were filling the casks. The second involved one or two "visits" to a village during which some of the French were taken inside a house, where they were asked to have intercourse with a young girl.

Limited as his experience of Samoan culture was, La Pérouse's opinion – condensed in these concluding sentences that abruptly summarise the upbringing and the rules of behaviour applying to Samoan girls – became an accepted part of Western anthropological "knowledge" about Polynesia. A century and a half later, in a vast compilation of Polynesian customs, which developed into several treatises – standard works of reference for any student of Polynesia – Williamson (1924, 1933, 1939), who had been instructed by Seligman to gather all the information available on this part of the Pacific, quoted that same sentence (from the 1797 publication of La Pérouse's journal) in order to characterise the absence of "chastity" in pre-Christian Samoa (Williamson 1939, 156). And then, in the 1980s, when the heated debate initiated by Freeman (1983) focused on Mead's 1926 fieldwork dealing with Samoan adolescence and her conclusions in *Coming of Age in Samoa* (Mead 1928; Tcherkézoff 2001a, 2001b, 2001c), one of the champions of Mead's views called on La Pérouse as a witness:

> Williamson (1939/1975) carried out an extensive review of all of the early accounts of Polynesian cultures. ... With respect to premarital sex in general, he said that in Samoa:
>
> "According to Turner and Brown [early missionaries], chastity ... was more a name than a reality ... Lapérouse tells us that girls were, before marriage, mistresses of their own favors, and their complaisance did not dishonor them" (p. 156).
>
> ... From these many accounts, there can be little doubt that sexual behavior in Samoa before it was Christianized was more casual for virtually everyone, including young females. The denial of this by Freeman and some contemporary Samoans can be understood in terms of the concerted efforts of missionaries and the local pastors to create, and then maintain, a hegemony of Victorian sexual values and practices (Côté 1994, 80–2).

Tahiti

It so happens that, twenty years earlier, in Tahiti very similar scenes had been played out, and these were similarly absorbed into the Western canons about Tahitian customs. On only the second or third day of their Tahitian visit (7 or 8 April 1768), a small group of French officers (we can identify three of them from the journals) told their captain, Louis-Antoine de Bougainville, that they had been "offered" sex with a "young girl" in the chiefly household that they had visited. Bougainville recorded this in his journal, and in his book of 1771, famous throughout Europe, he repeated this almost without alteration: "several Frenchmen" had told him what kind of "hospitality" they had enjoyed, "in the custom of this island." He immediately drew this generalisation: "we are offered all the young girls" (Bougainville 1966 [1771], 194–5; 2002, 63). He later reflected upon this extraordinary society that had clearly remained as it was in Eden, untouched and spared the consequences of the Fall: Tahitian girls were "as was Eve before her sin" (as his companion Fesche expressed it; see my section below "Tahitian Facts: The Scenes of April 7–9"). Notably, Bougainville spoke of "the young girls."

A close study of the journals written by the members of Bougainville's expedition (Tcherkézoff 2004b, 114–239) shows how the Frenchmen immediately imagined that this kind of behaviour had always been the local "custom" among Tahitians. The Frenchmen, like many early European visitors to Polynesian islands, could not imagine that they were perceived as not-entirely-human creatures and even as envoys from the realm of the gods (Tcherkézoff 2004a, 109–53). They thought that they were received merely as voyagers to whom "hospitality" was offered.[6] The Frenchmen had no conception that the way in which the girls behaved toward them was extraordinary.

They were also blind – and how strange this seems given the scenes they were witnessing – to the fact that the girls were forcibly presented by adults. They were apparently deeply convinced that, among people who had remained in a "state of nature," females engaging in sexual acts were only following the impulses of their "female nature."[7] And that here in this society they were "free" to follow those impulses.

The misconceptions of the voyagers meant that Polynesian societies appeared to scholars of the time to grant more freedom to women, and hence they were labelled more "civilised," in contrast to "Melanesian" societies where sexual presentations during the first encounters had not been staged. There, the women's absence led the voyagers to believe that the local women had been forbidden by their fathers and husbands to meet the newcomers and, hence, that they were more dominated by men than in Polynesia. The social position of Melanesian women was therefore thought to be "lower," and Melanesian societies were labelled more "barbarian" and "backward." Of course, the European – and exclusively male – assessment as to the "progress" of women was restricted to looking at (and misinterpreting) their roles in relation to men's roles: division of work tasks, access to "chiefly" positions, and apparent sexual behaviour.[8]

Everything that the French saw during this encounter in Tahiti they understood as being an integral part of the local way of life. They concluded that, during Tahitian adolescence, "girls were free" to follow their desires and thus to "offer their favours." From then on, up until the present, commentators in Europe and the Western world could write that, "as is well known," Polynesian females – at least before marriage – were "free to offer their favours" and were quite "willing" to do so. One of a host of examples is Irving Goldman's *Ancient Polynesian Society* (1970). The book is a classic example of a long and well-researched study, its subject, quite unrelated to sexuality, being social organisation and social hierarchies. It is therefore all the more significant to find in it this sentence, given as a universally accepted fact: "In Polynesia, where pre-marital sexual freedom was everywhere established custom ..." (1970, 564). Such statements, offered *en passant*, can be found throughout the historical and anthropological literature on the Pacific (Tcherkézoff 2004b, 455–510).

Samoan Facts: The Scene Observed by La Pérouse

Internal distinction: Description and interpretation

La Pérouse's narrative gives us some clues about the scenes in which the Samoan girls made the French believe that they were "mistresses of their own favours." In the conclusion to his narrative, La Pérouse adds a passage which, given his typically cautious style, he was clearly hesitant about including in his official journal:[9]

> As the story of our voyage can add a few pages to that of mankind I will not omit pictures that might shock in any other kind of book and I shall mention that the very small number of young and pretty island girls I referred to soon attracted the attention of a few Frenchmen who in spite of my orders endeavoured to establish links of intimacy with them; since our Frenchmen's eyes revealed their desires they were soon discovered; some old women negotiated the transaction, an altar was set up in the most prominent hut, all the blinds were lowered, inquisitive spectators were driven off; the victim was placed within the arms of an old man who exhorted her to moderate her sorrow for she was weeping (*qui lexortoit à moderer sa douleur,*[10] *car elle pleuroit*); the matrons sang and howled during the ceremony, and the sacrifice was consummated in the presence of the women and the old man was acting as altar and priest. All the village's women and children were around and outside the house, lightly raising the blinds and seeking the slightest gaps between the mats to enjoy this spectacle. Whatever navigators who preceded us might say, I am convinced that at least in the Navigators Islands girls are mistresses of their own favours before marriage, their complaisance casts no dishonour on them ... (1995, 419–20).

If the last sentence – which unerringly made its way into the twentieth-century literature as we have seen – is a typical example of European over-interpretation and over-generalisation, the preceding lines tell us what La Pérouse actually saw or at least what he had been told by some of his officers.

Ethnographic analysis and extrapolating backward

The "girls" and the "sacrifice": Comparison with Samoan ceremonies of the period 1830–1850

In La Pérouse's entire narrative of his stay in the Samoan archipelago, the only actual description he gives of a sexual act is this "sacrifice" in the "prominent hut." We have seen that this incident concerned only, as he says, "the very small number of young and pretty island girls I referred to." As to these "young girls" and the "sacrifice," the description is self-explanatory. The "victims" were only "girls." Each girl was "weeping." She was presented by the "old women," and then "placed within the arms of an old man" (a "chief-orator" or *tulafale* most probably) who spoke with her. She was apparently held by the orator during the "operation," since this "old man" is said by La Pérouse to have himself been the "altar" on which the "sacrifice" was performed. She was presented in "the most prominent hut," which seems to indicate a high stone base, which identifies the hut as the house of the main chief. All the blinds were lowered, and the women "sang and howled."

What La Pérouse describes corresponds to the enactment of a nineteenth-century Samoan marriage ceremony, where the young bride was a virgin and was ceremonially deflowered. Two types of ceremony have been recorded: one (see below) where the bride was presented on the sacred ground of the village, in front of the whole community, and deflowered by an orator (of the groom's family), and one where she was deflowered in the house, with the blinds lowered (personal notes, 1984), without any clear indication of whether the act was performed by an orator (*tulafale*) or the bridegroom (see discussion in Tcherkézoff 2003a, 350–70). Let me quote some passages from the first detailed descriptions available, dating from the early 1830s (the time of the first missionary visit) and the 1850s.

John Williams' account of 1830–32 tells us how girls could be "dragged by force" and held by older people while the operation was performed, particularly "if the female objects to submit …" The bridegroom was seated in front of his group, on the village's central, sacred ground (*malae*):

> The female now prepares herself to meet him which in general is attended with considerable delay. The preparation is mostly attended with furious crying & bitter wailing on the part of the young woman while her friends are engaged in persuading her that what is about to take place will not hurt her. She at length consents & is taken by the hand by her elder brother. … If she does not consent to go she is dragged by force to him. She is dressed [with] scented oil … finely wrought mats edged with red feathers … on arriving immediately in front of her husband she throws off her mat and stands before him perfectly naked. He then ruptures the Hymen of the female with two fingers of his right hand [when everyone sees the blood, the women of the girl's family] throw off their mats & commence dancing naked. … If the female objects to submit to the above ceremony which is sometimes the case persons are employed to hold her—some to hold her down others to hold her arms others her legs. She is thus held in the lap of another person while the husband ruptures the Hymen. On some occasions the parties bed immediately after the ceremonies are concluded (Williams 1984, 255–6).

Thus, these final sentences of Williams' account likely describe the procedure that was used for the "marriages" with the French in 1787.[11] We can see that this marriage ceremony took the form of that described later by Williams, one in which "the female objects to submit." If Samoan girls routinely expressed fear and hesitation in a marriage with a Samoan husband, we can easily imagine the terror of those girls who were brought to be married to such unknown and awesome creatures.

La Pérouse's reference to the "matrons singing and howling" almost certainly corresponds to what William T. Pritchard (son of a pastor and briefly "consul") observed in the 1850s: at the crucial moment the girl stood naked, greeted by the cheers of the crowd, "which were acknowledged only by her tears":

> All her mats were taken off by the old duennas;[12] who then slowly paraded her, naked and trembling, before the silent gaze of the multitude, then she was seated, with her legs crossed, on a snow-white mat spread on the ground, in the centre of the square, or *malae*. There the chief approached her and silently seated himself also cross-legged, close to and directly facing her. Then was the critical moment. Though perhaps more than a thousand spectators looked on, of all ages and both sexes, not a word[,] not a sound was heard. Then, placing his left hand on the girl's right shoulder, the chief inserted the two forefingers of his right hand into the *vulva*, while the two old duennas held her round the waist from behind. In a moment, the chief's arm was held up, the two fingers only extended, when her anxious tribe watched eagerly for the drops of blood to trickle down the sight of which was the signal for vehement cheers ...
>
> Once more, the old duennas loud in songs that told of rivers flowing fast water no banks could restrain, seas no reefs could check – figurative allusions to the virgin blood of the chaste bride – once more those stern old duennas led their trembling and bashful girl, still naked as before, to the gaze of the cheering and excited multitude, to exhibit the blood that trickled down her thighs. Cheers of applause greeted her, which were acknowledged only by the tears which silently stole down her cheeks.[13]

"The blinds lowered": Comparison with ethnography of the 1930s to 1980s

La Pérouse's remark that "all the blinds were lowered" is also very important. As far as I know from my discussions with Samoans in the 1980s, there were only two cases where an activity would be conducted inside a house with all the blinds lowered. One was a defloration ceremony (some of the old people remembered such ceremonies from the 1930s). The other was a "meeting with the spirits" (*fono ma aitu*), when chiefs of the village faced with making an important and difficult decision, and needing some superhuman inspiration, met at night and silently. In all other cases, even when there is a storm, Samoans have told me that some of the blinds – or at least one – should remain up because, if all are lowered, "it becomes very dangerous." It seemed to me, from their tone and the way they suddenly changed to speaking in a hushed voice, that having all of the blinds lowered enabled the "spirits" (*aitu*) to enter the house. This, therefore, posed a great danger to the people staying there. (Even as late as 1982, in several places I was told that spirits can steal the soul of a sleeping person, particularly the soul of a baby).

Although paradoxical, it should be understood that a Samoan house that is closed and has all its blinds down is in fact open to the spirits' movement, because the social "sacred ring" of posts is then not operative. The "sacred ring," which gives the house its significance in terms of genealogical and territorial history, is the circle of posts supporting the roof. When there is a formal meeting, each chief leans against one of the posts of the circle, sitting cross-legged. Chiefs of lesser rank sit in between posts and are called precisely that: "in-between-posts chiefs." When the blinds are up, the "space between the posts" (*va* – the word is also used in the general sense of "social relation") is significant. Each man must then choose his point of entry into the house and his sitting position according to his rank in relation to the ranks of those already seated. From these elements we can hypothesise that, when *all of the blinds* are down, the social circle – which is the "sacred circle" defining every Samoan social context of belonging to a group (Tcherkézoff 2003a: ch. 2, 2005a) – is no longer active, no longer socially efficacious. The house reverts back to the "Night" (*Po*) side of the world, where the sources of life are located, but are hidden, and must be seized from the gods and the spirits. This communication with the "Night" side was necessary when a difficult decision needed to be made (by the council, the "meeting with the spirits") – *and it was also necessary for a marriage*, at least if we take into consideration the hypothesis that, at the moment of defloration, a superhuman principle had to come into contact with the bride (see below, "Conclusion (II)").[14]

The presence of the "women" and "very young girls"

At dawn on 11 December 1787, de Langle, one of La Pérouse's officers, and about sixty men landed with their longboats at a village in a cove on the north coast. This is where the so-called "massacre" took place. La Pérouse stayed on board his ship, and later obtained the account of the survivors who managed to get back to the ships. His journal cites only the narrative of one of the officers who was with de Langle, a certain Vaujuas. Vaujuas reported that in the cove the same arrangements had been made as during the previous day's watering expedition at which La Pérouse had been present:

> We peacefully rolled out, filled and reloaded the water casks, the natives allowing themselves to be fairly well contained by the armed soldiers,

there were among them a certain number of women and very young girls [*femmes et filles très jeunes*] who made advances to us in the most indecent fashion, of which several people took advantage (La Pérouse 1995, 407).

The journal does not tell us how, exactly, the men "took advantage." But, soon after, stones began to fly and the attack was launched.

These are Vaujuas' only lines on the topic of sexual encounters. If we relate these lines to La Pérouse's description of the "sacrifice," we must conclude that the French only "took advantage" of the "advances" made by the young "girls." We must therefore put forward the hypothesis that the "advances" made by the "women" were in fact only sexual gestures inviting the French to "take advantage" of the girls – we shall see that such was the case in Tahiti. If the Samoan women were really "offering" their own favours, there is no reason why the French would not have accepted them as well. And there is no reason why La Pérouse would not have mentioned it in his concluding pages and would have decided to mention only – with some hesitation – the sexual act with the young "girls." Let us now move to Tahiti and the events of almost twenty years before.

Tahitian Facts: The Scenes of April 7–9 (According to Nassau and Fesche)

Nassau, April 7, 1768

When we compare the French journals and examine the dates of daily entries we find that the first "offering of girls" reported to Bougainville by his men occurred on April 7, the first full day the French spent on land. (On the previous day, Bougainville and a group of officers had made a brief first landing; see below). The Prince of Nassau, who had been with Chevalier d'Oraison, tells us that they were "keen to call on their chief":

> When I arrived at his home, they served us fruit, then the women offered me a young girl. The Indians surrounded me and each was eager to share with his eyes in the pleasure I was about to enjoy. The young girl was very pretty but European preconceptions require more mystery. An Indian used very singular means to further excite my desires. Happy nation that does not yet know the odious names of shame and scandal (Nassau 2002, 283).

We can note that a presentation, understood by the French as an "offering" (of a sexual gift), was made as soon as the French came on land. The adults were so keen for Nassau, as the apparent leader of the group, to be able to act his part that they tried to get him "excited" in a "very singular" way (of which we are told nothing more). Was this merely a matter of sexual "hospitality" staged by the dominant males of the place for their visitors – with women fully participating (they were bringing in the girl)? The French assumed that it was, but they were blind to the exercise of masculine power, since for them these scenes only showed how in Tahitian society "women" were generally "free" to "follow their natural drives" (see quotations in Tcherkézoff 2004b, 169–72, 202–7, 223–39). But, even given the gendered complexities of the "offer," a gift of sexual hospitality would surely not have involved rushing upon the new arrivals in this manner and trying to force them into accepting their offers. (See, too, the discussion below about the "signs" that the Tahitian adults made to the French to ensure that they understood what was expected of them).

All this was in vain. Nassau was struck by performance anxiety when he realised that he had to perform in a "public festival." He had at first agreed to play his part and would have done so "had not," as Fesche puts it, "the presence of the surrounding 50 Indians, through the effect of our prejudices, put the brake on his fierce desires" (2002, 257).

Nassau reported that in the chief's house which he visited, the "young girl" was "offered," and that this offer was made by "the women." He does not say that the women offered their own favours. Nassau also tells us that there was a crowd who "surrounded" him and the girl. This led the French to believe, as they noted in their journals and as Bougainville noted in his official voyage account, that "Tahitian custom" required, or at least allowed, the performance of the sexual act to occur "publicly" and even made of it a "public festival." The French would continue to interpret any event involving their own presence in terms of the imagined *everyday* practices of Tahitian life. They did not for a moment suppose that all of this might be quite exceptional or, at least, occasioned specifically by families ceremonially giving their young daughters in marriage to powerful strangers imagined as akin to high chiefs.

Fesche on April 7

Together in the chief's house with Nassau and Chevalier d'Oraison was the young adventurer Fesche, who had volunteered to join Bougainville's voyage of circumnavigation. Even if it is likely that his narrative was polished in editing by de Saint-Germain, a professional writer who was also a member of the expedition, the events Fesche describes are too specific and out of tune with the European male imagination of the time to have been merely the product of a fantasy invented by de Saint-Germain (Taillemite 1968, 7; Tcherkézoff 2004b, 134–5).

Fesche begins with a summary of the first day:

> The very day after we anchored, Mr de Bougainville went ashore accompanied by several officers; they were received by the chief who

accompanied them everywhere with a thousand demonstrations of friendship.

Fesche describes the meal, makes no mention of any presentation of females, and describes the "theft" of a pistol. He then goes on to relate the events of the next day:

> The next day we went ashore, the chief brought back the pistol lost on the previous day and received gifts in exchange.
>
> I shall outline facts that will appear to many to be falsehoods, but those who know me can be sure that what I shall report as having seen is absolutely correct ...
>
> There were three of us, we go off with the intent of taking a walk escorted by a group of islanders, we arrive at a hut where we are welcomed by the master of the house, he firstly shows us his possessions, making us understand that he was waiting for his wives who were due to arrive shortly. We go together, he shows us the tree the bark of which is used to make the loincloths they wear as their clothing and tells us the names of all that country's fruits. After some time spent strolling, we returned to his home where we found his wife and young girl aged 12 or 13. We are made to sit, they bring us coconuts and bananas, we are invited to eat, we conform to their wishes. We then see each one of them pick up a green branch[15] and sit in a circle around us, one of those present took a flute from which he drew pleasant soft sounds and they brought a mat that they laid out on the open space and on which the young girl sat down.
>
> All the Indians' gestures made us clearly understand what this was about, however this practice being so contrary to those established for us and wanting to be sure of it, one of us [Nassau[16]] goes up to the offered victim, makes her the gift of an artificial pearl that he attaches to her ear, and ventures a kiss, which was well returned. A bold hand led by love slips down to two new-born apples [*deux pommes naissantes*] rivals of each other and worthy like those of Helen to serve as models for cups that would be incomparable for their beauty and the attraction of their shape. The hand soon slipped and by a fortunate effect of chance, fell on charms still hidden by one of their cloths, it was promptly removed by the girl herself whom we saw then dressed as Eve was before her sin. She did more, she stretched out on the mat, struck the chest of the aggressor, making him understand that she was giving herself to him and drew aside those two obstacles that defend the entrance to that temple where so many men make a daily sacrifice.

> The summons was very appealing and the athlete caressing her was too skilled in the art of fencing not to take her right away had not the presence of the surrounding 50 Indians, through the effect of our prejudices, put the brake on his fierce desires, but however great the ardour that drives you, it is very difficult to overcome so quickly the ideas with which you have been brought up. The corruption of our morals has made us discover evil in an act where these people rightly find nothing but good. It is only someone who is doing or thinks he is doing evil who fears the light. We hide in order to carry out such a natural action, they do it in public and often. Several Frenchmen, less susceptible to delicacy, found it easier, that same day, to shrug off these prejudices.
>
> After some time spent in that hut, our eyes finally weary of looking and touching, we withdrew, the residents quite displeased at seeing us so reluctant to share the spoils and even telling us so. We walked to the place that had been chosen to set up a camp and a hospital (Fesche 2002, 257).

It should be noted that the girl was presented wearing a "loincloth," that is barkcloth, which shows that she had been intentionally dressed for a ceremony. (If she had just come from work in the garden, she would have had on a belt of leaves).

We can judge the girl's youth from the expression used to describe her breasts, together with Fesche's own assessment that she was "aged 12 or 13." And if, as Fesche says at the beginning, the man went to look for his "wives," it was only the young girl who was offered. If we are to believe Nassau and Fesche, the role of the "women" was in fact to tell the girl what she had to do (Nassau: "the women offered me a young girl," see above) and, by means of gestures, together with the other adults, to make the French understand what was involved (Fesche: "All the Indians' gestures made us clearly understand what this was about," see above).

In the following days: Bougainville and Nassau

One or two days later Bougainville himself received propositions. He does not give any details, but this does not prevent him from enthusing about Tahiti and its inhabitants. He pays a visit to the chief, Eriti, and notes in his journal:

> We had to repay their visit in the afternoon. The chief offered me a woman from his household (*le chef m'a proposé une de ses femmes*),[17] young and fairly pretty, and the whole gathering sang the wedding anthem. What a country! What a people! (2002, 66).

Here again the Tahitian woman was "young." She could have been a daughter, even if Bougainville's sentence can be taken to mean that he assumed that she was one of the chief's wives. But the main point is that if she had been a wife, this proposal would have meant that the context was already one of "sexual commerce" where all women could be offered (see below). In that case there would not have been a circle of adults surrounding the scene and singing. The singing rather evokes the atmosphere of the solemn presentation as described by Nassau and Fesche.

During this same period of April 7 to 9, there was another encounter that Nassau related:

> These Indians offered us women as being the objects they most cherished, undeniably these well deserved this distinction. They each in turn used all their charms to please us. Here is one example. I was strolling in a charming place, carpets of greenery, pleasant groves, the gentle murmur of streams inspired love in this delicious spot. I was caught there by the rain. I sheltered in a small house where I found six of the prettiest girls in the locality. They welcomed me with all the gentleness this charming sex can display. Each one removed her clothing, an adornment which is bothersome for pleasure and, spreading all their charms, showed me in detail the gracefulness and contours of the most perfect bodies. They also removed my clothing. The whiteness of a European body delighted them. They hastened to see whether I was made like the locals and pleasure quickened this research. Many were the kisses, many the tender caresses I received! Throughout this scene, an Indian was playing a tender tune on his flute. A crowd of others had lined up around the house, solely preoccupied with the spectacle. We were living amidst this gentle nation like allies and friends. The chief, the leading men constantly made us gifts (2002, 284).

The passage offers a perfect example, one of many that can be found in the journals kept during this voyage and in Bougainville's narrative, of the young French visitors (Nassau and Fesche) only being able to see these cultural encounters from their masculine and Eurocentric perspective: the exchanges were between "us" (the French men) and the "Indians," while the objects of exchange were "the women" (the "girls").[18] Their views apparently influenced Bougainville. Only naturalists like Commerson (or Forster with Cook), older men and eager to come up with theories about the whole society, stressed on the contrary what appeared to them to be the women's agency and "freedom" in those sexual matters. Of course, it could not have been otherwise for these young French men. But later readers of Bougainville's voyage narrative had no conception of the intercultural and gender issues involved here either and took Bougainville's framing and interpretation of the encounters for accurate "observation." We see, too, how Nassau reduced the Tahitian perception of the advent of these strangers to their shores, and the kind of beings they were, to the arrival of mere "allies and friends."

Here again, the "women" offered (see the first sentence: "Indians offered us women") are in fact "girls," when the description becomes precise. This is one of many examples of the way in which the European narrators of these early encounters with Polynesians, whether French or British, used the term "women" in their general commentaries and conclusions about sexual offers, while they specified "(young) girl(s)" in their descriptions of particular scenes, as Nassau does five lines later. The same goes for the question of Tahitian females taking the initiative in sexual encounters when we read in the general commentaries that "women" or "girls" were "offering themselves," while in more precise descriptions we are told that they "were brought by" elders. We should also note Nassau's implication at the beginning of the description that if the girls did "use their charms" to attract the Frenchmen, they did so "in turn" once they were "offered." These more precise forms of expression about the conduct of these sexual offers are to be found in the journals and in the published accounts as well. But later, because commentators tend to use short quotations, only the more general passages from the accounts came to be remembered and quoted. *Thus the idea of "women" "offering themselves" concealed and replaced the descriptions of "young girls" forcibly "brought" to the Europeans by elders.*

We should also note that while this scene is being played out for the admiring Nassau "a crowd" has gathered "around the house" and throughout the whole episode a Tahitian man is in attendance, playing his flute. The fact that the Tahitian girls examined Nassau intimately —"to see whether I was made like the locals" — is also significant (see section below, "Conclusion (II)").

"Tahitian Marriages" (Fesche)

Fesche, the only observer to give us specific details about the first sexual presentation of a young girl, also provides us with a summary that either takes this scene up again, adding a number of points, or combines it with other similar scenes at which he had been present or that other men had described to him.

Indeed, Fesche prides himself on describing "their marriages" for us. Like the rest of the French visitors, he of course knows nothing about how Tahitians might have conceived such marriages, the French only having stayed for ten days. At least, he admits straight away that he is only hypothesising. What is interesting for us is that he admits that he is relying only on the sexual offerings made to the French (see his text below). For that reason, we need to pay his account some attention. It is not an imaginary tale about Tahitian marriages, but the presentation of points in common between the several scenes of sexual presentation that were enacted for the benefit of the French.

The description provides an important piece of information that I shall comment upon in a later section, namely the performance of an "operation" that made the young girl "cry." But first of all let us note two aspects, namely that the Tahitians tried to force the French to take action, and that the girl was still young and was "brought forward" by the adults. The Tahitian adults were surely following a definite strategy:

Fesche's text

> Their marriages are, I believe, made in public. I make this supposition on the basis of what happened to possibly two-thirds of the Frenchmen: the fathers and mothers who brought their girls [*amenaient leurs filles*], presented them to the one who pleased them, and urged them to consummate the task of marriage with them [*consommer l'oeuvre de mariage avec elle*]. The girl [*la fille*] struck the chest of the one to whom she was being offered, uttered a few words that expressed, from the meaning we have attributed to them,[19] the surrender she was making of herself, lay down on the ground and removed her clothing. Several made a fuss when it came to the point [*Plusieurs faisaient des façons quand il s'agissait d'en venir au fait*], however they allowed themselves to be persuaded. During the operation [*Durant l'opération*], the islanders assisting[20] [with the operation], always present in large numbers, made a circle around them, holding a green branch, sometimes they threw one of their cloths over the actor,[21] as in Cythera they covered the happy lovers with greenery. If one of them happened to have a flute, he would play it, others accompanied him singing couplets dedicated to pleasure.[22] Once the operation was over, the girl would cry [*L'opération finie, la fille pleurait*], but would easily recover her composure and make a thousand caresses to her new spouse as well as to all those who had been witnesses.

> There is some evidence that these are the same ceremonies as are used in their weddings; there may be some other formalities required, I believe this all the more readily because an officer from the *Etoile* to whom a young Indian girl had offered herself, but who was not favourably disposed, a Cytheran [Ahutoru], the same one who joined us on board to follow us in our travels, took the girl and showed him how he should act. If there were no other formalities than those for a marriage, he would not have acted in this way. Moreover, all they did for us can only be viewed as honours they wished to pay to strangers.

> Married women are a model of faithfulness ... but those who are unmarried are free and prostitute themselves with whomever takes their fancy (Fesche 2002, 259–60).

A forced encounter

Fesche begins his passage by saying, "Their marriages are, I believe, made in public." But let us go straight to the conclusion: seeing the officer's difficulty, Ahutoru gave a demonstration of what had to be done. Fesche saw in this further confirmation that "marriage" (what he was really interested in was the act of intercourse) was performed in front of everyone.

But his remark about what Ahutoru did on this occasion is very useful. It confirms something that comes up on at least five occasions in the French accounts, namely that the Tahitians did everything they could to force the French to engage in sexual intercourse. These were the episodes (Tcherkézoff 2004b: ch. 5–6):

(1) the first contact at sea (April 5) involving two young girls "from thirteen to fourteen years old" who were presented in a canoe while the adults made gestures that clearly mimicked the act of intercourse (2) and (3) the presentation of "Venus" (the first Tahitian woman who went on board, an adolescent who was accompanying Ahutoru: April 6) and of "Helen" (the scene of April 7: Nassau caressed her breasts but found himself unable to go any further), where these two girls were brought forward by the adults or even the "elderly men." Onlookers made explicit gestures, with one of them even using "very singular means" to attempt to arouse Nassau's sexual interest (4) Nassau's walk around the village, when on going into one of the houses he was surrounded, undressed and examined and touched intimately (see section above "In the following days: Bougainville and Nassau") (5) the escapade of Bougainville's cook (April 5 or 6), who experienced the same fate, but with less solicitude apparently (he swam to shore before the official landing was felt over, and once the examination had been made, he was pressed up against a girl, gestures being made to show what was expected of him – absolutely terrified, of course, he could do nothing at all).

On each of those occasions, the Tahitians wanted the French to perform the sexual act that they expected of them. This time, as Fesche describes it, Ahutoru also gave a practical demonstration. But Fesche only draws from the attitude taken by Ahutoru toward the officer an additional argument in support of the idea that Tahitian "marriages" always take place in this fashion, that is, "publicly." And he sees the Tahitians' attempt to extend this offer of "marriage" to the French merely as "honours they wished to pay to strangers" (or new "allies and friends," as Nassau put it; see above).

The youth of the victims and the ceremonial framework

The generalisation made by Fesche suggests important elements in the forced presentations of young girls. The Frenchman speaks of "girls" and generalises by referring to "the fathers and mothers who brought their girls," meaning, therefore, that in every case the victim was young. It will be recalled that apart from the generalising expressions about "women" which merely express the fantasies of the Frenchmen, both of our French reporters (Nassau and Fesche), when they describe the exact situation of the first presentations, use only the words "girl" and "young girl."

In every case the girl was brought forward by others. The Western image of young women adorned with flowers, living only for love and throwing themselves at unexpected voyagers, and only too delighted to have yet more opportunities for making love, is shattered by this account where Fesche generalises from what happened on April 7 and a number of other scenes that must have happened in the same way.

Moreover, we have seen that during these presentations of young girls to the French, the onlookers always formed a circle and held a "green branch" in their hand. From many concurring sources we know of the ritual role of these branches in Tahiti: they allowed a taboo to be set aside so that one could enter into contact with a superior (Tcherkézoff 2004b, 424–6). The formal, ceremonial aspect is quite clear.

And there is another element: a piece of *tapa* cloth might be thrown over the girl at the crucial moment. Therefore, it was not a question of voyeurism on the part of the audience with the aim of arousing collective sexual excitement. This further discredits the notion of the Tahitian taste for lovemaking performed "publicly." It similarly calls into question the theory prevailing in the nineteenth and twentieth centuries which held that Tahitians made offerings to please the gods in the form of acts of human copulation performed in the open, so that they would be visible from the heavens (Moerenhout 1837; Handy 1927; see Tcherkézoff 2004b, 463–6, 474–7). But this gesture also points to something tangible. If we move forward in time and take into account more detailed Polynesian ethnography of the nineteenth and twentieth centuries, we invariably see that the fact of wrapping a person in tapa cloth is always a ritual gesture, whose aim it is to call down the presence of the sacred forces from the world of the gods onto the earthly stage and to give efficacy to their actions (Valeri 1985; Babadzan 1993, 2003; Tcherkézoff 2002, 2003c, 2004a: ch. 10).

The question of virginity in the French accounts: The girls' very young age, deflowering and tears

Finally, a spectre haunts these texts: that of deflowering. The words for which I have added the original French version in Fesche's description of "marriages" strongly imply something never explicitly stated, either in Bougainville's official account or in any of the journals. Let us reiterate these elements: the likely age of the girls presented; phrases indicating that they "made a fuss" before proceeding to the awaited act; the fact that the girl "was crying," and especially the word "operation," which in French as in English, when used in reference to the human body, implies some kind of serious surgical procedure. All of these things, when considered together, lead us to conclude that the sexual act offered to the visitor implied defloration.

We can see that Bougainville's readers, who were presented with nothing but delightful and beguiling scenes and visions, had no conception that the young women of "New Cythera," whose "only passion is love," as Bougainville told them, were in fact – in the arms of these Frenchmen – not women gaily displaying their flower necklaces and their desires, but girls weeping: girls who were undergoing their first act of sexual intercourse. Only Fesche speaks of this directly. In the other accounts of the French stay in Tahiti, there is nothing to be found on the subject of defloration. However, one of Bougainville's sentences, brief as it is, suddenly reveals that the officers and sailors had not hidden the truth from their captain. It was always, if we take Fesche's generalisation as a guide or at least sometimes, the case that the girl brought forward and presented to the French was a virgin. If at least some members of the expedition had not so remarked to Bougainville, it would be difficult to see why, at the moment of his departure, he wrote, in reference to the peaceable character that seemed to him to typify Tahitian society,

> ... love, the only God to which I believe these people offer any sacrifices. Here blood does not run on the altars [presumably a reference to human sacrifices] or if sometimes it reddens the altar the young victim is the first to rejoice at having spilt it (2002, 72–3).

"Without Asking For Any Reward": From Ritual to Sexual Commerce (Fesche)

Fesche was not only a keen observer of daily events. He also, like the others, made various generalisations and hypotheses. The main difference between Fesche's method and that of Bougainville and the other officers is that he did not forget to include his observations when he was speculating or making general comments, and thus provides us some "ethnography" to reflect upon. We have seen the importance of this when we looked at his views on marriage. But we also need to consider some of his notes which, while they may seem unimportant, in fact lead us in the direction of a complete reconsideration of the historical record relating to sexual encounters at a pan-Polynesian level.

Fesche describes the funeral rites at which a number of the French were present. The corpse is kept for several days on a ceremonial stage, is rubbed with oil and receives other such attentions before being interred:

> The women, no doubt out of propriety, weep abundantly, but several of the French who happened to be present at their ceremony easily caused this to be followed by most immoderate laughter through the signs and

propositions they were making to the prettiest of them, propositions that were accepted. Let one draw from this whatever conclusion one wishes (Fesche 2002, 261).

This is an interesting anecdote and it applies to numerous first contacts between Polynesians and Europeans. At the very beginning the European captains and officers who were received by the chiefs were astounded to discover that girls were being offered to them. So it did not take long before all the sailors and soldiers wished to receive the same treatment, and let it be known, as we see here.

Now, on the Polynesian side, this had different consequences. From that moment the Polynesians understood that these presentations of girls – which for them served a cosmological purpose, I believe – could also be used as a medium of commercial exchange. It was at that point that the men brought forward more girls, as well as women perhaps, and asked for objects in exchange. And then the women did this themselves. A key phrase in Fesche's narrative should be quoted here. Fesche first of all explains that married women do not grant their favours, but that "those who are unmarried are free and prostitute themselves with whomever takes their fancy, and so one can appreciate the kind of life most of the French led in this fortunate island" (2002, 260). We see again how the statement about the local ways and the rules regulating sexual behaviour rests solely on the interpretation that the French had made of the sexual relations they themselves had entered into with Tahitian women/girls. Fesche then immediately adds, "they gave themselves to us at first without asking for any reward, simply eager to give us some pleasure, but soon self-interest became their guide, they insisted on presents" (260). We can disregard Fesche's interpretation that the women/girls were "simply eager to give us some pleasure," but we should remember his observation that they made their overtures to the French "at first without asking for any reward." This remark leads us to make a distinction between two stages, something that up until now historical researchers have not done in their studies of the accounts of first sexual contacts.

The Frenchman also describes the way in which, once the first days of the encounter had passed, the Tahitians took all that they could when they went aboard the French ships: "These people have minds that are very disposed toward theft, they are the cleverest scoundrels I know" (Fesche 2002, 262). Some of them came dressed in many layers of *tapa* and hid the objects that they took underneath the layers, but they were sometimes caught out when they left:

> Others, aware of the special esteem we had for women, brought several very pretty ones on board who offered themselves to the first come. An elderly man, held in special respect by them as far as we could tell, led three of them into Mr de Bougainville's room and urged him most pressingly to enjoy their favours. Mr de Bougainville resisted but it was

impossible for him not to be distracted to the point where, while they were there, an achromatic glass was stolen from him (Fesche 2002, 262).

Fesche is intelligent enough to note that "aware of the special esteem we had for women," the Tahitians started to come forward with girls (and/or women, we do not know) who offered themselves to the "first come" on the ship in order to distract attention. But, significantly, this began when the Polynesians noticed this "special esteem" on the part of their visitors. We should also take note of the fact that, even at the beginning of this second phase of sexual encounters, it is again the men who "led" the women on board, and in this case even an "elderly man held in special respect by them" (Fesche 2002, 262).

So, transformation had indeed taken place by which the ritual presentation of young girls quickly turned into sexual commerce. At least this applied in the case of contacts with Polynesian societies that did not enjoin a marriage with a public defloration. The girls could therefore have a sexual relationship with the visitors without putting their future in danger. That is why this sexual commerce took place in Tahiti, Hawai`i and Tonga, but apparently not in Samoa.[23]

But the emergence of this trade in a second phase (which could be set up in a few days, or only after one or even several new arrivals of Europeans) is in no way an argument for interpreting the first presentations of girls in terms of hospitality or sexual commerce. We know now that these presentations took place in the same way in Tahiti and Samoa.

Beyond Tahiti And Samoa: Also Forced Presentations of Young Girls?

The explicit nature of the French journals

Armed with this knowledge, we must now call seriously into question what is commonly believed about Tonga or Hawai`i or the Marquesas. These are always cited as the classic examples, with Tahiti (including Wallis' stay, just before Bougainville), and again Aotearoa, of episodes of sexual license during the first contacts. The question needs to be asked even where the journals do not describe specific scenes of very young girls who act under coercion. It is possible that the first moments have not been related in detail and that too much has rather been written about the second phase in which sexual commerce featured. Moreover, if the description of such scenes seems to be lacking for Hawai`i, we have some clues, only too brief, for Tonga, Aotearoa and the Marquesas (see below).

The absence of reporting of such scenes does not mean that they did not take place. Here we need to be careful to distinguish between and compare not only the countries visited by the Europeans but equally the nationalities of the European narrators. For Tonga, Hawai`i and Aotearoa, our first sources are Dutch or English. In the case of these authors, during the seventeenth century, or even at the end of the eighteenth century, inhibition about raising questions of sexuality meant that all discussion was a matter of allusion ("amenities of decorum forbid," as Pritchard (1866, 139) wrote in relation to the defloration ceremony in Samoa). Admiration in the French manner is not expressed, but rather reserve or outright condemnation. Therefore, the authors do not permit themselves to describe the bodies and the ages of the "women," and confine themselves to a general denunciation. These allusions do not allow us to reconstruct anything specific, and they therefore leave the door wide open to the usual over-interpretation about "Polynesian sexuality." The constant references to lascivious dances and attitudes, to obscenities that cannot be described and the like could only lead the readers to believe that anything and everything was possible.

In this respect it is the French sources that are most valuable, as their authors were less prudish about telling things as they were. No Dutchman or Englishman of the seventeenth or eighteenth century described the body of a young girl in the way that Fesche did in his journal entry for 7 April 1768, nor did they reveal with such frankness the youth of such girls.[24]

Another exemplary passage is where Fesche refers to the first case of Frenchmen who were too inhibited to perform the act expected of them because of the crowd (here it is the famous scene of the Tahitian Venus, when the first young woman was brought on board by the chief Ahutoru). Fesche complained that this failure would give a "poor impression of the gallantry and burning ardour so generally attributed to Frenchmen" (*piètre idée de la galanterie et la bouillante ardeur si généralement reconnue aux françois*) (Fesche 2002, 256). Fesche's concern reveals another French fantasy about sexuality – this time about their own. The myth of the sexual prowess of French men, who surpassed all other nations in this respect and, as the French assumed, were universally acknowledged as doing so, was quite familiar in the early twentieth century, as we know, but we discover now that it was already in existence in 1768. This is one reason why French narrators were not reluctant to go into such details, while their British counterparts, including Joseph Banks, even though he also was very taken by Tahitian girls, never in their journals crossed the boundary set by the "amenities of decorum." The French showed no such restraint.

To take another example, Vivès, the young surgeon with Bougainville's expedition, even compared the length of the penises of the Tahitians and the French (see Tcherkézoff 2004b, 131). Which British surgeon on any of Cook's voyages would have done that, and then written about it? (Of course, Vivès declared the French winners over the Tahitian men!) And again, at the royal court, Ahutoru, the Tahitian chief whom Bougainville had brought back to Paris, was on one occasion seen to be looking at a painting of a woman. The subject in the painting was clothed and when Ahoturu touched the lower part of her body, the French imagined that he was fantasising about her nude state (Tcherkézoff 2004b, 149–53). As it was, in Tahiti, when Ahutoru got them to understand that he wanted to accompany them to other countries, the French could only conclude that here was a Tahitian man "eager to enter into temporary marriage with white women."[25] And that is why they took pity on him – his motive for visiting Europe being such a noble one to the French masculine way of thinking –and accepted his request to be taken on board.

It happened by chance that the French were almost the first to land in Tahiti (and the first on this eastern side of the island) and the very first to land in Samoa. So it is that we have detailed descriptions in both cases which allow us to see the high degree of congruence between them and not to let our imaginations run riot. This congruence is not a question of something that the French had devised on their own but comes out of the attention paid to sexuality typical of Frenchmen of the time.[26] Because of this they have been able to provide us with a comparison between the two geographical extremities of the Polynesian region. If Tasman in Tonga – or Cook, for that matter, in Tonga or in Hawai`i – had been a Frenchman of the late 1700s, perhaps we would have similar scenes from Tonga or Hawai`i to compare with the Samoan and Tahitian cases. In any event, it is better to leave the question open, rather than choosing to ignore it by affirming that narratives of encounters in other Polynesian archipelagoes do not provide any such scenes.

As it happens, there are a few indications in parts of other narratives to suggest that similar scenes did in fact occur elsewhere. These can provide significant supplementary evidence, when we read them in light of what we have now learned from the Samoan and Tahitian cases. If the information remains too scanty to be conclusive, at least we can note that, contrary to what is usually assumed, Tongan, Maori or Marquesan material may also include scenes of young girls deflowered and forcibly brought to European visitors.

Hamilton in Tonga, 1791

The date is 1791, the observer is Hamilton, surgeon on board the *Pandora* under the command of Captain Edwards, whose mission it was to find the mutineers from the *Bounty*. The period is still one in which the arrival of the Europeans represented a noteworthy event.[27] But the Tongans had, of course, already experienced a number of visits and the presentation of women was already taking place in the context of sexual commerce, because we note that the Tongans expected a gift in return. Notwithstanding the exchange aspect, the Tongan attitude to this situation still demanded, for whatever reason, that the female victims be young virgins. And so I am confident that the comparison is justified.

Hamilton describes what he believed to be the "sale" of "many girls": "Many beautiful girls were brought on board for sale, by their mothers" (Hamilton 1793, 87; 1915, 134). In exchange for their daughter the mothers demanded a small axe (an exchange item at the time). Captain Edwards refused this as too high a price and, after three days of refusing, Hamilton tells us, *"la pucelage* fell to an old razor, a pair of scissors or a very large nail. The quarter deck became the scene of the most indelicate familiarities" (1793, 87; 1915, 134). The original text carries no ambiguity as to the question of virginity: *"la pucelage ..."* Hamilton was surprised to see that the mothers stayed on board and seemed to be happy with the proceedings: "Nor did the unfeeling mothers commiserate with the pain and suffering of the poor girls, but seemed to enjoy it as a monstrous good thing" (1793, 87; 1915, 134).

The narrative continues and again confirms the fact of defloration, referring to it, as we see in the following quotation, as an "accident of this kind." It also reveals a further stage in the process of victimisation:

> It is customary here, when girls meet with an accident of this kind, that a council of matrons is held, and the novitiate has a gash made in her fore finger. We soon observed a number of cut fingers amongst them; and had the razors held out, I believe all the girls in the island would have undergone the same operation (Hamilton 1793, 87; 1915, 134).

Suffice to say that there is no source about Tonga, either at that time or later, that gives any indication that an act of sexual intercourse or the marriage of a girl to a high chief (there are descriptions of families bringing their daughters to the Tongan king, the Tui Tonga) had to be concluded by cutting the girl's finger. But there are many sources on Tonga from all periods, from the early Dutch visits to the mid-nineteenth century, that show how this cutting of the fingers (beginning with the top of the little finger) was a sacrificial offering (these sources are listed in Tcherkézoff 2004b, 191–4). Propitiatory or expiatory, such an offering was made to gods and ancestors in times of great fear, when someone in the family was very ill, or grieving, following a death. These sources indicate that adults would do it to themselves and that mothers would cut the fingers of their children. The operation could be repeated according to circumstances and several fingers would be cut as well (191–4). Other considerations lead to the hypothesis that the European ship may have been seen as an Island-of-the-dead, or at least that it was thought to have come from beyond the human world (Tcherkézoff 2004c). In that case, a mother's cutting of her daughter's finger would have been a propitiatory act whose aim was to ensure that the girl returned safely to land (or, if here too an idea of sacred conception and reproduction was involved, to ensure that the process was efficacious).

Whatever the reason for this practice, we must note from Hamilton's observations that in Tonga, in 1791, as in Samoa and Tahiti, *"la pucelage* fell ..." by the acts of these early European visitors and that it resulted in "the pain and suffering of the poor girls."

J.R. Forster in Aotearoa, 1774

The following lines by J.R. Forster are well known, but until now it was thought that they showed how the situation in Aotearoa had differed from the warm and smiling sexual welcome (to summarise two centuries of Western commentaries) that the early European visitors had enjoyed in Tahiti and in other places in Polynesia. The quotation is of course too decontextualised to provide conclusive information and could not be held to represent the main trend of Maori–European early encounters. But it does show that similar violent scenes could occur there as well:

> In New-Zeeland [sic] the fathers and nearest relations were used to sell the favours of their females to those of our ship's company, who were irresistibly attracted by their charms; and often were these victims of brutality dragged by the fathers into the dark recesses of the ship, and there left to the beastly appetite of their paramours, who did not disdain them, though the poor victim stood trembling before them, and was dissolved in a flood of tears (Forster 1996 [1778], 259).

Captain Marchand in the northern Marquesas, 1791

The southern Marquesans had experienced the arrival of the Spanish in 1595. Mendana's landing was brief and was sealed by a massacre perpetrated by his men. The next visit took place almost two centuries later, during Cook's second voyage. But the people of the northern Marquesas had not yet witnessed the arrival of Europeans. An American trading vessel arrived there in April 1791, but without making a landing. Two months later, a French trading vessel, commanded by Captain Marchand, reached the same place. On one of the islands, Uapou, the French made a brief landing. They were the first Europeans to set foot on this island. Captain Marchand sent a rowboat ashore. In his journal he relates what the officer told him on his return some hours later:

> They landed in the southern cove ... Several huts [were] scattered here and there ... The inhabitants resembling the first men whom we are told inhabited the earth during the Golden Age ... nonetheless approached our gentlemen with confidence, almost certain proof that they had never heard tell of Europeans or of the excesses that they have committed in these seas, or of their fearful weapons.[28] Respectable old men leading young girls by the hand came to present them to [the men who had gone ashore] as the surest sign of, and the most sacred testament to, the hospitality which they were extending to us, these young creatures,

victims of a holy duty, obeyed, trembling, and with their eyes lowered, at the command of their parents (Marchand 1961, 251).

This is a scene that is now becoming very familiar. Adults approached offering "young girls," the young girls obeyed the adults, but they were "trembling" as they did so. This is no longer Tonga or Aotearoa, but the Marquesas, the islands that were to become, in the work of the anthropologist Edward C.S. Handy (1923), "Polynesia" par excellence – the Polynesia where teenage girls throw themselves at any man who comes their way. But far from it: in June 1791, at least on the day that Marchand anchored in front of Uapou, the northern Marquesas were no different from the other archipelagoes – and there is no reason why they should have been.

Wallis in Tahiti, 1767

Finally, without entering into a consideration of the whole succession of events during Wallis' "discovery" of Tahiti, it is worth noting that, on the topic of sexual encounters, one of Wallis' companions wrote in his journal that the sexual offers concerned not "women" but "very young and small girls":

> Their love of Iron (nails) is so great that the women (or rather Girls, for they were very young and small) prostitute themselves to any of our People for a nail, hardly looking upon knives (Henry Ibbot in Corney 1913, 2: 460).[29]

Conclusion (I): One Thing is Certain: Neither Love nor Pleasure

If we consider our two cases from Samoa and Tahiti, we should note that the presentation concerned "young girls." The girls were even "very young," as Vaujuas observed in Samoa, and indeed as Fesche's physical description of the Tahitian girl presented on April 7 attests. Furthermore, a detailed analysis of all the published narratives and journals for each of these two visits leads us to the certain conclusion that the very first presentations concerned *only* the "young girls." The "women" were not involved. Their role was to bring forward the young girls and surround them, and to make sexual gestures (in the same way that they would stand behind the young virgins in the ceremonial dances performed to invoke the procreative powers of the male gods). This they did repeatedly, the most likely reason being that they wanted to explain to the visitors what was expected of them.

However that may be, the explicit references to defloration as well as the constant references to the girls' young age must henceforth completely invalidate the main hypothesis initially proposed by the French and then recycled in the form of a Western myth persisting until today. We now know that there is not a shred of truth in the proposition that the sexual encounters were organised by the Tahitians and the Samoans in the name of love and pleasure.

Two conclusions are to be drawn, one from the feminine perspective, one from the masculine. The hypothesis put forward by certain Frenchmen about these young girls being driven to satisfy their desire in the constant search for new lovers is totally untenable for the type of encounters we have seen described when we take into account the girls' young age and their fear – not to mention their "suffering" during the "operation." On the other hand, if we consider the situation from the chiefs' perspective and imagine that their motive for presenting the French with young girls, even ones shrouded in tears, was to offer sexual pleasure to their visitors, we come up against two obstacles. Firstly, this would suggest that the Polynesians had immediately seen the French as ordinary men; but I have conclusively shown elsewhere, drawing on a wide range of examples, that this hypothesis must be abandoned, because it is incompatible with too many other aspects of Polynesian society and culture of that time and as described by the same early visitors.[30] Secondly, one could ask why these men, if their idea had been to please their visitors with a "sexual gift," would have chosen for this purpose young or very young girls, always or often virgins, distressed and physically tense, rather than young women who were just as attractive but more experienced. Young women, who did not have to endure the physical pain of defloration and who would most likely have been less frightened, would have been preferable sexual partners and surely a more likely choice for sexual hospitality.[31]

In Polynesia the person of the young girl or young woman who is still a virgin, or at least who has not given birth, holds an essential place in the "human" collectivity, or *ta(n)gata*. Throughout Polynesia, societies have reserved a quite specific vocabulary for such a person, distinguishing her thus from the child, from the mother, from the woman as a sexual partner and from women in general.[32] But we are still waiting to see persuasive ethnographic information that could show us that the distinctive place given to the person of the young girl or woman in the social whole flows from the high cultural value put on the sexual pleasure of adolescent girls. All we have, though, is Handy's unreliable reconstruction of a hypothetical Marquesan culture and claiming that the overriding purpose of this period of a woman's life was to collect lovers.

Mead followed close behind and thought she had confirmed this for Samoa when she heard her foremost masculine informant, a young teacher who was rather full of himself, smugly tell her about his sex life and his many feminine conquests. Mead made the grave error of attributing to the two sexes a vision that was an exclusively Samoan male view conveyed to her by this favourite informant.[33] This male vision, which one finds elsewhere in Polynesia as well, was itself the expression of the normal fantasy life of young men that derived in turn from the myths glorifying the sexual appetite of the male gods and of the chiefs. It must be understood within the double standard[34] of the male conquest of virgins *versus* the female preservation of virginity until marriage. An important consequence flowed from this: Mead did not pay any attention to the fact that the detailed account that this teacher gave her of his real or imaginary conquests also indicated that the young girl was often coerced and that she would subsequently have to suffer the reproaches and even blows of her family, if the affair became public.[35]

Conclusion (II): A Hypothesis: Virginity, Conception of the First Child

The child of the god

We have seen that there are strong reasons to think that the scene described by La Pérouse belongs to the very specific context in which brides were presented for "marriage." The same possibility should then be raised in relation to Tahiti. After all, Fesche's perception that the presentations to the French could convey some idea of Tahitian marriages (at least those that were hypergamic) was useful, had he not been inclined to make the comparison in relation to the act of intercourse staged "publicly," instead of reflecting upon the young age of the girls.

It is well attested, from many sources from all over Polynesia, that the forced presentation of young girls who were to enter into marriage with a high chief, where the brides had to be virgins (or at least girls who had not yet given birth), was common practice.[36] Other myths describe how young virgins would get pregnant by sitting nude in front of the rays of the rising sun.[37] In the ritual dances, the first row was reserved for these young virgins.[38] What was the special significance of virginity in all of these cases?

The answer could well lie in the dialogue that Captain Bligh held with a number of Tahitians in 1789. He relates that he had numerous conversations with the "Queen" and with other "principal" people. Among other subjects, he made a "long enquiry," he says, about a belief that the "Queen" would have her first child "through the inspiration of the Eatua" [*atua*, the god]:

> The Queen, whoever she is, has her first Born Son, or the one that becomes the Heir to the Crown, through the inspiration of the Eatua. Nay more than that, they assert that while the Woman is asleep and the Husband by her, the Eatua hovers over her, and literally explaining their expression, says he has connection with her & she conceives, but that all the other children are begot by the Husband (Bligh 1789, quoted in Oliver 1974, 442).

A partial confirmation of this is to be found in the reconstitution by Teuira Henry of the rites surrounding birth "when a queen was about to be delivered of her first child, called the *matahiapo*" (Oliver 1974, 414 ff). The songs chanted by those in attendance praise "the cord of the child, the sacred cord of the god that has flown hither" (*te pito o te tama, te pito tapu o te aitu o mahuta mai nei*). Later, the child is called "the child god" (*te tama aitu*).[39] Next the body is rubbed with the tender inside part of a banana tree and oil.[40] We should note in passing the term *matahiapo*. This is an ancient term, used throughout Polynesia, the etymology of which could derive from the notion that "the child has come out from under the tapa." *Tapa,* like feathers, is the attire of the gods and even a "way" for the gods to descend to earth (Tcherkézoff 2004a, 160), and also has the property of enabling the sacred to be present in what has been wrapped in it (see section above, "The youth of the victims and the ceremonial framework"). Thus, the same range of hypotheses applies to the interpretation of rites attending the birth of the first child as to the conduct of the sexual encounters.

Morrison, who lived in Tahiti from 1789 to 1791, does not raise the general question of this belief, as Bligh does, but he explains that the high chief of the time (Pomare II) had a divine father. This is the relevant passage from Morrison as quoted by Oliver, who has added the correct spelling of the proper names:

> The present Earee Nooi [*ari'i nui*] (or King) is the Son of Matte or O'Too [*Tu* or Pomare I], his name is Toonooeayeteatooa [*Tunuia'eiteatua*] which may be translated "Too, the Great begotten of God", and his title Eatoa Raa [*e Atua Ra'a*] or Sacred God—which Sacraligous [sic] Name and title He obtained by His Mother declaring that the Deity (Taane) Cohabited with her in her Sleep and, proving Pregnant soon after, the Child was declared to be the offspring of the Deity and is rever'd as something supernatural (Oliver 1974, 774).

The three partners involved in conception

Was Bligh's understanding of Tahitian beliefs about conception correct? Was it held that only the first child was a divine work? Or was this thought to apply to all children, but with the sacred quality diminishing according to their order of birth? Was it the case that the husband was thought to play no role at all? Or was he thought to play a facilitating role, as seems to have been an almost universal conception encountered from west to east, from Tonga to Rapa? In fact an obviously ancient notion sees men and gods intervening in different and sometimes complementary ways in relation to women. First of all let me emphasise that in Polynesian mythology concerning relations between the gods and human beings the sexual relationship is always asymmetrical favouring the side of masculinity. The male god meets a mortal female. But no earthly hero would impregnate a goddess. Moreover, it is well attested that throughout the region the Polynesians held to the principle of the complementarity of substances.

So it is that the woman possesses a substance – her blood – that can bring life. An external principle must be added to this. But here the system bifurcates. The husband's sperm acts to obstruct the woman's blood, with "life" quickening in the blood through divine agency. Or alternatively, as it is told in certain Hawaiian legends, the masculine role in the act of sexual intercourse is needed to open the way for divine action (Sahlins 1985: ch. 1).[41] Or again, in the Samoan case, it was the correct handling of the virginal blood of the female partner that was necessary (defloration and spreading of the blood on a sacred cloth, which was then displayed outside).[42] Thus every child is divine, and the action of the husband does no more than enable divine action. But it is still necessary for conception to occur.

Conception therefore involves three main elements, even if they are not always present at the same time. First of all there is the female partner's blood. Next comes the man's contribution, which itself can take three forms enacted singly or together: a "forced" opening by means of manual or sexual intercourse to allow divine action to operate (or both); his displaying of the hymeneal blood; and the penetration of his sperm acting to obstruct the menstrual blood. Finally there is the divine element of "life" quickening in the blood via the agency of a superhuman principle. These elements are found in Samoa, Tonga, Puka-puka, Tahiti, Rapa, Raivavae, Rurutu and Aotearoa New Zealand.[43] Specialists of eastern Polynesia (see Hanson 1982) overwhelmingly record the obstruction of the woman's blood and the relationship between menstrual blood and impregnation (in Samoa a relationship to hymeneal blood is also adduced). But, in what is certainly an excessively reductive formulation, they combine different elements of the non-feminine role into a unitary "male principle," without distinguishing between the respective human and divine acts involved. Moreover, they attribute the *tapu* state of the woman to the "pollution" inhering in the menstrual blood, instead of seeing that the female body as a whole, or at least female blood, was a channel for divine action: a "sacred side," *itu sa*, as the Samoans say, and not a pole of impurity. In 1982 Hanson first shed light on these erroneous conceptions and was the only anthropologist who at the time criticised the idea that there existed a Polynesian ideology of feminine pollution. The Samoan case supports Hanson and provides all the counterevidence necessary to discredit any such theorising about the Polynesian representation of pollution (Tcherkézoff 2003a, 372–94).[44]

Whatever the exact details of the conceptual framework that explains the precise mechanism of conception and its variant forms, its broad outlines are quite clear: three partners, one of whom was divine, and not two, were essential to the process. It is quite plausible, therefore, that how the coming into being of the first child was conceptualised in Polynesian cosmology was one of the reasons why girls who had not yet given birth were presented to the Europeans.

It would also be valuable to be able to assess the importance we should place on Bligh's observation that the notion of the divine conception of the first child concerned the "Queen" —that is, it applied only to girls from a high-ranking family. Indeed, if this was really the case, we might envisage that, before the arrival of the Europeans, the production of "divine" children required that the young woman already be reasonably close to the divine (through the rank of her family). But then, what about the success of the Arioi? (This was a Tahitian brotherhood whose members performed as theatre the myth of Oro coming down to earth to bring fecundity and to make the women pregnant). Were the young women or girls presented to the Arioi for planned acts of intercourse because the Arioi could divinely impregnate even the daughters of ordinary families, owing to their being representatives of the gods? And what happened when the Europeans landed? Quite clearly the chief Reti led the French to his house and got his daughter to come forward. But if Fesche was correct in saying that during their stay "two thirds" of the French sailors had received the same propositions, we would have to conclude that a broader receptiveness to the newcomers held sway. Perhaps because the male partner – to wit the European visitor – was both divine and able to play the enabling role at the same time (as the Tahitians had discovered having disrobed and "touched" Nassau and other Frenchmen), access to divine conception and birth was seen to be more certain? Families of low or middle rank perceived the novel possibility of theogamy (or at least hypergamy) up until that time reserved for the families of the chiefs (*ari'i*). Whence this attitude, well noted by the French and confirmed by Cook (in relation to Tahiti, but also in relation to Hawai`i), even if Cook only refers to it in a few lines: in no time, all the adults were taking every opportunity to lead the newcomers to their daughters (see references in Tcherkézoff 2004b).

There is perhaps proof that the Europeans were compared to the Arioi and that they were being asked to play the same role. Let me recall that in Fesche's account (see section above, "Fesche's text") the girl took care to "strike the chest" of the Frenchman before lying down. Then the audience made gestures to the French simulating what was expected of them. The sources on the Arioi indicate that, when they arrived in a village where they were authorised to remove the women's barkcloth and to take the young women by force, they struck themselves on their chest to announce that the cloth or the young woman had to be brought to them.[45]

"Very young age": The question of the threshold of pubescence

The first Polynesian females who were forcibly "married" to the Europeans were young girls – girls of around twelve years old, according to Fesche in relation to the encounter of April 7. Indeed, they could on occasion be extremely young: Dumont d'Urville gives a figure of "8 to 10 years old" when he called at the Marquesas.[46] This was the age at which girls learned the dances offered to the gods (in fact, instruction in the dances took place within schools devoted to the whole realm of cosmological learning, as is well known in relation to the Hawaiian "dance," the *hula*). Apparently, such dances became a feature of some of the presentations to the European male visitors.

For the acquisition of cosmological learning, it did not particularly matter if the girls were very young, even prepubescent, because, as long as their involvement was limited to dancing with the male gods and to the mythical idea of "virgin birth" (girls impregnated by the rays of the sun, by the god Oro, etc.), practical considerations about impregnation did not come into play. But how can we explain the fact that very young, and therefore (we may assume) in some cases prepubescent, girls were presented to the Europeans, if the idea was to bring about conception and to force the male Europeans to take on the role of the god "Eatua" and the role of the mortal husband at the same time?

In fact, it is possible that the idea of presentations of prepubescent girls to chiefs was already in existence at the time. Mead's male informant mentioned sexual acts with girls "under ten years old" (Tcherkézoff 2003a, 370–1). This discussion leads on to another point. In Samoa (but again there is no reason why Samoa should be unique) there was also a belief, recorded in the nineteenth and twentieth centuries, that the marriage ceremony (defloration) could provoke the onset of menstruation if the bride was prepubescent. Somehow, the very action of this flowing of hymeneal blood and the spreading of it on the sacred cloth was symbolic of menstrual blood and of the divine action which quickened life in the girl's blood (Tcherkézoff 2003a, 352, 365, 372ff.). Significantly, for Samoa and also Eastern Polynesia in the twentieth century, there is clear evidence for the belief that the only days when impregnation could occur were those right at the end of the menstrual period (see Tcherkézoff 2003a, 372ff.; Hanson 1970).

In addition to the more specialised ethnographic questions raised in the course of this discussion, the main hypothesis elaborated here has sought to explain a fact that rather surprised the Europeans, some of whom mentioned it in their journals, namely the young and sometimes very young age of the girls presented to them during these early encounters. My contention is that, at the initiative of the chiefs and/or orators, the total cosmological framework – the mythical structure, underpinning the Polynesian idea and practice of theogamy, one in which a girl's physically having reached pubescence or not was not at issue – was transposed without modification onto the scene of the encounters with the Europeans, the cosmology demanding the presence of a female agent who had not yet given birth.

Conclusion (III): European Male Vision

Of course, European male visitors could rationalise this in only one way. It gave them a further reason to conclude that the main goal of the young girls' education, according to the "customs" of the islanders, was the proper or even "artistic" performance of the act of sexual intercourse – in effect an apprenticeship in what would later be the "main preoccupation" and activity of their adolescent and adult lives.[47]

John Hawkesworth was an even more active proponent of this particular misinterpretation than Bougainville and his companions. In 1773, when he was given the task of editing the manuscript of Cook's journal of his first voyage for publication, he unfortunately rephrased Cook's and Banks' observations noted in 1769 in Tahiti, to accord with this view. He did so particularly when he dealt with a scene which later came to be called the "Point Venus scene" in the literature. It happened just a year after Bougainville's visit, and the circumstances add another ethnographic example to our file on the young age of the girls presented. On this occasion Tahitian dignitaries brought before the British a young man ("a young fellow above 6 feet high") and a "little girl of about 10 to 12 years of age," as Cook wrote in his journal, and they ordered them to have intercourse – which they could not do, as they were terrified.[48] Being himself the director of a girls' college, Hawkesworth misunderstood what he read in the journals, erroneously interpreting this scene in terms of an educational and cultural value specific to these societies. He saw fit to add a paragraph of his own on the topic, presenting the act of intercourse as the main "religious" value of Tahitian society, as if these were Cook's own words.

Shortly afterward, in 1775, the French philosopher Voltaire, from his reading of Bougainville's book (where this metaphor of "love as the only religion of the place" is present) and of Cook's voyage (as retold by Hawkesworth), concluded and made known to all of Europe that, as the French and the British "observations in Tahiti are identical," this account, however incredible, of a "Tahitian custom" which describes how intercourse must always be staged in public, how it constitutes the whole of the local "religion" and how it is the main educational goal, had indeed to "be true." And the explanation for this could only be that in this society sexuality came to be the main preoccupation, indeed the Tahitians' "whole religion."[49] Voltaire did not realise that Hawkesworth had rephrased many passages from Cook's journal, and that Hawkesworth, who knew French, had of course read the short piece by Commerson, the naturalist with Bougainville's expedition, published in Paris in 1769 (*Post-scriptum sur l'île de Taïti*), who affirmed that indeed the only religion of the place was "love." Hawkesworth would also have had the time to read Bougainville's book, which came out in May 1771, while he was working on his version of Cook's journal.

The Western myth of Polynesian sexual freedom was poised to spread in every direction. Twelve years later La Pérouse arrived in Samoa. His interpretation about the offering of female "favours" and his blindness to the very facts he had noted only a few lines earlier were already a consequence of that myth. The interpretations of Williamson one hundred and fifty years later and, of Margaret Mead's supporters and exponents, two centuries later, are no less due to the cultural misreadings that created the Western myth of "Polynesian sexuality."[50]

REFERENCES

Aiavao, Ulafala

1994 Strange ways of the European race. *Islands Business Pacific* (November): 74.

Babadzan, Alain

1982 *Naissance d'une tradition: Changement culturel et syncrétisme religieux aux Iles Australes (Polynésie française)*. Paris: Éditions de l'ORSTOM.

1993 *Les dépouilles des dieux: Essai sur la religion tahitienne à l'époque de la découverte*. Paris: Maison des Sciences de l'Homme.

2003 The gods stripped bare. In *Clothing the Pacific*, ed. Chloe Colchester, 25–50. Oxford: Berg.

Baré, Jean-François

1985 *Le malentendu Pacifique: Des premières rencontres entre Polynésiens et Anglais et de ce qui s'ensuivit avec les Français jusqu'à nos jours*. Paris: Hachette.

1987 *Tahiti, les temps et les pouvoirs: Pour une anthropologie historique du Tahiti post-européen*. 2 vols. Paris: Éditions de l'ORSTOM.

Bougainville, Louis Antoine

1771 *Voyage autour du monde par la frégate du roi La Boudeuse et la flûte L'Etoile ... 1766, 1767, 1768, 1769*; 1 vol. Paris: Saillant & Nyon.

1772 *Voyage autour du monde . ...* 3 vols, 2nd edn. with a supplement. Paris: Saillant & Nyon.

1966 [1771] *Voyage autour du monde*. Series "10/18." Paris: Union Générale d'Éditions.

1968 *Journal de Bougainville* (transcribed by Étienne Taillemite). In *Hommage à Bougainville. Journal de la Société des Océanistes* 24 (24): 11–34. Special issue.

2002 [1768] Journal. In *The Pacific Journal of Louis-Antoine de Bougainville*, trans. and ed. John Dunmore. London: Hakluyt Society.

Cook, James

1773 *An Account of the Voyages Undertaken by Order of Her Present Majesty for Making Discoveries in the Southern Hemisphere and Successively Performed by Commodore Byron, Captain Wallis, Captain Carteret and Captain Cook, in the Dolphin ... / Drawn Up from the Journals ...*, ed. John Hawkesworth. London: W. Strahan and T. Cadell.

Corney, Bolton G., ed.

1913 *The Quest and Occupation of Tahiti by Emissaries of Spain during the Years 1772–1776.* 3 vols. London: Hakluyt Society.

Côté, James E.

1994 *Adolescent Storm and Stress: An Evaluation of the Mead–Freeman Controversy.* Hillsdale, NJ: Lawrence Erlbaum.

Danielsson, Bengt

1956 *Love in the South Seas*, trans. from Swedish by F.H. Lyon. First published 1954. New York: Reynal.

Dening, Greg

1980 *Islands and Beaches: Discourse on a Silent Land, Marquesas 1774–1880.* Carlton, Vic.: Melbourne University Press.

1984 *The Death of Captain Cook.* Sydney: Library Society (State Library of NSW).

1988 *History's Anthropology: The Death of William Gooch.* ASAO Special Publications, no. 2. Washington: University Press of America. Rev. ed. *The Death of William Gooch: A History's Anthropology,* Honolulu: University of Hawai`i Press, 1995.

1992 *Mr Bligh's Bad Language: Passion, Power and Theatre on the Bounty.* Cambridge: Cambridge University Press.

1996 *Performances.* Chicago: Chicago University Press.

1998 *Reading/Writings.* Carlton, Vic.: Melbourne University Press.

2004 *Beach Crossings: Voyaging across Times, Cultures and Self.* Philadelphia: University of Pennsylvania Press.

Diderot, Denis

1964 [1796] *Oeuvres philosophiques.* Paris: Garnier Frères.

Douaire-Marsaudon, Françoise

1998a *Les premiers fruits: Parenté, identité sexuelle et pouvoirs en Polynésie occidentale (Tonga, Wallis et Futuna).* Paris: Éditions du CNRS et de la Maison des Sciences de l'Homme.

1998b *Le meurtre cannibale ou la production d'un homme-Dieu. Théories des substances et construction hiérarchique en Polynésie (Tonga)*. In *Le corps humain supplicié, possédé, cannibalisé*, eds Maurice Godelier and Michel Panoff, 137–67. Paris: Archives contemporaines.

Dumont d'Urville, Jules-Sébastien-César

1842 *Voyage au Pôle sud et dans l'Océanie, sur les corvettes l'Astrolabe et la Zélée, sous le commandement de M.J. Dumont-d'Urville: Histoire du voyage (tome quatrième)*, vol. 4. Paris: Gide.

Dunmore, John, trans. and ed.

1995 *The Journal of Jean-François de Galaup de Lapérouse, 1785–1788*. 2 vols. Trans. of *Le voyage de Lapérouse, 1785–1788*. London: Hakluyt Society.

2002 [1768] *The Pacific Journal of Louis-Antoine de Bougainville*. London: Hakluyt Society.

Dunmore, John, and Maurice de Brossard, eds.

1985 *Le voyage de Lapérouse, 1785–1788: Récit et documents originaux*. Paris: Imprimerie Nationale.

Fesche, Félix

2002 [1768] Journal. In *The Pacific Journal of Louis-Antoine de Bougainville*, trans. and ed. John Dunmore. London: Hakluyt Society.

Forster, George

2000 [1777] *A Voyage Round the World by George Forster*, eds Nicholas Thomas and Oliver Berghof. 2 vols. Honolulu: University of Hawai`i Press.

Forster, Johann Reinhold

1996 [1778] *Observations Made during a Voyage Round the World*. New edition, eds Nicholas Thomas, Harriet Guest, and Michael Dettelbach; with a linguistic appendix by Karl H. Rensch. Honolulu: University of Hawai`i Press.

Freeman, J. Derek

1983 *Margaret Mead and Samoa: The Making and Unmaking of an Anthropological Myth*. Cambridge, MA: Harvard University Press.

Goldman, Irving

1970 *Ancient Polynesian Society*. Chicago: University of Chicago Press.

Grijp, Paul van der

1994 A history of misunderstandings: Early European encounters with Tongans. In *European Imagery and Colonial History in the Pacific*, eds Toon van Meijl and Paul van der Grijp, 32–48. Nijmegen Studies in

Development and Cultural Change, vol. 19. Saarbrücken: Verlag für Entwicklungspolitik Breitenbach GmbH.

Hamilton, George

1793 *A Voyage Round the World in His Majesty's Frigate "Pandora," Performed under the Direction of Captain Edwards in the Years 1790, 1791 and 1792.* London: Berwick.

1915 *Voyage of H.M.S. "Pandora" Despatched to Arrest the Mutineers of the "Bounty" in the South Seas, 1790–1791: being the narratives of Captain Edward Edwards, R.N., the Commander, and George Hamilton, the surgeon,* with introd. and notes by Basil Thomson. London: Francis Edwards.

Handy, Edward C.S.

1923 *Native Culture of the Marquesas.* Bulletin 9. Honolulu: B. P. Bishop Museum.

1927 *Polynesian Religion.* Bulletin 34. Honolulu: B. P. Bishop Museum.

Hanson, Allan F.

1970 *Théorie rapaienne de la conception. Bulletin de la Société des Études Océaniennes* 14 (170): 281–4.

1982 Female pollution in Polynesia? *Journal of the Polynesian Society* 91: 335–81.

Jolly, Margaret

1992 "Ill-natured comparisons": Racism and relativism in European representations of ni-Vanuatu from Cook's second voyage. In *Colonialism and Culture,* ed. Nicholas Thomas. *History and Anthropology* 5 (3–4): 331–64. Special issue.

1993 Lascivious ladies, beasts of burden and voyaging voyeurs: Representations of women from Cook's voyages in the Pacific. Paper presented to 9th David Nichol Smith Memorial Seminar "Voyages and Beaches, Discovery and the Pacific 1700–1840," University of Auckland, New Zealand, August 24–28.

1996 Devils, holy spirits, and the swollen god: Translation, conversion and colonial power in the Marist Mission, Vanuatu, 1887–1934. In *Conversion to Modernities: The Globalization of Christianity*, ed. Peter van der Veer, 231–62. New York and London: Routledge.

1997a From Point Venus to Bali Ha`i: Eroticism and exoticism in representations of the Pacific. In *Sites of Desire, Economies of Pleasure: Sexualities in Asia and the Pacific,* eds Lenore Manderson and Margaret Jolly, 99–122, 303–6. Chicago: University of Chicago Press.

1997b White shadows in the darkness: Representations of Polynesian women in early cinema. In *Imaging, Representation: Photography and Film in the Pacific*, ed. M. Quanchi. *Pacific Studies* 20 (4): 125–50. Special issue.

2002 Introduction: Birthing beyond the confines of tradition and modernity? In *Birthing in the Pacific: Beyond Tradition and Modernity?* eds Vicki Lukere and Margaret Jolly, 1–30. Honolulu: University of Hawai`i Press.

n.d. Women of the East, Women of the West: Representations of Pacific women on Cook's voyages. In *An Ocean of Difference?: Revisioning Gender, Sexuality and Race on Cook's Voyages*. In preparation.

Keate, George

2002 *An Account of the Pelew Islands*, eds Karen L. Nero and Nicholas Thomas. London and New York: Leicester University Press.

Lamb, Jonathan, Vanessa Smith, and Nicholas Thomas, eds.

2000 *Exploration and Exchange: A South Seas Anthology, 1680–1900*. Chicago: University of Chicago Press.

La Pérouse, Jean-François Galaup de

1995 Journal. In *The Journal of Jean-François de Galaup de Lapérouse, 1785–1788*, trans. and ed. John Dunmore. London: Hakluyt Society.

Linnekin, Jocelyn

1991 Ignoble savages and other European visions: The La Pérouse affair in Samoan history. *Journal of Pacific History* 26 (1): 3–26.

Malinowski, Bronislaw

1927 *Sex and Repression in Savage Society*. London: Routledge & Kegan Paul.

1929 *The Sexual Life of Savages in north-western Melanesia: An Ethnographic Account of Courtship, Marriage and Family Life among the Natives of the Trobriand Islands, British New Guinea;* with a preface by Havelock Ellis. London: Routledge.

Marchand, Etienne

1961 *Journal de bord du Capitaine Etienne Marchand, Commandant le "Solide" trois-mâts marseillais qui fit le premier tour du monde commercial français de 1790 à 1792*, ed. Robert Suteau. *Bulletin de la Société des Études Océaniennes* No. 135 11(10): 247–60.

Mead, Margaret

1928 *Coming of Age in Samoa: A Psychological Study of Primitive Youth for Western Civilisation*. New York: William Morrow.

Moerenhout, Jacques Antoine

1837 *Voyages aux îles du Grand Océan, contenant des documents nouveaux sur la géographie physique et politique, la langue, la littérature, la religion, les moeurs, les usages et les coutumes de leurs habitants; et des considérations générales sur leur commerce, leur histoire et leur gouvernement, depuis les temps les plus reculés jusqu'à nos jours.* 2 vols. Paris: Adrien Maisonneuve (Librairie d'Amérique et d'Orient).

Nassau, Prince de

2002 [1768] Journal. In *The Pacific Journal of Louis-Antoine de Bougainville*, trans. and ed. John Dunmore. London: Hakluyt Society.

Oliver, Douglas L.

1974 *Ancient Tahitian Society.* 3 vols. Honolulu: University of Hawai`i Press.

1981 *Two Tahitian Villages: A Study in Comparisons.* Laie: Institute for Polynesian Studies, Brigham Young University.

Orans, Martin

1996 *Not even Wrong: Margaret Mead, Derek Freeman, and the Samoans.* Novato, CA: Chandler & Sharp.

Pérez, Christine

1996 *Fantasmatique égéenne, fantasmatique polynésienne.* In *Le Pacifique ou l'odyssée de l'espèce: Bilan civilisationniste du grand Océan,* ed. Serge Dunis, 141–231. Paris: Klincksieck.

Pritchard, William T.

1864 Notes on certain anthropological matters respecting the South Sea islanders. *Memoirs of the Anthropological Society* 1: 325–6.

1866 *Polynesian Reminiscences; or, Life in the South Pacific Islands.* London: Dawsons.

Sahlins, Marshall

1981 *Historical Metaphors and Mythical Realities: Structure in the Early History of the Sandwich Islands Kingdom.* ASAO Special Publications, no. 1. Ann Arbor: University of Michigan Press.

1982 The apotheosis of Captain Cook. In *Between Belief and Transgression: Structuralist Essays in Religion, History, and Myth,* trans. John Leavitt, eds Michel Izard and Pierre Smith, 73–102. Chicago: University of Chicago Press.

1985 *Islands of History.* Chicago: University of Chicago Press.

1989 Captain Cook at Hawaii. *Journal of the Polynesian Society* 98 (4): 371–423.

1995 *How "Natives" Think: About Captain Cook, for Example*. Chicago: University of Chicago Press.

Salmond, Anne

1991 *Two Worlds: First Meetings between Maori and Europeans, 1642–1772*. Honolulu: University of Hawai`i Press.

1997 *Between Worlds: Early Exchanges between Maori and Europeans, 1773–1815*. Auckland: Viking.

Taillemite, Étienne

1968 *Hommage à Bougainville*. In *Hommage à Bougainville. Journal de la Société des Océanistes* 24 (24): 1–2. Special issue.

1977 *Bougainville et ses compagnons autour du monde: 1766–1769, journaux de navigation / établis et commentés par Etienne Taillemite*. 2 vols. Paris: Imprimerie Nationale.

Tcherkézoff, Serge

1993 The illusion of dualism in Samoa: "Brothers-and-sisters" are not "men-and-women." In *Gendered Anthropology*, ed. Teresa del Valle, 54–87. London: Routledge.

2001a *Le mythe occidental de la sexualité polynésienne: Margaret Mead, Derek Freeman et Samoa*. Paris: Presses Universitaires de France.

2001b Is anthropology about individual agency or culture? Or why "Old Derek" is doubly wrong? *Journal of the Polynesian Society* 110 (1): 59–78.

2001c Samoa again: On "Durkheimian bees," Freemanian passions and Fa`amu's "confession." *Journal of the Polynesian Society* 110 (4): 431–6.

2002 Subjects and objects in Samoa: Ceremonial mats have a "soul." In *People and Things: Social Mediations in Oceania*, eds Bernard Juillerat and Monique Jeudy-Ballini, 27–51. Durham: Carolina Academic Press.

2003a *FaaSamoa, une identité polynésienne (économie, politique, sexualité): L'anthropologie comme dialogue culturel*. Paris: L'Harmattan.

2003b A long and unfortunate voyage towards the "invention" of the Melanesia/Polynesia distinction 1595–1832. In 'Dumont d'Urville's Divisions of Oceania: Fundamental Precincts or Arbitrary Constructs?', ed. Geoffrey Clark. *Journal of Pacific History* 38 (2): 175–96. Special issue.

2003c On cloth, gifts and nudity: Regarding some European misunderstandings during early encounters in Polynesia. In *Clothing the Pacific*, ed. Chloe Colchester, 51–75. Oxford: Berg.

2004a *"First Contacts" in Polynesia: The Samoan Case (1722–1848). Western Misunderstandings about Sexuality and Divinity.* Canberra/Christchurch: Journal of Pacific History Monographs/Macmillan Brown Centre for Pacific Studies.

2004b *Tahiti 1768—Jeunes filles en pleurs: La face cachée des premiers contacts et la naissance du mythe occidental.* Papeete: Au Vent des Îles.

2004c *Visions européennes et polynésiennes de l'espace-temps insulaire du XVIIIe siècle à nos jours.* In *Le Grand Océan: Le temps et l'espace du Pacifique,* ed. Serge Dunis, 277–302. Geneva: Georg Éditeur S.A.

2005a Culture, nation, society: Secondary changes and possible radical transformations in Samoa. Towards a model for the study of cultural dynamics. In *The Changing South Pacific: Identities and Cultural Transformations,* eds Serge Tcherkézoff and Françoise Douaire-Marsaudon, 245–301. Canberra: Pandanus Books.

2005b *La Polynésie des vahinés et la nature des femmes: une utopie occidentale-masculine.* CLIO: Histoire, Femmes et Sociétés 22: 61–80.

2005c *Le désir féminin, l'anatomie de Priape et l'ardeur du French Lover: stéréotypes de la sexualité chez les voyageurs français lors des premiers contacts en Polynésie.* In *Stéréotypes et représentations en Océanie: Actes du 17ᵉ Colloque CORAIL,* eds Véronique Fillol and Jacques Vernaudon. Nouméa: CORAIL Publications.

2005d The anatomy of Priape and the ardour of the French Lover: Stereotypes of masculinity among 18th-century male French arriving in Polynesia. Paper presented at the *Moving Masculinities: Crossing Regional and Historical Borders* conference, held at ANU, Canberra, 30 November – 2 December.

Thomas, Nicholas

1990 *Marquesan Societies: Inequality and Political Transformation in Eastern Polynesia.* Oxford: Clarendon Press.

1997 *In Oceania: Visions, Artifacts, Histories.* Durham, NC: Duke University Press.

Valeri, Valerio

1985 *Kingship and Sacrifice: Ritual and Society in Ancient Hawaii,* trans. Paula Wissing. Chicago: University of Chicago Press.

Williams, John

1984 *The Samoan Journals of John Williams, 1830 and 1832,* ed. and introd. Richard M. Moyle. Canberra: Australian National University Press.

Williamson, Robert Wood

1924 *The Social and Political Systems of Central Polynesia*. 3 vols. Cambridge: Cambridge University Press.

1933 *Religious and Cosmic Beliefs of Central Polynesia*. 2 vols. Cambridge: Cambridge University Press.

1939 *Essays in Polynesian Ethnology*, ed. Ralph Piddington. Cambridge: Cambridge University Press.

Notes

[1] Sahlins for Hawai`i; Salmond and her team for Aotearoa-New Zealand; Dening for the Marquesas, Tahiti and Hawai`i; and Baré for Tahiti, while Thomas has added numerous comparative remarks and has also worked on early encounters in the Marquesas Islands: Sahlins (1981, 1982, 1985, 1989, 1995); Salmond (1991, 1997); Dening (1980, 1984, 1988, 1992, 1996, 1998, 2004); Baré (1985, 1987); Thomas (1990, 1997). Thomas and others have also edited numerous early accounts (Forster 1996 [1778]; Forster 2000 [1777]; Thomas; Lamb et al. 2000; Keate 2002). But, at the time of writing, only two articles had appeared in relation to western Polynesia (Linnekin 1991; van der Grijp 1994).

[2] Until very recently, these pages were only available in French. In 1968 a Chief Conservator at the French Archives, Étienne Taillemite, made the first transcription of extracts from Bougainville's and his companions' accounts of their stay in Tahiti (Taillemite 1968). Ten years later he published all of the journals kept during the circumnavigation (a limited edition from the French Imprimerie Nationale) (1977). And it was only in 2002, thanks to Professor John Dunmore's great work of translation, that these journals became available in English through the Hakluyt Society. La Pérouse's journal, published in 1797 by the French naval authorities in an "edited" version, became available in its original form in 1985 (Dunmore and Brossard 1985) and ten years later in an English translation, also thanks to John Dunmore (1995). Throughout this chapter I shall use Dunmore's translation. Dr. Stephanie Anderson translated the short excerpts from other French authors, namely Buffon and Captain Marchand.

[3] Although Diderot himself really only proposed this idea in jest. Diderot's *Supplement*, written in 1772 – immediately after Bougainville's book appeared – but banned for fifteen years, is an imaginary dialogue between a Polynesian elder and a European priest. In it the Polynesian elder relativises, even mocks, European certainties of the time about religion and political systems. He also explains that Europeans are naïve in their exchanges with non-Europeans. He describes what his people had really planned in Tahiti. The French, he says, thought they had been offered sexual hospitality and gave the Tahitians many gifts in return, when in fact they had been cunningly used. Firstly, they had been depleted of their seed to give some of the local women a chance to get pregnant, so that the Tahitians could secure the "intellectual abilities" of this "new race." Secondly, Tahitian men, too busy with their wars and garden work, could not waste their time and their own seed with the "sterile women" (the elder does not comment on the presence of these women). It is these women, he says, that were offered first. Then he generalises about human nature: everywhere in the world, in every exchange, one party tries to cheat the other (Diderot 1964 [1796], 499–501).

[4] The sexual encounters were not Sahlins' main topic. In this lecture and in a book published in 1981, he dealt mainly with the rise and fall of Captain Cook's fortunes in Hawai`i (Sahlins 1981, 1985: ch. 1). Many other works on this question were to follow (see references in Sahlins 1995).

[5] See pictorial portfolios in Tcherkézoff (2004a, 2004b): La Pérouse refers to the drawing by John Webber (the artist on Cook's third voyage) of a Tahitian girl bringing gifts of barkcloth and necklaces (we can see the extent to which the Tahitian scene played on La Pérouse's mind when he visited Samoa).

[6] We shall see this expressed explicitly by Fesche and Nassau.

[7] In his book, Bougainville only admitted to having noticed a temporary shyness or hesitation when the girls were presenting "themselves" to the French; but he was convinced that it was ingrained in the "nature of women" always to "claim not to want what they desire the most" (*prétendent ne pas vouloir ce qu'elles désirent le plus*) (Tcherkézoff 2004b, 128, 203).

[8] Forster (1996 [1778]) was among the first voyagers to the Pacific to express these views, preceded only by his French fellow naturalist of the Bougainville expedition, Philibert Commerson, who raised the issue in his famous letter of 1769 published in the main Parisian newspaper (*Post-scriptum sur l'île*

de Taïti) which was written on his way back from Tahiti (Tcherkézoff 2004b, 210ff.). See the discussion about the European views concerning a supposed West/East (later called Melanesian / Polynesian) contrast in Jolly (1992, 1993, 1997a, 1997b, n.d.) and Tcherkézoff (2003b).

[9] A record that he knew he would be sending to the French authorities from his next port of call, which was Australia. This is how the narrative of his voyage up until early 1788 came to be left for posterity, since, once he left southern Australia, no further word was heard from the expedition. See Tcherkézoff (2004a, 28–9, 49) for discussion of the fate of the expedition, which was shipwrecked in the Solomons (Vanikoro), and the recent archaeological findings that relate to it.

[10] The French expression may imply physical pain as well as sorrow.

[11] La Pérouse's journal gives no details about digital/penile penetration. In the nineteenth-century sources there seems to be general agreement that in Samoan marriages the first sexual act was preceded by an act of digital defloration, performed by an officiant or by the bridegroom, because it was important to collect the hymeneal blood on a sacred cloth (Tcherkézoff 2003a, ch. 8). Was it the case in the 1787 meeting that the Samoans did not perform this initial procedure? Or did the French account fail to mention it because it was seen as unimportant or perhaps embarrassing?

[12] The word is of Spanish origin. Pritchard is referring to the old women who were the guardians of the unmarried daughters of Spanish royalty or nobility.

[13] The description was published by Pritchard in his "Notes on Certain Anthropological Matters" (1864, 325–6) and is cited by Danielsson (1956, 116–7). In his well-known book *Polynesian Reminiscences*, published two years later, Pritchard did not include this description as "amenities of decorum" forbade it, he said, and he only alluded to it: "The ordeal by which the virtue of the chief girl of Samoa was tested was as obscene as severe, and the amenities of decorum forbid the description here" (1866, 139).

[14] The "spirits" (*aitu*) of today may appear to be ranged only on the negative side and opposed to any idea of life. This was not so in pre-Christian times, as the first missionaries specifically note a constant mixing in the Samoan language of references to various *atua* (later translated as "God") and to various *aitu* (later translated as "spirits"). Jolly (1996) describes a comparable case for Vanuatu.

[15] This was a ritual gesture which made the way open for stepping into a sacred and tabooed area (Tcherkézoff 2004b, 424–6).

[16] As we now know from his own journal.

[17] Dunmore translates this as "one of his wives," but rightly explains to his reader that the French *femme* can mean "woman" or "wife," and that he had to "guess" the meaning. But when the expression includes the possessive adjective as in *sa femme*, it usually means "his wife," so his guess was correct. Nonetheless, I have departed from his translation at this point in order to maintain the possible ambiguity.

[18] In these French journals a mixed Tahitian crowd is always described as "the Indians," a male Tahitian (such as a flute musician) is referred to as "an Indian," while Tahitian women and girls are simply "women" and "girls." During this period French men, particularly in educated discourse, were able to refer to the female gender, of any nation, in its entirety as *le sexe* (the more usual expression being *les femmes*), while the only term used for the male gender was *les hommes*.

[19] We should remember that the French only communicated by signs, as we know from the descriptions of other scenes, as in the negotiation between Bougainville and the chief Eriti about the question of knowing whether the French could set themselves up on the shore. They could not understand and, as Fesche tells us, they just tried to guess the meaning from the context. In fact, the words uttered at this moment were certainly not meant to inform the French about "the surrender she was making of herself," which was already obvious and did not need any further explanation, but were probably ritual words linked to the act of striking the chest, a gesture that appears in the rites of the Arioi cult (see this chapter, Conclusion (II)).

[20] *Les assistants insulaires*; Dunmore translates this as "the islanders themselves" rather than as "island assistants/participants." It is not clear whether Fesche means "assisting" (helping with the procedure) or just "attending" (merely present at the scene). Still, the ritual gestures of these people (i.e. holding the branch, singing) suggest that their presence was a meaningful component of the whole ceremony.

[21] *Sur l'acteur*, thus singular. Fesche probably means that the girl was partly dressed, or temporarily covered, with a ceremonial barkcloth.

[22] See previous notes. As the French were unable to understand what was being sung, this is only Fesche's interpretation.

[23] For Samoa, sources as late as the 1830s continue to note that sexual advances on the part of European male visitors were rejected (Tcherkézoff 2004a, 82).

[24] Physical descriptions only became more exact in the nineteenth century with the advent of the theoretical framework of "sciences" such as raciology and phrenology. By that time the period of early encounters in Polynesia was over and the "naturalists" of the eighteenth century were now naval medical officers concerned with measuring facial angles and the volume of skulls. It was not until the 1920s that there was a revival of interest in the "sexual life" of "savages" (see Malinowski 1927, 1929). This was precisely the time when the theme of sexuality in the narratives of the early voyages to the Pacific was beginning to be considered as a source of knowledge (and even as a model for the West by philosophers such as Bertrand Russell), after the relatively general condemnation of "heathenist" practices according to the European conceptions of Pacific cultures that had prevailed during the nineteenth century (Tcherkézoff 2001a, ch. 4).

[25] As Fesche wrote in his journal, "*l'envie qu'il a de se marier pour quelque temps avec des femmes blanches*" (Tcherkézoff 2004b, 152).

[26] See Tcherkézoff (2005c, 2005d). In his theory of the nature of Man, the French naturalist Buffon held that the size of the penis and the level of male sexual prowess were an expression of the original masculine condition as created by God – and for Buffon "white people" best exemplified this original humanity. In his view, men who were "coloured" had obviously departed ("degenerated") from this original design, and were found to be "small in the size of their sexual organs" (*petit par les organes de la génération*) and with "no passion for their female partner" (*nulle ardeur pour sa femelle*) (see Tcherkézoff 2004b, 212–3).

[27] See the chapter by Douaire-Marsaudon (this volume).

[28] Captain Marchand's particular perspective on the voyages of discovery was rare for the time. A little later he tells us that he felt obliged to nail a copper plaque attesting to his "taking possession" of the island, an act he undertook for "His Majesty Louis XVI, King of the French," although acknowledging "I have never been able to conceive how and by what right a civilised nation could take over an inhabited land without the consent of its inhabitants." He relieves his conscience, however, by adding immediately that the act of taking possession is a preventive measure against "oppression if some European nation ever tried to enslave them" (Marchand 1961, 253; my translation).

[29] Wallis, in the official "edited" publication of his narrative in 1773 by Hawkesworth (I have not been able to consult the unpublished manuscript of Wallis' journal), speaks of "women" who "openly trafficked with our people for personal favours" (hence he declares – or Hawkesworth makes him declare – that "chastity does not seem to be considered as a virtue among them"). But even so he specifies that these women "were brought down by their fathers and brothers" (see reference in Tcherkézoff 2004b, 248).

[30] For Samoa see Tcherkézoff (2004a, 60–2); for Tonga, Hawai`i, Cook, etc. (109–53); in relation to the term "*Papala(n)gi*" used in Western Polynesia, (193–6); and for Tahiti see Tcherkézoff (2004b, 200–1).

[31] As shown by various chants, all Polynesian cultures plainly recognised the desirability of sexual pleasure for both sexes (and practices involving sexual mutilation were quite foreign to them).

[32] As *tapairu* in Maori or, in Samoan, *tamaitai, tausala, augafaapae* (in sharp distinction to *fafine*).

[33] Aside from the whole question of how the Western myth about Polynesian sexuality obviously influenced her interpretation in the field, the main thrust of the revised view that we must now adopt in relation to Mead's interpretation of girls' adolescence in Samoa bears on gender roles. She thought that she had understood the feminine perspective on sexuality in Samoa, but in fact it was her male informant, absent from the published book but crucial in her field notes, who was her source (Tcherkézoff 2001a, ch. 8 *passim*). As these girls were constantly "joking-and-lying" (*pepelo*) when telling her the story of their supposedly free and easy private lives, their discourse (quite at odds with what they were actually experiencing, but Mead did not realise it) appeared to Mead to correspond well enough with what her male informant had told her (Tcherkézoff 2001b).

[34] I use this expression for the sake of brevity. But it does not reflect accurately the *two levels* of the ideology involved here. On one level, where the ideology is governed by ideas of family inheritance, the ancestors' cult, etc., girls as "the relationship to the whole," *feagaiga*, are seen as somewhat asexual, while boys, who are all their "brothers," "serve" them. On another level, according to a universalistic notion of gender dualism and heterosexuality, boys as "males" are supposed to become full males by showing their ability to conquer the "females" (Tcherkézoff 1993, 2003a: ch. 7).

[35] I have analysed and published the informant's account (Tcherkézoff 2003a, 366–71; for the original English text see Orans 1996).

[36] See Tcherkézoff (2003a, 384) on Tongan and Hawaiian cases quoted by Douaire-Marsaudon (1998a, 182–3) and Sahlins (1985), in addition to the description of Samoan "marriages" given here at the beginning of the analysis.

[37] For this theme in Tonga, see Douaire-Marsaudon (1998a, 182–3); for Tokelau, see Tcherkézoff (2003a, 48–9). There are also Samoan legends on this topic.

[38] There are very precise descriptions of the Samoan dances of the 1830s in Williams' journal (Tcherkézoff 2003a, 384–7). In relation to Tahiti, Cook and Banks had noted that the young girls learning and practising the dances had to give up this specialised learning "as soon as they have form'd a connection with man" (Tcherkézoff 2004b, 303–4).

[39] The word *aitu* is equivalent to *atua*. In Tahiti as in Samoa, ancient practices show the use of these two words even if in Samoa today we find two quite distinct notions: "God" is *O le Atua*, while *aitu* generally refers to spirits (spirits of place and the wandering souls of the dead who have returned to trouble the living).

[40] The complete account told by Teuira Henry is quoted by Oliver (1974, 414–6).

[41] With one more element to be added: in the case recorded by Sahlins (1985), a chief must perform this operation for the husband (the fact that the body of the woman is taboo and that not just anyone may touch her certainly comes into it). In Samoa, too, it seems that a distinction was made between marriages where it was the orator of the family group of the husband who manually performed the act of deflowering before the newly-wed couple themselves engaged in intercourse, and cases where the husband was of sufficiently high rank and performed the defloration himself.

[42] With the idea that this display was intended for the sun, the wind and the gods, and not simply the crowd of villagers who had come to see that the "honour" of the husband was intact (according to the Eurocentric interpretation of the missionaries and first ethnographers).

[43] See Douaire-Marsaudon (1998a: 187–8, 1998b); Pérez (1996, 168ff.); Oliver (1974, 442; 1981, details recorded by Bligh, Morrison and Henry); Babadzan (1982); Hanson (1970); Best (1975); Tcherkézoff (2003a, ch. 8).

[44] See also the discussion regarding Melanesian examples in Jolly (2002).

[45] Babadzan (1993, 274, quoting an observation recorded in 1797). On the dual figure of Oro and the Arioi cult, see Babadzan 1993. For a discussion of the whole context of the Arioi in relation to the Western over-interpretation of their "orgies," see Tcherkézoff (2004b, 304–14, 411–21).

[46] In September 1838, in Nuku-Hiva, Dumont d'Urville was surprised to see how young the girls were who were being offered: "from 12 to 18 years of age" and "some much younger, no more than 8 to 10 years" (1842, 6). We are still at the time of early encounters, as there were no missionaries, he said. Unfortunately, he does not give any details of the encounter, and that is why it cannot be included as primary evidence along with the other comparative cases.

[47] This was an application to the specific context of these encounters of a general male vision of the mid-eighteenth century about the "nature of females": "desire" and "love" were said to be the main components of that "nature" (see note 7; Tcherkézoff 2005b, 2005c).

[48] From Hawkesworth's interpretation, and, two years later, Voltaire's in the same vein, to references in all the books on "Old Polynesia," the chain of over-interpretations was a long one. If the hypothesis presented in this chapter is valid, it also provides an explanation of this famous scene (see discussions in Tcherkézoff 2004b, 273–83).

[49] See Voltaire's correspondence quoted in Tcherkézoff (2004b, 286).

[50] In the course of its development, this analysis has been strengthened by many discussions with colleagues. My thanks go particularly to the participants in the following seminars and workshops: the RSPAS Department of Anthropology Seminar (Head, Mark S. Mosko, RSPAS, ANU, Canberra, October 2001), the Macmillan Brown Centre for Pacific Studies Seminar (organised by the Centre's then Director, Ueantabo Neemia-Mackenzie, University of Canterbury, March 2002), the "Second Western Polynesia – including Fiji – Workshop" (CREDO, Marseilles, May 2002; organised by Steven Hooper, Françoise Douaire-Marsaudon, Serge Tcherkézoff; Marshall Sahlins as discussant), and our RSPAS–CREDO symposium on "Oceanic Encounters" (Marseilles 2002, Canberra 2003) which is part of the RSPAS–CREDO program of ongoing cooperation under the guidance of Darrell Tryon (see Preface to this volume). For this published version, the analysis has been considerably enlarged in scope thanks to the very hospitable and academically exciting environment of the Gender Relations Centre of the RSPAS at the ANU, where this work was undertaken during my appointment there in 2004–05 as an Australian Research Council Linkage Fellow. I would like to extend my special thanks and appreciation to Margaret Jolly, Head of the Gender Relations Centre and of the ARC projects *Oceanic Encounters* and *Enlightened Explorations*,

who made it all happen. Thanks also for her reading of this chapter: her numerous commentaries have been very helpful. I also thank Dr. Stephanie Anderson, who translated a number of passages of this chapter from a first French version and edited others that were written in my often uncertain English.

Chapter 5

Uncertain Times: Sailors, Beachcombers and Castaways as "Missionaries" and Cultural Mediators in Tonga (Polynesia)

Françoise Douaire-Marsaudon

Introduction: How the South Sea Islands Were "Invented" Before They Were Discovered

This chapter focuses on a particular period in the history of the first European contacts with Tonga, that is, between 1796 and 1826, a period which was unmarked by any events sufficiently important to have interested contemporary chroniclers or historians, which is why I refer to it as "uncertain times." But in order to explain my choice of this phase of Tongan history, I would like to first describe the analytic framework within which I have situated my work on "first contacts."

We may consider "first contacts" as a particular period in the history of cultural globalisation. From this perspective, we have to take into account the fact that this historical phase may vary considerably from one country to another and may be much longer and consequently more heterogeneous than was affirmed when academic interest in this topic began. For Tonga, the very first contact between the indigenous inhabitants and European sailors took place in the year 1616, when the Dutch vessel *Eendracht*, commanded by Captain Schouten, with the merchant Lemaire on board, visited the archipelago for purely economic reasons. If we agree that the period of first contacts came to an end with the first successful installation of the Christian mission in about 1826, the history of the first contacts in Tonga lasted more than two centuries. Of course, during these two hundred years, all European visitors were not of one type, did not share the same vision of the world and did not have the same intentions toward the populations they encountered. However, a lot of them, particularly those who narrated their adventures in the South Seas, did share, as we shall see, a kind of a common heritage, which appears to be a many-faceted representation of an imagined world of adventure.

The "beginnings" of a situation are always and by their very nature of interest to social scientists, as has been emphasised by Pierre Bourdieu and others. This is the case with these "first contacts." Certain situations, however, are doubly "beginnings" and this is precisely the case for these "uncertain times" in Tonga. It is a time of "first contacts" in that for the first time the Tongans saw Europeans settle and live on their land; but it also coincides with the commencement of a particularly significant process, Christianisation. However, this period is not well known because, from a European point of view, no decisive events occurred and it was a time of total failure for the first "missionaries." Accordingly, this period is rarely mentioned in books and articles dedicated to the history of Christian missions.[1] However, these "uncertain times" are particularly crucial for the understanding of the whole history of "first contacts" in Tonga, because it was during this period that the first European communities settled in the islands. Ten young proselytes of the London Missionary Society and also a small group of white people – runaway sailors, castaways and escaped convicts – became the first white residents of the Tongan islands. For the first time, the indigenous people could observe white people as they really were.

If the European vision of the South Seas may be considered a long-lasting story which began in the sixteenth century, long before the Enlightenment, the representation of Pacific peoples may be considered more complex than the commonly quoted myth of the "noble savage." As we know, the whole story of the myth of the "noble savage" began on the shores of America at the end of the fifteenth century. The discovery and the conquest of the Americas during the sixteenth century showed the Europeans that peoples existed who could not be confused with the concept of "savage" as it was perceived during the middle ages: a sort of wolf-man, a monster, directly born from the imagination and fears of the medieval age, and much closer to animals than to man. With the discovery of the populations of America, the "savage" became for Europeans a permanent subject of fascination, corresponding precisely to the slow birth of anthropology. Faced by these new peoples, navigators, princes, theologians and missionaries were confronted with the necessity of defining the nature of this new "savage": those inhabitants of the New World could hardly be relegated to the extreme limits of humanity.[2] Finally, the conquest of America constrained the pope to take a position.

The first text which speaks about the nature of the "savages" is the papal bull *Sublimis deus*, promulgated in 1537 by Pope Paul III. This text established the humanity and the divine origin of all the "savages" with whom the Europeans would come into contact. However, the colonisation of the New World led to the slaughter of the Indian populations and the ruin of the pre-Columbian empires, despite the efforts of some men, like Bartolomé de Las Casas, who drew up a veritable indictment of colonisation and pleaded for the defense of the Indian populations, presented as "noble savages."[3]

In other words, when the first European voyagers after Magellan sailed into the Pacific waters, they had already, and long before J.J. Rousseau, their vision of the "noble savage." As it has been suggested by Eric Vibart (1987), it is probable that the European "bad conscience" following the tragic episodes of the American colonisation played a role in the idea that confrontation in the Pacific would *not* be as disastrous as was the case in America. Nothing echoes these preoccupations more than the myths and legends of the Terra Australis:

> Mythical territory for geographers, the austral continent also soon became an imaginary landscape for philosophers. A place of fantasy that in their minds already had an existence, it gave rise, in the years preceding the scientific exploration of the Enlightenment, to scope for creative thinking, the source and confluence of all utopias (1987, 22).

The Portuguese Pedro Fernandez de Quirós was, from the start of the exploration of the southern seas, one of the principal architects of the myth of a welcoming, beneficial land, perfect from all points of view as opposed to the violence and corruption of the Western world. Basing himself on the few islands discovered during his expedition, he launched into an a priori description of the Terra Australis. The riches of nature met the needs of all. The inhabitants, white-skinned natives, were represented as easy to approach, convert and civilise, and therefore superior to the American races by their physical and moral qualities. In fact, Quirós' text prefigured later paintings of Polynesian Edens (cf. Jolly, this volume).

This vision was to be adopted and developed in the narratives called "philosophical odysseys," which flourished on the eve of the eighteenth century. Among these narratives, we may cite *L'Histoire des Sévarambes* (Vairasse d'Alais 1715). In this book, originally published in 1675 in London, England, Denis Vairasse d'Alais, who claimed as authority Plato and Thomas More, presented an ideal city, where community law created perfect harmony between the individual and society (Vibart 1987, 28ff.), where everything – families, institutions, trade associations, groups – was in permanent osmosis. This ideal city was also a veiled criticism of the France of Louis XIV.[4]

All these philosophical travellers' tales preceded, and up to a point prepared for, the rapid development in the eighteenth century of the natural history of man. People turned away from their religious preoccupations and made man the centre of their literary and philosophical discourse. For natural philosophers, men were not united by a common genesis, but by their common – therefore universal – nature, source of both highly civilised societies and the most remote tribes. This natural history of man was born in England with Hobbes (*Leviathan*, 1651), then Locke (*An Essay Concerning Human Understanding*, 1690). For the latter, we know that the state of nature was a state where all were free, equal and independent, the only obligation being to conform to the law of nature. The necessity of respecting this natural law imposed the creation of a civil society (*Two Treatises of Government*, 1690). These writers were the precursors of what will later be called "cultural primitivism."

These examples are sufficient to show that Europeans had "invented" the South Seas and their inhabitants, even before they were "discovered". We can say that the arrival of the Europeans in the Pacific, and particularly in Polynesia, fleshed out an imaginary preconception built up over nearly two centuries. European travellers would come to the South Seas at different times and with very different, even divergent, ideas. However, "all show a strong intellectual proclivity, based on three elements: the American heritage, the myth of the South Seas and the principles of the natural history of man" (Vibart 1987, 46).

To conclude this long introduction and before turning to my discussion on Tonga, I would like to add a brief remark about one of the items which was exchanged between Europeans and Pacific Islanders: writing. Writing is, of course, both a knowledge and skill, and in the relations between the Europeans and the Pacific Islanders it had a status equivalent to that of healing. Many accounts show that writing and healing were both considered by indigenous people as practices related to religious and cosmic forces. But we have also to take into account that, in these societies of oral culture, the discovery and learning of writing not only transformed the system of oral transmission but also had profound effects on cognitive processes and social organisation as a whole.[5]

Missionary Fervour

At the end of the eighteenth century, England, roused by the preaching of the Methodist John Wesley, experienced a veritable religious revival, shaking up both traditional Anglican society, ensconced in its privileges, and dissenters, split into rival factions. The reports of Cook's voyages came just at the right time: they depicted a people given over to sin, whose salvation depended on those who had received the Word of God. Missionary work was seen in all its glory as the highest expression of religious fervour. At the end of the eighteenth century, an extraordinary flowering of missionary societies was seen: the Baptist Society (1792); London Missionary Society (1795); Church Missionary Society (1799); and Wesleyan Missionary Society (Julien 1971 [1942], 68ff.) were all established.

In 1796, the London Missionary Society, in order to save the South Sea Islanders from heathenism, sent an expedition to the Pacific on the missionary ship *Duff*, under Captain James Wilson, with thirty missionaries on board. They were young men, most of them in their twenties, all artisans, sometimes accompanied by their families (Latukefu 1974, 25). They had a strong professional background, but not much intellectual education and no missionary experience at all (Farmer 1855, 78). Only four of them were ordained. They were all Calvinists and saw themselves as saved sinners, and different from worldly men (Gunson 1977, 98). They shared a passion for the salvation of lost souls, a salvation for which each of them was convinced God had called him. The London Missionary Society had been founded with the idea of "civilising" the natives before converting them; for that, it was necessary first to teach them practical skills, like carpentry, to engage their interest before turning them toward the Christian religion (Wood 1932, 27).

First Mission, First Setbacks

On the way to Tahiti, ten missionaries were left behind in Tonga (of those ten, none were ordained). On their arrival, in April 1797, the missionaries were surprised to see two fellow countrymen coming aboard, Ambler and Connelly. The two were prisoners who had escaped on their way to the penal colony of New South Wales. They belonged to a group of six beachcombers, composed of a sailor and five escaped convicts, who were the first European settlers in Tonga, and the start of a small community of Europeans.[6] At first, the missionaries made use of these beachcombers as translators – Ambler and Connelly were fluent in Tongan.[7] However, their relations soon deteriorated. According to Niel Gunson, these first missionaries "were an unusual category of men. In class and background they had much in common with their beachcombing rivals. For the most part, they were lower class, aspiring to the next rung up on the social ladder; they were provincial, and enthusiastic about their religion" (Gunson 1977, 98).

From the start the Tongans, the chiefs in particular, were more interested in the missionaries' iron tools and other equipment than in their teachings. The missionaries were generous with the chiefs and soon they became the recognised source of European goods. For a brief time, they appeared to have superior *mana* compared with that of the beachcombers: "their stocks of material goods were greater and they had influence with the ship which brought them" (Gunson 1977, 98). The beachcombers, too, asked to be supplied with this material, but, since the missionaries quickly understood that their precious stock should last as long as possible, they began to refuse. The beachcombers then incited the Tongans to steal from the missionaries, which made their relationship worse. The missionaries explained to the Tongans that the beachcombers had violated the law of their own country and had come to Tonga to try to escape their punishment. The beachcombers, in their turn, said that they themselves were men of high rank in England, but that the missionaries were only *tua*, that is, commoners or "low people," that they were sent by the king of England to settle amongst them, destroy their chiefs and get the country into their own hands. They were singing and praying in order to invoke their gods, and they used their big book for witchcraft. Unfortunately for the missionaries, four chiefs of high rank died within months of their arrival (Gunson 1977, 99; Wilson 1799, 257). This seemed to confirm the rumours propagated by the beachcombers. For the missionaries, the situation deteriorated until 1799, when a civil war broke out in which three missionaries were killed. They became the first martyrs of the Pacific, although the reason for their deaths had nothing to do with religion. The other missionaries left, except one, Vason, who decided to abandon the Christian religion and to live like a Tongan (*fakatonga*). He stayed in Tonga for four years under the protection of a chief of royal blood, Mulikiha`amea, married his daughters and received a large piece of land, which he cultivated with great success (Vason 1840). In January 1800, he took advantage of the arrival of a European ship to escape to Australia. Tonga would not see another missionary for almost a quarter of a century.

Beachcombers and Castaways: Mercenaries, Wreckers and ... Teachers

The beachcombers, however, became more and more numerous, particularly with the development of whaling. Some of the runaway sailors became wreckers with the help, and often for the benefit, of chiefs. We know that, at this time, at least a dozen whites, beachcombers or castaways, lived in Tonga and served like mercenaries for the chiefs under whose authority they were living.[8] At first, these Europeans explained the handling of firearms (guns and canons) seized from ships.

However, the exchange between Tongans and Europeans was not limited to trade in tools and firearms only. Some better educated beachcombers, at least better educated than the others, took up the function of teacher-advisers to the chiefs. One of them, named William Brown, became a valued retainer of the Finau family (chiefs of very high rank). According to Gunson, his life and influence resembled that of a secular missionary (1977, 105) and he taught some of the more intelligent and enterprising chiefs to read and write. William Brown and another beachcomber, William Singleton, became the official scribes of chiefs of royal rank. Soon it became fashionable for every high chief to have a white man as his official scribe. These beachcombers transmitted the art of writing to the chiefs and, because the only available texts were those in the Bible, they taught the Tongans some basic knowledge of the Christian religion.

In Vava`u, the northern group of the Tongan islands, another beachcomber, Samuel Blackmore, had the distinction of being the first runaway sailor to teach the people about the Christian god, before any missionaries: the story of Jehovah in the Bible, recounted by this English sailor, so influenced a young chief of high rank (Lolohea) that he became the first recognised Christian convert in the group. A shipwrecked 16-year-old English boy, William Mariner, became famous because his adventures were reported in detail in a book which is, today, considered as a major source of Tongan history.[9] In 1806 his ship, the

Port-au-Prince, was captured by Tongans, looted and burnt, and some of the crew were murdered. The survivors formed the mercenary artillery force of an ambitious chief, Finau Ulukalala, who adopted the English boy as his son. William Mariner succeeded in saving some books from the ship. The first reaction of Finau Ulukalala, his adoptive father, was to burn the books. For him, in the words of William Mariner "those books and papers were the means of invocation to bring down some evil upon the country" (Martin 1981, 65), and "he would not allow him to practise witchcraft to the injury of the Tongan people" (65). He told William Mariner that, some years before, several white men had come and built a house in which "they used often to shut themselves up, to sing and perform ceremonies" and that, after a while, many chiefs died (65). Later, William Mariner discussed literacy with this chief. He told him that in several parts of the world messages were sent great distances through the medium of writing. The chief acknowledged this "to be a most noble invention," but added that it would not do at all for the Tongan islands; that there would be nothing but disturbances and conspiracies, and he would not be sure to live, perhaps even for another month. He said, however, that he would like to know it himself and for all the women to know it, so that he might make love with less risk of discovery, and not so much chance of incurring the vengeance of their husbands (93–4). And so it passed that the young Mariner transmitted the knowledge of reading and writing to many Tongan chiefs together with notions of the Christian religion.

Learning to Read with the Bible

When Christianity was adopted by the people of Lifuka, the central group of the Tongan archipelago, Captain Samuel Henry reported that they had "actually made a sailor their teacher. He teaches them to read and write on the sand, and prays in the chapel on Sunday. One of the chiefs has given up his house as a chapel" (Farmer 1855, 174–5, cited in Gunson 1977, 106).

In 1822 three missionaries from Tahiti went ashore in Vava`u, the northern Tongan archipelago. Their reports, sent to Tahiti, testified to the situation: "So desirous are the adjacent islands to obtain native teachers that those sent to Vava`u are kept in the centre of the inhabitants lest the kings of the neighbouring islands should come and steal them away" (Gunson 1977, 110). These Tahitian missionaries, however, fled after the destruction of their chapel, some months later.

The desire for literacy seems to have spread to Samoa. After the arrival on Savai`i of the first Christian party from Tonga some of its members were appointed by the Tongan chief to teach the Samoans to read. "Although there were some Tahitian teachers there already, American, English and Hawaiian sailors were soon in demand as teachers" (Gunson 1977, 106). Finally, certain Tongan chiefs went to visit places such as Sydney, Tahiti and Canton, and came back after having learned to read and write – and also gained some basic knowledge of the Christian religion. In their turn, they served as teachers. The missionaries who came at the end of these "uncertain times" acknowledged that amongst the first Tongans to become Christian there were many young chiefs who had already learned to read the Bible.

The Role of Literacy in the First Missionary Successes

Thus, in 1800, Tonga had been abandoned by the missionaries of the London Missionary Society. After an unfruitful effort in 1822, the Wesleyan Methodist Church in Sydney decided to send two missionaries to Tonga in 1826. At first, they had many difficulties and the mission was on the point of being abandoned. In 1827, however, the chapel built by them in Nuku`alofa was filled with people every Sunday. What had happened? Firstly, the Wesleyans from Sydney had sent help in the form of two more missionaries, and one of them, Turner, had a solid intellectual background, some medical skills and missionary experience among the Maori of New Zealand. Soon, Turner decided to organise the new converts in classes where they were prepared to become active members of the mission. In these classes, the missionaries used the Bible as the basis for instruction in reading. The missionaries also decided to open a public school in March 1828. In September, the school received 150 students, boys and girls. Turner asked their colleagues to write down everything they taught, and to write it down in Tongan. In 1829, the missionaries decided to translate the Bible into Tongan, each of them having to translate a part of the Bible. In 1831, the mission received a small printing press and the first Tongan book was published on April 14 of the same year.

As from 1831, the main role in the Christianisation process was played by a young and ambitious chief, Taufa`ahau, who was to become the first Christian king and the founding father of the Tongan nation. Before his conversion Taufa`ahau, as the governor of the central archipelago, paid several visits to the main island, where he met the missionaries and also some of his relatives who were already converted. Back again in Ha`apai, he decided to use an ungodly runaway sailor "to trace the letters of the alphabet upon the sand of the seashore, for the benefit of those who wanted to learn." (West 1865, quoted by Latukefu, 1977, 126). He also obliged the sailor to celebrate the Christian god through prayers in a house which he reserved for this purpose.

After his conversion in 1831, Taufa`ahau waged long wars against the traditionalist chiefs, including the paramount chief, the Tu`i Tonga. Although these wars were mainly political, they were undertaken in the name of the Christian god, and with the active support of the missionaries. Meanwhile, education continued to receive high priority in the work of the mission. At a district meeting in May 1850, the members of the mission unanimously declared: "We must have schools in every place ... thus elevating the rising race with the

Bible in their hands, far above the darkness and baseness of heathenism and the wicked intrigues of Popery" (Latukefu 1974, 129–30). Taufa`ahau, then King George Tupou I, supported the missionaries' efforts to build schools in every way possible.[10] The promotion of education culminated in the establishment, in 1866, of Tupou College, where chiefs and commoners were treated alike.[11] Many commoners proved themselves to be outstanding scholars and formed a new educated elite, the basis of the future middle class.

Conclusion

In the Pacific region, the period of the so-called "first contacts" may vary considerably from one country to another, in terms of length and processes. In some cases, such as in Tonga, this period lasted more than two centuries. During this long-lasting time of "first contacts" the European voyagers were not of one kind, did not share the same vision of the world and were not armed with the same intentions toward the Pacific Islanders. However, it seems possible to sketch a sort of common "European" heritage, which was shared by some of them at least. When attested, this long-lasting period of "first contacts" is generally constructed in different phases, some of which are well known, while others appear blurry. The turn of the eighteenth century in Tonga is precisely one of these "uncertain times" during which, through the existence in their country of a small community of white people, Tongans came to know the new foreigners. Their goods, abilities and skills came to be regarded as more and more desirable, but at the same time they put into question the Tongan system of representation and values.

The "heroes" of these uncertain times were not only the young and inexperienced missionaries but also the beachcombers and castaways. Curiously enough, these white men who were supposed to be "undesirable," prepared the ground for the future Christian missions and played an important role in the relationship between the European and Tongan systems of values. With the missionaries, but also without them, they were the first cultural mediators between Europeans and Tongans.

Many things have been said about the natives' greed for European goods, particularly metal tools, weapons and cloth, those goods for which natives were – to use the missionaries' words – "dying from desire." There is no doubt that, in Tonga, these goods attracted the indigenous people and convinced them of the missionaries' *mana* and the powerfulness of the Christian god. Together with these objects, certain European skills helped the missionaries' work considerably. In many countries, the medical skills of some missionaries constituted a powerful tool in the work of evangelisation. The healing part of the mission's work was also important in Tonga, but writing must be considered as having played a role at least as important in the process of Christianisation. However, literacy had a particular effect on the Tongan system of values and power.

For Tongans, writing was at first suspected of being witchcraft: like firearms, writing appeared as a secret skill, the property of a few (white) experts, who used the magical power to kill at distance. Soon, however, Tongan chiefs understood the multidimensional character of writing, as the Tongan chief, Finau Ulukakala perceived: a technical means of communicating at a distance; a privileged way to get access to secret knowledge; and thus, a means of power. No doubt Tongans were conscious that writing could serve purposes other than religion. However, because it was learned through biblical texts, literacy was, for Tongans, intrinsically associated with the religious interests of the white people: their god, their mythology, their rituals. For Tongans, literacy was therefore conceived as a privileged tool to get access to the white people's world. And, because the evangelical undertaking was by definition a global one, in principle every Tongan – not only chiefs – willing to be Christianised could get access to writing. Thus, for commoners, the art of writing was soon to become a powerful means of challenging the traditional hierarchy of rank. In many respects, it is still the case today, in contemporary Tongan society.

References

Derlon, Brigitte

1997 *De mémoire et d'oubli: Anthropologie des objets malanggan de Nouvelle-Irelande*. Paris: Editions de la Maison des sciences de l'homme.

Farmer, Sarah S.

1855 *Tonga and the Friendly Islands: With a Sketch of Their Mission History*. London: Hamilton Adams.

Foigny, Gabriel de

1705 *Les avantures de Jacques Sadeur dans la découverte et le voiage de la Terre Australe: Contenant les coutumes et les moeurs des Australiens, leur religion, leurs exercices, leurs études, leurs guerres, les animaux particuliers à ce païs et toutes les raretez curieuses qui s'y trouvent*. Paris: Christophe David. Originally published in 1675 as *Le nouveau voyage de la Terre Australe de Jacques Sadeur*.

Goody, Jack

1979 *La raison graphique: La domestication de la pensée sauvage*. Paris: Les Editions de Minuit.

2000 *The Power of the Written Tradition*. Washington DC: Smithsonian Institution Press.

Gunson, Niel

1977 The coming of foreigners. In *Friendly Islands: A History of Tonga,* ed. Noel Rutherford. Melbourne: Oxford University Press.

Hobbes, Thomas

1651 *Leviathan*. London: Andrew Crooke.

Julien, Charles André

1971 [1942] *Histoire de l'Océanie*. Paris: Presses Universitaires de France.

Las Casas, Bartolomé de

1983 [1552] *Très brève relation de la destruction des Indes*. Paris, La Découverte/Maspéro.

1974 *Très brève relation de la destruction des Indes* (after *Les trente propositions très juridiques*). La Haye: Mouton.

2002 *Histoire des Indes*, translated from the Spanish by Jean-Pierre Clément and Jean-Marie Saint-Lu, 3 vol., Paris: Éditions du Seuil.

Latukefu, Sione

Church and State in Tonga: The Wesleyan Methodist Missionaries and Political Development, 1822– 1875. Canberra: Australian National University Press.

1977 The Wesleyan Mission. In *Friendly Islands. A History of Tonga*, ed. Noel Rutherford. Melbourne: Oxford University Press.

Locke, John

1690 *An Essay Concerning Human Understanding*. London: T. Basset.

1690 *Two Treatises of Government*. London: A. Churchill.

Martin, John

1981 *Tonga Islands: William Mariner's Account. An Account of the Natives of the Tonga Islands, in the South Pacific Ocean. With an original Grammar and Vocabulary of their Language. Compiled and Arranged from the Extensive Communications of William Mariner, several Years Resident in Those Islands*. Tonga: Vava`u Press.

Pope Paul III

1537 *Sublimis deus*.

Vairasse d'Alais, Denis

1715 [1675] *Histoire des Sévarambes, peuples qui habitent une partie du troisième continent communément appelé La Terre Australe: Contenant une relation du gouvernement, des mœurs, de la religion, & du langage de cette nation, inconnue jusques à présent aux peuples de l'Europe*. Rev. and expanded edn. Two parts in one volume. Amsterdam: Pierre Mortier.

Vason, George

1840 *An Authentic Narrative of Four Years Residence in Tongatapu, One of the Friendly Islands, in the South-Sea.* London: Longman, Hurst, Rees & Orme et al.

Vibart, Eric

1987 *Tahiti, naissance d'un paradis au siècle des Lumières.* Bruxelles: Editions Complexe.

West, Thomas

1865 *Ten years in South-Central Polynesia: Being reminiscences of a Personal Mission to the Friendly islands and their Dependencies,* London: J. Nisbet.

Wilson, William

1799 *A Missionary Voyage to the South Pacific Ocean, Performed in the Years 1796, 1797 and 1798, in the Ship Duff, Commanded by Captain James Wilson. Compiled from Journals of the Officers and Missionaries; and Illustrated with Maps, Charts and Views ... With a Preliminary Discourse on the Geography and History of the South Seas Islands.* London: T. Chapman.

Wood, Alfred Harold

1943 [1932] *A History and Geography of Tonga.* Nuku`alofa: Government Printer.

Notes

[1] We do have sources, but they did not yield lengthy narratives as did the voyages of discovery. It must be noted that the last years of the eighteenth century corresponded precisely to the slowing down of the "narratives of discovery" all over the Pacific (Vibart 1987).

[2] In some late descriptions, Europeans still confused Amerindian peoples with Medieval-style ideas about savages. However, generally speaking, the continued confrontation with these peoples during the conquest and the colonial period, their mutual frequenting on an increasingly daily basis, tended to impose, little by little, the *"principe de réalité"* (reality principle) at the expense of the fiction.

[3] In the years following his return to Spain in 1546, Bartolomé de Las Casas published the *Très brève relation de la destruction des Indes* (after *Trente propositions très juridiques* (1974)) and other texts (cf. *Histoire des Indes,* Paris: Éd. du Seuil, 2002). Throughout his writings, he stayed true to the image of the "noble savage." Until his death in 1566, Las Casas spoke for all those who sought to modify the status of the Indians and to put an end to their extermination.

[4] In another odyssey of the same type, *Les avantures de Jacques Sadeur dans la découverte et le voiage de la terre Australe* (Christophe David, Paris, 1705), Gabriel de Foigny presents his hero Jacques Sadeur, a hermaphrodite, who reaches Terra Australis after a long and difficult voyage (Vibart 1987, 30). His hermaphroditism saves his life, because Australians are hermaphrodites and systematically massacre any unisexual beings who fall into their hands (Vibart 1987, 30).

[5] Compare the work and comments of Jack Goody (1979, 2000) on the implications of literacy. See also Brigitte Derlon's article concerning the association of cargo and books with Europeans' *malanggan,* an association around which a cargo cult developed. This association left a highly significant trace in the verb that designates the act of writing in Mandak, which is itself formed from *malanggan* (Derlon 1997, 135–66).

[6] The beachcombers who arrived in Tonga before 1797 appear to have been convicts from New South Wales who left the American ship *Otter* in March 1796. Morgan Bryan, an Irishman, was perhaps the most influential of these; "he was the prototype of the hedonistic low-cultured beachcomber, skilled in the use of iron tools and weapons but otherwise deficient in communicating the advantages of western

civilisation. The first missionaries ... found him singularly depraved and they did not like him near them" (Gunson 1977, 96; see also Wilson 1799, 246).

[7] Connelly resided with Fatafehi, the Tu`i Tonga (paramount chief) designate, while Ambler was married to the daughters of the chief of the fleet of Tuku`aho, the *hau,* or "working king" (see Gunson 1977, 96).

[8] According to Gunson, from 1796 to 1826 over eighty aliens from Europe and distant Pacific islands resided in Tonga (Gunson 1977, 90).

[9] His adventures were written by an English doctor, John Martin, in 1817 (see Martin 1981).

[10] In a memorable sermon, he exhorted his fellow countrymen with these words: "See what knowledge has done for the white man! See what ignorance has done for the men of this land! Is it that white men are born more wise? Is it that they are naturally more capable than the others? No: but they have obtained knowledge ... This is the principal cause of the difference (Latukefu 1977, 130).

[11] As soon as the hostilities ceased, Taufa`ahau concerned himself with evangelisation as much as education, the two going together as far as he was concerned. Tupou College was intended to form an elite with the mission of enforcing the new laws. In this school it should be noted that while they evidently learned English, the Tongan language was used for religious instruction (from which stems the development of a body of religious – and also literary and scientific – studies in Tongan). Girls were admitted into the school from 1880.

Chapter 6

In the Event: Indigenous Countersigns and the Ethnohistory of Voyaging

Bronwen Douglas

Introduction

This chapter combines an ethnohistory of French voyagers' representations of indigenous people in Oceania[1] with an ethnohistory of cross-cultural encounters in which those representations were generated and about which they speak. It does so for both epistemological and pragmatic reasons: to illustrate the entanglement of discourse, text and event that underpins historical writing; and to construct a comparative history of specific cross-cultural interactions in the Pacific Islands and Van Diemen's Land during one exemplary voyage in the classic era of European scientific voyaging (1766–1840) – the expedition of *La Recherche* and *L'Espérance* (1791–94) led by Antoine-Raymond-Joseph de Bruni d'Entrecasteaux (1737–93) (see figure 6.1). The chapter foregrounds embodied ethnohistorical moments and moves inductively from them to anticipate aspects of the wider intellectual context of an emerging science of race, which is merely outlined in the introduction. I not only problematise the assumed centrality of European actors in actual cross-cultural encounters but argue for an ongoing, mobile dialectic of discourse and *expériences* [2] – that the presence and agency of indigenous people infiltrated the writings and pictures produced by sailors, naturalists and artists in the course of scientific voyages and left ambiguous countersigns in the very language, tone and content of their representations. Indigenous countersigns permeate voyagers' representations but are often camouflaged in the ignorance, prejudices and ethnocentric perceptual processes of European observers. They can be identified through critical attention to disparities and correspondences between particular representations and their different genres or media (see also Douglas 1999a, 1999b, 2003, 2006, 2007). Such countersigns are a key resource for ethnohistorians.

The political backdrop to d'Entrecasteaux's voyage was revolution in France; the intellectual context of the voyage comprised the unstable scientific discourses or artistic conventions which programmed European modes of seeing and representing exotic people. Violent political ferment at the end of the eighteenth century paralleled dramatic flux in anthropological ideas and vocabularies. This intellectual and semantic volatility registered an analogous series of discursive shifts which in some respects were embodied or prefigured in the written and pictorial legacy of d'Entrecasteaux's voyage. In art, empirical naturalism supplanted neoclassicism. In literature, Romanticism displaced classical Enlightenment values including idealisation of the primitive. In the natural history of man, holistic humanism gave way to the rigid physical differentiations of the science of race and in the process the modern biological conception of race was distilled out of the term's older, ambiguous, environmentally-determined connotations of "variety," "nation," "tribe," "kind," "class" or, sometimes, "species."

Eighteenth-century discourses on human similarity and differences were always ethnocentric and often racially obnoxious with respect to "Negroes" and other non-white people. Yet racial discriminations were rarely categorical while most savants in principle attributed a common origin and the possibility of development toward "civilisation" to all human beings. Nineteenth-century discourses varied widely but moved steadily toward a consensus that racial differences were permanent, hereditary, formative and, possibly, primordial. This transition was epitomised with respect to Oceania in the writings of d'Entrecasteaux's celebrated successor, the multiple circumnavigator Jules-Sébastien-César Dumont d'Urville (1790–1842), whose hierarchical division of the indigenous people of Oceania into "two distinct races" used race in its modern biologised sense and reviled the "black race" of "Melanesia" (1832, 3, 19).

Tale of a Voyage

This chapter refers to cross-cultural encounters during the visits of d'Entrecasteaux to the Admiralty Islands (in what is now Papua New Guinea), Van Diemen's Land (later Tasmania), Tongatapu and New Caledonia. I draw on a range of texts both published and unpublished at the time: the *Voyage* (1808) of d'Entrecasteaux; the *Relation du voyage* (1800a) of the naturalist Jacques-Julien Houtou de La Billardière (1755–1834); the shipboard journal of one of the officers (Richard 1986b); original drawings by the artist Piron; and the forty-six plates engraved by Jacques-Louis Copia (1764–99) for the *Atlas* to La Billardière's *Relation* (1800a; 1800b).[3] Like its French and English precursors and successors, this expedition combined patriotic and scientific goals "in the name of humanity, the arts and the sciences." Its "double mission" was to search for the missing French navigator Jean-François de Galaup de La Pérouse (1741–88), whose ships had vanished in 1788 after leaving Botany Bay, and "simultaneously to undertake research relative to the sciences and to commerce."[4] The quest for La Pérouse was unsuccessful, but the voyage made significant contributions to the sciences, including the natural history of man.

Figure 6.1 Map of d'Entrecasteaux's voyage, 1791–94.

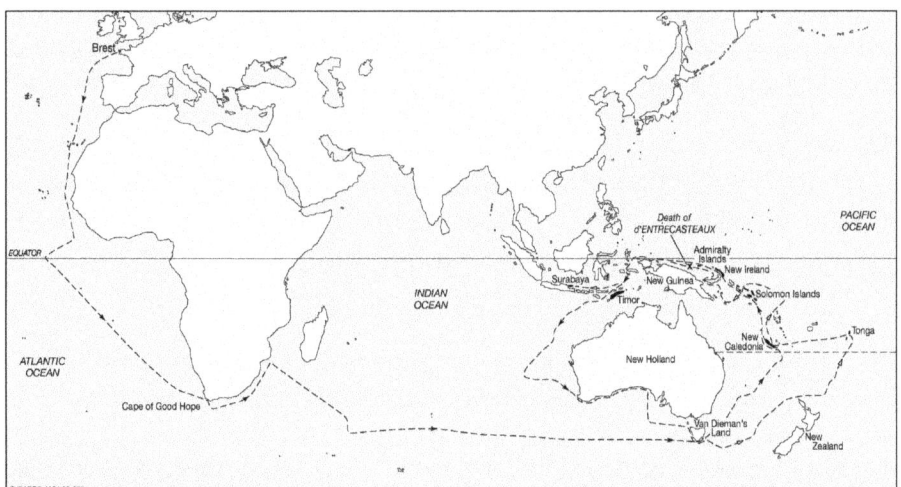

Map courtesy ANU Cartographic Services, Research School of Pacific and Asian Studies, The Australian National University, Canberra.

The narrative trajectory of d'Entrecasteaux's *Voyage* is one of dissolution — literally so in its conclusion with the death of the commander but also metaphorically, in Anthony Pagden's sense: "The spaces that separated the European from those 'others' he was eventually to encounter were spaces of dissolution, menacing areas where civility could so easily dissolve into barbarism" (1993, 3). This *Voyage* is a synecdoche for the era's dawning disenchantment with primitivist idealisation of the noble savage (*le bon sauvage*) and its supplanting by negative, ultimately racialised attitudes better aligned with a new age of intensifying European imperialism. In his seminal work on the impact of Oceania in European art and science, the Australian art historian Bernard Smith argued that the transformation in the weight of European opinion about "savages" from sentimental approval to disgust owed much to "the death of famous navigators" at indigenous hands in Oceania (1960, 86–7, 99–105). In France, a specific trigger was the disappearance of La Pérouse and the publication of his *Voyage* in 1797 with its shocking climax in the apparently unprovoked killing of twelve crew members by Samoans. These people had seemed to La Pérouse to be "the most fortunate inhabitants of the globe," but their inexplicable actions forced him to the bleak conclusion that "man living in anarchy in a nearly savage state is a more vicious being than the most ferocious animals" (1798 [1797], 3: 223–63, 238).

However, neither *le bon sauvage* nor *le mauvais sauvage* ("the ignoble savage") was *sui generis* in European art and literature or merely a matter of imaging. Both positive and negative representations of indigenous people took initial shape on the ground, in particular equations of discourse, authorship and located encounter which saw voyagers' words and pictures colonised by countersigns of indigenous agency – their demeanour, actions and desires. Indigenous countersigns were filtered through distorting screens of European preconception, precedent, perception, fantasy and phobia, and cloaked in loaded epithets, such as welcome, friendship, indifference, hypocrisy, treachery, rejection, or hostility. The narrative transition in d'Entrecasteaux's *Voyage* from initially rapturous approval of "natural man" to eventual bitter disillusionment with "ferocious savages" is thus a *signifiant* "signifier" of this author's unsettling experience of a variety of unpredictable indigenous behaviours (1808, 1: 230, 359). Yet d'Entrecasteaux's descriptive shifts do not denote the logical unfolding of a deductive racial scheme that was yet to be conceived. In this chapter, I juxtapose samples of the emotive idealism of d'Entrecasteaux's *Voyage* with the more pragmatic, republican optimism evinced in La Billardière's *Relation* and the unsentimental "hard" primitivism of Piron's neoclassical portraits.[5] This interior contrast between varied narrativisations of d'Entrecasteaux's expedition foreshadows an inductive comparison of shifting discourses in the science of man, epitomised in Dumont d'Urville's theory of "two distinct races."

"By Their Conduct Toward Us"[6] – Admiralty Islands, July–August 1792

At the end of July 1792, a false rumour about a possible relic of La Pérouse's passage sent d'Entrecasteaux on a long detour through the Admiralty Islands, north of the island of New Guinea, where the expedition had its first significant interactions with indigenous people (d'Entrecasteaux 1808, 1: 133–42; La Billardière 1800a, 1: 249–69). The negative precedent set by Hawkesworth's account of the "perfidy of the inhabitants of the southern Admiralty Islands towards [the English navigator] Carteret" in 1767 had inspired "misgivings" in the French, who did not land (Hawkesworth 1773, 1: 382–5; La Billardière 1800a, 1: 251). In the event, however, they were generally impressed by the behaviour of the men who came out to the boats or the ships seeking nails, axes or "bits of iron" in exchange for their foodstuffs, weapons, ornaments and implements. "Only iron," said d'Entrecasteaux, "seemed to have some value in their eyes" (1808, 1: 138, see also 134–5). The naturalist La Billardière enthused that, by and large, "the exchanges took place with the greatest good faith imaginable," notwithstanding some early instances of theft (1800a, 1: 260–1, 252–4).

For the naturalist, the only shadow on this idyllic setting of "a fine climate in a fertile island" was the affront dealt to his republican and primitivist sensibilities by acts of violence and cupidity committed by supposed "chiefs" toward their underlings: "We did not expect to see man treated in this way in a tribe which had seemed to us to be so close to the state of nature" (1800a, 1: 255, 252–3, see also 262).[7] Forty years later, Dumont d'Urville, a republican of far more conservative hue, appropriated this story approvingly in his popular semi-fictional work, *Voyage pittoresque autour du monde*, as a sign that "a certain social hierarchy existed on these islands" (1834–35, 2: 171). By this stage, the relative level of hierarchy was taken as an unproblematic index of the "degree of [political] perfection" achieved and was one of the complex of "numerous and essential traits ... as much moral as physical" by which "races" were presumptively characterised (1832, 3). Each of these judgements is a version of the "uniformitarianism" that has variously but consistently informed European evaluations of alien mores since classical times, but together they exemplify the different moral valences with which such judgments were historically inflected (Porter 1990; Rousseau and Porter 1990, 2). The complacent, racially-based assumption of European superiority evident in the nineteenth-century equation contrasts with the more circumstantial and ambiguous – if no less ethnocentric – eighteenth-century linkages, as will be seen again with respect to Tonga.

I have previously identified a common motif in first-hand Oceanic voyage texts: a rhetorical sequence from relief at approved indigenous conduct or demeanour to positive depictions not only of the character of local people but also of their physical appearance, notwithstanding skin colour or hair type that was often seen as unappealing (Douglas 1999a: 70–3, 2003). These textual elements are indigenous countersigns, oblique reflexes of indigenous strategies and behaviour that have infiltrated voyagers' representations after being processed in European perception via the unstable dialectic between discourse and experience: "This arduous voyage," as La Billardière put it, "through seas strewn with reefs, and amongst Savages against whom we had to be continually on guard" (1800a, 1:x). The rhetorical sequence recurs in the d'Entrecasteaux voyage literature, beginning in the Admiralty Islands. It is explicit in La Billardière's declaration: "If we can judge the character of these inhabitants by their conduct towards us they are extremely mild: a look of goodness was stamped on their features" (1800a, 1: 262). Somewhat earlier in the *Relation*, the following verbal portrait succeeds several pages of mostly positive description of Islanders' actions: "These islanders have skin of a not very deep black: their physiognomy is agreeable and differs little from that of Europeans. ... they seem happy, if one is to judge by the air of satisfaction imprinted on all their features: they have frizzy hair" (255).

The sequence is equally clear in d'Entrecasteaux's *Voyage*: his report of the initially pacific reception received by the French in the Admiralty Islands is followed by the pronouncement that "all displayed an assured air, an open, confident countenance which betokened nothing sinister." He recounted a similar series of reactions by de Rossel, a lieutenant on the *Recherche*, who had taken a boat close inshore and been surrounded by a crowd of apparently well-disposed men: "He thought they had a trusting nature; their faces seemed agreeable to him; there is nothing hard in their features; they have a fine stature" (1808, 1: 134–5). Both authors maintained the comforting fiction of welcome by configuring thefts committed during the initial encounter as individual acts of opportunism by certain older men who lacked the "honesty and candour" of the young (d'Entrecasteaux 1808, 1: 135; La Billardière 1800a, 1: 254–6). However, La Billardière's idealism was consistently more empirical and pragmatic than that of d'Entrecasteaux (see Douglas 1999a, 73–83). His delight in the "marks of great probity" subsequently shown to the French by men at another island in the group was doubly qualified: by astonishment "at encountering so great a difference in the manners of Savages so little separated from each other and with the same arts"; and by a realistic acknowledgment that variations in indigenous conduct might have been strategic since the men the French met initially "had had to deal only with ship's boats, whereas the others dealt with ships which inspired respect" (1800a, 1: 262).

The overt moral and physical approval of the word portraits was implicitly rehearsed in Piron's flattering rendition of a *Man of the Admiralty Islands* in the neoclassical guise of a Greek warrior.[8] Piron's drawing was engraved by Copia (figure 6.2) and published in La Billardière's *Atlas* as *Savage of the Admiralty Islands* (La Billardière 1800b, pl. 3; Smith 1960, 110–1). In the introduction to his *Relation*, La Billardière assured his readers that Piron's drawings were "strikingly truthful." The apparent lack of naturalism of this and Piron's other portraits might sit oddly with the author's assertion, except that the compliment referred directly to "drawings of *costumes* ... made in the course of the campaign" (1800a, 1:x; my emphasis). Piron's Admiralty Islander, then, is an example of the venerable classical mode of portraying foreigners that Smith labelled the "ethnographic convention," which "defines by means of costume and adornment" and represents people "as type specimens, accompanied by detailed verbal descriptions" (Smith 1992, 80–1; Joppien and Smith 1985–87, 1: 8). Indigenous dress and accoutrements, rather than actual physiognomies, were the prime objects of Piron's artistic endeavours and were understood as such by his shipmates, but so too was his generalised compliment to these particular indigenous subjects.

Figure 6.2 *"Sauvage des îles de l'Amirauté"* (engraving).

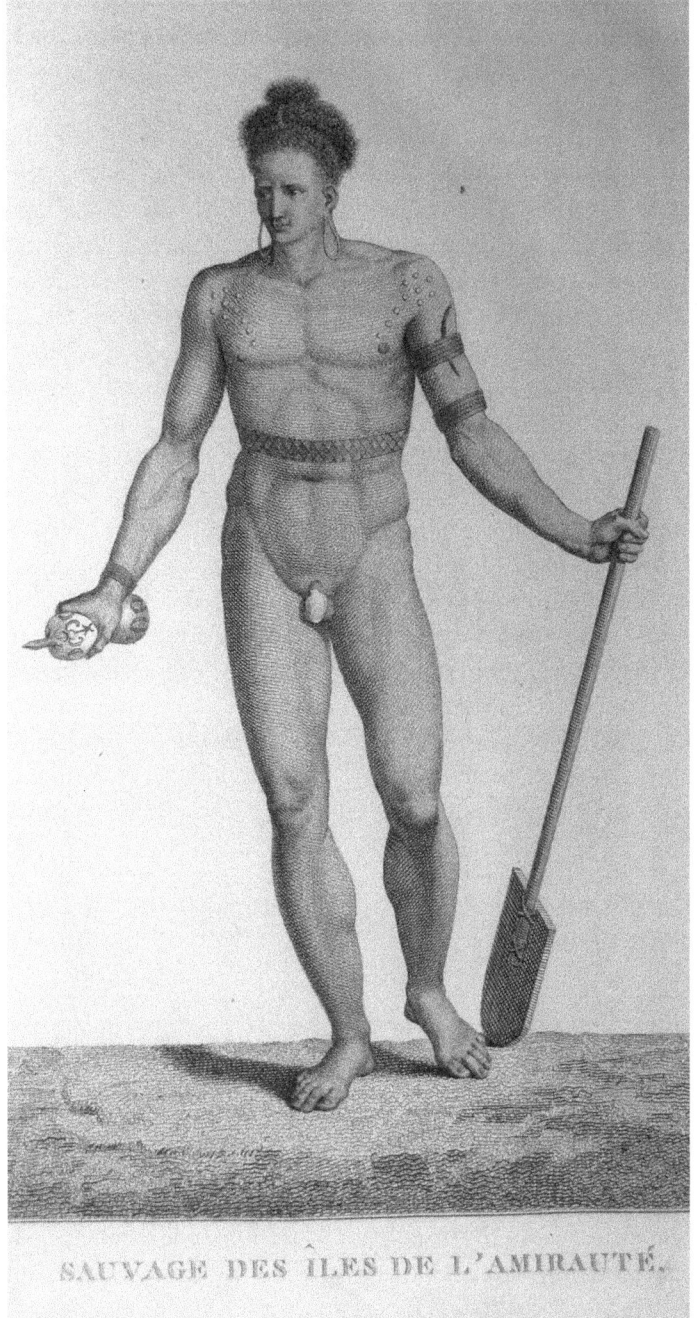

Artist, Piron; Engraver, Jacques-Louis Copia. Source: La Billardière 1800b: pl. 3. Photograph: Bronwen Douglas.

The "Man/Savage of the Admiralty Islands" is undoubtedly objectified by a Eurocentric aesthetic – a "spirit of heroic humanism," Smith called it (1960, 111). Yet neither Piron's picture nor the accompanying text is demeaning to Islanders, racially or otherwise. In sharp contrast, racial preoccupations suffused Dumont d'Urville's reinscription of La Billardière's text in *Voyage pittoresque* to characterise the Admiralty Islanders whom he had not personally seen. "Assuredly," Dumont d'Urville concluded, "they are one of the finest varieties of the Melanesian race" (1834–35, 2: 171). But this was faint praise given his opinion and ranking of "the Melanesians." As citizens of Papua New Guinea, Admiralty Islanders are today often classed collectively as Melanesians and identify themselves as such regionally. In these modern indigenised usages, the term has largely shed (or sometimes reversed) the racialised connotations of its ugly history. The term *Espèce Mélanienne* "Melanian species" was invented in 1825 by the polygenist French soldier-biologist Jean-Baptiste-Geneviève-Marcellin Bory de Saint-Vincent (1778–1846) to designate the "penultimate" of the fifteen separate species into which he divided the human genus (1827 [1825], 1: 82; 2: 104–13). Dumont d'Urville (1826) adopted *Mélaniens*, "from the dark colour of their skin," to label one of the "three great divisions" into which he initially classified Oceanian people.[9] He subsequently reworked *Mélaniens* into *Mélanésiens* to name the so-called "black Oceanian race" and characterised them in highly derogatory terms: "disagreeable features"; "often very thin and rarely well-shaped limbs"; "women ... hideous"; "far more debased toward the state of Barbarism than the Polynesians and the Micronesians"; "institutions ... still in their infancy"; "dispositions and intelligence ... very inferior to those of the copper-coloured race"; "natural enemies of the whites" (1832, 6, 11).

"Men So Close to Nature"[10] – Van Diemen's Land, February 1793

Such a priori racial differentiation of Oceanian people was unknown in 1792–93. D'Entrecasteaux referred in passing to the fluid, circumstantial classification of "two great varieties of people in the South Seas" that the German Johann Reinhold Forster (1729–98), senior naturalist on the second voyage of James Cook (1728–79), had initially mapped in 1778 (1996 [1778], 153). But for d'Entrecasteaux, it was a possibly useful hypothesis rather than fact – "if, as Mr Forster thinks, ... [the Pacific Islands] are peopled only by two races of men ..." The reference occurs in the context of a comparison between the Tongans, whom d'Entrecasteaux saw as the most "beautiful race of men" imaginable, and a single "native of Fiji," who was less handsome but had "an equally fine stature" and "seemed endowed with more intelligence, and had more desire to educate himself" (1808, 1: 312–3). Like Forster, d'Entrecasteaux used race in the loose, mutable sense of "variety."

Unlike Dumont d'Urville, the ethnological discriminations made by La Billardière and d'Entrecasteaux were flexible and contextual. They were shaped by cumulative particular experiences of indigenous reception and actions, which each author tried to correlate with his general values and preconceptions, desires and place-specific expectations derived from reading voyage literature. The terms of these overlapping equations were discourse and precedent on the one hand, experience and indigenous agency on the other; the products were representations infused with indigenous countersigns. The Admiralty Islands vignette suggests particular permutations of these relationships: here, perceived experience of indigenous actions redefined precedents but confirmed the discourse of primitivism to which d'Entrecasteaux, especially, was ambivalently attracted. Relieved and charmed by the behaviour of Admiralty Islanders, at the end of his stay d'Entrecasteaux remarked on the lessons of experience, reporting that the "ferocity" and "hostile attitudes" of these people had been "exaggerated" (1808, 1: 140). From this point on, the voyage added its own precedents to those learned from earlier literature.

After a break in Ambon, d'Entrecasteaux headed for Van Diemen's Land, where in February 1793 the French found uncorrupted, natural man:[11] "so good and so different from the idea that one forms of savages from the accounts of different voyagers" – specifically from accounts of the visit to Van Diemen's Land in 1772 of his compatriot Marc-Joseph Marion du Fresne (1724–72), who had clashed violently with the inhabitants and thought them "wicked." "On the contrary," for d'Entrecasteaux, the "peaceable dispositions" of the Tasmanians with whom his crews enjoyed amicable relations over ten days in Recherche Bay and Bruny Island proved to him "that they are good and trusting" – indigenous actions and demeanour here determined the voyager's evaluation of their character.[12] He delighted in these "simple and good men," "so close to nature, whose candour and goodness contrast so strongly with the vices of the state of civilisation," and who seemed to him also to lack the "vices" – especially the "disposition to theft" – that he attributed to the more "advanced" but also often more "ferocious" Pacific Islanders (1808, 1: 230–6, 241–3, 287–8, 307).

The Van Diemen's Land section of d'Entrecasteaux's *Voyage* is almost irresistibly quotable for examples of the ethnocentric, infantilising universalism of Enlightenment primitivism, with tropes like "this first natural affection" and "this school of nature" (1808, 1: 234). There is little realism in his ecstatic, self-indulgent prose portraits – perhaps unsurprisingly since, by La Billardière's report, the commander did not have "the pleasure of seeing" any Tasmanian until the final day of the stay in Recherche Bay (1800a, 2: 57). Yet, at least as much as its more empirical counterparts, d'Entrecasteaux's narrative bears the imprint of Tasmanian actions and demeanour toward their visitors. Indigenous countersigns inflected the tone and content of the narrative from its opening scene of "the first meeting" which "established such confidence that it was followed by several others, all just as friendly, and giving the most favourable idea of the inhabitants of this country" (d'Entrecasteaux 1808, 1: 230). During this first meeting, a Tasmanian man made it clear "by unequivocal signs" (La Billardière 1800a, 2: 32) that he had inspected the four-man French party as they slept in the open the previous night, providing d'Entrecasteaux with further evidence that Tasmanians "are not evil-minded," because they had not molested the Frenchmen (1808, 1: 232).[13] His near-to-final passage on the Tasmanians of Recherche Bay paid tribute to "their open and cheerful countenance" but infantilised it as the "reflection of a happiness untroubled by upsetting thoughts or impotent desires" (243). I argue, by contrast, that indigenous demeanours toward newcomers, however they were experienced, were always strategic – even if I cannot begin to fathom the reasons – and that their textual inscription is yet another enigmatic countersign of indigenous agency.

At this stage of the rhetorical sequence, local conduct encouraged positive evaluations of indigenous appearance as well as character: a single man agreed to go to the ship where his "confidence" delighted d'Entrecasteaux and gave "the most favourable impression of this tribe, but especially of this man," who was still more "remarkable" for his "fine physique and his intelligence" (1808, 1: 238, 243). The sequence is patent in the contemporary journal of the first officer of the *Recherche*, Alexandre d'Hesmivy d'Auribeau, who was usually more empirical and pragmatic than d'Entrecasteaux: the natives' unaggressive behaviour toward the sleeping Frenchmen was "an infinitely interesting deed," which at the outset established their "goodness and humanity"; their general lack of suspicion or fear of the French showed "a nature as good as it is trustful"; finally, he remarked, their "agreeable physiognomy" and "mild gaze" (Richard 1986b, 308, 312). D'Entrecasteaux's largely vicarious experience of indigenous actions in Van Diemen's Land confirmed the recent precedent set by Admiralty Islanders, further reinforced the discourse of primitivism, and refuelled his expectations for future encounters.

"Hypocritical and Treacherous"/ A "Fine Race of Men"[14] – Tongatapu, March–April 1793

D'Entrecasteaux concluded the narrative of his stay in Van Diemen's Land with a burst of heavily gendered primitivist enthusiasm for this "most perfect image of the first state of society, when men are not yet troubled by the passions or corrupted by the vices which civilisation sometimes brings in its wake," had "no cause for dissension" because their only property consisted of "their wives and children," and enjoyed the "mutual affection" of a simple, family-based patriarchy (1808, 1: 242–3). This echo of La Billardière's ambivalence about assumed chiefly abuses in the Admiralty Islands also anticipated d'Entrecasteaux's own deep misgivings about the "much more advanced" Tongans whom he encountered in Tongatapu in March and April 1793 (1808,

1: 343). He likened their political situation to "the old feudal regime," reduced to "general anarchy" by the "weakness of the principal chief" and the fractionating effect of the "division of two things which ought to be inseparable" – those "who exercise power from those to whom honours are paid."[15] The resultant "factions between the family possessing the sovereignty and that which only exercises it" meant that the government was "powerless," the people were out of control and "the warrior class" seemingly "recognised no authority" (1808, 1: 305–6, 309).

Supposedly guileless "natural" man in Van Diemen's Land and devious "warrior chief" in Tonga are visually juxtaposed in an unattributed plate in La Billardière's *Atlas* (1800b, pl. 8) (figure 6.3):

Figure 6.3 *"Homme du Cap de Diemen; Finau, chef des guerriers de Tongatabu"* (engraving).

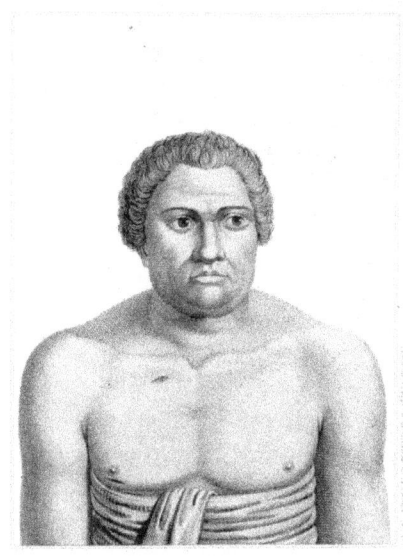

Engraver, Jacques-Louis Copia; Artist, anon. Source: La Billardière 1800b: pl. 8. Photograph: Bronwen Douglas.

Though the Tasmanian is a nameless, idealised neoclassical type rather than an individual, La Billardière insisted that the portrait "provides a much more exact idea of the characteristics of their face than everything I could teach about them by [writing] lengthy details" (1800a, 2: 33–4). The aristocratic d'Auribeau similarly endorsed the "truth" and "naturalness" of the classical depiction of Tasmanian figures by "this clever artist" (Richard 1986b, 313). The cursory attention paid to physical appearance in the written texts of d'Entrecasteaux's voyage was an eighteenth-century norm in sharp contrast to the obsessive primacy of physical differences in the naturalised racial agenda of Dumont d'Urville and his naturalists.[16] In contrast to the generalised Tasmanian, the Tongan portrayed was an actual individual known to the French as Finau, a "chief of the warriors." La Billardière described him as being "of middling height and very fat" and as having, like his compatriots, "all the features of a European." The naturalist approved this likeness also as "extremely truthful" (1800a, 2: 95).

I see no invidious racial comparison in these portraits, though their juxtaposition implies an ethnological agenda and there is some differentiation of skin colouring. Textually, any implied moral comparison is mainly to the Tasmanians' advantage, though La Billardière did take exception to aspects of their gender relations. He pitied the "poor women condemned" to the "arduous labour" of diving for shellfish while their husbands dined by the fire, heedless of sanctimonious French suggestions to "share their toil at least" (1800a, 2: 54). By contrast, in Tonga d'Entrecasteaux "noted with pleasure that the women are better treated" than in the most westerly Pacific islands, where they did all the hard work, because they were "here destined uniquely for housework and child rearing" (1808, 1: 310). On the other hand, contrasting indigenous actions saw the weight of French censure bear more heavily on Tongans with respect to female chastity: two young girls in Van Diemen's Land won La Billardière's approval by fleeing the sexual advances of several sailors (1800a, 2: 46), whereas d'Entrecasteaux was disgusted at the Tongan "market ... in prostituted girls, ... whom the chiefs offered with a licence which is not seen even among the most corrupt peoples" (1808, 1: 288).

Class- and culture-bound conceptions of propriety in gender relations apart, the voyagers were consistently disconcerted by the behaviour of Tongan men who seemed all too well-endowed with "the passions" and "the vices" supposedly consequent on a degree of "civilisation" (1808, 1: 242).[17] D'Entrecasteaux expressed affront and apprehension at the repeated "turbulent" and "insulting" conduct of "badly-intentioned" men who displayed an "irresistible proclivity ... for theft" (1808, 1: 279–81, 299, 287; see also 294–5, 297). The seemingly arbitrary brutality of Finau's public treatment of ordinary Islanders inspired "horror" in d'Entrecasteaux and offended the ethnocentric humanism he shared with La Billardière, producing the global assertion that Tongans "are not, it is true, naturally ferocious; but ... sentiments of humanity are unknown to them" and they "attach no value to human life" (d'Entrecasteaux 1808, 1: 283–4, 308; La Billardière 1800a, 2: 96, 115, 174–5).[18] D'Entrecasteaux attributed this dismal state of affairs to "the nature of government" in the Pacific Islands, where the "abuse of force" by chiefs toward "the inferiors" provoked their "disposition to theft," which in turn rendered "their character ... hypocritical and treacherous, especially toward strangers, whose goodwill they seek in order to have a better chance to rob them" – though here he did acknowledge a strategic element in friendly indigenous reception of visitors (1808, 1: 307–8).

Nonetheless, disapproval of Tongan conduct did not deter voyagers from aesthetic appreciation of their looks. La Billardière praised their "fine shape" and the "very agreeable and very animated physiognomy" of the women (1800a, 2: 175, 176–7). D'Entrecasteaux applied the same phrase – "a very agreeable physiognomy" – to "most women belonging to the chiefly *class*" and professed himself unable to envisage "a finer *race* of men ... especially that of the chiefs" (1808, 1: 310, 313; my emphasis). Race here signified in its Enlightenment sense as a synonym for "class" or "kind," a usage confirmed in d'Entrecasteaux's subsequent speculation that "the people" belonged to "a different race," though still enjoying a healthy and comfortable existence (320).[19]

Yet, general Pacific precedents, notably in La Pérouse's journal,[20] and specifically Tongan precedents in the Cook voyage narratives meant that d'Entrecasteaux had not expected to find "uncorrupted, natural man" in Tonga. From the outset he took precautions because he knew that "in these countries, ... the inhabitants' dispositions must always be regarded as very suspect" (1808, 1: 277). Forewarning, though, did not forearm against fear consequent on the vulnerability of isolated expeditions or a sense of betrayal at frustrated good intentions: "I attached very great value to finishing this campaign without shedding blood," he wrote in the wake of a lethal clash with Tongan warriors,[21] and "so I am acutely affected by this unfortunate event: but I could wait no longer [before firing on them]" because of "the danger threatening some of our people" (1808, 1: 298; see also 308). Of course there was self-exculpation here. D'Entrecasteaux's official instructions cautioned against using arms against native people except "as a last extremity," and significant sections of his audience would be expected to deplore the necessity.[22] There is no reason, though, to doubt the sincerity of his regrets or the extent to which his pre-emptive strike and the manner of its textual inscription were compelled by indigenous agency: by Tongans' desire for European property and use of violence to obtain it – a material motivation that d'Entrecasteaux morally reconfigured as "this passion for theft" (1808, 1: 290).

"Ferocious Savages"[23] – New Caledonia, April–May 1793

I have previously published detailed ethnohistorical critiques of the narratives of d'Entrecasteaux's subsequent sojourn in New Caledonia and shall not rehearse the details (Douglas 1970, 1999a: 73–83). Enough to say that Kanak actions – attacking and stealing from the French; and providing "incontestable proofs" that they were "anthropophagous: [that] they are avid for human flesh and do not hide it" – quickly pushed the authors of both narratives into angry disenchantment with the favourable accounts of Kanak behaviour, character and appearance published by Cook and Georg Forster (1754–94). The Kanak practice of cannibalism particularly appalled d'Entrecasteaux and drove him to "reclassify [them] amongst the most ferocious of peoples," reconstituting Cook's "good-natured" Kanak as "barbarous men" and "ferocious savages" (Cook 1777, 2: 114; d'Entrecasteaux 1808, 1: 332–4, 358–9; La Billardière 1800a, 2: 191).

Piron's neoclassical pencil drawing of a "Man of Balade"[24] was engraved by Copia (figure 6.4) for La Billardière's *Atlas* as "Savage of New Caledonia hurling a spear" (1800b: pl. 35). Copia's figure is at once as rampant as the original, but more ferocious in expression. "Hard" primitivist in style, neither figure is at all naturalistic – though the bodily proportions of the engraving are somewhat more realistic – since the classical ideal precluded depiction of the drought-induced emaciation of the people described in the texts. "They have little corpulence," said d'Entrecasteaux, "their arms and legs are very spindly: an excessive thinness betrays their wretchedness. ... [T]heir means of subsistence are very insufficient" (1808, 1: 330). In an earlier paper I argued that the symbolic significance of the "Savage of New Caledonia" is considerably more than ethnographic (Douglas 1999a, 73–83). It is the only engraving out of forty-six in La Billardière's *Atlas*, which represents an indigenous person in aggressive pose and one of only two in which male genitals are prominently displayed – the other being the Admiralty Islander. The "Savage" is an intensely confrontational representation, surely intended to be so by the artist, the engraver, the publisher and, presumably, the author. I maintain, moreover, that the drawing is also a countersign of confrontational collective agency on the part of many of the Kanak of whom this figure was meant to be an ideal type. This case is sustained by a parallel scrutiny of the written texts.

La Billardière's *Atlas* conveys strongly discordant visual messages about Kanak and Tongans, which might be seen to oppose New Caledonian cannibalism and violence to Tongan beauty and sociality, thereby anticipating Dumont d'Urville's categorical opposition of Melanesians and Polynesians (Thomas 1997, 139–41). Forty-two percent (11 out of 24) of the objects representing "Effects of the *Savages* of New Caledonia" are weapons or things associated by the Europeans with war and cannibalism; in contrast, only 15 percent (6 out of 41) of the "Effects of the *Inhabitants* of the Friendly Islands" are weapons. The *Atlas* also contains several portraits of Tongan individuals as well as three elaborate scenes of Tongan social interactions (La Billardière 1800b, plates 8, 26–33, 37–8; my emphasis). On the other hand, any such disjunction is far less marked in the written texts which express profound ambivalence about Tongan actions and recount repeated instances of cross-cultural friction and violence during the French visit – as exemplified above. D'Entrecasteaux called Tongans "less wicked" than Kanak, but that was hardly strong approval given his opinion of Kanak (1808, 1: 359).

In the Event: Indigenous Countersigns and the Ethnohistory of Voyaging

Figure 6.4 *"Sauvage de la Nouvelle-Calédonie lançant une zagaie"* (engraving)

SAUVAGE DE LA NOUVELLE CALÉDONIE LANÇANT UNE ZAGAIE.

Artist, Piron; Engraver, Jacques-Louis Copia. Source: La Billardière 1800b: pl. 35. Photograph: Bronwen Douglas.

Within the total textual corpus of this voyage, visual and verbal, the apparent polarity in visual representations of Tongans and Kanak clearly did not signify the racialisation of observed human differences in the Pacific Islands and should not be taken as a precursor to Dumont d'Urville's named racial types. It was not pro-"Polynesian" prejudice that inspired these eighteenth-century voyagers to represent Tongans as less violent than Kanak. Rather, their antithetical representations are countersigns of dominant motifs in the collective self-presentations of significant numbers of Tongans and Kanak respectively. As d'Entrecasteaux (1808, 1: 308) acknowledged, Tongans generally dissimulated their intentions the better to plunder the visitors, using force as required, while many Kanak endeavoured openly to intimidate and control them. Indeed, what prejudice there was favoured Kanak, thanks to the precedents set by Cook and Forster, and inflected the d'Entrecasteaux voyage narratives with the added bitterness of thwarted expectations. In contrast, ambivalence was the norm in European voyagers' accounts of meetings with Tongans, a countersign of Tongan unpredictability as judged by European standards of propriety, consistency and order. Years later, de Rossel, who had sailed with d'Entrecasteaux and edited his dead captain's journal for publication, wrote an official report on Dumont d'Urville's voyage of 1826–29. He found Dumont d'Urville's relations with Tongans painfully familiar:

> These men, in appearance so sociable, and in actual fact so seductive, are never more to be feared than when one believes one can abandon oneself to live among them with the most complete confidence; it is then they indulge in acts of violence that one is obliged rigorously to repress. … [Like Cook and d'Entrecasteaux,] M. d'Urville was in turn forced to punish the audaciousness and guile of these islanders (Rossel 1830, lxxxii–lxxxiii).

Nearing the end of his voyage and, indeed, his life, d'Entrecasteaux's optimistic curiosity to engage with natural man on a friendly, mutually beneficial basis had dissolved into despair in the face of cumulative indigenous intransigence, unpredictability, seemingly unprovoked violence, or cannibalism in Tonga, New Caledonia and, subsequently, in islands further north toward New Guinea. By this stage rumour alone sufficed for him to damn whole groups as "cannibals" and to deplore "the excesses in which the human species can indulge when customs are not moderated and softened by civilisation" (1808, 1: 422–3). It was a far cry from d'Entrecasteaux's "simple and good," "natural" Tasmanians and his early strictures against the corrupting "vices of the state of civilisation" (1808, 1: 242). Indigenous agency – their largely inscrutable demeanour, actions and desires – forced d'Entrecasteaux to confront the paradox and the dilemma of the Enlightenment vision of peaceful, philanthropic, scientific encounters with so-called "savages" who were also regarded as fellow human beings: that ethnocentric, hierarchical, paternalist, prescriptive and acquisitive strands in Enlightenment humanism would not accommodate other people's assessments and exercise of their rights, desires and autonomy. "[I]t seems certain to me," he wrote on leaving New Caledonia, "that [either] we must renounce visiting [Pacific Islanders] ... , or we must inspire respect in them by very great severity" (1808, 1: 359). This was a chilling portent.

Race

In the course of his extensive voyaging in Oceania, Dumont d'Urville never met the indigenous people of New Caledonia. He nonetheless classed them with Tasmanians on the basis of previous voyage literature: "It appears that in New Caledonia ... the Melanesian essence has undergone scarcely perceptible modifications: so La Billardière *naturally* approximated the New Caledonians to the Tasmanians" (Dumont d'Urville 1832, 15; my emphasis). La Billardière had, indeed, noted a physical resemblance: "The black colour of ... [Kanak] skin is almost as deep as that of the natives of ... [Van Diemen's Land], whose characteristic physiognomy much resembles theirs" (1800a, 2: 186). D'Entrecasteaux remarked not only a physical likeness between Kanak and Tasmanians but explicitly distinguished both from Tongans: "[Kanak] have the same physique and adopt the same postures as the inhabitants of Van Diemen's Land. This tells us that their height is much inferior to that of the natives of the Friendly Islands" (1808, 1: 330). Yet, as has been seen, La Billardière and his shipmates had unstintingly admired Tasmanian behaviour, sociality and appearance, whereas they were revolted by Kanak cannibalism, dismayed by their aggression toward the French, and represented them accordingly (Richard 1986b, 308–23; La Billardière 1800a, 2: 28–79, 182–248). D'Entrecasteaux himself compared the physical appearance of the Tasmanians and the Maori (later to be Dumont d'Urville's favourite Polynesians) to Maori disadvantage: "[Maori] are less black; their limbs are more muscular and their height greater: but their physiognomy proclaims much less goodness; it even has in it something dark and ferocious" (1808, 1: 271). For Dumont d'Urville, La Billardière's analogy between Tasmanians and Kanak was *ipso facto* damning and literally naturalised his own low racial ranking of Kanak, but he had to wrench the physical comparison out of textual and experiential contexts and construe it in terms of an anachronistic racial grammar. The descriptions of skin colour, hair type and facial features in La Billardière's *Relation* are incidental and empirical rather than systemically ethnological or biological, as was the nineteenth-century norm. Neither he nor d'Entrecasteaux argued for a broad differentiation or hierarchisation of Oceanian people on the basis of race or even Forster's flexible "varieties."

Both d'Entrecasteaux and his naturalist were Enlightenment men – La Billardière was a committed republican – whose evaluations of indigenous people were muted, fluid, mainly aesthetic and at least as significantly shaped by experience of native actions and demeanours as by their own preconceptions. Both undoubtedly took for granted the reality of an environmentally-determined developmental hierarchy of humanity ranging from "natural" man in a state of "savagery" to "civilisation," within which the different indigenous groups encountered were implicitly located on the basis of experience; but no fixed evolutionary trajectory was implied and neither author was uncritical of "advance" or "civilisation" as he knew it. D'Entrecasteaux remarked that while the Tasmanians were "undoubtedly less advanced in civilisation than the peoples of New Zealand, neither do they have their ferocious temperament." Elsewhere he opined that "the inhabitants of the Friendly Islands [Tonga] are ... much more advanced than the inhabitants of New Caledonia" (1808, 1: 243, 343). It is clear from the foregoing, however, that he regarded "advance" as an equivocal blessing, which in Tonga had produced a "feudal"-style government with "weak," "effeminate" chiefs, whose "voluptuous" lifestyle and arbitrary "abuses" led to a "state of anarchy" and forced the ordinary people into dissimulation and theft (298, 305–12). For his part, La Billardière conceived social and material progress as strongly influenced by environment and did not doubt that Aborigines were ultimately civilisable – he hoped that a pregnant female goat and a young male left by d'Entrecasteaux at Adventure Bay in Van Diemen's Land might multiply and "occasion total change in the lifestyle of the inhabitants, who, able to become a pastoral people, would abandon the coast without regret and enjoy the pleasure of no longer having to dive for their food, at risk of being devoured by sharks." The women, "condemned to this arduous labour," would benefit most, though he feared that the goats would be killed before they could reproduce (1800a, 2: 79). An ethnocentric, quixotic vision perhaps, but in stark contrast to Dumont d'Urville's bleak, racially-determined prognostication thirty-five years later: "Everything suggests that the Tasmanian, and later the Australian, incapable of ever being civilised, will end up disappearing entirely" (1830–33, 5: 96).

Conclusions

The details of indigenous motivations, the content of their strategies, the meanings of their words and actions reported in long-ago encounters with European voyagers are now difficult, if not impossible, to recover, even where rich local traditions subsist (but cf. Salmond 1991, 1997). For example, we cannot now know, though we can speculate, what "one of the chiefs" standing on the platform of a canoe in the Admiralty Islands said in his "speech" to the French, or why he made "signs" which "did not allow us to doubt that he wished to induce us to land," or what his actual relations were with the "paddlers" who "probably did not have permission to speak, but joined their signs of invitation to the chief's" (La Billardière 1800a, 1: 258). But I am convinced not only that there was — obviously — always a range of local strategies and motivations, conscious and unconscious, in play in every situation of encounter but also that what indigenous people wanted, meant and did — and how they looked — profoundly influenced European reactions, expectations and representations in the always fraught and vulnerable settings of voyaging in frail, wooden sailing ships in unknown or little-known waters (see Douglas 2003).

The theory of indigenous countersigns developed in this chapter decentres — though it does not discount — European authors and their "pre-programmed" systems of knowledge and language which are assumed by most scholars to determine travellers' "perceptions, consequent interpretations, and consequent actions" (Porter 1990, 122; Strack 1996, 286 n. 4). This is notably the case in text-focused disciplines, like literary studies, cultural studies, art history and the history of ideas (e.g. Guest 1992; Pagden 1993; Porter 1990; Strack 1996). The historical strategy implemented here, in contrast, takes seriously the complex interplay of discourse, presupposition, personality, experience, action and indigenous countersigns, which is encoded in voyagers' representations of Oceanian people and particular encounters with them. In the late eighteenth century and much of the nineteenth, travellers' narratives, drawings and ethnographies provided important raw material for the emergent anthropological science of race. The indigenous countersigns that permeate voyagers' written and visual representations were usually vitiated in the process of appropriation of such knowledge by metropolitan savants, but they remain key building blocks for the construction of modern ethnohistorical narratives.

REFERENCES

Anderson, Stephanie

2000 French anthropology in Australia, a prelude: The encounters between Aboriginal Tasmanians and the expedition of Bruny d'Entrecasteaux, 1793. *Aboriginal History* 24: 212–23.

Banks, Joseph

1962 *The* Endeavour *Journal of Joseph Banks 1768–1771*, ed. John C. Beaglehole. 2 vols. Sydney: Public Library of NSW, in association with Angus and Robertson.

Bory de Saint-Vincent, Jean-Baptiste-Geneviève-Marcellin

1827 [1825] *L'homme (homo): Essai zoologique sur le genre humain.* 2 vols, 2nd edn. Paris: Rey et Gravier.

Bougainville, Louis-Antoine de

1771 *Voyage autour du monde par la frégate du roi la Boudeuse et la flûte l'Etoile en 1766, 1767, 1768 & 1769.* Paris: Saillant & Nyon.

Carrier, Achsah H., and James G. Carrier

1991 *Structure and Process in a Melanesian Society: Ponam's Progress in the Twentieth Century*. Chur, Switzerland: Harwood Academic Publishers.

Cook, James

1777 *A Voyage Towards the South Pole and Round the World Performed in His Majesty's Ships the Resolution and Adventure in the Years 1772, 1773, 1774, and 1775* ... 2 vols. London: W. Strahan and T. Cadell.

Douglas, Bronwen

1970 A contact history of the Balad people of New Caledonia 1774–1845. *Journal of the Polynesian Society* 79 (2): 180–200.

1999a Art as ethno-historical text: Science, representation and indigenous presence in eighteenth and nineteenth century Oceanic voyage literature. In *Double Vision: Art Histories and Colonial Histories in the Pacific*, eds Nicholas Thomas and Diane Losche, 65–99. Cambridge: Cambridge University Press.

1999b Science and the art of representing "savages": Reading "race" in text and image in South Seas voyage literature. *History and Anthropology* 11: 157–201.

2003 Seaborne ethnography and the natural history of man. *Journal of Pacific History* 38: 3–27.

2006 Slippery word, ambiguous praxis: "Race" and late 18th-century voyagers in Oceania. *Journal of Pacific History* 41: 1–29.

2007 The lure of texts and the discipline of praxis: Cross-cultural history in a post-empirical world. *Humanities Research* 14: 11–30.

Dumont d'Urville, Jules-Sébastien-César

1826 Sur les peuples de l'Océanie. MS. 7GG$_2$ 30 (2). Paris: Service historique de la Défense, département Marine.

1830–33 *Voyage de la corvette l'Astrolabe executé ... pendant les années 1826–1827–1828–1829 ... : Histoire du voyage*. 5 vols. Paris: J. Tastu.

1832 Sur les îles du Grand Océan. *Bulletin de la Société de Géographie* 17: 1–21.

1834–35 *Voyage pittoresque autour du monde: Résumé général des voyages de découvertes, de Magellan, Tasman, Dampier* ... 2 vols. Paris: L. Tenré et Henri Dupuy.

Dunmore, John, trans. and ed.

1995 *The Journal of Jean-François de Galaup de la Pérouse 1785–1788*. 2 vols. London: Hakluyt Society.

d'Entrecasteaux, Antoine-Raymond-Joseph de Bruni

1808 *Voyage de Dentrecasteaux, envoyé à la recherche de La Pérouse* ..., ed. Elisabeth-Paul-Edouard de Rossel. 2 vols. Paris: Imprimerie impériale.

Forster, Johann Reinhold

1996 [1778] *Observations Made during a Voyage Round the World*. New edition, eds Nicholas Thomas, Harriet Guest, and Michael Dettelbach; with a linguistic appendix by Karl H. Rensch. Honolulu: University of Hawai`i Press.

Guest, Harriet

1992 Curiously marked: Tattooing, masculinity, and nationality in eighteenth-century British perceptions of the South Pacific. In *Painting and the Politics of Culture: New Essays on British Art, 1700–1850*, ed. John Barrell, 101–34. Oxford: Oxford University Press.

Gunson, Niel

1979 The *hau* concept of leadership in Western Polynesia. *Journal of Pacific History* 14: 28–49.

Hawkesworth, John

1773 *An Account of the Voyages Undertaken by the Order of His Present Majesty for Making Discoveries in the Southern Hemisphere* ... 3 vols. London: W. Strahan and T. Cadell.

Joppien, Rüdiger, and Bernard Smith

1985–87 *The Art of Captain Cook's Voyages*. 3 vols. Melbourne: Oxford University Press in association with the Australian Academy of Humanities.

La Billardière, Jacques-Julien Houtou de

1800a *Relation du voyage à la recherche de La Pérouse ... pendant les années 1791, 1792 et pendant la 1ère et la 2ème année de la République Françoise*. 2 vols. Paris: H.J. Jansen.

1800b *Atlas pour servir à la relation du voyage à la recherche de La Pérouse* ... Paris: H.J. Jansen.

La Pérouse, Jean-François de Galaup de

1798 [1797] *Voyage de La Pérouse autour du monde, publié conformément au décret du 22 avril, 1791*, ed. Louis-Antoine Milet-Mureau. 4 vols. Paris: chez Plassan.

Pagden, Anthony

1993 *European Encounters with the New World: From Renaissance to Romanticism*. New Haven: Yale University Press.

Porter, Roy

1990 The exotic as erotic: Captain Cook at Tahiti. In *Exoticism in the Enlightenment*, eds George S. Rousseau and Roy Porter, 117–44. Manchester: Manchester University Press.

Quoy, Jean-René Constant, and Joseph-Paul Gaimard

1830 *Voyage de découvertes de l'Astrolabe ... pendant les années 1826–1827–1828–1829 ... : Zoologie,* vol. 1. Paris: J. Tastu.

Richard, Hélène

1986a *Le voyage de d'Entrecasteaux à la recherche de Lapérouse: Une grande expédition scientifique au temps de la Révolution française.* Paris: Comité des travaux historiques et scientifiques.

1986b Rapport de d'Auribeau: seconde relâche à la terre de Van Diemen. In *Le voyage de d'Entrecasteaux à la recherche de Lapérouse: Une grande expédition scientifique au temps de la Révolution française,* 301–31. Paris: Comité des travaux historiques et scientifiques.

Rossel, Elisabeth-Paul-Edouard de

1830 Rapport sur la navigation de l'Astrolabe ... lu à l'Académie royale des sciences, dans la séance du 17 août 1829. In *Voyage de la corvette l'Astrolabe exécuté par ordre du Roi, pendant les années 1826, 1827, 1828, 1829 ... : Histoire du voyage,* by Jules-Sébastien-César Dumont d'Urville, vol. 1, lxxv–xcxv. Paris: J. Tastu.

Rousseau, George S., and Roy Porter

1990 Introduction: Approaching enlightenment exoticism. In *Exoticism in the Enlightenment,* ed. George S. Rousseau and Roy Porter, 1–22. Manchester: Manchester University Press.

Salmond, Anne

1991 *Two Worlds: First Meetings Between Maori and Europeans 1642–1772.* Auckland: Viking.

1997 *Between Worlds: Early Exchanges Between Maori and Europeans 1773–1815.* Auckland: Viking.

Smith, Bernard

1960 *European Vision and the South Pacific, 1768–1850: A Study in the History of Art and Ideas.* Oxford: Oxford University Press.

1992 *Imagining the Pacific: In the Wake of the Cook Voyages.* Carlton, Vic.: Miegunyah Press/Melbourne University Press.

Strack, Thomas

1996 Philosophical anthropology on the eve of biological determinism: Immanuel Kant and Georg Forster on the moral qualities and biological characteristics of the human race. *Central European History* 29: 285–308.

Thomas, Nicholas

1997 *In Oceania: Visions, Artifacts, Histories*. Durham, NC: Duke University Press.

Notes

[1] In modern usage, the term *Oceania* is often limited to the Pacific Islands, but I give it its inclusive nineteenth-century sense, which encompassed Australia, the Pacific Islands, Aotearoa New Zealand, New Guinea, and adjacent islands in eastern Indonesia. All translations are my own.

[2] The French term *expérience* retains the dual meaning of "experience" and "experiment," whereas English has lost the second sense since the mid-seventeenth century; "empirical" can connote either or both meanings (*Oxford English Dictionary*, online). Both apply to the ethos of scientific voyaging.

[3] Following d'Entrecasteaux's death in New Guinea waters in the latter stages of the voyage, the expedition disintegrated in the East Indies under the multiple pressures of external war, national political divisions and disease. On La Billardière's departure from Batavia, Piron had "begged" him to accept a duplicate set of "the drawings of costumes and landscape, which he had made in the course of the campaign" (La Billardière 1800a, x). La Billardière's *Relation* was duly illustrated by Copia's engravings of Piron's drawings. Two separate English translations appeared the following year, testimony to the huge popularity of voyage literature. A collection of Piron's drawings, long held by the Musée de l'Homme, is now in the Musée du Quai Branly in Paris. None is included in this chapter because the fee charged for reproduction rights is exorbitant. D'Entrecasteaux's narrative was edited belatedly by a surviving officer, Elisabeth-Paul-Edouard de Rossel (1765–1829) and finally published in 1808 accompanied by a magnificent collection of charts, but without pictures.

[4] "Décret de l'assemblée nationale," Feb. 9, 1791 (La Pérouse 1798 [1797], 1: 1–3). See also "Mémoire du roi, pour servir d'Instruction particulière au sieur Bruny-Dentrecasteaux, chef de division des Armées navales, commandant les frégates la Recherche et l'Espérance" (d'Entrecasteaux 1808, 1: xliii–xliv; Richard 1986a, 21–82, 133–48).

[5] "Hard" primitivism was Smith's term for a discourse which extolled "the harsh but virtuous primitive life" in counterpoint to expressions of distaste for "the luxuries and excesses of civilization" (1960, 126–27).

[6] La Billardière (1800a, 1: 262).

[7] In their historical reconstruction of early colonial political relations in Ponam – a small island north of Manus, the largest of the Admiralty Islands – Achsah and James Carrier discussed the position of *lapan* "leader, rich man," who sought to strengthen his own and his group's position by dominating ceremonial exchanges and recruiting new members to the group. The Carriers' argument that "economic success and political prestige" depended on the ability to "manage trade intelligently" and "control" people, together with their production and labour, has suggestive implications for the actions of "chiefs" described in the d'Entrecasteaux voyage texts (Carrier and Carrier 1991, 55–72).

[8] Piron, "Homme des iles de l'amireauté," pencil drawing, 34 x 43 cm. MQB ICONO PP0154838 (Paris: Musée du Quai Branly). Online <http://www.quaibranly.fr/fr/documentation/le-catalogue-de-l-iconotheque/index.html>.

[9] In 1826, following his initial voyage in Oceania as first officer on the *Coquille* but before his return to the Pacific in command of that vessel, renamed *Astrolabe*, Dumont d'Urville wrote a long, unfinished essay in response to the offer by the Société de Géographie of one of its annual prizes for work on "the peoples of Oceania, revealing their differences and their similarities to other peoples, with regard to their form and physical constitution, ... their morals, customs, civil and religious institutions and languages." His "three great divisions" were: (1) "Australians," "Blacks," or "Melanians"; (2) "peoples of Tonga," the "true Polynesians," "adherents of *tabou*"; (3) "Carolines." The "Malay race properly speaking" remained outside the classification (Dumont d'Urville 1826). This manuscript anticipated the

well-known, far more pithy and schematic paper on the same theme that he read to the Société in January 1832 and published in its *Bulletin* (Dumont d'Urville 1832).

[10] D'Entrecasteaux (1808, 1: 230).

[11] See Stephanie Anderson's (2000) recent interpretation of cross-cultural encounters during d'Entrecasteaux's visit to Van Diemen's Land.

[12] The French were evidently able to do a careful census of the people they met in Recherche Bay – another marker of the cross-cultural intimacy of this episode. D'Entrecasteaux enumerated, as follows, the "forty-eight individuals" comprising "the tribe we saw": ten old or young men, fourteen women of various ages, and twenty-four children from 1 to 12 years divided equally between girls and boys (1808, 1: 245; see also Richard 1986b, 311–2).

[13] The meeting and its gratifying antecedent event were described in detail by La Billardière, who was a participant along with the expedition's gardener and two armed seamen. He counted forty-two "savages," amongst whom were seven men and eight women, while "the others appeared to be their children" (1800a, 2: 27–40).

[14] D'Entrecasteaux (1808, 1: 308, 313).

[15] In Tonga, the highest-ranking titleholder was the deeply sacred Tu`i Tonga, while the pragmatic exercise of power was the domain of the *hau* or paramount ruler. Niel Gunson has discussed the relationship between sacred and secular leadership, Tu`i Tonga and *hau*, both in general terms and historically, at the end of the eighteenth-century when contending chiefs engaged in lethal competition for the position of *hau* and local leaders rejected the authority of the *hau* over their districts, with resultant violent conflict and political fragmentation (1979, 28–43).

[16] See, for example, Dumont d'Urville (1832); Quoy and Gaimard (1830, 15–59); see also Douglas (1999a: 86, 1999b).

[17] For accounts of the French stay in Tonga see d'Entrecasteaux (1808, 1: 276–99); La Billardière (1800a, 2: 92–177). For the commander's ethnographic reflections on Tongans, see d'Entrecasteaux (1808, 1: 300–23).

[18] The stark variation in the cultural construction of punishment was graphically displayed in La Billardière's report that a chief who advocated the execution of a captured thief nonetheless "begged that he be pardoned" and "seemed to be extremely affected" when the man was flogged (1800a, 2: 140).

[19] D'Entrecasteaux's predecessor Louis-Antoine de Bougainville (1729–1814) had applied the term *race* to Tahiti in a similarly ambiguous sense, when he discerned "two very different races of men, yet with the same language, the same customs and seeming to mix together without distinction" (1771, 214). He did not correlate colour difference with class, whereas Joseph Banks (1743–1820), the naturalist on Cook's first voyage, linked class, climate and lifestyle to account for "the colours of different Nations." In "the South sea Islands," he wrote, "many of the Better sort of people who keep themselves close at home are nearly as white as Europeans, while the poorer sort, oblig'd in their business of fishing &c. to expose their naked bodies to all the inclemencies of the Climate, have some among them but little lighter than the New Hollanders" (Banks 1962, 2: 124). For his part, La Billardière attributed an analogous difference in the colour of Tongans to gendered behaviours rather than class: whereas men "have swarthy skin because they very often expose themselves to the ardour of the sun; ... the women, who stay fairly constantly in their houses or in the shade of trees, have a very white complexion" (1800a, 2: 176–7).

[20] D'Entrecasteaux's expedition was provided with a very well-equipped library, including a copy of La Pérouse's manuscript journal (Richard 1986a, 70).

[21] The blacksmith of the *Recherche* was seriously wounded while in pursuit of a thief, and in reprisal at least two Tongans died, one reportedly a chief, and two high-ranking chiefs were taken hostage (d'Entrecasteaux 1808, 1: 294–8; La Billardière 1800a, 2: 155–61).

[22] D'Entrecasteaux's orders here replicated those of La Pérouse (Dunmore 1995, 1: cxlviii). Published reports of Cook's use of violence against Pacific Islanders had inspired widespread controversy (Smith 1992, 199–202). Both d'Entrecasteaux (1808, 1: 359–60) and La Billardière (1800a, 2: 175) reported that many Tongans complained of "the harsh treatment he had inflicted on them."

[23] D'Entrecasteaux (1808, 1: 359).

[24] Piron, "Homme de Balade," pencil drawing, 41 x 46 cm. MQB ICONO PP01544787. (Paris: Musée du Quai Branly). Online <http://www.quaibranly.fr/fr/documentation/le-catalogue-de-l-iconotheque/index.html>.

Chapter 7

Watkin Tench's Fieldwork: The Journal of an "Ethnographer" in Port Jackson, 1788-1791

Isabelle Merle

> Whether plodding in London; reeking with human blood in Paris; or wandering amidst the solitary wilds of New South Wales – Man is ever an object of interest, curiosity, and reflection.
>
> (Tench 1979, 274)

Today Watkin Tench belongs to the Australian pantheon as a popular historical figure of early Sydney. His narrative, republished in paperback in 1996 and 2000, is available cheaply in any bookshop in Australia (Flannery 1996, 2000). It is one of the most accessible First Fleet narratives. It can be presented easily to schoolchildren as a well-written and lively testimony of the foundational years of the nation. It has long been prized for its literary and descriptive qualities. In 1923 the historian G.A. Wood considered Tench's narrative "the most accurate, most orderly, and most valuable description of life in the colony in the first days" and wrote of his "style of generous vivacity" (Tench 1979, xxi). In 1938 it was chosen above all other First Fleet journals, some written by people historically more important than Tench – Governor Phillip, Judge-Advocate David Collins or future Governor John Hunter – to be partially republished for the 150th anniversary of British settlement in Australia (Tench 1938). It was republished in full in 1961 by the prestigious Royal Australian Historical Society, which was engaged in a program of publishing all the First Fleet narratives. Tench's editor in 1961, L.F. Fitzhardinge, stated that Tench had some claim to:

> be considered the father of Australian literature, if not Australian history. ... Less detailed than Collins, less matter-of-fact than Phillip or White, Tench is the first man to mould Australian experience into a work of conscious art. ... Nor is he, for this reason, less valuable as an historian: rather does his humanity and insight enable him to see further than his fellows. If we wish to know what it was like to be in Sydney through the famine, or to get the "feel" of the primeval bush as the first explorers saw it, we turn to Tench. Not only the externals, but the very atmosphere

and moods of the settlement are reflected in his measured, smoothly flowing prose, which with its careful periods, its balanced rhythms and antitheses, and its precise choice of words might challenge comparison with Gibbon himself (Tench 1979, xxi).

Tench's narrative has been widely used by historians as one of the most informative historical sources on the early years. In her book *Dancing with Strangers* Inga Clendinnen lavished praise on it:

> The best reason for reading Watkin Tench is that he reminds us of two important things surprisingly easy to forget: that the past was real, and that this likeable man whose words are on the page before us was actually there. In his writings Tench lives again, as he makes the people he sees around him live, especially the men and women rendered near-invisible or unintelligible in too many other accounts: the indigenous inhabitants of the Sydney region (Clendinnen 2003, 58).

It is because I myself have been touched by the charm and the quality of Tench's description that I feel a need to create some distance from the text and try to analyse it as an "historical source" written in a precise context by a specific person for a particular purpose and audience. I feel a need to return to what might seem a rather classical historical methodology of "internal and external critique" of the document, but I am also interested in the "source" as such – the circumstances of its making, its material forms, its history. It seems to me that this is useful, because analyses of the history of First Fleet narratives are rare. Although First Fleet narratives are widely used by historians to describe events and issues in Port Jackson, they have usually been treated as "neutral sources" – as providing the factual framework of the events (see as an example, among others, Willey 1979). Historians such as Alan Atkinson (1997) and Inga Clendinnen (2003) have used them in a more sensitive way, asking, for example: Who said what? Who saw what? In which circumstances? Clendinnen's book, in particular, offers interesting conclusions about Tench's position as an observer of Port Jackson's scene, but her analysis is incomplete, since this is not her central focus.

This chapter considers Tench as a person and as an author, and his journal as an historical construction. The idea is to evaluate the narrative precisely, particularly concerning the first inhabitants, later called Aborigines. If Tench can compete with Gibbon and those first "ethnographers" (scientists or missionaries) travelling and later settling in the Pacific, we have to take his narrative seriously and try to understand its nature as a text. I have noted that little has been written on First Fleet narratives as texts. Further, only two biographies of First Fleet officers have been written to date, one by Alan Frost on Governor Phillip, the other by John Currey on David Collins (Frost 1987; Currey 2000). Tench himself is known only through the introductions written by the successive editors of his narrative. As Inga Clendinnen notes, "almost all we know of the man is here, in the two and a half hundred pages of his two books" (2003, 57). In fact we can add Tench's few surviving letters and a third book written while he was a prisoner in Quimper (France) during the Revolution (Edwards 2001).[1] But nothing more. No private diary or personal comments are known which might throw light on Tench's life, personality and experience.

Tench's account is the only First Fleet journal that has specifically interested literary scholars. Two articles have been published from this perspective, giving us a sense of Tench's compositional practices and the literary influences on his text (Edwards 2000; Mitchell 1994). These show that Tench had a strategy as an author and wrote for an audience at a particular time, the late eighteenth century, when the genre of "travel accounts" flourished. Yet, at that time, as studies of travel literature show, the genre was very unstable and "hybrid." According to one French specialist, it was a genre that:

> knew no laws ... which allied the quest for literary perfection with the pleasures of seduction and entertainment and to which voyagers contributed in different ways depending on whether their writing lent itself to description with a generally geographical bent or to accounts potentially rich in adventure (Le Huenen 1990, 14; my translation from the French).[2]

Tench's narrative is highly representative of the uncertainty of the genre, written for the "amusement of the public" but also for scientific purposes. Tench aspired to be a popular author and wrote, as we shall see, a series of narratives of dramatic events and adventures. But he also claimed to be an accurate observer, describing what he saw in the manner of the prestigious navigators in the Pacific before him. Following Cook's tracks, Tench wanted, as Greg Dening (1994, 451) would put it, to be part of "the season for observing."

Tench's account raises questions concerning his identity, the context of his writing, the choices he made in describing the world of Port Jackson, and the composition of his two Australian volumes, particularly the modalities of their description, writing and publication. Such simple questions as who he was, how he wrote and published, in what circumstances, for what audience and with what editorial changes (as was then common) are not simple to answer. Tench's description itself and what it tells us of what happened in Port Jackson also needs to be interrogated. This chapter is a work in progress and it raises more questions than it answers. As a first exploration, I focus on Tench's description of the Aboriginal world, an important part of his account and his main interest in Port Jackson. I will suggest that the "past" Tench describes is greatly influenced by his construction of it, so much so that his text cannot simply be regarded as an empirical account.

Watkin Tench and his "Journal"

Tench's account was based on his "regular journal" and diverse notes that no longer exist. He wrote the first part of his narrative "on the spot," during his first six months in Port Jackson, between January and July 1788, and quickly sent it back to England on the transports returning to Europe. It was published as *A Narrative of the Expedition to Botany Bay* in London in 1789, by John Debrett of Piccadilly. According to Tim Flannery, before they left, Tench and surgeon John White were contracted by this publisher to write "an interim report on the state of the colony" (Flannery 1996, 2). Other First Fleet officers were similarly approached by London publishers before their departure: Arthur Phillip and John Hunter by John Stockdale publisher, and David Collins by Cadell R. Davies. Unlike previous scientific expeditions to the Pacific, no demand for publication was made from the naval authorities. The demand came from publishers who anticipated that books on Botany Bay would be popular with a British audience.

In 1789 *The Voyage of Governor Phillip* (a compilation of Phillip's notes) and Tench's *A Narrative* became the first two accounts published on Botany Bay. The manuscript Tench sent to Debrett apparently no longer exists. This bars discussing possible editorial changes to the manuscript – a pity, because the scandal created by Hawkesworth's 1773 revision of Cook's *First Voyage* was still in people's minds, yet it remained common for an editor to revise manuscripts of travel like Tench's first volume.[3] However, the success of *A Narrative* was immediate, with three English editions, an Irish edition, a translation in Dutch, two in French, two in German and a number of book reviews during 1789. It was translated even more quickly than Phillip's work, which itself received great attention. Tench's second volume was published in London in 1793 under the title *A Complete Account of the Settlement at Port Jackson* by G. Nicol, the editor who likely also published Cook's *Third Voyage* in 1785 (Cook and King 1785). Tench reached home in July 1792, so had less than a year to complete his second volume. He was able to read John White's journal, published in 1790, and extracts from Governor Phillip's letters, published by Debrett in 1791 and 1792. His own account was published at the same time as John Hunter's journal, and received less attention than his first narrative. The interest aroused by the novelty of the subject had died away. No second edition was published,[4] but it was translated into German in the following year and into Swedish in 1797.

Tench was twenty-nine years of age when in May 1787 he joined the fleet, anchored in Portsmouth, which was going to ship the first British convicts to Australia. He was an officer of the Marine Corps, and knew only military life. Recruited at eighteen years of age in 1776, he was sent to fight the rebellious American colonies. That war ended in 1783 and Tench was placed on half-pay in 1786. In this context he decided to sign on for a three-year tour of duty to Botany Bay. As he wrote in the introduction to the first part of his account, he knew that he was getting involved in an expedition "which has excited much curiosity, and given birth to many speculations, respecting the consequences to arise from it" (Tench 1789, xxvi).

The expedition was much publicised for two main reasons. First, its aim was to establish on the far side of the world a penal colony in an unknown territory inhabited only by "savages." This was an extraordinary project, which provoked intense debate among specialists of penology and criminal affairs in Europe. Second, the expedition was to settle these convicts in Australia, the main land of the South Seas, visited by James Cook twenty-eight years earlier. We know how famous Cook was at that time in Britain, and how successful the publications written by members of his prestigious scientific expeditions had been. The publicity the expedition to Botany Bay attracted in 1787 placed Tench and his companions in a particular situation. As Marines, they were sent to Botany Bay "for the protection of the settlement intended to be made there, as well as for preserving good order and regularity among the convicts" (Tench 1979, xvi). But, as earlier noted, they were also contacted by London publishers eager to publish travel accounts of this extraordinary expedition.

Tench, then, signing for three years' service in Botany Bay, was offered an improbable opportunity in a soldier's life: to write for the public. In introducing his first volume he wrote:

> In offering this little tract to the public, it is equally the writer's wish to conduce to their amusement and information. … An unpractised writer is generally anxious to bespeak public attention, and to solicit public indulgence. Except on professional subjects, military men are, perhaps too fearful of critical censure. For the present narrative no other apology is attempted, than the intention of its author who has endeavoured not only to satisfy present curiosity, but to point out to future adventurers the favourable, as well as adverse circumstances which will attend their settling here (Tench 1979, 5–6).

Lieutenant Watkin Tench presents himself as an unskilled author and asks "the candid to overlook the inaccuracies of this imperfect sketch, drawn amidst the complicated duties of the service in which the Author is engaged" (Tench 1979, 5–6). Writing was for Tench a new and unusual task, but he obviously had some initial skills. Born in Chester in 1758, Watkin Tench's father was a master of dance and director of a boarding school, an educated man and a protégé of a great landed family in north Wales, the Williams-Wynn family. Apparently he gave his son a sound schooling, to judge by the quotations Tench used. Tench was obviously a reader and was fond of English literature, quoting by heart such authors as Shakespeare, Milton and Goldsmith. He had also read the philosophers of the time, including Hobbes, Rousseau and Voltaire – these three names appear in the general comments he made on Aboriginal society. He knew

Latin and spoke French. In his edition of Tench's narrative, Fitzhardinge described Tench as "the most cultivated mind in the young settlement on Sydney Cove" (Tench 1979, xv), although his young friend Dawes was more scientifically oriented. Despite his sound education, Tench was far from being able to compete with the *savants voyageurs* of his time, such as Humboldt, Volney and Potocki, who all belonged to the privileged classes, had been through the best universities in Europe and could travel at their own expense.

Both Tench's narratives are written "as if" they were journals. They are divided into chronological episodes, organised in narrative chapters describing a series of events, followed by summing-up chapters taking stock of the characteristics of the country, the progress of the settlement, and the convicts or the natives. According to Gavin Edwards (2000, 2), Samuel Johnson's *Journey to the Western Islands of Scotland* (1775) or Caesar's commentaries on the Gallic Wars (58–51 BC) could have been Tench's models. Another name is evoked throughout Tench's narrative: James Cook. Like his fellow officers, Tench had read Hawkesworth's description of Cook's first voyage. He repeated many descriptions given by the great navigator "as a pair," sometimes with some annoyance, as when he got stuck in "a rotten spungy bog," which Cook had described as "some of the finest meadows in the world" (Tench 1793, 215). "It has often fallen to my lot to traverse these fabled plains and many a bitter execration have I heard poured on those travellers, who could so faithlessly relate what they saw" (215).[5] Tench undoubtedly wished to be part of the making of a scientific knowledge of the Pacific. The words "observers" and "observations" occur more than ninety-two times in his account. His introduction clearly reveals his intent:

> As this publication enters the world with the name of the author, candour will, he trusts, induce its readers to believe, that no consideration could weigh with him in an endeavour to mislead them. Facts are related simply as they happened, and when opinions are hazarded, they are such as, he hopes, patient inquiry, and deliberate decision, will be found to have authorised. For the most part he has spoken from actual observation; and in those places where the relations of others have been unavoidably adopted, he has been careful to search for the truth, and repress that spirit of exaggeration which is almost ever the effect of novelty on ignorance (Tench 1979, 5).

We can see in this preoccupation with truth and this principle of direct observation the imprint of the Enlightenment, a philosophy based on the requirement of Reason, which influenced the travel accounts of Tench's predecessors in the Pacific. After Wallis, Bougainville, Cook, Banks and the Forsters, Tench wrote in Port Jackson along the same lines – a chronicle of events carefully reported. In conformity with the inventory model adopted by the *savants voyageurs* of his time, he wished to conduct an exhaustive investigation, describing all he could see: fauna, flora, landscapes, climate, "Indians"[6] (as Aborigines were then called) and, because of the singularity of this British expedition, the convicts and the state of the colony.

But beyond these scientific interests Tench was also writing "a work of conscious art" for "the amusement of the public." Mainly interested in man and context, his narrative can be read as a book in two parts, a part for adventures (the chronicle) and a part for scientific description and philosophical debate. It can be read as two stories in one, each separate from the other and each with its own tempo and suspense. On the one hand, he described the difficulties of survival, the imposition of public order, the conditions of control and repression of the penal population, the corrosive effect of the long and anxious wait for British news and supplies. On the other, he described new animals, plants and new people, telling of contact with the "Indians" and the very slow process by which the British tried to establish regular contact with these "Others."

Chronicles of the Encounters between British and Aborigines

In his first volume, this story of discovery and contact starts in January 1788 with a description of a "first contact" episode, followed (from Tench's point of view) by the sudden and incomprehensible disappearance of the "Indians," who then stayed aloof and later attacked unarmed convicts on the fringe of the settlement. The general conclusion of *A Narrative*, written after six months of "petty war" and little contact with the "Indians," reflected the uncertainties of the situation, the impossibility of Tench conducting a "patient inquiry," the increasing tension, and the deterioration of his own judgments of "Indians." His observations reflect the great gulf existing between the British and the Aborigines. His description is limited to aspects of material culture or to behaviour observed from afar. Tench's views were fuelled by his prejudices, but he also recognised the limits to his knowledge and his lack of comprehension.

The second volume starts with "a retrospect," probably written in 1792 in London, which admitted a "reversal of opinion":

> With the natives we were very little more acquainted than on our arrival in the country. Our intercourse with them was neither frequent or cordial. They seemed studiously to avoid us, either from fear, jealousy, or hatred. When they met with unarmed stragglers, they sometimes killed, and sometimes wounded them. I confess that, in common with many others, I was inclined to attribute this conduct, to a spirit of malignant levity. But a farther acquaintance with them, founded on several instances of their humanity and generosity, which shall be noticed in their proper places, has entirely reversed my opinion (Tench 1793, 135).

Starting with this positive statement, the second volume recounts a series of episodes *chosen* by Tench as "significant events" in the "politics" of British relations with Aborigines. He thought these "events" important to narrate, even though he was not present at most of them.

(1) The kidnapping and first meeting with Arabanoo, Baneeloon and Colbee. Tench related by hearsay the kidnapping of these people but was present when they first came in the camp.

(2) The famous scene of meeting Aborigines around a dead whale, the spearing of Governor Phillip and the ensuing interaction between British and Aborigines. Tench detailed all these events, including dialogue. But he was not there.

(3) The spearing of the gamekeeper McIntyre. Again, Tench was not a witness.

(4) The punitive expedition in retaliation. Tench *was* there, in charge of this very first punitive expedition against Aboriginal people. The expedition was a failure and Tench described it as a farce.

(5) The vignette of the Aboriginal potato thieves and the British attack against their Aboriginal campsite. The discovery of an Aboriginal victim who was obviously an important person. Tench acquired all this information by hearsay.

(6) The description of an inland expedition based on a journal chosen "among my numerous travelling journals into the interior" (Tench, 1793, 223). Tench made this choice to conclude his chronicle concerning Aboriginal people: "I select the following, to present to the reader, as equally important in their object, and more amusing in their detail than any other" (223).

It is useful to note that Tench used the singular form "*I*" when he was a direct witness, and "*we, us*" or another plural form when he was not present. But that apart, he did not clearly state whether or not he was a participant. He could have organised his narrative concerning Aboriginal people differently, keeping to his own observations and experiences –for example, to his conversations with Arabanoo, Colbee, Baneelon and others. But like most of his fellow officers he chose to relate this particular series of "events," which became, in the course of the consolidation of Australian history, "historical events." It is useful to note that these successive episodes give the story a rhythm, with a slow increasing tension. Power and potential violence is at the heart of the story, especially with the attack on Phillip, the killing of the gamekeeper and the consequent retaliation against the Aboriginal campsite. The punitive expedition Tench led could have been presented as a moment of high tension. Instead Tench described it as a farce. For Clendinnen, Tench's choice is explained by the fact that the governor was organising only a "theatrical statement about the new order" (Clendinnen, 2003, 180) and did not himself believe in the efficacy of this military action. Tench pointed out the complete inadequacy of the British military response: soldiers heavily armed and lost in the bush going after Aborigines running fast and light. But what would have happened had Tench and his company seized some Aborigines? The expedition could then no longer have been merely "a theatrical statement about the new order" (180). Whatever the significance of the "event" for the actors of the time, the fact remains that Tench describes it as farce in a highly amusing scene, and this releases the narrative from the tension previously described. It is as if Tench did not want to pursue the theme of violence and preferred to privilege "the amusement of the public." In the following chapter he describes the attack on the Aboriginal campsite, but concludes these "events" by taking the reader on a safe "ethnographic" inland expedition for the "amusement of the public." This reveals an ambivalence between Tench the observer and Tench the author. It also reveals in Tench an ambivalence toward violence and the consequences of colonisation for the Aboriginal world: ambivalence between the soldier upholding the colonial order, and the "enlightened" person attached to Aborigines by true feelings of friendship.

Tench's Ambivalence: General Considerations on Aboriginal Society

As Bernard Smith observed, Tench's account encapsulates the ambivalence of his time toward "the state of nature of primitive societies" (Smith 1984, 175–8). On the one hand, the state of nature was valorised as a happy stage of humanity following Bougainville's famous *Voyage autour du monde* and Rousseau's thesis; on the other, it was condemned as a state of backward heathen savagery by evangelical groups and defenders of progress and civilisation. For Smith, Tench's account reflected the cross-currents of the time. It is important to know that Tench, writing his conclusions in 1792 on the basis of his experience of Port Jackson, was not a Rousseauist. On the respective natural physical strength of the British and the Aborigines, Tench quoted Rousseau: "Give to civilised man all his machines, and he is superior to the savage; but without these how inferior is he found on opposition, even more so than the savage in the first instance" (Tench 1793, 274), but Tench immediately added, "These are the words of Rousseau; and like many more of his positions, must be received with limitations" (274).

Tench's anti-Rousseauist position was made even more clear later, when he mocked,

> those European philosophers, whose closet speculations exalt a state of nature above a state of civilisation ... [If they] could survey the phantom, which their heated imaginations have raised: possibly they might then learn, that a state of nature is, of all others, least adapted to promote the happiness of a being, capable of sublime research, and unending ratiocination: that a savage roaming for prey amidst his native deserts, is a creature deformed by all those passions, which afflict and degrade

our nature, unsoftened by the influence of religion, philosophy, and legal restriction: and that the more men unite their talents, the more closely the bands of society are drawn; and civilisation advanced, inasmuch is human felicity augmented, and man fitted for his unalienable station in the universe (Tench 1793, 291).

These words are written just after an evocation of the violence and ill treatment exerted against women in Aboriginal society. This will become a "marker" for Europeans in the nineteenth century of the "rank" of a primitive society. But Tench referred also to the "vicissitudes of their climate, the lack of clothes, the precariousness of supply, the sharpness of hunger, their ignorance of cultivating the earth" (Tench, 1793, 281). In a way, increasingly common in the nineteenth century, he underlined "the lack of" (habitat, tools, agriculture, clothes) to describe the backwardness of the people on a scale of technical advancement. "If they be considered as a nation, whose general advancement and acquisitions are to be weighed, they certainly rank very low, even in the scales of the savages" (281). But this backwardness is mainly due to the context, and not to a supposed deficiency of *nature* in the Aborigines themselves.

> Let those who have been born in more favoured lands, and who have profited by more enlightened systems, compassionate, but not despise, their destitute and obscure situation. Children of the same omniscient paternal care, let them recollect, that by the fortuitous advantage of birth alone, they possess superiority, that untaught, unaccommodated man, is the same in Pall Mall, as in the wilderness of New South Wales (1793, 293).

If Aborigines are backward because of the unfortunate context in which they live, they are by no means the "miserablest People in the World ... setting aside their Human Shape ... [who] differ but little from Brutes," as the navigator Dampier put it at the end of the seventeenth century (1998 [1697], 218). On the contrary, Tench affirmed that "the Natives of New South Wales possess a considerable portion of that acumen, or sharpness of intellect, which bespeaks genius" (1793, 281). And "if they resist knowledge, and the adoption of manners and customs, differing from their own, it is because the progress of reason is not only slow, but mechanical" (281): "Of all the lessons peculiar to man, that which he learns the latest, and with the most difficulty, is reason itself" (281).[7]

Tench defended the *quality* of Aboriginal people – their intelligence, comprehension, ingenuity and celerity, courage and honesty, freedom of judgement. According to the categories used by the philosophers to describe society, he also defended Aboriginal societies as organised, testified to by the fact that they had principles of government based on equality (he recognised that he knew little about their law), religious beliefs, sophisticated language (he worked with Dawes on a dictionary but never finished it). The people were "divided in tribes" (Tench 1793, 285), but Tench gave little information on their names or location. Cameragal is one of the few tribal names in his account. Interestingly, he made no reference at all to property or its lack. The only "possession" he mentioned was a "fishing ground." On the whole Tench's observations on Aboriginal social organisation are vague. He kept, rather, to what he could easily describe – the material culture, the physical appearance, the dances and so on – then made general remarks which slotted readily into the European debate on "primitive societies." From his experience in Port Jackson, he arrived at another set of considerations, referring mainly to the discovery of *individuals*, men and women with whom "he cannot but feel some share of affection" and proven to belong to humanity with all the qualities required: civility, feelings, intelligence (293).

> To appreciate their general powers of mind is difficult ... if from a general view we descend to particular inspection and examine individually the persons who compose this community, they will certainly rise in estimation. ... In the narrative part of this work, I have endeavoured rather to detail information, than to deduce conclusions; leaving to the reader the exercise of his own judgement. The behaviour of Arabanoo, of Baneelon, of Colbee, and many others, is copiously described and assuredly he who shall make just allowance for uninstructed nature, will hardly accuse any of those persons of stupidity, or deficiency of apprehension (Tench 1793, 281).

Encounters with "People": The Fieldwork of Watkin Tench

First Contacts

Tench sailed on the *Charlotte*, which reached Botany Bay two days after Phillip in the *Supply*. Describing "on inquiry" – by hearsay – the first sighting between Aborigines and British, Tench reported "not less than forty persons, shouting and making many uncouth signs and gestures" (Tench 1789, 35) and noted the prudence of the governor in landing on the opposite shore, "in order to take possession of his new territory, and bring about an intercourse between its old and new masters" (35). Tench does not question this immediate act of appropriation. The only problem at stake is the "delicacy" requisite on the British side "as on the event of this meeting might depend so much of our future tranquility" (35). The description is extremely short and the conclusion is quick – "both parties pleased each other." He also alludes to the gift of a looking glass, some beads and other toys (35).

Tench describes in much more detail his own "first contact," made on a beach three days later, as he was walking with a boy and a few soldiers. They sighted twelve "Indians." After careful approaches from each side, an old man came close. What does this beautifully described scene tell us, and what does it not?

Tench described how the old man and his comrades were struck by the skin colour of the intruders, the absence of beards and so their indefinite sex, the strange nature of the clothes (which might have been confused with skin). This description gives few clues as to what these Aborigines thought. Did they see the intruders as ghosts, ancestors, deities, monsters, or what? Tench does not contemplate this, and the context (contrary to the arrival of Cook in Hawai`i) does not help him. He noted the gentleness of the old man toward the boy, the reluctance of the Aborigines to exchange goods and their lack of interest in British toys.

Tench later reported various "interviews," again insisting on the need to make the "Indians" understand the new order of things: "Our first object was to win their affections, and our next to convince them of the superiority we possessed: for without the latter, the former we know would be of little importance" (Tench 1789, 37). Superiority meant muskets and their display, but to calm "fears and jealousy," an officer whistled *Malbrooke*, "which they appeared highly charmed with, and imitated with equal pleasure and readiness" (37).

In describing "first contacts" Tench showed how pragmatic he was. His interpretation of "events" is strongly influenced by awareness of the power game at stake and the necessity for the British to show their force, their superiority of arms, the fact that they are the new masters. However, he also revealed his empathy with the feelings and capacities of Aboriginal people: the gentleness of the old "Indian" toward the boy, their "fear and jealousy" when muskets are fired, their capacity to appreciate a song and their talent in mimicry. Tench was ready to see in those "savages" men with human qualities, and his first contacts confirmed his opinion. But his description provides little interpretation of "what the natives thought" or saw or understood.

Tench as an Ethnographer?

Tench met "Indians" again a year later, when Phillip decided to try to facilitate interaction with the Aborigines by kidnapping one of them to act as a "go-between." Using hearsay again, Tench evoked the kidnapping scene in a lively style and reported the "most piercing and lamentable cries of distress" (Tench 1793, 139) of the prisoner. "I went with every other person [in Sydney] to see him" (139). He described the man, his physical appearance, "his manliness and sensibility, his curiosity and observation despite the situation, his astonishment at the novelty" (139–40). The tone is positive, the account very detailed, with sustained attention to the feelings of the man and his reactions to this new world; the food, the houses, the bath, images of animals and a print of the Duchess of Cumberland. Among several pictures of people which he recognised as human beings, he identified a large print of a portrait of the Duchess of Cumberland as "woman" (the English word that he had learnt to call the female convicts). He pointed to and spoke about several plates of birds and animals but they must not have been only ones he was familiar with since this included an elephant and a rhinoceros (140). The first Aboriginal words pronounced appear in the text – *Ben-gà-dee* for "ornament", *Weè-rong* for "Sydney". Tench's description then turned to Phillip's expedition, which intended to show the Aboriginal man to his compatriots in order to "open an intercourse" (140). It did not work.

The man was Arabanoo. Tench gives no indication of his origins. How close Tench was to him we do not know. Tench merely reports Arabanoo's close relations with Phillip and he observes his reactions to British habits and practices (e.g. flogging) and to his own people (e.g. their behaviour toward smallpox victims) as well as his *qualities*: "a portion of gravity and steadiness, a thoughtful countenance," "fidelity and gratitude," "gentle and placable temper" (Tench 1793, 150). Tench underlined his independence of mind, his humour, the fact that he allowed no superiority.

Tench paid attention to Arabanoo but ignored the two young orphan children adopted by the British who would become the real go-betweens: Nanbaree and Abaroo. They were too young to be of interest to him. He paid attention to some new prisoners, kidnapped six months after Arabanoo died of smallpox. Again, his description of the kidnapping is brief; Tench emphasised the physical aspects of the men and their behaviour. He wrote nothing about their origins or their group affiliations. This must be found, rather, in Collins' or Phillip's journals. After Colbee's escape, Tench took great pleasure in describing Baneelon's very strong character: a hot Latin lover, who loved wine, food and women, was very bright and cunning, remarkable for his talent for mimicry and sense of humour, but violent and capable of a terrible temper. Tench tells us that Baneelon was a precious informant: "He willingly communicated information; sang danced and capered: told us all the customs of his country, and all the details of his family economy" (Tench 1793, 160). But Tench did not elaborate on any of these matters. We know that Baneelon had a special relationship with Phillip, but Tench says nothing of his own relationship with him. Was he an informant? A friend? Tench offers fragments of linguistic and ethnographic knowledge. We can guess that he accumulated notes and observations, which finally, he did not use. Perhaps he did know a great deal about Aboriginal society. But he did not report it. Presenting empirical material was not, in fact, his principal aim in writing his text.

Discrepancies of Description: Phillip's Spearing

In an illuminating chapter, Clendinnen reconstructs Aboriginal agency through a reading of the first narratives of Botany Bay. She observes:

> Historians of the episode [of Phillip's spearing] have usually chosen to select one of the accounts – often that of Watkin Tench, who wasn't there but who reads beautifully – to rely on, or have cobbled together bits from several mildly conflicting versions to construct a sufficiently coherent narrative (Clendinnen 2003, 114–5).

But, as she adds, "the difficulty is that while the discrepancies may be trivial, they may not be. Discrepancies need not be sinister. Even honest witnesses can disagree as to actions and sequences, as any traffic cop will tell you. But only the reconstruction of actual action-sequences can bring us closer to Australian intentions" (Clendinnen 2003, 115). Thus, Clendinnen chooses to use Tench's account in a second step, preferring instead to primarily rely on Phillip's and Waterhouse's narratives, since they were both witnesses to the scene. Waterhouse seems very reliable to her: "[He] was there, he had no investment in what happened, as a junior officer he was used to watching closely and getting orders straight, and (unlike Collins) he was not already antagonistic to Phillip's conciliatory enterprise" (118).

We know how important the scene of "Spearing the Governor" (Clendinnen 2003, 110ff.) is in the Australian historical narratives of the foundation years. Many historians have interpreted this event as "an accident" mainly due to the irrational behaviour of an Aboriginal man described in officers' accounts as a "stranger" panicking at Phillip's approach. Similar to Keith Vincent Smith in his book *Bennelong* (2001), Clendinnen proposes another interpretation of the whole scene. She views it as a ritual payback "swiftly organised over a couple of hours and with representatives from the local tribes already fortuitously gathered, where Phillip would face a single spear-throw in penance for his and his people's many offences" (Clendinnen 2003, 124). Baneelon is depicted as the "master of ceremony." He is described as an essential "go-between" acting as a political leader, attempting to take advantage of his privileged relations with the British in general and with Governor Phillip in particular, in order to impose negotiated relations and compensations. The hypothesis of a "ritual payback" would explain Baneelon's attitude: first, the deliberate aloofness of a man with a formal role to perform, and second, the prolonged acting-out of the intimacies he enjoyed with the British intruders. In showing off his familiarity with the whites and his capacity of claiming gifts, he was trying to elevate his position within his own world. In organising a "ritual payback," he was attempting to create a new political arrangement. This is why he refused to give "the special spear" to Phillip, throwing it to a "stranger," apparently in charge of the single spear-throw. To Phillip he gave a throwing-stick instead, and a club to defend himself as required in Aboriginal payback ceremonies. Phillip, however, did not defend himself and instead arrived at the "stranger," his empty hands spread out. The warrior gave signs of agitation and then threw his spear, waited to see it touching its goal, and disappeared in the bush.

The idea of Baneelon organising a "ritual" "fortuitously and in two hours time" on a territory (Manly) that is not his own (Baneelon was a Wangal from Parramatta), with only one spear-throw by another "stranger," could be seriously discussed and possibly challenged. But this is not the purpose here. What is rather interesting here is to analyse Tench's own "reading" of the scene.

Tench wrote this part of his account in 1792 when he was in London. He had his own journal to rely on, and possibly notes by fellow officers and memories of conversations with them.[8] Tench had talked first to the surgeon John White, who first encountered the Aboriginal party in September 1790 on the beach, feasting on a dead whale. White was accompanied by Nanbaree, one of the Aboriginal children adopted eighteen months earlier, serving as translator. For the first time, dialogues are included in Tench's account. This was a common practice in travel accounts of the time, to increase *l'effet de reel* – "reality effects" – by the inclusion of "reconstituted" dialogues. In Tench's narratives, this occurs when a translator (like Nanbaree) enabled a better understanding of Aboriginal words transmitted to Tench by hearsay. These words articulated by Baneelon contained a demand for hatchets.

To know the second part of the story, the "spearing," Tench had to talk to Phillip, Waterhouse, Collins and a seaman, these men being the only participants on the British side. And he was able to recreate, by hearsay, a complex set of interactions in great detail. This reveals his capacity of investigation among his main informants – his fellow officers – and his ability to reconstitute facts and events. Nevertheless, and curiously enough, Tench omitted all details that could shed light on Baneelon's agency and responsibility. He did not link the "stranger" to Baneelon and Colbee and ignored the fact that it was Baneelon who threw the "very special spear" in the direction of "this" stranger. Phillip's narrative questioned Baneelon's attitude – "the behaviour of Baneelon on this occasion is not so easily to be accounted for; he never attempted to interfere when the man took the spear up, or said a single word to prevent him from throwing it" – but to immediately excuse him, "he possibly did not think the spear would be thrown, and the whole was but the business of a moment" (Hunter 1968, 463–4). But Tench ignored the entire matter.

A week later he related another scene in which two "Indians" revealed the name of the culprit: Wil-ee-ma-rin. However, according to Phillip and Collins, it was Baneelon who divulged the name of the culprit (Hunter 1968, 466; Collins 1975, 113), but Tench omitted this detail. (Baneelon added that he had severely beaten the man for the aggression.) Instead, Tench, provides other information:

> These two people inquired kindly how his excellency did, and seemed pleased to hear that he was likely to recover. They said they were

inhabitants of Rose Hill and expressed great dissatisfaction at the number of white men who had settled in their former territories. In consequence of which declaration, the detachment at that post was reinforced on the following day (Tench 1793, 181).

By contrast, Phillip and Collins made no allusion whatsoever to such words critiquing the colonial context. They only considered the individual responsibility of an "irrational savage" (Hunter 1793, 463; Collins 1975, 111).

Why did Tench introduce in the conclusion of the description he gave of "spearing the governor" a sudden allusion to colonial violence? Who reported to him those Aboriginal words expressing anger against the whites? Was it his friend Dawes, the young astronomer of the First Fleet, the most sympathetic to the Aborigines, who refused in December 1790 to participate in the first punitive expedition set up under the command of Tench? According to Tench, Dawes was with the chaplain and Abaroo on a boat when they talked to the two "Indians" on 14 September 1790. But why wasn't there any allusion made to this in Phillip's journal when military measures were said to be taken? Why, in relating the whole scene of "spearing the governor," did Tench refuse to consider the meaning of Aboriginal actions and, in particular, the possible responsibility of Baneelon? All these questions remain open and reveal how difficult it is to understand Watkin Tench and his narrative.

Clendinnen, reflecting a common approach in Australian scholarship, remarks:

> What made Tench incomparable among good observers is that he treated each encounter with the strangers as a detective story: "This is what they did. What might they have meant by doing that?" This glinting curiosity is uniquely his. (Compare him with John Hunter, who also watches keenly, but at a condescending distance: the squire watching his beagles.) Tench always saw the Australians as fellow humans (Clendinnen 2003, 59).

Like many historians, Clendinnen uses a surprisingly sentimental approach toward Tench. Depicted as a "likeable" man," she praises him for his human qualities, which supposedly provided him with the capacity for a better understanding of the "other," the Aborigines (Clendinnen 2003, 58). But as we have seen, this explanation is far too simple. Tench, in fact, is an ambivalent person – at least, ambivalence emerges as a central feature in my analysis of his narrative.

Ambivalence saturates the form of description itself. Tench wants to observe and to relate facts "simply as they happened." He also wants to write "for the amusement of the public." To do that he must make choices, he needs to construct his narrative so that it reaches the audience. Tench's alternatives are not "science" or "fiction," but rather the question of the mode and purpose of his descriptions.

He could have described what he saw or what he learned from the society he confronted, but he chose rather to shed light on "the colonial encounter" as such, and more precisely on "specific events," which he and his fellow officers considered unavoidable in a narrative of Port Jackson's first years, even though he was not there when most of these "events" took place. The best quality of Tench as an informant is his capacity for enquiring among his fellow officers about interactions they had with Aboriginal people. This necessitated a kind of collective detective work. His narrative, being one of the first to be published in London with Hunter's account, gave, through the description of "important events," the impression of an "official history" of the foundational years. In that sense, as Fitzhardinge stresses, Tench can be considered the first Australian historian. But his aim was different. Tench wanted to be recognised as an author, and his narrative epitomises the typical ambivalence of the travel account of the time – between the will for observation and the desire for adventure.

Tench's ambivalence is also perceptible in his view of Aboriginal society. As an anti-Rousseauist, he refused to defend the state of nature as an enviable state and denounced the misery of the Aboriginal way of life. Aboriginal society was, according to him, low on the scale of humanity. The cause lay not in the nature of the people, but in the context in which they lived (cf. Douglas this volume). As with many philosophers of his time, Tench explains the "primitive state of nature" by external and contingent causes: climate, natural environment and local history, and refuses to see in the Aborigines only brutes and savages. Part of a common humanity, these societies like any others could be improved through the triumph of civilisation, good order and the Christian message.

Tench obviously had a strong sympathy toward individuals such as Arabanoo, Baneelon, Colbee and some unnamed women. He was keen to defend the human qualities of his friends, courage, honesty, pride, intelligence, skill and so on. He was obviously also fascinated by their culture, their beliefs and their practices. The effects of smallpox horrified him. He condemned convicts' wrongdoings and felt unease with military violence. But he was also a soldier proud of his duty and convinced of the necessity of colonisation. All these contradictions are encapsulated in his narrative. In Tench's account, colonial violence erupts on the surface at several occasions, but the author refuses to speculate on its meaning. He refuses to consider the possible role of Baneelon in the "spearing of the governor." He transforms the punitive expedition he leads into a farce. By the end of his narrative, after an allusion made to the first blind military retaliation following a potato theft, he takes the readers to a safer subject, an expedition in the search of a river south of Rose Hill (Parramatta) and the description of Aboriginals providing help to soldiers and sailors (Tench 1793, ch. 15). He concludes with some general reflections on the "Indians" and on "primitive societies." In using such a narrative strategy, Tench carefully avoids exposing the effects of colonisation on Aboriginal people, even though he seems to be conscious of what is going on. In the first place, he wants to become a popular author and write a travel account "for the amusement of the public."

References

Atkinson, Alan

1997 *The Europeans in Australia: A History – The Beginning* (vol. 1). Melbourne: Oxford University Press.

Carter, Paul

1988 *The Road to Botany Bay. An Exploration of Landscape and History.* New York: Alfred A. Knopf.

Clendinnen, Inga

2003 *Dancing with Strangers.* Melbourne: Text Publishing.

Collins, David

1975 [1798] *An Account of the English Colony in New South Wales, with Remarks on the Dispositions, Customs, Manners, etc, of the Native Inhabitants of that Country*, vol. 1, ed. B.H. Fletcher. Terrey Hills, NSW: A.H. and A.W. Reed, in association with the Royal Australian Historical Society. First pub. in 1798–1802 by T. Cadell & W. Davis, London.

Cook, James, and James King

1785 *A Voyage to the Pacific Ocean, undertaken by the Command of His Majesty, for making discoveries in the Northern Hemisphere. Performed under the direction of Captains Cook, Clerke and Gore, in His Majesty's ships the Resolution and Discovery, in the year 1776, 1777, 1778, 1779 and 1980.* 2nd ed., 3 vols (with Atlas); vols 1 & 2 written by Captain James Cook, vol. 3 by Captain James King. London: Printed by H. Hughs, for G. Nicol, Bookseller to His Majesty, in the Strand; and T. Cadell, in the Strand. London: G. Nicol and T. Cadell.

Currey, John E.B.

2000 *David Collins: A Colonial Life.* Carlton South, Vic.: Melbourne University Press.

Dampier, William

1998 [1697] *A New Voyage Round the World: The Journal of an English Buccaneer.* London: Hummingbird Press.

Dening, Greg

1994 The theatricality of observing and being observed: Eighteenth-century Europe "discovers" the ? century "Pacific." In *Implicit Understandings: Observing, Reporting, and Reflecting on the Encounters between Europeans and Other Peoples in the Early Modern Era*, ed. Stuart B. Schwartz, 451–83. Cambridge: Cambridge University Press.

Edwards, Gavin

2000 Watkin Tench and the cold track of narrative. *Southerly* 60 (3): 74–93.

2001 ed., *Letters from Revolutionary France: by Watkin Tench (1796)*. Cardiff: University of Wales Press.

Flannery, Tim F., ed.

1996 *1788: Comprising A Narrative of the Expedition to Botany Bay and A Complete Account of the Settlement at Port Jackson / Watkin Tench*. First published as 2 separate vols. Melbourne: Text Publishing.

2000 *Two classic tales of Australian exploration: 1788 by Watkin Tench / Life and Adventures, by John Nicol*. Melbourne: Text Publishing.

Frost, Alan

1987 *Arthur Phillip, 1738–1814: His Voyaging*. Melbourne: Oxford University Press.

Hunter, John

1968 [1793] Narratives from the official despatches of Governor Phillip. In *An Historical Journal of Events at Sydney and at Sea 1787–1792, with Further Accounts of Governor Arthur Phillip, Lieutenant P.G. King, and Lieutenant H.L. Ball, by John Hunter*, ed. John Bach, 305–14. [Sydney]: Angus & Robertson in association with the Royal Australian Historical Society.

Le Huenen, Roland

1990 Qu'est-ce qu'un récit de voyage? In *Les modèles du récit de voyage: Littérales*, no. 7, ed. Marie-Christine Gomez-Géraud, 7–26. Nanterre: Centre de Recherches du Département de Français de Paris X-Nanterre.

Linon-Chipon, Sophie, Véronique Magri-Mourgues, and Sarga Moussa, eds.

1998 *Miroirs de textes: Récits de voyage et intertextualité*. Nice: Publications de la Faculté des Lettres, Arts et Sciences Humaines de l'Université de Nice Sophia Antipolis.

Mitchell, Adrian

1994 Watkin Tench's sentimental enclosures. *Australian and New Zealand Studies in Canada* 11 (June): 23–33.

Smith, Bernard

1984 *European Vision and the South Pacific*. Sydney: Harper & Row. Second rev. ed.; first ed. 1960.

Smith, Keith Vincent

2001 *Bennelong: The Coming In of the Eora, Sydney Cove, 1788–1792*. East Roseville, NSW: Kangaroo Press.

Tench, Watkin

1789 *A Narrative of the Expedition to Botany Bay: with an Account of New South Wales, Its Productions, Inhabitants, &c. : to which is Subjoined, a List of the Civil and Military Establishments at Port Jackson*. London: Printed for J. Debrett.

1793 *A Complete Account of the Settlement at Port Jackson, in New South Wales: Including an Accurate Description of the Situation of the Colony; of the Natives; and of Its Natural Productions; taken on the spot*. London: G. Nicol and J. Sewell.

1938 *A Narrative of the Expedition to Botany Bay. By Captain Watkin Tench of the Marines*. Reprint of the 3rd ed., London, 1789; with an introductory note by C.H. Bertie. Sydney: The Australian Limited Editions Society.

1979 *Sydney's First Four Years: Being a reprint of A Narrative of the Expedition to Botany Bay and A Complete Account of the Settlement at Port Jackson, 1788–1791 by Captain Watkin Tench;* with introduction and annotations by L.F. Fitzhardinge; reprint of 1961 ed. Sydney: Library of Australian History.

Viviès, Jean

1999 *Le récit de voyage en Angleterre au XVIIIe siècle: De l'inventaire à l'invention*. Toulouse: Presses Universitaires du Mirail.

Weil, Françoise

1984 La relation de voyage: document anthropologique ou texte littéraire? In *Histoires de l'anthropologie: XVIe–XIXe siècles,* ed. Britta Rupp-Eisenreich, 55–65. Paris: Meridiens Klinksieck.

Willey, Keith

1979 *When the Sky Fell Down: The Destruction of the Tribes of the Sydney Region, 1788–1850's*. Sydney and London: Collins.

Notes

[1] A few short letters are on microfilm in the Mitchell Library, Sydney.

[2] The original French reads: *"sans loi ... qui allie à la finalité documentaire la séduction du plaisir et du divertissement, et à laquelle les voyageurs apportent des réponses diversement dosées selon qu'ils privilégient, dans leurs écrits, tantôt la description généralement tournée vers l'information géographique, tantôt le récit potentiellement riche en aventure"* (Le Huenen 1990, 14). Literary studies of voyaging accounts have expanded considerably in number over the last twenty years. Notable works consulted for this study include: Viviès (1999); Weil (1984); and Linon-Chipon et. al. (1998).

[3] This question is still open and needs further investigation. Fitzhardinge argued that "in the absence of manuscripts, the establishment of the text presents no problems. As all the editions of the *Narrative* appeared before Tench's return, they cannot have been revised by him, though some additional matter was included in the third" (Tench 1979, xxvi).

[4] It was reprinted in 1824 and again in 1954 by Angus and Robertson.

[5] See Paul Carter's discussion about Tench's attitude towards Cook (1988, 36–9). Carter argues that Tench, in his successive judgements, "hardly proceeds empirically. He defines and redefines his position dialectically – in terms of and against Cook's earlier descriptions" (37). "His outbursts are increasingly theatrical. [...] For all this, though, Tench's aim is clear. It is to dethrone Cook and substitute his own experience as authoritative" (38). Nevertheless, two things should be pointed out. On the one hand, Tench has practical experience of the field in Botany Bay, especially when he and his party find themselves in serious danger, trapped in the mud while running after Aborigines. Fear or anger could also explain Tench's outbursts against Cook's inadequate descriptions. On the other hand, Tench allowed himself to be increasingly critical of Cook precisely because he acquired a better and practical knowledge of the field in the area of Botany Bay. He progressively lost the respect he had when he was first assigned to read the already famous navigator. But I am not sure we can assert that he could really pretend to "dethrone" Cook and substitute his own experience as authoritative as he was only a simple mariner and he knew that his narrative could not compete with Cook's prestigious and official one.

[6] The term *"Indians"*, derived from the experience of the Americas, was more generally applied to indigenous people in this period.

[7] In French in the original text: *"De toutes les instructions propres à l'homme, celle qu'il acquiert le plus tard, et le plus difficilement, est la raison même"* (original source of quotation unknown).

[8] No narrative on the Botany Bay experience had been published in 1792 since Tench's first volume and Phillip's account. Hunter was preparing the publication of his own journal with compilation of Phillip's official papers.

Chapter 8

The Art of Encounter: Verisimilitude in the Imaginary Exploration of Interior New Guinea, 1725–1876

Chris Ballard

Jamais au Spectateur n'offrez rien d'incroyable.

Le Vrai peut quelquefois n'estre pas vraisemblable.

(*L'Art poétique*, Boileau, III.47–8)[1]

Encounters, Factual and Fictional

There is an enduring paradox in the art of writing about cross-cultural encounters: in trying to convey something of the alterity or strangeness of an encounter, writers invariably fall back upon a limited range of entirely familiar conventions, shared understandings that enable them to convey the meaning of the encounter to a like-minded or like-cultured audience. In order to be represented, difference must first be recognisable (Fothergill 1994, 40). Consequently, as Stephen Greenblatt proposes, Western narratives of encounter with native others often tell us less about those native others than they do about Western practices of representation (1991, 7):

> Travellers do not simply record what they see. They travel with a purpose. They journey with preconceptions. They observe and write according to established models, having these in mind even when they wish to query or depart from them (Youngs 1994, 209).

Bronwen Douglas and others have argued for the importance, and demonstrated the viability, of recovering indigenous or subaltern presence from Western texts, but our ability to attempt this sort of reading must be predicated on some prior understanding of the structured quality of these texts (Douglas 1998, and this volume; Beer 1996, 325; Guha 1983). Access to ethnographic insight and indigenous agency in these texts requires a form of reading that remains alert to the mediating effects of these representational conventions, and an acknowledgement that they are not "easily corrected for" (Greenblatt 1991, 7). "The things to look at," as Edward Said advises of Orientalist texts, "are style, figures of speech, setting, narrative devices, historical and social circumstances, not the correctness of the representation nor its fidelity to some great original" (1985, 21).

What I want to explore here is the possibility that an analysis of fictional accounts of exploration may offer a more ready means of identifying these representational conventions than consideration of the seemingly sober narratives of "real" exploration. Like engravings and other forms of visual imagery, explorer narratives establish their own "canons of authenticity" and their own lexicons of textual emotion through the "constant repetition of vaguely familiar scenes" (Steiner 1995, 224). The seduction of factual narratives, operating through the apparently singular reality of the events that they describe, tends to obscure or mask the familiarising role of these conventions, through which a series of unconsciously anticipated routines have the effect of investing the narrative with an air of authority. Travel fiction, however, is unencumbered by the requirement to report, by the exigencies of events or by the need to explain – although we shall see how each of these requirements is skilfully deployed in fictional narratives purporting to offer accounts of real encounters. A further and particularly intriguing feature of cross-cultural encounters is that these same representational conventions, reflecting a series of preconceptions and assumptions about difference, come to play a significant role in structuring the nature of the encounters themselves. An attention to fictional narratives of encounter and exploration thus potentially offers access both to the rhetorical strategies of textual authority and to the presumptions of actual explorers.

Popular travel fiction, quite evidently, draws upon factual accounts of exploration, often following closely the trajectories of explorer heroes and repeating details of the new lands encountered and their inhabitants. To this extent, it might be said to have "promoted, spread and entrenched the assumptions and images emerging from the scientific works" (Richards 1989, 90). But, in equal measure, travel and scientific accounts have endorsed the powerful imaginary canons of fiction: "such components of travel accounts as 'style, plot, [and] the character of the narrator-traveller bear a remarkably close relationship' to those that occur in 'strictly fictional' works" (Batten 1990, 132, quoting Hans-Joachim Possin). This recursive relationship has been further cemented through the assumed pedagogic value of adventure fiction, first affirmed by Rousseau, who actively promoted *Robinson Crusoe* as a fundamental and edifying text for the children of the Enlightenment (Green 1989, 37). Travel fiction, subsequently, could be considered part of the requisite baggage of any educated Western traveller. By the 1850s, what I refer to here as a European "colonial imaginary" for Africa (as a form of shorthand for collective representations that traversed public and professional domains) was widely available and commonly understood.[2]

It was found in children's books, in Sunday School tracts, in the popular press. Its major affirmations were the "common knowledge" of the educated classes. Thereafter, when new generations of administrators went to Africa, they went with a prior impression of what they would find. Most often they found it, and in their writings in turn confirmed the older image – or at most altered it only slightly (Philip Curtin 1963, as quoted by Fothergill 1994, 46–7).

Some scepticism about the fixity and impermeability of the categories of fictional, travel and scientific forms of narrative is thus in order. For the Western reading public of the late nineteenth century, "travel literature, ethnography and adventure novels were often consumed indiscriminately" (Dixon 2001, 102). Uncertainty persists, and has evidently reigned amongst writers in each genre, as to the historical or veridical status of many narratives of adventure. François Leguat's account of his seemingly fantastic voyage to the island of Rodrigues was alternately regarded as a truthful source or derided as fiction, from its publication in 1707 until the 1980s – currently, his tale is held to be largely factual (Rennie 1995, 70–3). In some respects, it may be more instructive to conceive of a veridical continuum of narrative forms with respect to historical events of exploration, or of a dense textual skein that extends between fiction, travel accounts and scientific writing, all of which reference, play off and plagiarise each other.

The European exploration of interior New Guinea – the "last unknown" of Karl Shapiro's poem and Gavin Souter's history of New Guinea exploration (Shapiro 1944; Souter 1963; Ballard 2006)[3] – came late in the long history of European expansion and its attendant literatures. If the narrative strategies common to factual and fictional accounts of travel had already been honed with reference to the Americas, Africa and sundry remote islands of the Indian and Atlantic oceans, then it might be argued that interior New Guinea, as the "last colonial imaginary" (Garnier 2002), was subjected to a more knowing form of literary exploration. Through consideration of a series of fictional explorations of New Guinea published between 1725 and 1876, it is possible to identify a range of rhetorical strategies that correspond to different narrative genres, and to track the resurgence in a novel form of the timeworn strategy of verisimilitude.

Verisimilitude, derived from the Latin *verisimilis* and cognate to the French *vraisemblance* and German *wahrscheinlich*, refers to the semblance of reality and specifically, as the *New Oxford Dictionary* insists, to "the quality of a representation that causes it to appear true." But the reality effect demanded of verisimilitude often exceeds the standards that we expect of the real or the true. Without the comfort of proof, it must convince through appeal to a logic of the real, to an anticipated, prefigured understanding of the semblance of the truth. The art of verisimilitude, then, is the art of persuasion, of the deployment of rhetorical devices that convey a sense of the real which improves on the poverty of reality itself. The art of the encounter narrative, whether fictional or factual, consists of strategies that achieve this reality effect for an audience that is already familiar with the anticipated categories of difference.

Verisimilitude in the Fictional Encounter – A Brief History

Histories of a European tradition of travel fiction conventionally hinge upon the publication in 1719 of Daniel Defoe's *Robinson Crusoe*, as the defining moment in the evolution of the genre.[4] Prior to Defoe, fictional interest in the exotic appears to have been largely utopian in mode, adopting locations such as the Americas principally for their value as conveniently distant settings for satirical critiques of contemporary European society. Thomas More's *Utopia* (1516–19), William Shakespeare's *The Tempest* (1611), and Henry Neville's *Isle of Pines* (1668) are amongst the best-known and most influential texts of this earlier period. By the late seventeenth century, travel narratives were increasingly replacing romances in popular taste, and Defoe's realist narrative of shipwreck and redemption through labour struck a powerful chord and spawned an entire genre, the Robinsonade, in its wake (Green 1989; Rennie 1995, 68). The influence on the emergent colonial imaginary of *Robinson Crusoe* and Defoe's other novels was immense, possibly exceeding that of the real voyage accounts of the period in their broad appeal and in the power of their imagery. Much as Defoe had drawn upon the voyage narratives of William Dampier, published between 1697 and 1709, and the tale of the marooned sailor, Alexander Selkirk, published in 1712, for the detail of his setting for *Robinson Crusoe,* so too the authors of subsequent Robinsonades turned to contemporary travel literature for inspiration.

During the course of the eighteenth century, the heroic figure at the centre of the Robinsonade came to take the form of the gentleman naturalist or scientist, with the British and French scientific expeditions to the Pacific supplying much of the necessary material (Batten 1990). Michael Bravo has demonstrated how "the language of accuracy and precision" became employed during this period "to scrutinize, combine, discard, evaluate, praise or criticize the scientific conduct and observations of travellers" (1999, 181). In step with this trend toward investing authority in the rhetorical vocabulary of precision, fictional travel became increasingly marked by the detail of its description of exotic places and peoples: "the romantic impulse to tell (and subsequently rework) Crusoe's tale [was] counterpointed by a stress on verisimilitude – to minimize, even conceal, the impropriety of fiction" (Bristow 1991, 97).[5] The digression to describe, often at great length, the characteristics of flora and fauna, or the morals of the indigenous inhabitants emerged as a staple element of the eighteenth and nineteenth-century adventure novel (Adams 1983, 273).

Although the Antipodes had furnished utopian authors with a suitably obscure setting since at least as early as Hall's *Mundus* (1607), Pacific exploration during the eighteenth and nineteenth centuries saw the region established as the preferred setting for Robinsonades (Dunmore 1988, 9; Green 1989, 46). The heroes of Wyss' *Swiss Family Robinson* (1812), Marryat's *Masterman Ready* (1970 [1841]) and Ballantyne's *Coral Island* (1858) all found themselves on islands located more or less loosely in the Pacific. In keeping with the general observation that adventure fiction has tended to follow closely on the heels of explorer narratives, it should present no surprise to find that New Guinea featured only scarcely in fiction prior to the middle of the nineteenth century.

New Guinea, the "Last Unknown"

While Europeans had been aware of New Guinea since at least 1511, exploration before the mid-nineteenth century consisted of little more than sporadic landings for water and victuals, or attempts to map routes circumventing the island.[6] Other than two short-lived and unsuccessful settlements, the British Fort Coronation at Doreh Bay (1793–95) and the Dutch Fort du Bus at Triton Bay (1828–36), there were almost no protracted engagements with the indigenous communities of New Guinea, and no forays beyond the narrow coastal strip. Perhaps the first sustained attempt to map portions of the coastal mainland was Captain Blackwood's surveying mission on HMS *Fly* to the Papuan coast between 1842 and 1846 (Jukes 1847). Fragments of the coastline had already been mapped in some detail (see Wichmann 1909–12), but this usually reflected little more than the duration and extent of a passing ship's contact with the island, rather than a direct commission to chart the coastal topography.

A degree of frustration at their inability to know New Guinea beyond its coastline was evident amongst navigators by the 1840s. In a widely cited passage, Joseph Beete Jukes, an officer under Blackwood on HMS *Fly*, speculated on the character of this unseen interior:

> I know of no part of the world, the exploration of which is so flattering to the imagination, so likely to be fruitful in interesting results, whether to the naturalist, the ethnologist or the geographer, and altogether so well calculated to gratify the enlightened curiosity of an adventurous explorer, as the interior of New Guinea. New Guinea! The very mention of being taken into the interior of New Guinea sounds like being allowed to visit some of the enchanted regions of the Arabian Nights, so dim an atmosphere of obscurity rests at present on the wonders it probably contains (Jukes 1847, 291).

Thomas Huxley, a member of the next surveying expedition to the Papuan coast, in HMS *Rattlesnake* under the command of Captain Owen Stanley during 1849–50, was equally sure in his view of New Guinea as:

> a grand continent, shut out from intercourse with the civilized world—more completely than China, and as rich if not richer in things

rare and strange. The wide and noble rivers open wide their mouths inviting us to enter. All that is required is coolness, judgment, perseverance, to reap a rich harvest of knowledge and perhaps of more material profit (Huxley 1936, 129).

That great harvester of knowledge, Alfred Russel Wallace, provided the first widely read account of the main island of New Guinea to be written on the basis of personal experience, in his enormously influential account of eight years spent in island Southeast Asia between 1854 and 1862. *The Malay Archipelago*, first published in 1869, ushered in a golden era of scientific exploration in New Guinea, as Wallace was followed during the 1870s by a wave of naturalist explorers and collectors consciously emulating his feats: Nikolai Miklouho-Maclay, Adolf Bernhard Meyer, C.B.H. van Rosenberg, Odoardo Beccari and Luigi Maria d'Albertis amongst them. D'Albertis, in particular, pioneered the exploration of the interior through his navigation of the Fly River on three successive visits between 1875 and 1877 (D'Albertis 1880). Collectively, Wallace and the second wave of explorers of the 1870s inspired a new round of fictional adventure writing, novel in terms of both its focus on the last unknown of New Guinea, and its particular emphasis on what might be termed "naturalist realism" as a narrative strategy.[7] Interior New Guinea presented a familiar fictional setting whose time had come, as implied by James Stanley, writing as Julian Thomas, during his passage along the coastline in 1883:

> The vastness of New Guinea ... makes it an attractive field for the traveller. As in our youth we believed in the African Mountains of the Moon, and the strange races which lived beyond them, so in New Guinea, the unknown land, we are ready to admit that great marvels and wonders may be hidden in the midst of its vast mountains (Thomas 1886, 377).

The Premised Land: Imagining Interior New Guinea

During the middle of the nineteenth century, as New Guinea began to impinge upon the European imaginary through the gathering tide of exploration reports with their teasing reflections on an unattainable interior, the first handful of fictional works speculated freely on what lay beyond the beach. As a space whose boundaries had already been described, the interior presented an irresistible canvas for the colonial imaginary, and the contemporary exploration of the interiors of Africa, Asia and the Amazon Basin supplied many of the elements of the interior imagined for New Guinea. Snow-capped mountains and towering forests, miniature humans or pygmies in the company of gigantic animals, and the promise of untold wealth and lost kingdoms were easily transposed from one interior to the other.[8]

A review of fictional adventures in New Guinea published between the 1830s and 1870s suggests something of the range of sources of inspiration for this imagined interior, in addition to those details gleaned from the naturalist explorers.[9] Few, if any, of the works considered here are well known and this perhaps reflects the signal absence of literary merit amongst them. They are all obviously and often inelegantly derivative, but that is precisely the attraction that they hold for this study. While I touch here upon a number of the published contributions to this first round of fictional exploration of interior New Guinea, attention is focused on the two most widely read and circulated novels: Louis Trégance's *Adventures in New Guinea* (1876) and Captain John Lawson's *Wanderings in the Interior of New Guinea* (1875a).[10] The first, a classic example of the meta-narrative of moral redemption for children, toys with the vocabulary of precision but wears its fabulous colours openly. The second introduces a much more serious challenge to the distinction between fictional and factual through its reference to the conventions of exploration, as practice and as narrative.

The earliest work of obvious fiction in which some part of the narrative is located explicitly in New Guinea appears to be Daniel Defoe's *A New Voyage Round the World* (1725), in which the unnamed author leads an expedition crossing the Pacific from west to east. Pausing on Guam while en route from Manila, the author clearly anticipated New Guinea and its surrounding islands as lands available for European discovery:

> And now, if ever, I expected to do something by Way of Discovery; I knew very well there were few, if any, had ever steer'd that Course; or that if they had, they had given very little Account of their Travels (1725, 120).

Approaching a "vast Tract of Land … which we call Nova Guinea" (1725, 121), the expedition's ships anchor close to shore, sending out boats to seek water and fresh food. In keeping with his general strategy of cautious realism (Scrimgeour 1963), Defoe dwells without great elaboration on a lengthy sequence of contacts with New Guinea's inhabitants, described initially as naked "black Creatures" (1725, 123) and later as "black, or rather of a tawny dark brown; their Hair long, but curling in very handsome Rings" (132); a "peaceable, quiet, inoffensive People" (131). Two young women are captured but clothed and then returned to their people during a foray upriver on small boats, an act of generosity which summons an equally generous response from their relatives, who provide the expedition with "Provisions, Cocoa Nuts, Roots, Cabbages, and a great Variety of Things which we knew little of" (1725, 129). Despite this more extended contact, the settlements prove too distant to be described, and the problem of translation precludes even the identification of names; the wide river explored by the expedition is named only by analogy, "being as broad as the Thames is about Fox-Hall" (127).[11] What Defoe seeks to convey here, as he does in Captain Singleton's earlier crossing of the interior of Africa (Defoe 1972 [1720]), is not the exotic specificity of New Guinea or its people but rather its general suitability for commerce.[12]

For more than a century after Defoe's *New Voyage*, New Guinea does not appear to have featured obviously in Western fiction. Scarcely touched by Captain Cook, who did no more than set foot briefly on a south coast beach in 1770 (Ballard 2008), New Guinea was passed over for other, more attractive and better-understood settings. The next series of fictional explorers were Americans engaged in commercial exploration of the southwest Pacific though, here, the genre was pioneered by authors who also travelled, blending their own experiences with those of others, often through the pen of metropolitan ghostwriters. American interest in New Guinea appears to have developed as their whalers first entered the waters around New Guinea in 1799; whaling activity increased through the 1830s, peaking at about 1840 (Gray 1999, 24). Amongst the whalers active during this heyday was a Captain Benjamin Morrell.

Morrell's account of his commercial voyages to the Pacific during the early 1830s was vigorous in its promotion of the southwest Pacific as a "golden harvest which now awaits the sickle of enterprise" (B. Morrell 1970 [1832], 461). Almost certainly, Morrell did visit the north coast of New Guinea and various islands of the Bismarck Archipelago in 1830, kidnapping several inhabitants, whom he later exhibited in the United States. Yet his narrative, together with that of his wife and voyaging companion, Abby Morrell (A. Morrell 1970 [1833]), appears to have been extensively embellished, largely as a means of maintaining the interest of the hapless backers of Morrell's financially ruinous expeditions.[13] When he ran out of locations on known maps that could be named after his friends and masters in New York, Morrell simply invented islands. Both narratives tended to excess, describing six volcanoes erupting in concert along the New Guinea coast, and flocks of four or five hundred birds of paradise flying between islands. However, husband and wife were outdone by the account of Morrell's final voyage to New Guinea, as captain of the *Margaret Oakley* in 1834. Written after Morrell's death by one of his crew, Thomas Jefferson Jacobs (1844), this remarkable work tacks bewilderingly between ethnographic detail on one hand, including recognisable illustrations of New Guinean artefacts and regular insertions of word lists, and irrepressible fancy on the other: marble obelisks, abandoned cities and baboons abound.[14]

The New Guinea adventures of John Coulter (1847) represent a further degree of fictionalisation of what may have been the events of real voyages. Lengthy accounts of interactions with the inhabitants of New Ireland, New Hanover, New Britain and mainland New Guinea at MacCluer Gulf and along the south coast provide an excess of ethnographic detail. The presence and intervention of no less than three white castaways at different points in the narrative enables Coulter to become involved in local conflict and to observe at close range the lives of members of New Guinea's two races, the Papuans and the Horraforas. A profusion of recognisable names for islands and bays, as well as for known trading vessels and real captains, serves to anchor Coulter's voyage. Yet none of the vessels or their captains prove to have been in the vicinity of New Guinea during 1835, the year of Coulter's visit, and neither the ethnographic detail nor the numerous gongs with which the Papuans signal to each other now ring true.

Charles Beach's *Andrew Deverel: The History of an Adventurer in New Guinea*, published in 1863, purported to represent events that had taken place during the 1850s.[15] The preface follows closely the "strategies of endorsement" for travel narratives described by Gillian Beer (1996, 323), advertising the narrative's claim to truth and neatly declining to declare it either strictly fictional or factual:

> The author is an entirely unlearned man, unaccustomed to literature, but he has actually been in all the scenes he describes, and has taken part in the adventures. If he can excite the curiosity and call the attention of the commercial world to the riches and unexplored resources of New Guinea, he will have conferred a benefit. That beautiful country offers a virgin field to enterprise which would well repay the dangers and difficulties of exploration.
>
> May 11, 1863 (Beach 1863, preface [n.p.]).

In an otherwise conventional tale of love lost, and the search for fame and fortune with which to win it back, Andrew Deverel, the novel's American protagonist, finances a gold-seeking expedition bound for New Guinea. Deverel's motives were self-consciously historical and literary:

> He knew the attention of mankind could not be turned upon New Guinea without some notice being taken of the one who had first drawn attention of others to it. He would be making a mark on the world that would last for ages. He would some time have his name written on the pages of the history of a country. He would be doing something towards making himself worthy of the one he loved, and would be winning a name that even her proud father might envy (1863, 115).

A brig carrying the gold-seekers from San Francisco via Manila anchors off the northeast coast of New Guinea, and short forays are made to shore.[16] A party of shooters seeking birds of paradise is ambushed by Papuan warriors, and the brig and its well-armed crew then approach the mouth of a wide river in order to deal out vengeance (this is surely the same river described by Defoe, though the hardening of Western attitudes towards Papuans, real and imaginary, in the intervening centuries is instructive). The attacking Papuans, massed on rafts, are decimated by cannon and rifle fire, and their white castaway leader is captured. When the brig is forced to enter the river to avoid a storm at sea, the battle rages on, with much loss of (largely Papuan) life. The expedition, accompanied by its white captive, is ultimately forced to retreat to Manila, where the author nurses the regret that "[h]is name would never be written in the future history of New Guinea" (1863, 170).

The sources for both Coulter and Beach were almost certainly other American writings, including those of the Morrells and perhaps the earlier narrative by Amasa Delano (1817, Chapter IV) of his voyage to New Guinea with MacCluer on the *Panther* in 1791. Nothing in the ethnographic detail or in the descriptions of coastal New Guinea resembles the principal contemporary source available to Beach in English author George Windsor Earl's *The Native Races of the Indian Archipelago: Papuans* (1853). As with Jukes and Huxley, Beach's narrative is confined to the coastal strip, and the interior is little more than a site for a vague and unbounded imaginary of gold and other forms of wealth. Beach may also initially have been influenced by Edgar Allan Poe's *Narrative of Arthur Gordon Pym of Nantucket* (1975 [1837]), but then Poe himself was directly inspired by Morrell, to the extent of borrowing or digesting many pages of text from the latter's voyage account.

If this sub-genre of American commercial voyagers published between the 1830s and 1860s stuck relatively closely to real sources and real voyages to New Guinea, a subsequent Australian strain of New Guinea explorer fiction was content to play more loosely with a New Guinea setting. Edward Cole's short, satirical pamphlet of 1873, *Account of a Race of Human Beings with Tails; discovered by Mr. Jones, the traveller, in the interior of New Guinea*, was written in flagrant self-advertisement for the wares of his Melbourne bookshop, and contained:

> the startling announcement which has just reached us of the discovery by a traveller of a race of men in the interior of New Guinea still possessing tails of unmistakable length, thereby once more triumphantly demonstrating to the world that the deductions of honest, laborious, scientific men are, as a rule, verified by later discoveries (1982 [c.1873], 4).

If his text had no pretensions to realism, Cole was nevertheless alert to the contemporary vogue for New Guinea's interior, and to the scope for pricking the vanity of metropolitan scholars and their learned societies. Of the claim of his traveller, a Mr. Jones, Cole wrote that,

> were it not for the high standing and well known integrity of the traveller, and high character of the "Calcutta Anthropological Review" – to the proprietors of which he has imparted the startling information – we should still doubt; but, of course, with such authorities before us, strange as is the fact our doubts must cease (1982 [c.1873], 5).

Gold was very much at the heart of the New Guinea imagined by Marcus Clarke in his short story "Gipsies of the sea, or the island of gold," which was serialised in the *Melbourne Herald* during December 1874. Clarke's band of gentleman adventurers declared that "[t]he only place left to be explored is New Guinea," as they embarked for "a new Eldorado in that mysterious Papua which has so long defied the conquering races of the west" (Clarke 1982 [1874], 13, 15).[17] The Americas were obviously the model for this imagined interior:

> This barbaric coast-line of New Guinea, inhabited only by savage monsters of huge stature, and unappeasable ferocity, is really the boundary of a great empire, the Saturn ring of a new planet. The interior of the vast island-continent which stretches away to the eastward is a fertile land more civilised than was ancient Mexico, more wild in religious extravagance than was ancient Egypt, more rich in metals than was the "Ophir" of Solomon. It is the Eldorado of Raleigh; the "Land of Gold" of which Cortez dreamed (1982 [1874], 21).

The centre of this fabulous island was dominated by

> the great Temple of Kitzpolchi, God of the Smoking Heart ... Here are still carried on those awful rites which horrified the stalwart Spaniards, and caused the destruction of the Palace of Axayacau. From this terrible centre radiate the tribal circles in ever-lessening civilisation until the forest-girt coasts give birth only to the uncouth and savage giants who – ignorant alike of religion and humanity – know but one law, to "kill the stranger" (23).

Clarke's deliberately overwrought romance, in which all but the narrator met grisly ends in pursuit of love or wealth, was a moral fable on the perils threatening young Australian men of the day, written shortly after the disastrous loss of life in 1872 during the shipwreck of an ill-fated gold-seeking expedition to New Guinea on the *Maria* (Maiden 2000). His vision of a lost civilisation at the heart of a continent of savages preceded by a decade Rider Haggard's *King Solomon's Mines* (1885), though I would argue that this suggests not so much a reverse flow of influence, from New Guinea to Africa, as a shared debt to a common imaginary.

There is little intertextual reference and considerable thematic diversity amongst this early fictional corpus on New Guinea, reflecting the absence of established conventions specific to this new field and the limited agreement evident even in explorer narratives about the ways in which New Guinea might be represented. Even as they imagined the unknown interior, authors returned repeatedly to the established sources, modelling their accounts of New Guinea on African, Asian or American precedents; thus, Morrell writes of wigwams and Jacobs of *wampum* shell wealth belts.[18]

Certain persistent themes can be detected, however, revolving around questions of the prestige associated with exploration, the authority of presence and experience and the possession of blankness. The twin desires for wealth and fame attach themselves in equal measure to this last unknown: colours of gold can be detected running through each of the texts, but the undying fame of priority is just as powerful a pull. Claims to experience, to actual presence in the interior, furnish the narrator with an unchallengeable authority; even as they approach the coast, Europeans recount rumours of Papuan savagery which they will seek to refute between passages describing desperate and violent clashes. Presence also confers rights to name and to possess. Morrell names islands and coastal features as an extension of his business enterprise, but Jacobs happily renames entire archipelagoes, substituting his own renditions of native terms for most of the established names of the islands of the Bismarck Archipelago.[19]

The "blankness" of New Guinea's interior offered not only the promise of a naming bonanza but also the projection of fantasies of possession, whether by virtue of its emptiness or through association with "natural" allies. Hence the manner in which the racial and moral topography of the imaginary interior is mapped, often in the form of an inverted gradient of civilisation, with barbaric black tribes on the coast barring or impeding entrance to a more civilised interior, settled by lighter-skinned and often shorter people who are blessed with riches, usually in the form of gold. Indigenous inhabitants encountered en route to this – not so much blank as white – heart of the island are thus impediments to progress and to the restoration of a true and natural alliance between Europeans and the denizens of the deepest interior.[20] Many of the elements of this earlier cohort of fiction are united in a single narrative in the adventures of Louis Trégance among the Orangwŏks, which serves in its turn as a counterpoint to the parodic precision of Captain Lawson.

Moral Redemption: Louis Trégance Among the Orangwŏks

The tale of Louis Trégance's adventures marries the well-worn theme in juvenile literature of moral redemption to this novel cartography in which a barbaric coastal fringe must be traversed to attain an inner kingdom of wealth, inhabited by a civilisation ripe for the Christian message. Notionally based on a manuscript written by Trégance and edited by "Henry Crocker,"[21] the volume's preface closes with the transparent statement that "the true character of the book is evident to the careful reader" (Trégance 1892 [1876], vi).

After a conventionally brief account of an unhappy French Catholic upbringing, and subsequent conversion to Protestant faith while in service with a bourgeois family in England, the narrator, Trégance, joins a ship bound for Australia. There he learns to dig for gold at Ballarat, and several pages are spent describing the technical process of creating amalgam (1892 [1876], 32–3). Inspired by "stories in Australia ... that the interior of the country [New Guinea] was rich in gold," he leaves on "an adventurous voyage" (1892, 60). Off the southern coast of New Guinea, the expedition encounters a hurricane, the ship strikes a reef and, like the *Maria* and its supercargo of gold-seekers in 1872, sinks. Trégance and some of his shipmates survive but are captured by a tribe of coastal "negroes," armed but otherwise naked. After a week of being fattened up, the crew are led off to be butchered for a cannibal feast. When Trégance grasps the hand of the tribe's priest he recognises the first of the Masonic grips and responds. He is duly rescued from the pot but attends the feast at which his former companions constitute the *plat du jour*.

As he lives among the Papuans, Trégance begins to learn their (conveniently uniform) language and hears tales of the dense forests that surround the interior kingdom of K'ootar and the high snow-covered peaks of the central mountains. The Australian rumours of gold are confirmed by the Papuan priest, and the two resolve to travel together to K'ootar. Before long they are captured by a troop of Orangwŏks, the people of the interior, mounted on little yellow-and-white striped ponies, and carrying shields and wearing armour of beaten gold. Valued for his gold-mining knowledge, Trégance is placed in the house of an old chief where, between long passages of ethnographic description of Orangwŏk customs, he wins the affections of his host's daughter, Lamlam. Sent to assist at the King's mines amongst the snow-covered mountains, he experiences a volcanic eruption and rediscovers the power of Christian prayer. Once at the mines, he introduces his novel Australian mining technology, and manages to boost production. When Trégance uncovers evidence of fraud on the part of the local governor, a civil war ensues and his prestige is further enhanced by assisting the King's forces in their defeat of the Governor's separatist rebellion. Now esteemed by his hosts, Trégance marries Lamlam (a long passage accounts to his readers for this interracial transgression)[22] and they have a child together. Fired increasingly with Christian zeal, Trégance and Lamlam preach to the Orangwŏks until their child, unhealthy product of a transgressive union, sickens and dies, commending his own soul to Jesus with his dying breath. Lamlam also dies shortly afterward, effectively freeing Trégance, who is accused of proselytising and expelled by the Orangwŏks, returning to the coast and ultimately to New Zealand, where he duly meets his editor.

Although Trégance's editor evidently had access to George Windsor Earl's (1837) description of Dayak communities and environments in the interior of Borneo,[23] and to the narrative of Owen Stanley's voyage on HMS *Rattlesnake* for knowledge of the southern coastline of New Guinea, there is no attempt made to disguise the volume's intentions as a moral charter for the lives of young Christian readers.[24] Once beyond the "ethnographic" frontier, the interior environment is entirely fabulous, with American, Asian and African fauna, including tigers, elk, antelopes, buffalo, bison and eagles thrown together in an ecological potpourri, along with more conventional New Guinea species such as the bird of paradise (here termed the *wawkoo*). Shorter than the coastal Papuans, between 4'6" and 5' in height, the Orangwŏks of the interior are also fairer in skin colour, with straighter hair: "An Orangwŏk reminded me of a Malay, and yet he was something like a Negro too, but very much superior to the ordinary Papuan" (Trégance 1892 [1876], 70). Trégance writes admiringly of the "habit of restraint and silence which was so observable in the Orangwŏks, especially when contrasted with the Papuans proper, who were a highly excitable and boisterous people" (74).[25]

In what amounts to little more than a gesture in the direction of verisimilitude, the accompanying map of New Guinea (figure 8.1) traces the coastline of New Guinea in some detail and with much care for established geography before striking out into a more fanciful interior.[26] The inclusion of a map is itself a claim to truth, a form of reality effect, establishing at least an internal correspondence with places and features named in the text (Joyce 2002, 151). Yet, the temptation evident in Trégance's map to complete the imaginary interior by filling most of the blank space proclaims the presence of an all-seeing (and thus indubitably fictional) authority. Positioned somewhere between Wyss and Marryat in terms of narrative strategy, and largely unencumbered by dates or figures, Trégance's tale marks a tentative step toward a limited, naive form of verisimilitude, in which claims to veracity serve primarily to convey the necessary context of credibility for the truth of the novel's moral charter. Published just a year before Trégance's account, a very different narrative of adventure to New Guinea's interior moved much more boldly toward a highly precise parody of explorer convention.

Parodic Precision: The Wanderings of John Lawson

In November 1871, just as Captain John Moresby was leaving Sydney for the southeast coast of New Guinea on the surveying expedition of HMS *Basilisk*, another captain, John Lawson, had "formed the resolution of exploring the interior of New Guinea, a country that had a great charm for me ..." (Lawson 1875a, 1). On 24 June 1872, he landed near the village of Houtree, on the south coast of New Guinea, where he enlisted the services of two Papuans to augment his motley crew of two Australian aborigines and a Lascar (the generic colonial term for ship's crew in the Indian Ocean).[27] With a flourish of precision, the party departed:

> Having completed my arrangements, I started for the interior at four o'clock on the morning of the 10th of July, taking a north-west direction. The village of Houtree, my starting point, is situated on the Torres Strait,

and my observations place it in longitude 143°17'8" E., and latitude 9°8'18"S (1875a, 12).

Lawson's adventures in the interior of New Guinea during the following eight months demonstrated all of the qualities required of an explorer by Huxley, "coolness, judgment, [and] perseverance" amongst them. His achievements, as documented in his 1875 account, *Wanderings in the Interior of New Guinea*, were unparalleled.

Lawson had walked across the island at its widest point, from Houtree to within twenty or thirty miles of the north coast, before turning back and retracing his steps – a route traced diligently, if somewhat vaguely, in an elegant fold-out "sketch map" (a small portion of which is shown in figure 8.2). In the course of this expedition, during which three of his five assistants met hideous deaths, Lawson had ascended the world's highest mountain, Mt Hercules, stopping just short of the snow-covered summit in order to return to his base camp within the same day. Armed with a rifle and a modicum of navigational equipment, he traversed and mapped a series of vast savannah plains teeming with wildlife, the mighty Lake Alexandrina and the wide and sluggish Gladstone and Royal rivers. Contacts with Papuan inhabitants of the interior were sporadic but increasingly violent, and Lawson and his team were forced to subsist on the abundant game: catching more than a hundred fish in just two hours, bringing down nineteen ducks with two shots and, once his rifle was lost, knocking down three dozen quail with a stick.

While he was disarmingly modest about his physical prowess, Lawson evidently derived great pride from his naturalist discoveries. New species abounded, including a giant striped tiger, the Moolah, one of which he was able to kill and skin, various new birds of paradise and ducks, a bison-like ox, human-like apes, spiders, beetles, fish and the tallest tree in the world. Where the species were already known, he found them in profusion: herds of thousands of deer and buffalo, three hundred and fourteen crocodiles spotted in an hour, and a colony of birds in twenty thousand nests. If his account of the ascent of Mt Hercules appeared abbreviated and casual, Lawson was positively prolix on the finer detail of his specimens, devoting five pages to the description of a new trapdoor spider. "I have no wish to weary the peruser of this little book with monotonous descriptions," he declared, before launching into the particulars of three more unknown butterflies (Lawson 1875a, 58–9). So much of what surrounded him was new to science that Lawson ultimately tired of the seemingly endless tasks of description and nomenclature; encountering "a few ostriches or emus," he added that "the reader is left at liberty to call them which he pleases" (240).

Figure 8.1 Map of Papua or New Guinea

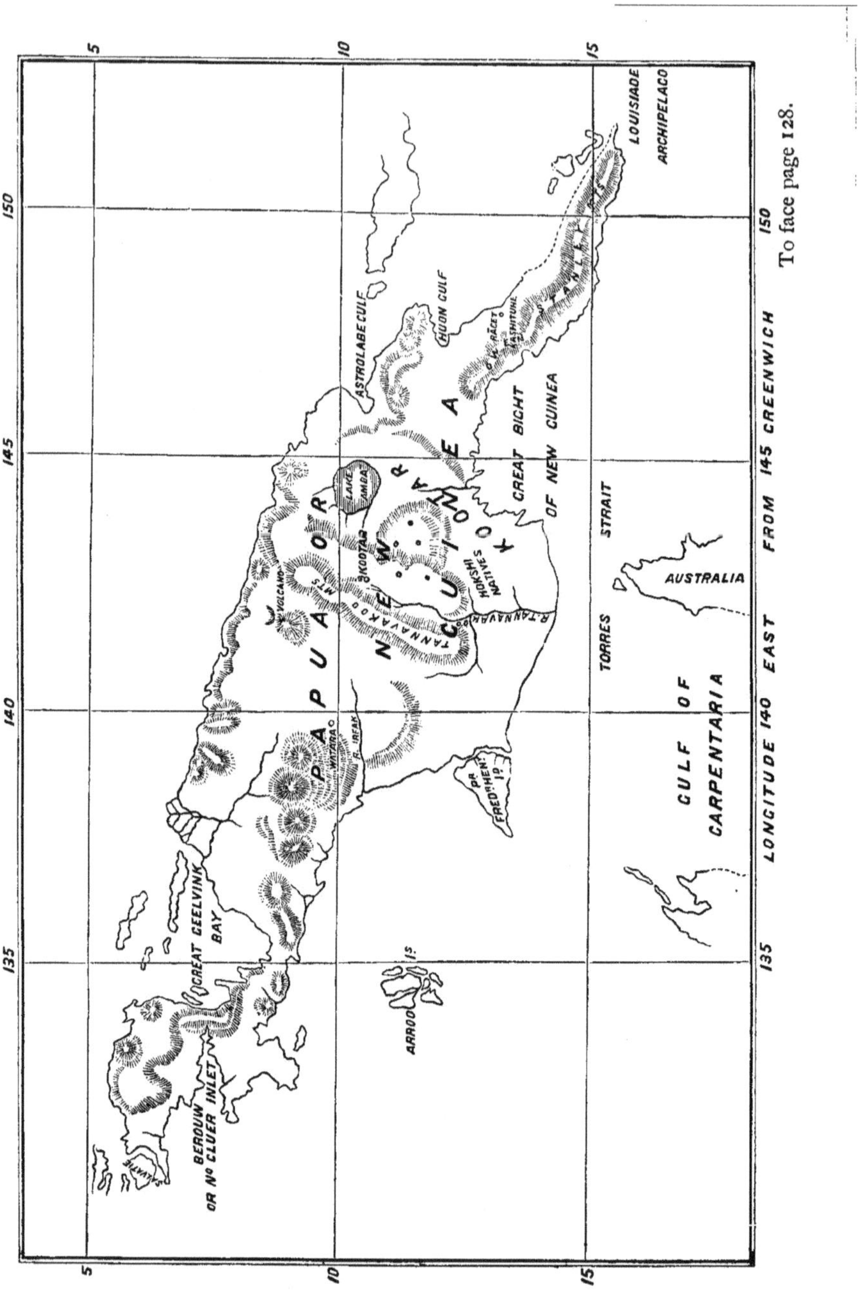

Source: Trégance, Louis. 1892 [1876] *Adventures in New Guinea: The Narrative of Louis Trégance, a French Sailor, Nine Years in Captivity among the Orangwŏks, a Tribe in the Interior of New Guinea*, ed. Rev. Henry Crocker. Facing p.128

Figure 8.2 Detail from "Sketch Map of a Journey across the Island of Papua by J.A. Lawson"

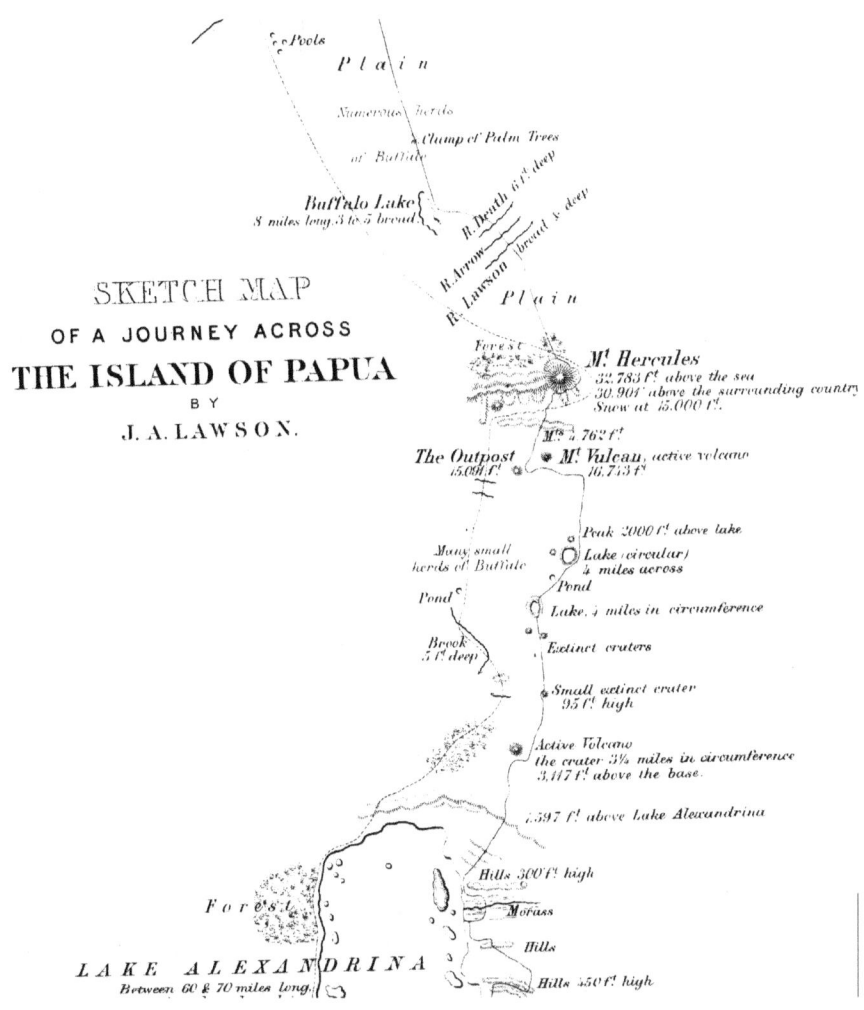

Source: John A. Lawson. 1875a *Wanderings in the Interior of New Guinea*. London: Chapman & Hall.

Lawson's ethnography of the Papuans is a study in the terms of amateur observation of the period. Physically, his Papuans bore little resemblance to the Papuans of Earl or Wallace, being "repulsive-looking men, having coarse and ugly features, exceedingly short, squat bodies, black matted and dirty hair, and a little monkeyish manner" (Lawson 1875a, 5). With "skin of a tanned, yellowish hue" (11), Lawson's Papuans had never seen a "Blackman" before (209). Curious "to learn something about Papuan law," Lawson offered ethnographic sketches of Houtree Village, describing Papuan morality and customs ("the men showing great regard for their wives and children, and treating the aged with reverence and respect") on the basis of interviews with Chief Kilee.[28] As prescribed by ethnographic convention, Houtree lives were traced from birth through to death, via marriage ("they feast and get fuddled for a week or ten days") (276); a long excursion on Papuan polygamy leads to pointed remarks about the nefarious influence of contact with the Dutch (69–70).[29] Through regular trade with Malay and Chinese vessels, the Papuans at Houtree and further inland had become entirely familiar with long Dutch smoking-pipes and armed themselves with brass six pounder cannon, horse pistols, pikes and curved swords. The principal foodstuffs and commercial products all appear to have been Asian or American in derivation, including yam, maize, rice, spice trees, mango, tamarind, lime, peach, teak, roasted monkey and herds of cattle bearing "a great resemblance to the yak." The debt of Lawson's Papuans to Asia was most evident in their speech:

> But one language appears to be spoken on the island, and of that, many of the words are, without doubt, derived from the Malay, Hindoostanee, Chinese, and other tongues. It is easily learned, or, at least I found no difficulty in mastering it ... (1875a, 277–8).

Lawson's tale was published by Chapman & Hall of London, and sales of the book were obviously sufficiently strong to enable Lawson to publish two further volumes of his travels (neither related to New Guinea) (Bradley 1876; Lawson 1880). Good sales are not always reflected in the reviews, however, and the book met with uproar in the press, attracting unfavourable comment in the *Times* and the *Geographical Magazine*, and in magazines such as the *Athenæum*, many of which cast doubt on its veracity. Alfred Russel Wallace himself undertook the review for *Nature*, in order to counter some more favourable responses which had appeared to accept some of Lawson's claims, as "a duty to inform our readers that it is wholly fictitious. It is not even a clever fiction" (1875, 83). Most reviewers appear to have been divided between outrage and mild amusement:

> None of these animals have been met with hitherto in New Guinea by other travellers, who were content with tree-kangaroos and wild pigs, neither of which Captain Lawson has been fortunate enough to observe there (*Geographical Magazine* 1875).

In a letter to the *Athenæum*, the Alpine Club waxed sceptical about the precise details of Lawson's ascent of Mt Hercules, calculating his rate of ascent as three or four times faster than the best climbers of Mont Blanc (Barlow 1875). The more pedantic reviewers observed unaccountable fluctuations in the strength of Lawson's arsenal and supply of fortifying spirits, and queried his credentials as a captain.[30] Yet the literary critic, Henry James, writing in the *Nation*, captured well the ambivalence experienced by many reviewers for whom there remained some slight chance that this was at least a partially true account of travel:

> There was a certain vagueness about some of the author's statements, and many of his stories bordered closely upon the marvellous; but his manner of narration seemed most plausible, he gave, first and last, a good deal of detail, his work was published by a most respectable house (Messrs. Chapman & Hall), and, above all, the things he had seen and done were so curious that, if they were not true, the more was the pity (James 1984 [1875], 1136).

Unexpectedly, Lawson took his critics head on, engaging in a lengthy correspondence with the *Athenæum* after its publication of a derisory review which demonstrated that the coordinates, carefully recorded by Lawson for the village of Houtree, actually placed it well out to sea: "[T]he gentleman who wrote this article knows nothing whatever about New Guinea, except such information as he has gleaned from text-books and gazetteers of doubtful accuracy" (Lawson 1875b, 585), to which the *Athenæum* retorted that "our knowledge of New Guinea has ... been derived ... from a study of the original writings of travellers who have actually visited the island" (*Athenæum* 1875, 586). Lawson countered with the assertion that Captain Moresby, as the only other possible source of recent first-hand information on New Guinea, was most likely the origin of the *Athenæum*'s intelligence; and, as a parting shot added: "[L]et a traveller explore and describe what he will, there are always wiseacres at home who know more than he does" (Lawson 1875b, 622).

There matters might have rested but for the intervention of Captain Moresby himself, freshly returned from his surveying expeditions on HMS *Basilisk* along the southeast coast of New Guinea and busily preparing his own account of adventures for publication. In a lengthy letter to the *Athenæum* (subsequently reprinted as an appendix to his own sober narrative of exploration, *Discoveries and Surveys in New Guinea and the D'Entrecasteaux Islands*, 1876) Moresby laboured, point by point and page by page, through the least plausible of Lawson's claims, while grounding his own observations upon the "truth" of his presence in New Guinea during exactly the period that Lawson claimed to have been there: "Proas do not exist in Torres Strait ... No tame fowl were seen by us in New Guinea ... Rice is unknown amongst the Papuans, and no trace of monkeys was ever seen by us," etc. (Moresby 1875).

Moresby and the other indignant letter writers to the *Athenæum* had fallen, like a herd of his mythical Papuan bison, into Lawson's trap, and he pilloried his critics mercilessly:

> My ascent of Mount Hercules has, also, provoked something more than mere astonishment in the minds of the delicate city gentlemen and podgy professors who are in the habit of ascending Mont Blanc, with the aid of sherry and sandwiches, and half-a-dozen greasy, garlic-fed guides, and then devoting a quarto volume to an account of their exploits (Lawson 1875b, 585).

Lawson openly mocked Moresby's solemnly stated objections to his claims, objections that were frequently buttressed by Moresby insisting that he "never saw" the animal species or ethnographic details contained in Lawson's account:

> A due sense of modesty should have kept [Captain Moresby] silent, especially as he is not a qualified judge as to what is or what is not to be found in the interior of New Guinea ... "We never saw," "we never saw"; when Capt. Moresby does see, he will be deeply mortified to think he is numbered amongst those who have tried to throw discredit upon my narrative (1875b, 787).

In a turn of satirical bravura, Lawson then queried whether Moresby was even the author of his own letter: "Surely the letter in the *Athenæum* bearing Capt. Moresby's name cannot be a forgery; if so, I am wasting my powder" (787).

At the height of this storm of controversy, Captain Lawson achieved perhaps his finest moment, when he had a paper read for him before a meeting of the Anthropological Society on 22 June 1875, with Colonel A. Lane Fox, the President, in the chair. Sadly, his paper, "The Papuans of New Guinea," was not reproduced in the society's journal. Perhaps more tellingly, no vote of thanks was offered to its author (Anthropological Society 1876, 322; *Athenæum* 1875, 858). Challenged by the editor of the *Athenæum* to appear with the skin of his Moolah tiger, Captain Lawson finally fell silent.

Lawson's principal rhetorical strategy harnessed the obsessive descriptive detail commonly associated with naturalist explorers but couched it in the modest, bluff language of plain-speaking gentleman amateurism. Lengthy parodies of naturalist narratives are present throughout Lawson's account, but parodic precision need not always entail verbose description. Just as effective are the passages of *ennui* – of short, terse entries for those days unmarked by events of any note: "Dec 4. Passing over exactly the same kind of country as yesterday. Still less forest" (Lawson 1875a, 249).[31] Restraint itself becomes a marker of truth.

Similarly, Lawson's map (figure 8.2) is both minutely detailed and restrained in its observance of the voyager's line of sight. Rivers are crossed, though their sources and subsequent outflows are not known, and villages glimpsed in the distance, though they remain unvisited and unnamed. The extent of the map is limited to the scope of his route – no claims are made for New Guinea beyond the reach of Lawson's eye and his surveying equipment (in contrast with Trégance's all-seeing map). A similar contrast is evident in the illustrations for the two volumes. Trégance is shown being wrecked at sea, captured by the Orangwŏks, and tried before a toga-clad jury of Orangwŏk chiefs. Lawson restricts the illustration of his text to just the map and a delicate watercolour sketch of Mt Hercules, reproduced as the frontispiece to his book (figure 8.3) – the immediacy of the sketch and the presumed agency of the author lending further weight to the claim of his presence in the interior.

Figure 8.3 "Mount Hercules"

Source: John A. Lawson. 1875a *Wanderings in the Interior of New Guinea*. London: Chapman & Hall, frontispiece.

Finally, like his map, Lawson's achievements, while admirable in their ambition, proved to be modest (and thus equally admirable) in their execution: Mt Hercules remained unclimbed and New Guinea uncrossed.

The question of Captain Lawson's identity has engaged bibliophiles, librarians and scholars ever since (see MacFarlane 1951; Romilly 1893, 189–90; Souter 1963, 11; Stone 1960; Tudor 1961a, 1961b, 1961c). Although several candidates have been proposed, including William Edington Armit (1848–1901), a policeman in Queensland, later employed in British New Guinea, and Robert Henry Armit (1844–?), a lieutenant in the Royal Navy with experience as an assistant surveyor in Australian waters and later Honorary Secretary of the New Guinea Colonising Association, the case is far from closed.[32] Later private – and previously unknown – correspondence by Lawson (still writing in character) includes the heavily qualified confession that:

> a great part of the book is a correct description of the island of New Guinea and was at the time derived from an original source. In fact it is a work of fiction drawn largely from nature; and I say that many of my assertions remain to be disproved (Lawson 1895).

Lawson's "original source" is not identified, but his account is strikingly devoid of reference to or evidence of any familiarity with the few texts that might have provided him with more credible ecological or ethnographic material. The narratives of the natural scientists exploring New Guinea during the early to mid-1870s would have been available to him only as reports to newspapers and letters to journals, but a glance through Earl's (1853) ethnography of the Papuans or Wallace's *Malay Archipelago* might have spared Lawson some of the criticism from his reviewers.

This seemingly fatal poverty of sources is more than compensated for by the precision of his parody, and the confidence with which Lawson met his detractors in the press reflects the sureness of his style. Indeed, the ecological and ethnographic blunders appear almost deliberate, as part of his satirical stand on the privilege of presence in an interior to which no one else – Captain Moresby included – could claim access. Lawson's parodic precision was rendered still more effective by occasional evidence for sober restraint interspersed with passages of wild excess in which familiar elements of a global exotic were knowingly transposed to New Guinea in breach of naturalist expectation.[33] Such niceties mattered little to Lawson, whoever he (or she) might have been, but they mattered greatly to real explorers such as Captain Moresby, who suffered the final indignity of having his own hard-won discoveries belittled by the Admiralty's Hydrographer:

> "Discoveries, Captain Moresby!" he replied; "I was not aware that you had made any. I suppose New Guinea was discovered before you went there. We have work like yours coming in every day."... Thus my hopes vanished; the word 'discovery' was henceforth officially eliminated by the Admiralty (Moresby 1913, 306).

Lawson could take possession of interior New Guinea, sculpting its topography as he pleased and stocking it with whatever he fancied, secure in the knowledge that no standards of proof could dispossess him entirely. As David Glen observes,

Lawson's New Guinea imaginary was "watertight in the way he effaced other texts and unified a disparate scene of writing" (2000, 27).

Wallace may have dismissed his account as poor fiction but Lawson's parody achieved something altogether more interesting by identifying the rhetorical strategy of precision and the vocabulary of field naturalist explorers as the critical narrative devices conferring authority, not just on documents or their authors but on what Gillian Beer describes as the entire "international gentlemanly community of enquirers" (1996, 323). Membership of this community was critical to the intellectual legitimation or registration of one's discoveries: Paul du Chaillu's 1861 narrative of exploration in interior Africa had previously been subjected to intense scrutiny and scepticism, particularly in the pages of the *Athenæum*, as his "class, educational background, and race quickly became key issues in the debate over the scientific worth" of his book (McCook 1996, 179).[34] The acceptance of new discoveries thus hinged upon the successful incorporation of their discoverers within the scientific community, and of their narratives of discovery within a canonical archive (Pratt 1992, 204; Withers 2004). Securing an audience at one of London's learned societies was amongst the very highest of honours to which colonial explorers could aspire; Lawson claimed later that he had also received personal speaking invitations from Sir John Lubbock of the Royal Society, as well as from the Royal Geographical Society and Zoological Society (Lawson 1895, 1–2).

That Lawson's outrageous claims were even briefly entertained by these societies would appear to confirm his most inspired insight, which was that the truth-claiming narrative strategies of actual explorers and their own appeals to a privilege or rhetoric of presence could be turned against them. The intense competition and exclusivity that characterised learned metropolitan society, and the gathering professionalism and boundary maintenance of the natural sciences were the game in Lawson's sights, and his aim proved as true in London as it had been in interior New Guinea. Climbing mountains, documenting native customs, discovering vast lakes, collecting new butterflies and fighting off natives with equal ease, Lawson aligned each of the classic avenues of colonial advancement and subjected them collectively to the satire of his modest wandering in New Guinea's interior.

The Last Colonial Imaginary

Travel narratives are as old as journeys themselves, if not older.

(Todorov 1996, 287)

The success, or fleeting notoriety, of Lawson's *Wanderings* owed much to the fortuitous timing of its appearance, during the brief interlude between the identification of New Guinea's interior as a novel field for enterprising explorers and the English publication in 1880 of the first comprehensive account of travels into the interior, the bluntly titled *New Guinea: What I Did and What I Saw*, by Luigi Maria d'Albertis (see Mosko, this volume). The expectation that adventure fiction in the realist mode should follow closely the more factual reports of actual explorers appears largely to be borne out in the case of interior New Guinea. Yet, in the course of their own adventures, these real explorers also reacted to or even emulated the New Guinea imagined in fiction. Thus d'Albertis acknowledged the stimulus of Lawson in launching his ambitious second expedition up the Fly River in 1876:

> Although I had thrown aside with contempt the book relating Captain Lawson's travels across New Guinea, still I actually had perused it; and it will not be wondered at that when I came to converse with the people who had actually beheld the huge birds, and seen the tracks of the buffaloes, and when, moreover, I heard of the probable existence of the rhinoceros, as asserted by Captain Moresby, my unbelief was staggered, and in my heart I begged Captain Lawson's pardon for having doubted his veracity (D'Albertis 1880, vol. 2, 2).

Lawson's fauna may have appeared ridiculous from the zoological security of London, but explorers approaching New Guinea were less certain of the integrity of Wallace's line: Sir William MacGregor's dinosaur or megafauna, MacFarlane's giant bird and Monckton's "gazeka" were all the productions of otherwise sober explorers (Souter 1963, 13–4).

While it is not my intention to suggest that Lawson's claims were seriously received by his readers, there are grounds for asserting that his *Wanderings* contributed in some measure to, or at least prefigured, the shift from the apparent polyphony of representations of New Guinea and of Papuans before the 1870s toward a more unified, if no more coherent, series of conventions guiding subsequent narratives about the exploration of interior New Guinea. Factual and fictional narratives of interior exploration would continue to leapfrog each other, from d'Albertis through to the self-conscious accounts of first contacts in the Highlands written by patrol officers and prospectors during the 1920s and 1930s, but the imaginative freedoms exercised by Trégance had been lost.

The broader argument being put forward here for the influence of a diffuse but all-pervasive colonial imaginary draws its strength from the permeability of the boundaries between fictional and factual writing, amongst academic, scientific, administrative, popular and juvenile literatures, and within the reading libraries of travellers. From at least the eighteenth century onward, travellers read fiction as they travelled and as they wrote, having been exposed as children to juvenile Robinsonades and other travel fictions. It may be possible to trace the intertextual genealogies that extend from the personal, first person singular narrative (whether fictional or factual) through to the plural forms of observation and witness, to generalised narratives and thence to a broader colonial imaginary, which in turn informs further personal narratives. Perhaps the more rewarding challenge is to consider not just the mutual implication of fictional and factual accounts but the manner in which this collective literature has drawn upon and further nourished a common imaginary.

The notion of a colonial imaginary may obscure the multiple histories and cultures of colonialism, but the extent to which the elements of this imaginary traversed these histories and cultures is striking. Much as Defoe and other seminal travel fictions were translated into most European languages – and then rewritten to further embed them in local, national understandings – so, too, Trégance and Lawson were both swiftly translated, indicating a ready market and an anticipated appreciation for these fictions across Europe. Mary Louise Pratt describes the product of this gathering uniformity of representation as a "monolith" (1992, 220) and, while that may be too concrete a metaphor for the entangled and often elusive transfers between narratives that we can often scarcely distinguish as either factual or fictional, it does resonate with the sense of the power and pervasiveness of the resulting conventions that operate throughout colonial literatures and imaginaries.

The travel encounter is a classic site for the enactment of these conventions, allowing as it does for the projection of preconceptions, relatively uncomplicated by more substantial engagement. Pratt writes of the European project of circumnavigation as "a double deed that consists of sailing around the world then writing an account of it" (1992, 29). In much the same way, encounters are almost invariably a "double deed," but one in which the conception of the account prefigures the act of encounter as much as the encounter determines the content of the narrative. If we are to appreciate the terms of the travel encounter – in Pratt's double sense as both event and narrative – we shall have to incorporate fictional accounts within our analysis, in order to understand how they have assisted in prescribing and embedding those terms. As the authors of travel narratives – fictional and factual – have long appreciated, the real often finds itself standing in the shadow of the semblance of the real.

References

Adams, Percy G.

1983 *Travel Literature and the Evolution of the Novel*. Lexington: University Press of Kentucky.

Anthropological Society

1876 [Meeting of] June 22nd, 1875. *Journal of the Anthropological Society of Great Britain and Ireland* 4: 301–22.

Armit, Robert Henry

1875 *Light as a Motive Power: A Series of Meteorological Essays*. 2 vols. London: J.D. Potter.

Athenæum, The

1875 The interior of New Guinea. 17 April, 2477: 518–9; 1 May, 2479: 585–6; 8 May, 2480: 622; 26 June, 2487: 858.

Ballantyne, Robert Michael

1858 *The Coral Island: A Tale of the Pacific Ocean*. London: T. Nelson & Sons.

Ballard, Chris

2000 Collecting pygmies: The "Tapiro" and the British Ornithologists' Union expedition to Dutch New Guinea, 1910–1911. In *Hunting the Gatherers: Ethnographic Collectors, Agents and Agency in Melanesia, 1870s–1930s*, eds Michael O'Hanlon and Robert L. Welsch, 127–54. Oxford: Berghahn Books.

2006 *The Last Unknown*: Gavin Souter and the historiography of New Guinea. In *Texts and Contexts: Reflections in Pacific Islands Historiography*, eds Doug Munro and Brij V. Lal, 238–49. Honolulu: University of Hawai`i Press.

2008 "Oceanic Negroes": British anthropology of Papuans, 1820–1869. In *Foreign Bodies: Oceania and the Science of Race 1750–1940*, eds. Bronwen Douglas and Chris Ballard, 157–201. Canberra: ANU E-Press. http://epress.anu.edu.au/foreign_bodies_citation.html

Barlow, F.T. Pratt

1875 The interior of New Guinea. *The Athenæum*, 15 May, 2481: 654.

Batten, Charles L., Jr.

1990 Literary responses to the eighteenth-century voyages. In *Background to Discovery: Pacific Exploration from Dampier to Cook*, ed. Derek Howse, 128–59. Berkeley: University of California Press.

Beach, Charles A.

1863 *Andrew Deverel: The History of an Adventurer in New Guinea*. 2 vols. London: R. Bentley.

Beer, Gillian

1996 Travelling the other way. In *Cultures of Natural History*, eds Nicholas Jardine, James A. Secord, and Emma C. Spary, 322–37. Cambridge: Cambridge University Press.

Boileau, Nicolas

1966 *Œuvres complètes,* introd. Antoine Adam, ed. Françoise Escal. Paris: Gallimard.

Boileau-Despréaux, Nicolas

1755 [1674] *The Art of Poetry: written in French by Monsieur de Boileau in Four Canto's. Translated by Sir William Soames, since revis'd by John Dryden, Esq.* Glasgow: printed and sold by R. and A. Foulis. Electronic reproduction available through Eighteenth Century Collections Online, Gale Group: <http://galenet.galegroup.com/servlet/ECCO>

Bradley, John

1876 *A Narrative of Travel and Sport in Burmah, Siam, and the Malay Peninsula.* London: Samuel Tinsley.

Bravo, Michael T.

1999 Precision and curiosity in scientific travel: James Rennell and the Orientalist geography of the new Imperial Age (1760–1830). In *Voyages and Visions: Towards a Cultural History of Travel,* eds Jás Elsner and Joan-Pau Rubiés, 162–83. London: Reaktion Books.

Bristow, Joseph

1991 *Empire Boys: Adventures in a Man's World.* London: HarperCollins Academic.

Clarke, Marcus

1982 [1874] Gipsies of the sea, or the island of gold. In *New Guinea Images in Australian Literature,* ed. Nigel Krauth, 13–34. St. Lucia, Qld: University of Queensland Press. Reprint. Originally printed in *The Melbourne Herald,* 31 December 1874: 24, 26, 28, 30; reprinted in 1890 as "A modern Eldorado," in *The Austral Edition of the Selected Works of Marcus Clarke,* comp. & ed. Hamilton Mackinnon, 343–61; Melbourne: Fergusson and Mitchell.

Cole, E.W.

1982 [c.1873] *Account of a Race of Human Beings with Tails; Discovered by Mr. Jones, the Traveller, in the Interior of New Guinea.* Fitzroy: A.T. Mason. Excerpts reprinted in *New Guinea Images in Australian Literature,* ed. Nigel Krauth, 3–11. St. Lucia, Qld: University of Queensland Press, 1982.

Conrad, Joseph

1973 [1902] *Heart of Darkness.* Harmondsworth: Penguin.

Coulter, John

1847 *Adventures on the Western Coast of South America, and the Interior of California: Including a Narrative of Incidents at the Kingsmill Islands, New Ireland, New Britain, New Guinea, and Other Islands in the Pacific Ocean; with an Account of the Natural Productions, and the Manners and Customs, in Peace and War, of the Various Savage Tribes Visited*. 2 vols. London: Longman, Brown, Green and Longmans.

D'Albertis, Luigi Maria

1880 *New Guinea: What I Did and What I Saw*. 2 vols. London: Sampson Low, Marston, Searle & Rivington.

Defoe, Daniel

1725 *A New Voyage Round the World, by a Course Never Sailed Before. Being a Voyage Undertaken by Some Merchants, Who Afterwards Proposed the Setting up an East-India Company in Flanders*. London.

1972 [1720] *The Life, Adventures, and Pyracies of the Famous Captain Singleton...* Facsimile edition. New York and London: Garland Publishing.

Delano, Amasa

1817 *A Narrative of Voyages and Travels in the Northern and Southern Hemispheres: Comprising Three Voyages Round the World; Together with a Voyage of Survey and Discovery, in the Pacific Ocean and Oriental Islands*. Boston: The Author.

Dixon, Robert

2001 *Prosthetic Gods: Travel, Representation and Colonial Governance*. St. Lucia, Qld: University of Queensland Press.

Douglas, Bronwen

1998 *Across the Great Divide: Journeys in History and Anthropology*. Amsterdam: Harwood.

Dunmore, John

1988 *Utopias and Imaginary Voyages to Australasia: A Lecture Delivered at the National Library of Australia, 2 September 1987*. Occasional Lecture Series, No. 2. Canberra: National Library of Australia.

Earl, George Windsor

1837 *The Eastern Seas, or Voyages and Adventures in the Indian Archipelago, in 1832–33–34: Comprising a Tour of the Island of Java, Visits to Borneo, the Malay Peninsula, Siam, &c, also an Account of the Present State of Singapore, with Observations on the Commercial Resources of the Archipelago*. London: Wm. H. Allen & Co.

1853 *The Native Races of the Indian Archipelago: Papuans*. London: Hippolyte Baillière.

Edinburgh Review

1875 Review of *Wanderings in the interior of New Guinea*. 142: 502–20.

Exman, Eugene

1965 *The Brothers Harper: a unique publishing partnership and its impact upon the cultural life of America from 1817 to 1853*. New York: Harper & Row.

Fausett, David

1995 *Images of the Antipodes in the Eighteenth Century: A Study in Stereotyping*. Amsterdam: Rodopi.

Fenn, George Manville

1887 *Nat the Naturalist; or, A Boy's Adventures in the Eastern Seas*. London: Blackie & Son.

Fothergill, Anthony

1994 Of Conrad, cannibals and kin. In *Representing Others: White Views of Indigenous Peoples*, ed. Mick Gidley, 37–59. Exeter: University of Exeter Press.

Garnier, Nicolas

2002 Le dernier imaginaire colonial: bilan d'un enquête sur la Papouasie Nouvelle-Guinée. In *Kannibals et vahinés: Les sources de l'imaginaire*, ed. Claude Stéfani, 77–83. Chartres: Musée des beaux-arts de Chartres.

Glen, David

2000 The Last Elusive Object. MA thesis, The Australian National University, Canberra.

Geographical Magazine, The

1875 Review of Lawson, "Wanderings in the interior of New Guinea," 1 May, 2: 148.

Gove, Philip Babcock

1975 [1941] *The Imaginary Voyage in Prose Fiction*. New York: Arno Press.

Gray, Alastair C.

1999 Trading contacts in the Bismarck Archipelago during the whaling era, 1799–1884. *The Journal of Pacific History* 34 (1): 23–43.

Green, Martin

1989 The Robinson Crusoe story. In *Imperialism and Juvenile Literature*, ed. Jeffrey Richards, 34–52. Manchester: Manchester University Press.

Greenblatt, Stephen

1991 *Marvelous Possessions: The Wonder of the New World*. Chicago: University of Chicago Press.

Guha, Ranajit

1983 The prose of counter-insurgency. In *Subaltern Studies II: Writings on South Asian History and Society*, ed. Ranajit Guha, 1–42. Delhi: Oxford University Press.

Haggard, Henry Rider

1885 *King Solomon's Mines*. London: Cassell.

Hamilton, R.V.

1870 On Morrell's Antarctic voyage in the year 1823, with remarks on the advantages steam will confer on future Antarctic explorers. *Proceedings of the Royal Geographical Society of London* 14 (2): 145–56.

Hordern House

2002 *Imaginary Voyages and Invented Worlds*. Sydney: Hordern House.

Huxley, Julian, ed.

1936 *T.H. Huxley's Diary of the Voyage of H.M.S. Rattlesnake*. Garden City, NY: Doubleday, Doran & Co.

Jacobs, Thomas Jefferson

1844 *Scenes, Incidents, and Adventures in the Pacific Ocean; or, The Islands of the Australasian Seas, during the Cruise of the Clipper Margaret Oakley, under Capt. Benjamin Morrell* ... New York: Harper & Bros.

James, Henry

1984 [1875] John A. Lawson. In *Henry James: Literary Criticism*. Vol. 1: *Essays on Literature, American Writers, English Writers*, eds Leon Edel and Mark Wilson, 1136–7. New York: The Library of America. Reprint; originally published in *Nation*, 24 June 1875.

Joyce, Simon

2002 Maps and metaphors: Topographical representation and the sense of place in late-Victorian fiction. In *The Victorian Illustrated Book*, ed. Richard Maxwell, 129–62. Charlottesville: University Press of Virginia.

Jukes, Joseph Beete

1847 *Narrative of the Surveying Voyage of H.M.S. Fly, Commanded by Captain F.P. Blackwood, R.N., in Torres Strait, New Guinea, and Other Islands of the Eastern Archipelago, during the Years 1842–1846*. 2 vols. London: T. & W. Boone.

Kingston, William Henry Giles

1874 *In the Eastern Seas; or, The Regions of the Bird of Paradise: A Book for Boys.* London: T. Nelson & Sons.

Krauth, Nigel Lawrence

1983 The New Guinea Experience in Literature: A Study of Imaginative Writing Concerned with Papua New Guinea, 1863–1980. Unpublished Ph.D. thesis, University of Queensland.

Krauth, Nigel, ed.

1982 *New Guinea Images in Australian Literature.* St. Lucia, Qld: University of Queensland Press.

Laracy, Hugh

2001 "Quixotic and utopian": American adventurers in the southwest Pacific, 1897–1898. *The Journal of Pacific History* 24 (1/2): 39–62.

Lawson, John A.

1875a *Wanderings in the Interior of New Guinea.* Chapman & Hall.

1875b The interior of New Guinea. *The Athenæum*, 1 May, 2479: 585; 8 May, 2480: 622; 12 June, 2485: 786–7.

1880 *The Wandering Naturalists: A Story of Adventure.* London: Remington.

1895 Letter to R.A.J. Walling, 5 December 1895. In Collections Held by West Devon Area Record Office Relating to Australia and New Zealand: 1800–1952. Canberra: Australian Joint Copying Project. NLA M2054.

MacFarlane, William H.

1951 Wanderings in the interior of New Guinea. *Cummins & Campbell's Monthly Magazine* 27 (11): 17.

MacGillivray, John

1852 *Narrative of the Voyage of H.M.S. Rattlesnake, Commanded by the Late Captain Owen Stanley, R.N., F.R S. &c. during the Years 1846–1850. Including Discoveries and Surveys in New Guinea, the Louisiade Archipelago, etc.* 2 vols. London: T. & W. Boone.

McCook, Stuart

1996 "It may be truth, but it is not evidence": Paul du Chaillu and the legitimation of evidence in the field sciences. *Osiris*, 2nd series, 11: 177–97.

Maiden, Peter

2000 *The Shipwreck of the New Guinea Gold Explorers: The Wreck of the Brig Maria off Hinchinbrook Island in 1872*. Rockhampton: Central Queensland University Press.

Marryat, Frederick

1970 [1841] *Masterman Ready*. London: Dent.

McKeon, Michael

1987 *The Origins of the English Novel, 1600–1740*. Baltimore: The Johns Hopkins University Press.

Moore, Clive

2003 *New Guinea: Crossing Boundaries and History*. Honolulu: University of Hawai`i Press.

Moresby, John

1875 The interior of New Guinea. *The Athenæum*, 29 May, 2483: 718–20; 26 June, 2487: 855.

1876 *Discoveries and Surveys in New Guinea and the D'Entrecasteaux Islands: A Cruise in Polynesia and Visits to the Pearl-Shelling Stations in Torres Straits of H.M.S. Basilisk*. London: John Murray.

1913 *Two Admirals: Sir Fairfax Moresby; John Moresby*. Rev. ed. London: Methuen.

Morrell, Abby Jane

1970 [1833] *Narrative of a Voyage to the Ethiopic and South Atlantic Ocean, Indian Ocean, Chinese Sea, North and South Pacific Ocean, in the Years 1829, 1830, 1831*, New York: J. & J. Harper. Facsimile ed.; Upper Saddle River, NJ: The Gregg Press.

Morrell, Benjamin

1970 [1832] *A Narrative of Four Voyages, to the South Sea, North and South Pacific Ocean, Chinese Sea, Ethiopic and Southern Atlantic Ocean, Indian and Antarctic Ocean. From the Year 1822 to 1831. Comprising Critical Surveys of Coasts and Islands, with Sailing Directions. And an Account of some New and Valuable Discoveries, including the Massacre Islands, where Thirteen of the Author's Crew were Massacred and Eaten by Cannibals. To which is Prefixed a Brief Sketch of the Author's Early Life*, New York: J. & J. Harper. Facsimile ed.; Upper Saddle River NJ: The Gregg Press.

Naranch, Laurie E.

2002 The imaginary and a political quest for freedom. *differences* 13 (3): 64–82.

Pearson, Bill

1984 *Rifled Sanctuaries: Some Views of the Pacific Islands in Western Literature to 1900*. Auckland: Auckland University Press.

Poe, Edgar Allan

1975 [1837] *The Narrative of Arthur Gordon Pym of Nantucket*. Harmondsworth: Penguin.

Pratt, Mary Louise

1992 *Imperial Eyes: Travel Writing and Transculturation*. London: Routledge.

Rennie, Neil

1995 *Far-Fetched Facts: The Literature of Travel and the Idea of the South Seas*. Oxford: Clarendon Press.

Richards, Jeffrey

1989 With Henty to Africa. In *Imperialism and Juvenile Literature*, ed. Jeffrey Richards, 72–106. Manchester: Manchester University Press.

Romilly, Hugh H.

1893 *Letters from the Western Pacific and Mashonaland, 1878–1891*. London: David Nutt.

Said, Edward W.

1985 *Orientalism*. Harmondsworth: Peregrine.

Scrimgeour, Gary J.

1963 The problem of realism in Defoe's *Captain Singleton*. *Huntington Library Quarterly* 27 (1): 21–37.

Shapiro, Karl

1944 *V-Letter and Other Poems*. New York: Reynal & Hitchcock.

Smith, Vanessa

2000 Abby Jane Morrell: philanthropic sympathy and the interests of commerce. In *Exploration and Exchange: A South Seas Anthology, 1680–1900*, eds. Jonathan Lamb, Vanessa Smith and Nicholas Thomas, 244–55. Chicago and London: University of Chicago Press.

Souter, Gavin

1963 *New Guinea: The Last Unknown*. Sydney: Angus & Robertson.

Springer, Haskell

2001 Entries for Abby Jane Wood Morrell and Benjamin Morrell. In *Encyclopedia of American Literature of the Sea and Great Lakes*, eds Jill B. Gidmark, 300–1. Westport, CT: Greenwood Publishing Group.

Steiner, Christopher B.

1995 Travel engravings and the construction of the primitive. In *Prehistories of the Future: The Primitivist Project and the Culture of Modernism,* eds Elazar Barkan and Ronald Bush, 202–25. Stanford: Stanford University Press.

Stella, Regis Tove

2007 *Imagining the Other: The Representation of the Papua New Guinean Subject.* Honolulu: University of Hawai`i Press.

Stommel, Henry

1984 *Lost Islands: The Story of Islands that Have Vanished from Nautical Charts.* Vancouver: University of British Columbia Press.

Stone, Walter W.

1960 Who was "Captain Lawson" – temporarily of New Guinea? *Biblionews* 13 (11): 36–8.

Sydney Morning Herald

1875 A modern Munchausen. 4 September 1875, 10.

Thomas, Julian

1886 *Cannibals and Convicts: Notes of Personal Experiences in the Western Pacific.* London: Cassell & Co.

Times

1875 Wanderings in New Guinea. 9 December 1875, 4.

Todorov, Tzvetan

1996 The journey and its narratives. In *Transports: Travel, Pleasure, and Imaginative Geography, 1600–1830,* eds Chloe Chard and Helen Langdon, 287–96. New Haven: Yale University Press.

Trégance, Louis

1892 [1876] *Adventures in New Guinea: The Narrative of Louis Trégance, a French Sailor, Nine Years in Captivity among the Orangwŏks, a Tribe in the Interior of New Guinea,* ed. Rev. Henry Crocker. London: Sampson Low, Marston and Company.

Tudor, Judy

1961a The mysterious spoof of "Captain Lawson." *Pacific Islands Monthly* 31 (10): 75–6, 97, 99.

1961b More clues on the trail of Lawson. *Pacific Islands Monthly* 31 (12): 79, 97, 99.

1961c When gentleman wanted to colonise New Guinea. *Pacific Islands Monthly* 32 (3): 73–6.

Urbain, Jean-Didier

1998 *Secrets de voyage: Menteurs, imposteurs et autres voyageurs invisibles.* Paris: Payot.

Wallace, Alfred Russel

1869 *The Malay Archipelago: The Land of the Orang-Utan and the Bird of Paradise; A Narrative of Travel with Studies of Man and Nature.* 2 vols. London: Macmillan and Co.

1875 Lawson's "New Guinea." *Nature* 12 (292): 83–4.

Wichmann, Arthur

1909–12 *Entdeckungsgeschichte von Neu-Guinea. Nova Guinea* vols I and II (1–2). Leiden: E.J. Brill.

Withers, Charles W.J.

2004 Mapping the Niger, 1798–1832: Trust, testimony and "ocular demonstration" in the Late Enlightenment. *Imago Mundi* 56 (2): 170–93.

Wyss, Johann David

1812 *Der schweizerische Robinson* [*Swiss Family Robinson*], ed. Johann Rudolf Wyss. Zürich: Orell, Füssli & Co.

Youngs, Tim

1994 Travellers in Africa: British Travelogues, 1850–1900. Manchester: Manchester University Press.

Notes

[1] John Dryden's revision of the translation of this famous couplet by Sir William Soames reads: "Write not what cannot be with ease conceiv'd; Some truths may be too strong to be believ'd" (Boileau-Despréaux 1755).

[2] See Naranch (2002) on the political and analytical implications of Lacan's substantivisation of the imaginary.

[3] Shapiro's poem offers an epigrammatic précis of New Guinea as it was imagined in children's fiction and approached by European explorers: "And children learned a land shaped like a bird, / Impenetrable black. Here savages / Made shrunken heads of corpses, poison darts / Pricked sudden death, no man had crossed their hills. / It fell from Asia: severed from the East; / It was the last Unknown. Only the fringe / Was nervous to the touch of voyagers."

[4] This very cursory summary of European travel fiction draws principally upon Adams (1983); Dunmore (1988); Fausett (1995); Gove (1975 [1941]); Hordern House (2002); Rennie (1995); and Urbain (1998). See McKeon (1987) for a comprehensive history of the tension between romance and history in seventeenth and early-eighteenth century English novels.

[5] This shift toward a heightened and more sophisticated verisimilitude in travel fiction can be identified in Frederick Marryat's *Masterman Ready* (1841), which was composed explicitly as an improvement upon the crude attempts at realism of Johann Wyss' *Swiss Family Robinson* (1812). Asked by his own children to write a sequel to the exploits of the Robinsons, Marryat found Wyss' factual errors

unpalatable: "it does not adhere to the probable, or even the possible, which should ever be the case, in a book, even if fictitious, when written for children" (Marryat 1970 [1841], xi).

[6] On the history of European contact with New Guinea, see Wichmann (1909–12); Souter (1963); and Moore (2003).

[7] Wallace's *Malay Archipelago* spawned a fictional sub-genre in its own right. An early example is William Kingston's *In the Eastern Seas, or, The Regions of the Bird of Paradise: A Book for Boys* (1874), which follows much of the route of Wallace's travels around what is now Indonesia, faithfully reproducing descriptive passages and even illustrations from the original. George Manville Fenn's *Nat the Naturalist; or, A Boy's Adventures in the Eastern Seas* (1887) covers much of the same ground.

[8] See Ballard (2000) for a preliminary analysis of this mapping of an African imaginary onto interior New Guinea.

[9] Extracts from many of these works have been assembled by Nigel Krauth (ed. 1982). Krauth's (1983) unpublished doctoral thesis provides the most comprehensive analysis of early European literature on Papua New Guinea, though it identifies Beach (1863) as the first fictional account of Europeans in New Guinea, and does not address the New Guinea fictions of Defoe (1725), the Morrells (B. Morrell 1970 [1832]; A. Morrell 1970 [1833]); Jacobs (1844) or Coulter (1847) (see below).

[10] Nigel Krauth (1983) offers the most detailed analysis available of these two works; Regis Tove Stella (2007, 21–8) has recently delivered a critique of both books from the perspective of a Papua New Guinean scholar.

[11] Defoe signals the forms of knowledge that would be desirable in such a moment of discovery, following the general expectations of the Royal Society's instructions (McKeon 1987, 100ff), if only to account for his author's failure to furnish them: "Our Stay here was so little, that we could make no Enquiry into their Religion, Manner of Government, and other Customs: nor have I Room to crowd many of these Things into this Account" (1725, 133).

[12] The author's verdict on New Guinea is suitably modest: "it seem'd to be very pleasant, but very hot; the Woods were all flourishing and green; and the Soil rich, but no great Matter, that could be the subject of Trade: But an excellent Place, to be a Bait Land, or Port of Refreshment in any Voyage" (1725, 134).

[13] Benjamin Morrell's narrative appears to have been written by Samuel Woodworth for the Harper brothers' publishing house (Exman 1965, 29–30); Woodworth's son, Selim, was one of only two survivors of Morrell's final and fatal voyage. Abby Morrell's account, which has recently been treated as a sober, self-authored text (Smith 2000), was written by a Colonel Samuel L. Knapp, also under contract to the Harper brothers. Quite how much liberty these writers took with tales – no doubt already enhanced in the telling by the Morrells – is unclear. A later attempt to revive Morrell's reputation as an explorer of the Antarctic was howled down at the Royal Geographical Society (Hamilton 1870), and subsequent critics have been equally as unforgiving (Pearson 1984; Springer 2001; Stommel 1984, 16ff; Wichmann 1909–12, II(i), 16–8, 27–31).

[14] Pearson has suggested that "this book contains what must be the earliest of the several hoax accounts of journeys to the interior of New Guinea," though the interior adventures described by Jacobs appear to be confined to the island of New Britain (1984, 47).

[15] Wichmann's almost obsessively comprehensive chronological listing of ships visiting New Guinea faithfully logs the accounts of the Morrells and of Coulter, dismissing the latter's claims as "fantasy" (1909–12, II (i), 34–5). Deverel, however, is so patently fictional that he fails to register. Krauth (1983, 18–21) identifies Captain Mayne Reid as the probable author writing as Charles Beach.

[16] Fiction would continue to inform real voyages with Beach and the other authors of fictional New Guinea inspiring at least two gold-seeking expeditions from San Francisco, their plans modelled closely on Beach's account (Laracy 2001).

[17] Clarke uses New Guinea and Papua interchangeably. Only with the advent of colonial boundaries, and particularly that between German New Guinea and Australian-administered Papua, did the terms assume their more limited spatial references. Here I tend to use *New Guinea* in reference to the island and reserve the term *Papuan* for its inhabitants (see Ballard 2008 for a brief history of the latter term).

[18] See also Bougainville writing of a *cacique*, as quoted in Tcherkézoff (this volume).

[19] "To name any of these delightful lands, basking in the light and heat of a tropical sun, and abounding in everything that can satisfy the physical wants or delight the sensual tastes, after the cold, damp, sterile regions of the Scottish or the Irish coast, as is now the case, is palpably absurd" (Jacobs 1844, 113–4, footnote). Thus New Britain became "Bidera" and New Ireland "Emeno," in an early satirical

20 The optimism of this interior imaginary of the mid- to late-nineteenth century stands in strong contrast to the subsequent pessimism of the moral topography conceived in Conrad's *Heart of Darkness* (1973 [1902]), in which nothing of moral value remains to be discovered in or recovered from the centre.

21 Henry Crocker appears to be a pseudonym for the Reverend Henry Crocker Marriott Watson, "a Tasmanian who migrated to New Zealand in 1873 and who published anonymously several other novels in the *voyages imaginaires* genre" (Krauth 1982, 35).

22 "Besides, Lamlam was not black by any means, she was fairer than any of the Orangwŏks, and they were usually of a dark olive complexion. ... Let those who feel inclined to condemn my feelings towards Lamlam, just place themselves in my position, an outcast from all civilised life, and their judgment will, I am sure, be greatly modified" (Trégance 1892 [1876], 154).

23 This point is made by Krauth (1982, 36). Earl's summation of the literature on Papuans, published in 1853, would have been of more use to Trégance.

24 Trégance's tale was evidently a popular title within the genre of children's fiction, and at least three further editions were published in English (in 1888, 1892 and 1894), with a translation into German under the title *Ludwig Freigang. Auf Neu-Guinea – Neun Jahre unter den Orang-Woks*, Leipzig (1878).

25 The "excitability" associated here with Papuans is probably derived, whether directly or indirectly, from Wallace's famous contrast between Papuans and Malays (1869, 317–8).

26 The dotted coastline of north-eastern Papua suggests that the author had not yet had access to Moresby's (1876) account of his surveying expedition to this area, with its accompanying map. However, he (or she) had obviously read accounts of Stanley's surveying voyage to southern New Guinea (published by MacGillivray in 1852), as Trégance identifies the Owen Stanley Mountains from the south coast (Trégance 1892, 43).

27 Companionship on both fictional and factual adventures to New Guinea deserves a study of its own. Of Lawson's companions, only two survive. D'Albertis (emulating Lawson?) would later hire an even more exotic blend of assistants for his voyages up the Fly River; tragically, most of them would prove as expendable as Lawson's crew.

28 Chief Kilee becomes "Kilu" on Lawson's return, symptomatic of the author's casual disregard for individual Papuans and for his readers alike (Lawson 1875a, 7, 11, 272).

29 The Dutch are not kindly treated by Lawson, who described them as the "oppressors" of Papuans (1875a, 267).

30 *Sydney Morning Herald* 1875, *Times* 1875. The reviewer for the *Edinburgh Review* enjoyed himself immensely: "The Captain's double-barrelled rifle must have produced others on the journey, for we only hear of one when they started, and yet it and three others had been lost and still two remained" (*Edinburgh Review* 1875, 517); "With Captain Lawson to see a mountain is to ascend it, and perhaps he would add to ascend a mountain is to see it" (512); "It is clear that as Captain Webb is among swimmers so is Captain Lawson, of whom we know not whether he be a land or sea captain, among climbers" (515), adding later, when Lawson lashes one of his companions, that his choice of "*ultima ratio*, a rope's end ... makes us think that he must be a sea-captain" (516). A search of the Navy and Army List for 1875 has produced no Captain Lawson, on either sea or land (Stone 1960, 38).

31 Compare Conrad: "Day after day, with the stamp and shuffle of sixty pair of bare feet behind me ... Camp, cook, sleep, strike camp, march" (1973 [1902], 28).

32 Krauth (1983, 39–46) has assembled the most detailed case for R.H. Armit as the true identity of Captain Lawson, largely on the basis of stylistic similarities and Armit's uncritical reference to Lawson at a time when his New Guinea Colonising Association was seeking to promote New Guinea as a destination for British settlers. An additional piece of evidence, not documented by Krauth, is the very close correspondence between Lawson's frontispiece illustration of Mount Hercules (figure 9.4) and Armit's (1875) frontispiece engraving of Mount Egmont in New Zealand.

33 As Lawson later commented on the reaction to his book: "The indignation of the naturalist portion of the Society was unbounded because I had made horned animals to exist eastward of Celebes; which would, it seems, upset all their preconceived ideas of 'geographical distribution'. That, of course, one could not expect them to tolerate" (1895, 7).

34 Lawson's adoption of the title of Captain was an obvious claim to the credibility conferred by status, and the *Sydney Morning Herald* review (1875) of Lawson's book opened with a lengthy diatribe against the abuse by authors of military commissions as "certificates of trustworthiness and responsibility."

Chapter 9

Black Powder, White Magic: European Armaments and Sorcery in Early Mekeo and Roro Encounters

Mark S. Mosko

"Actions speak louder than words", they say – especially if you are holding a gun. As a Euro-American I take this to mean there is something self-evidently coercive about the use and effects of firearms beyond their ability to wound and kill. And, as a social scientist, I recognise that the same is usually held to be true with regard to the deployment of "physical force" generally. Where non-Western people's responses to tokens of Western culture such as money, Christian missionisation, literacy, Hershey bars, Adidas tennis shoes, rock music and the internet seem necessarily variable and unpredictable, owing at least partly to the choices afforded by people's pre-existing cultural schema, physical force by definition allows little scope for subjects' volition.

In this chapter, I question the role that physical force, primarily in the form of guns and firearms, played in Pacific Islanders' experiences of Europeans in the earliest phases of the colonial establishment of British New Guinea at the end of the nineteenth century. While there might be some interest in examining these claims in relation to the long history of Western political philosophising, I am interested here in the initial meanings that physical force assumed in the particular form of firearms and explosives and specifically for the Mekeo and Roro peoples – Austronesian speakers living on the coast and sub-coast at the western margin of the Central Province of Papua New Guinea, some 150 kilometres to the northwest of Port Moresby. I suspect these meanings were instrumental in setting many of the parameters distinctive to subsequent interactions with subsequent colonial agents. Did guns and explosives have the same meanings for Mekeo and Roro, to whom they were directed, as for the Europeans who deployed them? If not, what were those meanings? For I do not accept that they were at all self-evident, either to Mekeo and Roro or to the Europeans. And, if Mekeo and Roro understandings of guns and armaments differed from the colonists' presuppositions about the compulsive character of physical force, what might this imply about villagers' responses to the colonial presence and their own agency? Eventually, how might the subsequent history of Mekeo/Roro-European encounters be re-read? Also, given the salience of guns in early Mekeo/Roro contact history, how did the asymmetry of their use and possession affect actors' perceptions of their own and others' identities and capacities?

Of course the written records of the early European colonial agents' experiences provide the most concrete available evidence of villagers' contemporaneous responses to Western armaments. But those Europeans' ethnographic comprehensions of Mekeo and Roro generally, and of endogenous Mekeo/Roro perceptions of *them and their guns* specifically, were necessarily very limited. Thus, I bring to bear on the events of a century ago, my own ethnographic knowledge of modern-day Mekeo and Roro cultural understandings accumulated over the past thirty-five years, to illustrate the value of conjoining ethnographic with historical approaches. For, in doing so, I believe it becomes possible to gain additional insight into subsequent colonial encounters up to the present. Of course, subsequent investigations may eventually challenge these findings but, for the time being, I believe the analysis which follows constitutes a considerable enhancement of our existing perceptions of the initial encounters between Mekeo and Roro peoples with European colonialists.

It just so happens that the role of physical force in these encounters is not at all straightforward in the existing historical accounts. Mekeo historian Michelle Stephen, who examined all of the early patrol and government reports held in the archives, reports numerous instances where guns and other firearms were employed by colonists, particularly government officers, in the first decade of official penetrations, even noting a few instances of "disturbances" and "revolutions" against colonial agents (1974, 63–115). Regardless, she concludes that there was a "smooth establishment of European control," and on the basis of villagers' oral traditions that she collected in the early 1970s the newcomers' military powers were accepted as signs of their "superiority" (92). This, she argues, allowed for a "reinforcement of certain underlying indigenous values" – namely, those associated with hereditary chieftainship and sorcery – enabling the "traditional structure of leadership to adjust without a great deal of difficulty to the imposition of control by a higher authority" (114). Noticeable change in Mekeo local authority structures for Stephen, therefore, did not arise until the time of World War II and its aftermath (1974: xxiii, 1979: 88). "This illusion of stability and permanence was to survive several decades of slow, seemingly unimportant changes" (1974, 114). In other words, Mekeo cultural values and social institutions, being already highly hierarchical, facilitated an easy and barely noticeable transition to colonial domination with relatively little reliance on interventions through physical force. Since colonial officials tended to administer their policies as far as practicable through local leaders, it was little more complicated than a gradual and barely perceptible augmentation of chiefs' and sorcerers' pre-existing powers (xxiii).

However, the Danish ethnographer Steen Bergendorff, who has poured over the same materials, has reached essentially the opposite conclusion (1996, 92–130). To establish peace, he writes, colonial authorities used physical force through the deployment of heavily armed police and patrol officers. Also, contra Stephen, he stresses the numerous cases of villagers' organised resistance to physical domination particularly in the decade 1890–1900 (94–5, 98, 100). And with reference to Sahlins (1981, 1985), rather than a mutual accommodation to the seemingly obvious superiority of colonial agents he argues that: "The encounter between the government and the Mekeo population was no mere clash of cultures, in the form of different mythopractices, or even differences in fighting techniques, or articulated exchanges of meaning; it was a case of the use of brute force and technological superiority by the Europeans" (1996, 102; see also 1996, 9–10, 94, 128, 129–30).

Thus, for Stephen, villagers' capacities to interpret and accept the Europeans' imposition of physical force was culturally conditioned by their prior experiences of chiefly and sorcery domination, especially as the Europeans, soon after arriving, tended to rely on local clan and village chiefs for enforcement of their policies. But, for Bergendorff, the events surrounding the arrival of missionaries and government officials was principally the consequence of an asymmetrical distribution of physical force which all parties understood more or less in the same terms, leaving little scope for Mekeo agency or cultural nuance. From these two perspectives, it is not at all clear what the roles of physical force *or* of cultural perceptions of the imposition of physical force were in the early encounters of Mekeo with European colonists.

Nevertheless, Stephen's and Bergendorff's otherwise discrepant interpretations do agree on one key point: that villagers' perceptions of the physical force imposed upon them coincided with the assumptions and intentions of the European colonists who did the imposing or who have subsequently done the interpreting. For Stephen, the Europeans' obvious military superiority was sufficiently similar to the chiefly domination with which they were already familiar that it facilitated a relatively easy acceptance of the colonial authorities. For Bergendorff, the facts of Europeans' military superiority through firearms were also obvious to the chiefs, sorcerers and warriors who resisted them. Neither Stephen nor Bergendorff, in other words, have allowed for the possibility that the meanings involved in the imposition of physical force may have been projected and perceived in altogether different terms by the various actors, and that these alternate understandings may have contributed significantly to the trajectory of early and subsequent events.[1]

There is an even more fundamental ethnological and historical issue at stake here. Mekeo and their coastal neighbours, the Roro, have been accepted as among the most hierarchical chiefly societies of Melanesia, and also two of the more sorcery-ridden (Haddon 1901, 262; Seligmann 1910, 278; Stephen 1974: xx, 15, 1979, 1995, 1996; Hau`ofa 1981; Monsell-Davis 1981, iii, xi; Godelier 1991; Bergendorff 1996; Scaglion 1996). Stephen and Bergendorff, like most other observers, presume that the systems of chieftainship and sorcery which were recorded by the early observers shortly after the imposition of European colonial domination at the end of the nineteenth century (and which tended in several respects to persist up until at least the 1970s) were more or less indicative of the state of affairs prior to European encounters. However, as I have argued elsewhere (Mosko 1999, 2005) and as I shall document below, there is considerable evidence that various exogenous factors introduced early on contributed to the very rapid and substantial escalation or inflation of both chiefly and sorcery power and authority in the wake of initial European encounters. The systems subsequently observed and taken as "traditional" by European observers were ones greatly changed by their own actions and intentions as well as villagers' interpretations of and responses to them. In this chapter I elaborate on the role that Europeans' superior physical force played in those dramatic transformations.

I shall attempt to shed some new light on these matters through consideration of two narratives of early encounters between Mekeo/Roro and Europeans, which, incidentally, Stephen and Bergendorff cite but basically disregard[2] – on the one hand, the journal of the Italian naturalist Luigi d'Albertis (1881), describing his experiences over eight months in 1875 living among Roro and Mekeo some fifteen years before they were "pacified" by government forces; on the other, C.A.W. Monckton's (1920) account of his experiences as a Resident Magistrate stationed among Mekeo for four months in 1898, just eight years following the start of the British campaign to establish colonial peace in the area. Certain patterns that arise from the juxtaposition of these two accounts, separated by a generation or so, are, I argue, indicative of some of the parameters that were set early on and that continued to affect subsequent Mekeo–European relations at least through to the end of the colonial period. It might be worth mentioning in passing that certain distinctive elements of these parameters resemble details of Sahlins' account of Hawaiians' initial perceptions of Captain James Cook and members of his crew as deities (Sahlins 1981, 1985, 1995).

Background

In the proto-contact era, Mekeo peoples were living much as they still do in consolidated villages along the Angabanga and Biaru waterways of the coastal plain at the western end of what is nowadays the Central Province of Papua New Guinea. They were bounded from the coast by a narrow strip of land occupied by Roro peoples, with whom they shared many features of language and culture. A key aspect of both Mekeo and Roro social organisation from pre-contact times to the present has been a complex system of chieftainship and official sorcery. Among Mekeo, every patrilineal clan ideally consists of patrilineages, each specialised in the performance of one of four politico-ritual functions: peace-chief, peace-sorcerer, war-chief, war-sorcerer. Ideally the most genealogically senior male member of a lineage would be installed as either the chief or sorcerer of the appropriate category, heir to the secret ritual powers of the lineage ancestors traced all the way back to the Mekeo creator deity, A`aisa (Akaisa among North Mekeo, Oa Lope among Roro). Details of Roro social organisation and politico-ritual specialisation differ from Mekeo but only slightly (Seligmann 1910; Monsell-Davis 1981).

The powers and authority of indigenous clan leaders were greatly enhanced following initial European contacts as a result of the complex interaction of various factors, including the introduction of epidemics of foreign diseases, a consequent increase in the intensity of inter-tribal warfare, and the imposition of numerous colonial policies including "pacification," Christian (Catholic) missionisation, the appointment of chiefs as Village Constables, and regulations for carrying out government patrols, for burying corpses in cemeteries and for suppressing the practice of sorcery (Mosko 1999, 2005). The epidemics of pneumonia/bronchitis and measles in 1874–75 and typhoid fever, bronchitis/pneumonia and dysentery in 1896–98 are directly relevant to the events discussed below (D'Albertis 1881, 28; Blayney 1898a: 52–3, 1898b: 86, 90, 1900: 68; British New Guinea Colonial Report 1898, 26–7; 1899a: 59–60, 1899b: 39–40, 1900: 22; British New Guinea Annual Report 1898a: xxiii, 1898b: 52–3, 1898c: 86, 90, 1898d: xxxiv–xxxv; MacGregor 1898a: xvi, xvii, xviii, 1898b: xvi, xxxv; Seligmann 1910, 196; Papua Annual Report 1912, 156; Monckton 1920, 124–6; Dupeyrat 1935, 118; Oram 1977).

By all ethnographic accounts of Mekeo, the specialised powers of the four categories of clan official and, for that matter, all other categories of indigenous "magic" or "cleverness" (*etsifa*), consisted in rigorous bodily preparations and abstentions, the manipulation of numerous charms (ancestral bodily relics), various "medicines" (*fuka*), and the recitation of chants or spells which instructed spiritual beings (*tsiange*) to perform the desired actions. Of particular relevance to issues of physical force, all knowledge of homicidal killing, whether in war or in peace, required the appropriate kind of "sorcery," for in "traditional" Mekeo and Roro cultures there apparently was (and still is) no recognition of death from natural causes. Most forms of death from sickness and poisoning as well as snakebite were attributed to official peace-sorcery (*ungaunga*), which is effective through the manipulation of various categories of spirits, especially spirits of the dead and the culture hero and creator deity, Akaisa. Several specific illnesses, such as tetanus, were attributed to knowledgeable specialists' secret control of non-human "bush spirits" (*faifai*). Deaths through violence – the wielding of spears, clubs or bows and arrows in warfare, or attack by wild pigs, cassowaries, crocodiles or falling tree branches – were typically attributed to official war-sorcerers (*faika, paiha*) and war-chiefs (*iso, i`o*) who similarly relied on manipulation of spirits. Also, the weapons that were regarded as particularly effective in killing were those that had already been successfully used in homicides, as the person wielding the weapon could draw upon the spirits of previously slain victims to assist him. The key point is, it was never enough among Mekeo merely to strike at one's enemy to kill him/her; one had to master all of the ritual ingredients of charms, spells, prayers, medicines, etc., through which spirits were bidden to assist. Thus, homicidal violence was as much a "sorcery" or "magical" skill as killing through the spiritual causation of illness, poison or snakebite.

Finally, as will be apparent in the narratives to follow, guns and other Western armaments figured significantly in initial direct contacts between Mekeo/Roro and Europeans. Unsurprisingly, firearms continued to have a salient role through the remainder of the colonial era. According to my North Mekeo respondents, their ancestors did not themselves acquire shotguns until several decades into the colonial era when the government allocated guns, ammunition and licences to village constables and, later, to other "responsible" men in compensation for their service as carriers on administrative patrols into the mountains. But well before they were allocated shotguns for hunting, villagers evidently presumed that efficacy in the use of firearms required secret knowledge and skills analogous to those they employed with their own weapons. Even today there are men in every North Mekeo village where I have conducted the majority of my enquiries who are expert hunters with shotguns. To be successful at shooting cassowaries, pigs, wallabies, flying foxes, crocodiles, etc., it is not sufficient merely to aim the gun at the quarry and pull the trigger; hunters must employ the spells, medicines, and other techniques to which they are heir in order to enlist the aid of ancestral and other spirits. And to the extent that over the course of Mekeo/Roro colonial history Europeans have demonstrated proficiency with firearms, it has been assumed that they have similarly relied upon the control of spiritual agents much in the manner of the indigenous sorcerers and other ritual adepts.

Luigi d'Albertis – "White Magician of the Mountain"

The record of known contacts between Europeans and the Roro and Mekeo peoples prior to the latter half of the nineteenth century is scanty. Available evidence suggests that initial encounters with explorers were relatively brief and intermittent, but not necessarily inconsequential. It is known that Roro, and very likely Mekeo living inland from them, suffered a devastating epidemic of either smallpox or chickenpox in the late 1860s, well before any Europeans had entered into sustained relations with villagers in the area (Chalmers 1887, 318; Seligmann 1910, 35; Mosko 1973: 66, 2005: 186-99; Oram 1977, 92; Monsell-Davis 1981, 40–2). Oral traditions indicate that the subsequent deaths were attributed to new kinds of sorcery that resulted in many deaths, not just single attacks as with indigenous peace- sorcery (Mosko 1985, 61, 271n).

The first European to enter into continuous relations with Roro and Mekeo peoples was the Italian naturalist Luigi d'Albertis, who left a fairly detailed and candid account of his daily experiences between 16 March and 8 November 1875 (1881, 223–421). D'Albertis did not arrive alone, however. Besides himself and a Genoese companion, Signor Tomasinelli, he was accompanied by two Cingalese servants (a cook and a preserver of specimens) and sixteen "Polynesians" (actually four men from the New Hebrides, and seven men and five women from New Ireland) (225, 233, 254–5). Soon after their arrival, d'Albertis established his camp on Yule Island opposite the strip of coast inhabited by several communities of Roro and, behind them on the plain toward the mountains, the Mekeo.

As a naturalist, d'Albertis was primarily concerned with the collection of as many specimens as possible of native fauna: insects, marsupials, reptiles, amphibians and, most particularly, birds. To acquire these, d'Albertis relied on three principal techniques. For many species, he bartered with villagers who procured specimens from the bush. Giving some idea of the intensity of these exchanges with local peoples, he reports that after six months, including several trips to inland Roro and Mekeo villages, he had collected "twenty thousand [butterflies], seven hundred reptiles, and a great number of fish, mammalia, and birds" (D'Albertis 1881, 374). Otherwise, he used dynamite exploded in rivers and streams to kill vast numbers of fish (330). And to bring down birds, given that his primary interest was ornithology, d'Albertis regularly used shotguns, as villagers' hunting techniques were inadequate to produce the number and variety of specimens he was seeking. On one mainland outing, for example, he notes: "When I arrived at Bioto, the natives took me to a lagoon, where I found an extraordinary number of waterfowls, among them *Porphyrius*, and *Parras*, water-rails, and ducks. In a couple of hours I killed such a number that I was forced to desist, because the canoe would hold no more" (373).

D'Albertis was personally responsible for all of the shooting and numerous other pyrotechnic demonstrations performed while his party lived among Roro and Mekeo. And the arsenal of weapons he had with him was considerable: twelve shotguns, ten fouling pieces, a double-barrelled rifle "with which explosives may be used," and five six-chambered revolvers (D'Albertis 1881, 254). Only one other member of his party – one of the Cingalese "boys" – knew how to use a rifle. D'Albertis notes: "I try to instruct them in the use of the gun, but most of them are so much afraid of it that my efforts have hitherto been in vain" (255; see also 379). Thus, on practically a daily basis, d'Albertis embarked on shooting and exploding forays either on Yule Island itself or in the grasslands and forests of the mainland. By my count, d'Albertis' text makes explicit reference to twenty-four separate occasions over eight months wherein he fired his munitions, but it is fairly clear that he was firing his guns or exploding dynamite on a more or less daily basis, which would have been easily detected, to say the least, by the local populace.

But on numerous occasions, d'Albertis relied on his munitions in his direct dealings with villagers. For example, he writes soon after his arrival:

> I seized that opportunity to show the natives what sort of things our guns are. I killed two hawks (*Milvius affinis*) with two successive shots. The natives were terrified at the report, but their wonder at seeing the two poor birds fall down from on high was still greater than their fright. I quieted them by signs; and they all then wished to see, touch, and examine the two birds, showing their astonishment by their gestures, their animated chatter, and a peculiar shooting out of their tongues (D'Albertis 1881, 247–8).

Eventually, d'Albertis' relations with the local villagers deteriorated, especially after his entire stock of cargo and supplies was stolen at the end of July – everything except his guns, ammunition and explosives, that is (see below). In the events that followed as he sought the return of his goods, he describes thirteen occasions when he deliberately fired at local peoples either to hit them or merely to impress upon them his ability to wound them. Not surprisingly, his account of these events is replete with references to the fear he had inspired in his neighbours. Several times also he detonated dynamite and "Bengal fire," i.e., flares emitting steady blue light (*Oxford English Dictionary*, vol. 2), in people's vicinity – where a few moments earlier people had been standing or sitting – as further demonstrations of his pyrotechnic abilities (D'Albertis 1881, 298, 331, 352–3). In nine further incidents, he relates how he threatened people with his guns if they resisted doing as he instructed them.

As explained above, in light of indigenous assumptions about the skills involved in killing through violence, there can be little doubt that d'Albertis' effectiveness in the use of firearms was perceived by Roro and Mekeo as a competence closely akin to their own notions of *faika* and *iso* war-magic. Also, d'Albertis was not the only European at the time who conspicuously used firearms in villagers' presence. Other parties of Europeans, who laid over on Yule Island to visit him while he was there, customarily participated in shooting forays (see below and D'Albertis 1881, 361–2). Thus, it is likely that the effective use of guns and explosives was perceived by the local peoples as a capacity characteristic of all Europeans and exclusive to them.

However, d'Albertis deliberately employed other tactics to communicate to the local peoples that he was in possession of powers of sorcery that surpassed those of their own peace- and war-sorcerers. In a section subtitled "Rival

Sorcerers", he relates events barely a month into his adventure that suggest he had begun to wear out his welcome:

> Several times during the day Oa and his friend Aicci disturbed me with their quarrels, to which I paid little attention; until, thinking perhaps to frighten me, they began to sharpen the points of their spears, and then I changed the cartridges of my revolver and gun. Towards evening they again began to make a disturbance, and soon worked themselves up into a state of excitement against me. Aicci, to insult me, made an insolent gesture with both hands, like one described by Dante in the 'Inferno.' I said nothing, and pretended not to have understood it, although I determined to administer a lesson to the impudent fellow.
>
> In the meantime some unusual occurrence had taken place outside, and one of my men summoned me in haste to Aira's house. I ran, and found the latter, spear in hand, near the stockade behind his house. A huge serpent [D'Albertis' pet python; see below] was trailing itself slowly along the stockade, while Aira was making signs at him. The serpent was looking at him, and from time to time thrusting out his head towards him. My men, who did not know that the snake was tame, tried to kill him before I could prevent them, but fortunately the reptile made its escape. Aira was fuming with rage, and began to vent his wrath by thrusting with his spear at an old cocoa-nut which was lying near his feet. At that moment he looked like a terrible and wrathful sorcerer; but I believe little in such sorcery, and know how to exorcise it. Oa, Aicci, Ocona, and the others, were, however, quite dismayed by his wrath, and came to me with threatening gestures and words, insisting that we should depart at once, and camp in the forest. Aira was then evidently a magician; and I determined to become one too, in order to bring him, and all the rest of them, to a sense of duty (D'Albertis 1881, 297–8).

After igniting some gunpowder that he had surreptitiously strewn on the ground, his guests became "terrified, and crying like children", begged him not to kill them. D'Albertis explains:

> I told them they had nothing to fear from me if they treated me with respect, but if they repeated their annoyance and insults I most certainly should be revenged. It will hardly be believed, that immediately after the explosion of the powder a violent storm, with lightning and terrific thunder set in; and I greeted every clap of thunder with studied smiles, while the terror of the poor creatures increased with each, as they were fully persuaded that I had invoked the storm (D'Albertis 1881, 299).

The python mentioned here had been taken as a pet by d'Albertis. As he attests, the typical Mekeo and Roro villager is greatly afraid of all snakes. Mekeo classify pythons as *faifai*, malevolent "bush spirits," and people who disturb them are thought to be at great risk of contracting *faifai* sickness. A few specialists, such as peace-sorcerers, however, are understood to possess knowledge of either inflicting powerful *faifai* sickness or curing it (Mosko 1985, 30–1, 151). At several points in his narrative, d'Albertis describes how he would impress horrified villagers with his casual intimacy with his pet python, caressing it, allowing it to crawl across his body while he was writing, wrapping it around his torso, kissing it, and so on. From the villagers' point of view, only an adept in *faifai* sorcery would dare to take such risks.

Just as importantly for his growing renown, on numerous other occasions d'Albertis demonstrated his utter lack of fear of smaller snakes, including poisonous ones, going so far as to skin and preserve many specimens (D'Albertis 1881, 280–1, 284, 298, 311–2, 315, 359, 370, 375, 376, 383). In local Roro and Mekeo understandings, peace-sorcerers are thought to keep poisonous snakes in clay pots, which they use in attacking their victims. These are not merely animal snakes, however; the snakes that sorcerers keep and that kill people are actually ancestral human spirits in snakes' bodies. Also, the skin of death adders, Papuan black snakes and taipans is used as a powerful *fuka* "medicine" in various categories of peace-sorcery for killing and love magic. There are simply no other cultural uses for poisonous snakes than these types of peace sorcery. Thus, anyone who keeps poisonous snakes in captivity or who seeks to capture their dead bodies is by definition *ungaunga*, a peace-sorcerer. But d'Albertis' sorcery powers in this context surpassed his peace-sorcerer contemporaries, for on one occasion he publicly ate the flesh of a nineteen-foot python he had shot, remarking upon the tastiness of its flesh and the soup made from it. People nowadays regard the meat of snakes as perhaps the most "dirty" of all meats, with the exception of human flesh. Contrary to villagers' expectations, d'Albertis is not struck down with sickness or death (312).

For the sake of brevity, I shall list several further indications from my own ethnographic data and d'Albertis' account which leave little doubt that villagers perceived him at the time as a particularly skilled and dangerous sorcerer:

- The indigenous counterpart of d'Albertis' intense interest in natural history is the entire spectrum of Mekeo and Roro "magic" and "sorcery" practices consisting in an intimate knowledge of a vast array of *fuka* medicines obtained from animals and plants of the bush, each of which is understood to embody the mystical essence of a particular spirit being. Anyone who goes about seeking animals and plants from the bush nowadays is by definition seeking powerful medicine ingredients for one or another kind of magical or sorcery practice.
- I have been told on numerous occasions that the sorcery for capturing birds of paradise (*opo ungaunga*) is the "hottest" or most powerful type of

peace-sorcery Mekeo possess, requiring greater (i.e. more *tsiapu* "hot" and *kapula* "strong") skills than are needed to kill fellow human beings with illness through spirit attack. D'Albertis' (1881, 279) ability to shoot down birds of paradise from the forest canopy with his shotgun was testimony to his possession of an extremely powerful type of peace sorcery.

- More than once, feuding villagers tried to recruit d'Albertis to employ his unique powers against their enemies (1881, 308, 355).
- Villagers nowadays and, I presume, in d'Albertis' time, argue that the only truly effective source for curing a particular malady is the sorcerer who is causing it. At one point, a number of villagers approached him to cure their ailments, and he attempts to do so (1881, 309).
- At one point, d'Albertis boasted of possessing the ability to control rain and drought, as noted above, when he claims to cause thunder. These are particularly powerful ritual skills monopolised among Roro by weather specialists (1881, 331; see also Seligmann 1910; Hau`ofa 1981, 36; Monsell-Davis 1981, 228–30).
- In addition to the pyrotechnics already noted, d'Albertis challenged local sorcerers numerous times to surpass his mysterious abilities which included the harmless "drinking [of] fire" (alcohol) and threatening to set the sea on fire while deftly brandishing white sheets and umbrellas and singing Verdi arias (1881, 257, 264, 321, 397).
- Stephen's (1974, 84, 86) and my own (Mosko 1985, 271) informants in the 1970s reported that their ancestors' initial impressions of Europeans was that they were shape-changing *faifai*, not human beings.
- Over the course of his visit, d'Albertis progressively acquired a limited ability for conversing in the local language, and at some point he abandoned his European clothes to wear the standard loincloth of male attire (1881, 338). These accommodations to local expectations of human behaviour would have probably facilitated interpretations of events surrounding d'Albertis' presence in accord with prevailing cultural assumptions.
- During his stay, d'Albertis received visits from representatives of numerous Roro and Mekeo villages who apparently had heard of him and his exploits. Thus it can be assumed that his presence created something of a regional sensation.
- The fact that the thieves of d'Albertis' belongings left behind all of his munitions, and nothing else, is testimony to the fact that they were locally regarded as equivalent to "hot" sorcerers' paraphernalia, as dangerous to anyone who is not knowledgeable in their use, as an indigenous sorcerer's bag with stones, medicines, ancestral relics and so on.

Additional evidence strongly suggests that Roro and Mekeo alive at the time had good reason to suspect the presence amongst them of an extraordinary being, human or otherwise, in possession of unprecedented powers for causing illness and death. As indicated above, following d'Albertis' arrival in 1875 the region to the west of Port Moresby including Mekeo/Roro was subjected to devastating epidemics of pneumonia/bronchitis and measles. D'Albertis himself makes numerous references to the prevalence of illness and death among the local inhabitants, occasionally expressing annoyance at all the coughing around him (1881, 265, 286, 371). At one point just a few weeks after his arrival, for example, he complains of passing a "sleepless night, owing to the continual coughing, crying, and shrieking on the part of the children, old people, dogs, and pigs" (entry of 28 April 1881; 306). During his stay, passing missionary or other European vessels landed on Yule Island to visit or deliver his mail and supplies at least six times (265, 315, 331, 361–2, 381, 387). It seems that the outbreak of respiratory illness that swept through the region was introduced either by the arrival of his own party on 16 March or by the London Missionary Society (LMS) missionary vessel, the *Ellengowan*, that arrived from Port Moresby on 26 March and on which all of the Polynesian missionaries were infected with "fever" (265). Oram (1977, 91) claims that the epidemic of measles that spread along the same stretch of coastal Papua later that year was also brought by the same vessel. Numerous elderly respondents whom I have interviewed over the past thirty-five years have indicated that their ancestors, alive at the time of the early epidemics, attributed them directly to Europeans or, at least, to the approximate time of Europeans' arrival in the area.

D'Albertis' stay on Yule Island thus coincided with the ravaging of the local population by disease epidemics of unprecedented scale that villagers would certainly have explained in terms of sorcery causation. And there, amidst this catastrophe, was d'Albertis doing his very best to convince everyone that he was a sorcerer in possession of exceptional powers of killing. As elsewhere in Melanesia with missionaries (e.g. Douglas 1989; Jolly 1996), it seems that d'Albertis' hosts attributed the illness and dying to him directly. Hence, as evidence of their agency at the time, villagers' several vigorous attempts to frustrate his various plans, to recruit his malevolent powers to their projects, to encourage him to leave, and even plotting to kill him (D'Albertis 1881; Chalmers and Gill 1885, 181–2; Chatterton 1969, 285; cf. Stephen 1974, 66; Monsell-Davis 1981, 47–50).

Unquestionably, for Roro and Mekeo actors at the time, d'Albertis' rather extreme deployment of "physical force" could only have been comprehended as evidence of new and enhanced kinds of sorcery ritual for both war and peace. However, there is considerable evidence that d'Albertis' impression as a white sorcerer extended beyond those Roro and Mekeo whom he encountered directly. Over eight months he had ample opportunity to set the mould for how other Europeans similarly equipped with guns were seen, at least in the eyes of villagers. But also, with the rapid publication and translation into English of his memoirs, it is very likely that d'Albertis was widely read by those Europeans who arrived in Roro and Mekeo soon after to establish British and Australian colonial governments, Christian missions and businesses. To them specifically, d'Albertis advised:

> In the midst of people who have never seen or heard of a white man, the most potent means of defence possessed by the latter is to act upon their superstitious fears. Courage avails much in most circumstances, though not in all; the natives dared not attack me face to face, nor perhaps even unawares; but when I was alone and asleep, surrounded by them, what availed courage? They could have planted a spear in my heart, or split my head with an axe or a club. How, then, can a man defend himself when he is asleep? The answer is simple enough. Make them believe you are something more than they; that you are not made of the same flesh and blood; make them as much afraid of you sleeping as waking; in a word, inspire them with a wholesome dread of approaching you at all. If there is an art my ignorance of which I regretted more than another in New Guinea, it was that of sleight of hand (1881, 397).

C.A.W. Monckton – "Charmer of Rifles"

At least one subsequent European colonist seems to have taken d'Albertis' advice to heart: Assistant Resident Magistrate C.A.W. Monckton, author of *Some Experiences of a New Guinea Resident Magistrate* (1920), which has been described as "quite likely the most read book ever written on New Guinea" (Lutton 1972, 5). Monckton was assigned to act as Government Agent in a relieving capacity at Mekeo Station, adjacent to Veifa`a village, between May and September 1898, more than twenty years after d'Albertis' departure. Upon close reading of the available documents including Monckton's narrative of his experiences, those several months emerge as among the most turbulent of early European contacts, not the least because of Monckton's considerable deployment of both military-cum-sorcery forces whilst a particularly virulent epidemic swept through the region.

Before proceeding to consider Monckton's narrative and exploits, questions about their veracity must be addressed. It is my understanding that some Pacific historians have more or less dismissed Monckton's account of his experiences, published a decade and a half after he left the colonial service, chiefly because of the extent to which the events he described seem consistently to revolve around him personally and thus to greatly exaggerate the effects of his actions over those of others (Hank Nelson, pers. comm. 2004; see also Lutton 1972, 36, 59; Nelson 1976).

No doubt Monckton reveals himself to be a man of considerable hubris, very much taken with his own self-importance. But it is exactly those personal qualities of Monckton's, which, I believe, fit in with the circumstances and events that he describes as well as with my analysis of them presented here. In *New Guinea: The Last Unknown*, Souter portrays Monckton as "The Veteran," epitomising colonial agents of the initial period of British administration:

> Monckton always took the most direct and violent course of action. If he suspected a man of malingering, he prescribed an emetic; if a native met with on patrol refused to disclose the nearest source of water, Monckton's police stuffed his mouth with salt and waited until thirst got the better of him; if carriers refused to work, the police beat them with steel rifle-cleaners; and if a village defied his orders, Monckton's policy was, in his own words, 'shoot and loot' ... 'The only way you can stop these beggars hurting their neighbours with a club is to bang them with a club' (1963, 84).

Moreover, Monckton apparently modelled himself on his superior, Lieutenant Governor William MacGovern, "a man of great physical strength ... the most formidable man that he [Monckton] had ever met" (Souter 1963, 60). In this circumstance, it seems reasonable to assume that Monckton's excesses were not entirely atypical. The sort of character who would compose a text such as Monckton's, I argue, was quite likely the kind of person who would have acted in the ways described.

Lutton, who attempted to sort out systematically the fact from the fantasy in Monckton's accounts, is in accord with this view. She concludes:

> Monckton drew extensively on published records, mainly those reports of his expeditions that had appeared in [British New Guinea] Annual Reports. ... The only difference is that anecdotes have been thrown in as they have occurred ... Nevertheless, despite the constant exaggeration of his own importance, *Some Experiences* and *Last Days in New Guinea* are on the whole reasonably careful attempts to write of events as he saw them (Lutton 1972, 88).

As for the relation of Monckton's descriptions and Mekeo and Roro villagers' experiences of the same events, she writes:

> Some of the most enjoyable parts of Monckton's books are the anecdotes in which he described the activity of the police and other Papuans. There is no reason to doubt the truth of the actual incidents, but Monckton's emphasis of his own importance in them and his interpretation of the motives of the Papuans was erroneous (Lutton 1972, 35–6).

It is precisely Monckton's misinterpretations of Mekeo and Roro actions (and possibly their motives) that this analysis aims to clarify. In any event, Monckton's record of his observations among Mekeo and Roro is directly relevant to the present discussion, as it is virtually certain that he read d'Albertis' text and modelled many of his own actions and subsequent writings upon it.

After d'Albertis, Before Monckton

Before examining Monckton's narrative in detail, it will be necessary to outline the course of Mekeo–European encounters that led up to his arrival following d'Albertis' departure a generation earlier.

The same ship that finally carried d'Albertis away from Yule Island near the end of 1875 left behind two English botanists, James and Thorngren, who several months later were killed by Roro, apparently in a dispute over payment for bird feathers. Their deaths and that of one of their assailants seem to have been conditioned, however, by villagers' continuing hatred toward d'Albertis. Several commentators have suggested that the deaths of James and Thorngren may have indicated to local peoples that Europeans were not spirits but human beings (Chalmers and Gill 1885, 181–2, 270, 220–3; Clune 1942, 95; Stephen 1974, 66; Monsell-Davis 1981, 47–50).

Over ensuing years, the LMS and Sacred Heart (SHM) missionaries intensified their activities in the area, which have been variously documented elsewhere (Dupeyrat 1935; Bergendorff 1966; Stephen 1974; Waldersee 1983, 1995). The Protestants began placing Polynesian missionaries in several Roro villages in 1882 and the Catholics set up a base on Yule Island in 1885–86, soon beginning their push inland to establish friendly relations with villagers there. At some early point, the SHM priests and lay brothers established the practice of devoting Saturdays to boisterous hunting forays into the bush with their guns (Monckton 1920, 141–3). The name for Saturday in North Mekeo is *auli tsina*, "steel" or "metal day," referring to the ongoing practice among villagers of weekly hunting retreats to the bush for meat. Also in the 1880s, the first of numerous European prospectors and traders in sandalwood, copra and rubber entered the area (Monsell-Davis 1981, 50, 52), who, it can safely be presumed, conspicuously carried firearms for their own protection, especially before the arrival of government forces. The British colonial government did not take an active role in the area until 1890, when the administrator himself, Sir William MacGregor, led a punitive expedition deep into Mekeo territory to "pacify" the internecine fighting between various Roro and Mekeo groups (MacGregor 1890a, 1890b, 1890c; Stephen 1974, 66–71). It is clear that he and the police contingent that accompanied him were heavily armed, and that on several occasions they fired their guns to demonstrate to villagers their command of superior force.

Soon after the local fighting was suppressed, the British established its administrative post, Mekeo Station, near one of the larger inland villages, Veifa`a, and in the vicinity of Amoamo village near the boundary of the previously warring tribes. Faced initially with violent resistance from villagers as regards the latter purchase, MacGregor had to despatch an armed party including twelve constables to secure the land at gunpoint (MacGregor 1892). For most of the next several years, Mekeo Station was run by the Agent for Mekeo, a German: Kowald. Consistent with MacGregor's prior actions, Kowald implemented government policies by appointing chiefs to become "Village Constables" or "VCs" and became himself regarded as a chief. Apparently, Mekeo Station was fortified and well armed with a contingent of native police besides Kowald. Interestingly, in light of villagers' experiences with d'Albertis, James and Thorngren, Kowald was a botanist and horticulturalist and he dedicated several acres of station grounds to experimenting on the suitability of various plants for the conditions on the Mekeo plain (Kowald 1893, 1894, 1897: 78; MacGregor 1897b; Monckton 1920, 117; Stephen 1974, 77–8). Needless to say, Kowald's careful attentions with exotic plants would have been viewed by villagers as corresponding closely with their own magical specialists' manipulations of secret *fuka* "medicines." Similarly, as Catholic missionaries established themselves in the various Roro and Mekeo villages, they planted food gardens with numerous exotic species (see below) (MacGregor 1894c, 44).

Official reports suggest that Kowald was warmly supported by local villagers who contributed considerable labour over the first several months in building the compound and assisting with road and garden work. By September 1891, however, various tensions in the relations between missionaries, prospectors and villagers themselves resulted in the members of a few villages rebelling against Kowald and his forces and attacking their old enemies, killing several. On numerous occasions as well, villagers' hostilities toward the missionaries and the government were met with arms and gunfire, with one man killed and several villagers shot and wounded (MacGregor 1893a, 1893b, 1893c: xvi–xviii; 1894c, 43). The matter was of sufficient seriousness that it drew MacGregor back from Port Moresby with a large armed force to quell the disturbances.

Relations did not greatly improve thereafter, however, as the area was ravaged by new epidemics of introduced diseases – scarlet fever and influenza – lasting from 1891 to 1894 (Kowald 1893, 91; MacGregor 1894a, 15–16; Winter 1896, xv). Undoubtedly these deaths were explained by villagers as the result of large-scale peace sorcery – what my contemporary informants claim refer to as *okauka ungaunga* "everyone (dies) sorcery". For villagers in those times and still today, it was imperative that surviving relatives watch over the graves in front of or underneath their houses so they could protect the corpses from sorcerers, who relied on rotting, bloody, human flesh for further killing. To counteract the spread of the epidemics, however, government passed regulations requiring villages to clear cemeteries away from villages, forcing people to bury their dead where, in the view of the latter, sorcerers would have easy access to them. And as noted above, it had eventually occurred in the minds of many Mekeo and Roro that these new kinds of sorcery-death were associated with the arrival of

Europeans. During 1891–94, therefore, relations between Kowald and Mekeo/Roro deteriorated primarily over the government's enforcement of the burial regulations (Kowald 1893: 90, 1894; MacGregor 1894b: xix, 1897a: xviii; Bramell 1898, 62) and its inability to remove the sorcerers, whom villagers apparently were blaming for the deaths (MacGregor 1898b, xvi).

Also in the same period, villagers mounted increasing resistance to supplying labour to Kowald. At first they were paid in tobacco, salt, steel tools, etc., for their assistance in clearing roads and carrying on patrols, but from 1894 villagers were required to work for the government without compensation. On several occasions, people deserted their villages at Kowald's or the police's approach, and there are reports of other "disturbances." As the situation intensified, in May 1896 a priest warned Kowald that a "revolution" was brewing over the regulations for road clearing (MacGregor 1897a: xxii, 1897b: 58, 1898a: xvi, 1898b: xvi; Kowald 1897, 79).[3]

The situation reached a crisis point in the months following December 1896 when Kowald, away in the Gulf District, was killed while handling a stick of dynamite (MacGregor 1898a, xvii, xxv). According to official reports, Mekeo and Roro took Kowald's death to signify the end of government domination. Thus, when Kowald's replacement, Bramell, arrived in January 1897 accompanied by police reinforcements, he found that the district had slipped beyond government control. People were refusing to work on the roads or carry for mission or government patrols, and there were incidents of villagers assaulting police (MacGregor 1897a: xvii, 1898b: xvi; Bramell 1898, 62; Blayney 1898b, 86).

This "irritation" and "discontent" was intensified in August 1897, when news spread across the district that two Mekeo carriers on a government patrol into the mountains had died and the others had suffered severe privations (Blayney 1898b, 86). Whenever Bramell or other government agents subsequently approached a Roro or Mekeo village, residents fled to the bush for fear they would be recruited as carriers. In desperation, Bramell spent several weeks touring all villages in the district unsuccessfully trying to recruit carriers, putting those who refused in irons – actions described by the Administrator, MacGregor, as "irregular" (1897a, xvii). Many who were recruited, however, deserted while on patrol, and Bramell's police were assaulted while they continued. Report reached Bramell and other officials that villagers were hostile to the government and were conspiring to attack patrols or Mekeo Station itself (Blayney 1898b, 86–7, 89; Monckton 1920, 113).

The government's policy of returning convicted sorcerers to their communities after they had served their jail terms contributed even further at this time to villagers' disaffection (Winter 1898, 74, 76–7). During 1897 and early 1898 the whole region was subjected to two deadly epidemics: first an outbreak of bronchitis or pneumonia and then, toward the end of the year, by dysentery. The bronchitis epidemic apparently caused a large number of deaths. At Waima, the largest of the Roro settlements, reportedly 50 of a population of 1,050 died (Blayney 1898b, 90; Winter 1898, 75). Many more died in late and early 1898 across the district when the dysentery epidemic erupted (Blayney 1898b, 90; see below). As with prior outbreaks of foreign disease, these and later epidemics were explained in indigenous terms as new types of sorcery (Mosko 2005).

In September, Bramell wrote to Port Moresby for police reinforcements, but when they were not forthcoming immediately he travelled to Port Moresby and returned with a contingent of twenty special constables to quell the disturbance. In October, joined by Resident Magistrate Blayney, Bramell with his police and jailer toured all the villages of the district arresting thirty-five "sorcerers" – i.e. any man who was caught with what appeared to be "sorcery implements" stored in his house – and transported them to Port Moresby (Blayney 1898b, 86–7). The suspected sorcery objects and all weapons the police could find, regardless of whether they were intended for good or evil purposes, were publicly burned in the centre of each village. Without discriminating between harmful and beneficial ritual forms, Bramell's actions amounted to removing villagers' primary means of defending themselves against sorcery, their own or foreigners'.

In the view of MacGregor in Port Moresby, Bramell had acted "with far too great precipitancy," and most of the presumed sorcerers were released (MacGregor 1898b, xv). Eventually, in May 1898, Bramell was reassigned to clerical duties under the Resident Magistrate in Port Moresby (Blayney 1898b, 89; MacGregor 1898b, xv-xvi; Monckton 1920, 112–3).

Bramell's Stockade, Sorcerers, Deadly Snakes and Monckton's Charmed Rifles

It was into this highly charged scene on 31 May 1898 that our second protagonist, Assistant Resident Magistrate Monckton, entered to relieve Bramell as Government Agent (Blayney 1898b, 89). Monckton's view of Mekeo and Roro was that they were "a cowardly, treacherous, and cruel lot, much under the influence of sorcerers, and averse to control by the Government" (1920, 113).

Upon his arrival at Mekeo Station, Monckton found Bramell secluding himself in his bedroom, with tables encircling his bed and loaded guns placed on top of them to confront possible attack from all directions (1920, 113–4). Bramell explained that sorcerers had been climbing over the stockade at night, leaving poisonous snakes around the compound and in his house and bed, firing arrows over the stockade walls and poisoning his food. He also claimed that local sorcerers had killed by snakebite three of his "boys" who were fetching his mail from the coast. It was apparently these attacks that triggered his previous call to Moresby for reinforcements to arrest the thirty-odd sorcerers he suspected of attacking him.

At a later point in his narrative, Monckton provides additional relevant information regarding the situation left to him by Bramell (Monckton 1920, 128–9). Through station gossip, he learned that members of his armed constabulary had also conspired to kill Bramell. The plan was that all of the police were to fire upon Bramell on the parade ground during inspection, but apparently only one man raised his rifle and shot, missing by some distance. Bramell did not report the incident to his superiors in Port Moresby because he was already in trouble with them, which was confirmed soon afterward with his removal, and he feared being blamed for the incident himself. Apparently, Monckton's discovery of Bramell's actions in this regard led to a breakdown in his own relationship with Bramell (128–9). I would suggest also that the breakdown in Bramell's relations with the local peoples contributed to the deterioration of his relations with his own police; namely, the poisonous snakes that villagers had released in the compound presented a serious threat to the native constables. And inasmuch as some of those police were themselves Mekeo from neighbouring villages, there is every reason to expect some of them would have viewed any deaths by snakebite in their midst in the same terms as the locals: as the result of peace-sorcery. Recall, as well, that three of Bramell's "boys" had died of snakebite while delivering the mail from the coast. Thus, Monckton was faced not only with rebellion from the local Mekeo sorcerers; he also had to deal with a rebellious police detachment which, in villagers' eyes, was itself in possession of powerful (firearm) sorcery.

Soon after Bramell's departure, a "sorcerer" was again detected scaling the compound wall leaving several snakes behind (Monckton 1920, 114). To stop these visitations, Monckton collected the guns of the sentries and other police – who, again, included several Mekeo recruited from neighbouring villages – and replaced the heavy-gauge lead shot with smaller "blue-stone" shotgun cartridges. Apparently, the heavier shot flew straight, but the police were either unskilled in their aim or intentionally missing their targets. Monckton's blue-stone, however, hit a wider target which he strategically exploited. "Now, I explained to the men, who hated the sorcerers as thoroughly as did Bramell, 'I'm going to play sorcery against sorcery; I have charmed these cartridges, so that if you hold your rifle firmly, take plenty of time in aiming at a sorcerer at night, and he is a true sorcerer, you can't miss him'" (114). Then he instructed four of his men to lie flat on their backs each facing one of the four walls of the compound, able then to detect the entry of bodies climbing over. When two intruders were later seen scaling the walls, the sentries shot and hit them both, wounding them, but not seriously enough to prevent their climbing back over. "For weeks after this, we were untroubled by nocturnal visitors; and by every one on the Station ... the plan was regarded as a gigantic success. My fame as a charmer of rifles, for use against sorcerers, spread throughout the land" (115).

Clearly, Monckton was exploiting villagers' perceptions established since the time of d'Albertis that European mastery of firearms consisted in knowledge and practices analogous to their own categories of sorcery. And in subsequent events, Monckton frequently sought to reinforce the impression that he was a sorcerer in unique possession of powers sufficient to outdo his Mekeo and Roro counterparts while remaining immune to their attacks. Moreover, Monckton's actions in these regards coincided with pre-existing indigenous expectations of how sorcerers establish their fame or renown as such. That is, when a man launches his public career as a sorcerer, other sorcerers will test whether he is truly in possession of the appropriate skills by attempting to kill him or make him sick. This is because competence in sorcery includes the capacity of protecting oneself from one's colleagues' sorcery attacks. Contemporary villagers' term for this form of qualification testing is *pipalau* "competition" (Seligmann 1910, 360–2; Stephen 1974, 60–2; Hau`ofa 1981, 277–82). The basic tenor of Monckton's relations with local village leaders (and Bramell's before him, whether he was aware of it or not) as mediated by firearms consisted basically in sorcery one-upmanship.

Contested Burials, Toothless Gums and Dirty Water

Monckton's European sorcery was not limited to his mastery of firearms, however. There is one extended example that is particularly significant, as it ties Monckton's interactions with local villagers directly to the prior history of epidemics and the resulting inflation in chiefly and sorcery power described earlier. In July 1898, he returned from an absence in the Gulf to find all of Roro and Mekeo villages in the grip of another virulent epidemic of dysentery (Monckton 1920, 120, 124–6). This was apparently the second large-scale outbreak of dysentery in the colony, which proved to be a serious scourge over subsequent decades and which, on its earlier appearance in 1897, had taken a heavy toll across the region. Apparently, a few weeks prior to the first outbreak, the entire southeast coast of Papua was inundated with a rush of four hundred gold prospectors heading up the rivers to the mountains of the Owen Stanley Range, including the Angabunga that traverses the Mekeo plain. It was recognised at the time in Port Moresby that these intruders had brought the illnesses with them, as many of them were forced by violent sickness to return to Port Moresby soon after heading inland (Blayney 1898a, 51; MacGregor 1898a, xviii).

Upon returning to Mekeo Station, Monckton found the neighbouring village of Veifa`a in considerable commotion. Ten people had died while he had been away, and it was reported that the sorcerers were claiming it was the fault of the government and/or the mission. A "savage" fight between two factions in the village had broken out, and the Catholic priests and lay brothers, in attempting to quell the violence, were at risk of being killed themselves. Monckton led an armed detachment of constabulary to the village. No one was shot, but several villagers were slain with bayonets or clubbed with rifle butts. Monckton left orders that his men were to:

> bully and bang the inhabitants about as much as possible, and also that they were to tell the natives that, if so much as a piece of soft mud touched the good fathers or sisters, I would make them believe that millions of devils were loose among them. 'Remind them,' I said to the patrol, 'of what happened to the two sorcerers climbing my fence, and tell them that I am devising a worse punishment still for them, if they offend further' (1920, 121).

Subsequently, the Veifa`a Village Constable explained that the bodies of the first to die in the epidemic had been buried in the village cemetery in compliance with government regulations. But, as other people continued to die, the sorcerers claimed that the deaths were the result of people's abandonment of their traditions "in favour of Government and Mission ways. 'Did we have deaths like this, when we buried our dead under the floors of the houses?' they asked, answering themselves, 'No!'" (Monckton 1920, 122). Under the sorcerers' instructions, villagers removed the fresh corpses from the cemetery, reburying them in the village. The Village Constable then sought the aid of the missionaries to persuade the people to conform to the government's burial strictures. Failing to dissuade the villagers, the Village Constable began to remove the bodies "by force" (122), which triggered the riot. With this report, Monckton ordered the Village Constable to bring the offenders to him, who numbered some forty. No doubt this group would have included many of the active leaders of the community. Monckton relates:

> They sat down; the v.c. [Village Constable], glad to get a little revenge, hastening the laggards by sharp blows with his truncheon. 'Now,' I remarked, 'I have heard a lot about sorcery since I came here, I am going to treat you to a little. Basilio [Monckton's Filipino station manager, who resumed care of Bramell's experimental plots], tell them to look at my eyes as I pass down the line, and tell me what they notice!' 'Well?' I asked, when they had all looked, 'what do they see?' 'They say your eyes are not as the eyes of other men, alike in colour, but differ one from the other.' 'Very true,' I said, as I stepped back a dozen feet where all could see me plainly. 'Now tell them to look at my mouth,' and I grinned, showing an excellent set of false teeth. They looked. 'Well?' 'They see strong white teeth,' Basilio interpreted, smothering a grin as he guessed what was coming. Turning my back for a second, I dropped my false teeth into my handkerchief and, swinging round again, exposed a row

of toothless gums. A yell of horror and amazement went up, and fearful glances were cast behind for somewhere whither to bolt. I swept my handerchief (sic) before my mouth, and again grinned a glistening toothful grin. There were no sulky or defiant glances now, nothing but looks of abject fear and horror. 'Ask them, Basilio, whether in all their villages, there is a sorcerer that can do such a thing as that?' 'No,' was the answer, 'the white chief is greater than them all.'

'Now explain to them,' I said, 'that the white men know more witchcraft than their own sorcerers, but they do not practise it, as it is an evil thing. I am going to make things uncommonly hot for the sorcerers in this district: the first one I catch, I will show to you what a feeble thing he is; for I will smell at a glass of clear water and then make him smell it, and he will jump into the air and fall as a dead man.' A wonderful effect can be obtained with half a wineglass of strong ammonia, I may remark in passing. 'Basilio, tell them I am going to punish them but lightly this time; but if I have to deal with this particular lot again, they will get something to remember. First of all, they will return to the village and remove the corpses to the cemetery; then they will clean up the village thoroughly; after that, they will return here and work in the gardens for a week without pay, and will cool their hot blood by living exclusively upon pumpkins' (1920, 122–3).

Here, once again, Monckton sought to establish for the assembled villagers the superiority of European force as sorcery, especially as, consistent with indigenous metaphors, he draws upon the relative "hotness" of his powers including his ability to "cool" theirs (Mosko 1985).

The epidemic was by then taking heavy tolls in all villages, even killing four LMS teachers and several of the SHM staff. The day following the Veifa`a "revolution," some dozen Village Constables from other villages arrived at the station to report that local sorcerers, after persuading the people to bury the recently dead underneath their houses, had fled to the bush (Monckton 1920, 123). Monckton determined that the illness was enteric (i.e. typhoid) fever or dysentery, spread from the still water sources that people were using nearby rather than walking the distance to the Angabunga River. [4] Monckton launched a flying patrol through all villages to dissuade people from drinking from the pools, "but still the natives died like flies" (124).

As he passed through each village, he ordered his police to look for fresh corpses by prodding the ground beneath houses with their bayonets. A common explanation that people gave me in the 1970s for the traditional practice of burying their dead relatives beneath domestic houses is that they can protect sorcerers from stealing the bodies or poking a spear into the flesh from above ground to remove traces of the deceased's, and thus the survivors', blood. The policemen's prodding of the graves with their bayonets under Monckton's direct orders would certainly have suggested to spectators that the police were trying to steal the hot, dirty blood of their dead kin, putting their own lives at risk (see Mosko 1985). In desperation, Monckton called a meeting of chiefs and village constables at which he:

> threatened and prayed them to stop the burial in the houses and the drinking of polluted water. 'We can't stop it,' they said; 'you are strong and wise, tell us what to do.' I racked my brains, and at last I thought I saw a way out. 'Take this message to your people,' I said: 'I am going myself to poison every hole from which they draw water, except running streams, and they can come and see me do it; after that, I shall burn down every house in which a man is buried, and if I find five corpses in one village, I shall burn the whole village. In the meantime they are all to leave the villages, and camp in shelters half a mile away' (Monckton 1920, 124–5).

One of the ways that some peace sorcerers have achieved renown for killing is through the use of poisons (*ipani*). Also, the sorcerers of at least one contemporary village (Imounga) are famous for knowing the secret location of a particular pool or spring, the water of which is poisonous. Monckton's "way out" in this instance was thus a further confirmation in villagers' terms of his sorcery prowess. Monckton continues:

> Then I wondered how I could make the people believe that their wells and pools were really poisoned; hunting amongst my supply of drugs, I found about half a pound of Permanganate of Potash, a few grains of which, placed in a bucketful of water, is sufficient to produce a red colour. 'Ah,' I thought to myself, 'now for a little sorcery.' I carefully filled up two wine glasses, one with Ipecacuanha wine, an emetic; the other with water, coloured by Permanganate to a passable imitation of it. Then I returned to my meeting of chiefs and village constables, carrying the glasses in my hands (1920, 125).

By this point, of course, villagers would have been familiar with the Catholic ritual of the Eucharist, in particular the feature where it is the priest only who drinks wine as the blood of Yesu Kristo (Jesus Christ). In contemporary Mekeo ethnography, the blood (or any other bloody tissue) of a human being contains his/her *tsiange* ("spirit") or *lalau* ("soul") and is particularly *iofu* ("dirty" and "life-threatening") to whoever might ingest it (Mosko 1985, 1997). Therefore, for Mekeo and also for Roro, any human who can drink human blood and not only survive but obtain from it enhanced spiritual power is by definition a sorcerer with capacities surpassing indigenous sorcerers.

Now other commentators have reported that villagers early on came to regard the Sacred Heart priests as *ungaunga* "sorcerers". A full documentation of this would require an effort comparable to the one here focusing on d'Albertis and Monckton.[5] I can nonetheless claim that one of the more intriguing obstacles to Christian conversion among Mekeo and Roro has been the notion that, by drinking the blood or consuming the flesh of another human, people's souls might be saved without the destruction of their bodies. Thus, given villagers' experiences of the Catholics, Monckton's drinking of a red fluid in the manner of wine would almost certainly have been interpreted as closely analogous to the sorcery-like Christian drinking of blood that contained the divine capacity of giving life and/or death.

Upon returning to the gathering, Monckton addressed the meeting with these words: "You see these glasses? They contain a virulent poison, the poison I am going to put in the wells and pools. I am going to drink one glassful and Maina, v.c., the other; ..." (Monckton 1920, 125).

This Village Constable, Maino (as his name is spelled elsewhere), was a clan war-chief at Aipeana village, a short distance from the station, and selected from the beginning by MacGregor himself to be the District Chief of all Mekeo.

> '... but the strength of my magic will save us from dying, though you will be able to see what a bad poison it is.' Maina was not at all keen on drinking his brew, but as his brother v.c.'s all told him to rely upon me, and I told him he would get the sack as a v.c., and gaol for disobedience of orders, if he did not, he plucked up courage and swallowed the nauseous draught with many grimaces. I then swallowed mine, passed round cigarettes, and awaited developments. In twenty minutes Maina asked whether I was certain of the efficacy of my protection against the poison I had given him, as he was feeling very ill. I explained that I was, and that he would be quite safe, unless at any time he had neglected his duties as a v.c.: should he have done that, he would be extremely ill for a few minutes, and then get quite well again. Somehow or other I think Maina must have been remiss in his duties, for in a few minutes he was most uncommonly sick, after which he rapidly recovered. The meeting then dispersed, fully convinced that my threat of poisoning the water was no idle one, and prepared to explain to the people the colour and nature of the poison I intended using.
>
> Village after village I then visited, drawing from each well or pool a bucketful of water, which I coloured red with Permanganate and exhibited to the natives: after which, I made some hocus pocus passes with my hands over the pool or well, whilst I poured in the mixture, dismally chanting all the time, 'Boney was a warrior, Boney was a thief, Boney came to my house and stole a leg of beef' (Monckton 1920, 125).

Very likely, assembled villagers interpreted these invocations as closely akin either to their own magicians' and sorcerers' spells, termed *menga*, or the priests' prayers (*mengamenga*) or both. Evidently, Monckton could not resist the temptation of including pyrotechnics in these performances. He continues:

> At very big pools, I constructed a little boat of leaves – like the paper boats made by children – and placing gunpowder in it, I focussed the rays of the sun through one of the lenses removed from my field-glasses, until it exploded in a puff of fire and smoke. Then, gazing severely at the village constable and assembled villagers, I would groan loudly, and explain that the poison devils I had placed in that particular pool were of the most malignant description, and I hoped that they would not be fools enough to allow them to enter their systems through the medium of the water. 'Not much!' was the equivalent of their reply; 'we are not going to risk magic of this sort. No! Not even if we have to walk miles for our water' (Monckton 1920, 125–6).

The result of contaminating villagers' water sources with poisons and spirits, however, seemed to have worked. Monckton continued his patrols to ensure that his orders were followed. At first, to his relief, the epidemic seemed to slacken and the mortality ebbed. But then a fresh outbreak occurred,

> sweeping like a wave with awful virulence through the people, who were now mostly camped away from villages. At my wits' end, I again assembled the chiefs and village constables. 'What foolery are you up to now?' I asked. 'Are you drinking the water from the poisoned wells, or burying the dead in the villages or houses?' 'Oh no,' they said, 'we have obeyed you most strictly; also we have carried out a precaution suggested by the sorcerers.' 'What was that?' I demanded. 'They have told us that when a death takes place, the body of the dead person is to be licked by all the relations.' Frantic with rage, I jumped to my feet and howled for the Station guard. 'Strip the uniform and Government clothes off these men, and throw them into goal, until I can devise some means of bringing them to their senses,' I yelled, as the police came running up. Pallid with funk, and loudly protesting that they were good and loyal servants of the Government, my village constables and chiefs were hauled away. Soon, from the villages, came streaming in the wives, friends, and relations of the imprisoned men, weeping bitterly and praying me to release their husbands, fathers, brothers, etc. Then I took counsel with Basilio. 'The men are not to blame,' he said, 'it is the sorcerers; you will do no good by punishing the v.c.'s and chiefs, who are trying to help you, merely because they are fools.' 'Very true; but how can I catch the elusive sorcerer?' I remarked. 'The v.c.'s are badly frightened now,' said Basilio; 'scare them a little more, and they will

drop a hint as to the whereabouts of some of them' (1920, Monckton 126–7).[6]

Monckton then called the Village Constables and chiefs back, threatening and abusing them, but they continued to deny knowing the whereabouts of the sorcerers. Those Village Constables, who were also chiefs, were, no doubt, in a precarious position, which very likely Monckton would not have fully appreciated. In the pre-colonial times as afterward, according to all ethnographers, peace-chiefs relied on their peace-sorcerers to enforce their rules and commands; indeed, all sorcery attacks were ideally perpetrated only at the expressed direction of chiefs (Stephen 1974; Hau`ofa 1981; Mosko 1985; Bergendorff 1996). Since most of Monckton's Village Constables were chiefs or closely related to installed chiefs, handing over the sorcerers to the government would have cut away at their own base of support in their own clans and villages and risked turning the sorcerers' hostilities toward them.

In any event, Monckton released the chiefs and constables "after uttering the most blood-curdling threats as to what would happen if they indulged in any more corpse-licking" (Monckton 1920, 130). He then led a patrol across the district overseeing the burial of the dead, "harrying the natives" (130) and incarcerating as many sorcerers as he could catch. Eventually, the epidemic died down, but events took another curious turn when, back at Mekeo Station, Monckton came down with black water fever, an often fatal complication of malaria. Evidently everyone at the station believed that he was going to die, including Monckton, as he issued instructions on his own burial under the flagstaff in the government compound, so "I can hear the feet of the men at drill," as he told his lieutenant (135). Probably Monckton did not recognise that to the local villagers this would have corresponded with the very burial practice that he and his predecessors had so fiercely tried to suppress. When news of Monckton's illness reached the jailed sorcerers, they started to sing in happiness (135). But Monckton recovered after being treated first by the SHM priests and then by a certain Dr. Seligmann who happened to be visiting the area on the Cambridge Expedition to the Torres Strait (136).[7] Nonetheless, Monckton left the area for Port Moresby and Thursday Island until he was sufficiently recovered that he could resume his duties, at which point he was likely regarded by villagers as having returned from the dead. Soon thereafter, however, Monckton caught enteric fever. Out of concern for his health and his dislike of Mekeo, he resigned from his posting and was eventually reassigned to the Southeast Division (143).

It appears that Monckton's actions, regardless of their tactical merits, were temporarily effective in suppressing the spread of the 1897 dysentery epidemic, at least among Roro and Mekeo (Blayney 1900, 68). However, by 1899 dysentery had become "endemic" once again causing many deaths, and it remained a persistent problem for many years throughout the Possession (Blayney 1901, 111).

Conclusion

The events I have recounted here as presented in Monckton's text culminated in an important turning point for the subsequent history of Mekeo and Roro relations with European colonists. Undoubtedly, because of the inability of government agents and missionaries to break up the traditional alliance of clan chiefs and sorcerers, the practice of selecting peace-chiefs as Village Constables, which had been government policy until then, was abandoned. Patrol officers were instructed to select Village Constables on the basis of their presumed fitness for bearing responsibility, although the endorsement of village chiefs and elders for these nominations was also encouraged. But also, Monckton's consistent insinuation of the white man's sorcery in his deployments of physical force, and villagers' evident interpretations and responses in those same terms confirms what had become by then, following the precedent set by d'Albertis, a generation of encounters overshadowed by contests of sorcery on various sides.

For the sake of Mekeo and Roro colonial history, it can thus be concluded that there was anything but an easy transition from chiefly to colonial hierarchy and that the changes represented by the European presence were for the people far more than "barely perceptible." Contrary to Stephen's view of the early colonial encounter, it was simply not a case where the authority of Roro and Mekeo chiefs and sorcerers were gradually transformed through incremental additions of administrative responsibility. And contra Bergendorff's claim that the encounter was dominated by the imposition of brute physical force free of intercultural dynamics, the key aspect of European relations with villagers was an intense struggle over what was perceived by villagers as the effectiveness of magic and sorcery. Certainly d'Albertis and Monckton represented their actions, including their wielding of physical force, as kinds of sorcery and, in light of the decimation through disease that accompanied their use, there is little reason to suspect that villagers perceived the European presence in terms other than those presented by Europeans themselves – that is, as consisting essentially in the monopoly of new forms of devastating spiritual power. And unlike the sorcery that ideally till then had been used morally – that is, only with the endorsement of chiefs – Europeans' sorcery, whether in the form of firearms or disease, was amoral to the extent that it attacked people more or less indiscriminately. As indigenous sorcery practices were already monopolised by clan chiefs and sorcerers, their struggles against colonial forces over ensuing decades became intensely moral contests – which perhaps go a long way toward explaining the subsequent reputations of both Mekeo and Roro for cultural conservatism, including the persistence of inflated chiefly and sorcerous authority, well into the 1970s and 1980s.[8]

This reconsideration of d'Albertis' and Monckton's encounters with Roro and Mekeo also underscores the significance that the introduction of foreign diseases would have had even before Europeans arrived physically on the scene. There is a particularly strong irony here though, as the reputation of Roro and Mekeo among European observers (including anthropologists and historians) for being traditionally preoccupied with magic and sorcery appears to be in large measure a result of encounters with Europeans.

In these encounters, we can thus discern the outlines of a mythopraxis in Sahlins' sense of the term where the Europeans, to be effective in imposing their wills, consciously revised their identities and actions in ways that happened to coincide with certain pre-existing presuppositions on the part of the village peoples, and accordingly the latter elaborated their views of themselves and their capacities in ways designed to enhance their effectiveness with the new foreign powers.

Finally, I think it is fair to say that "physical force" played a role in early encounters between Europeans and Mekeo and Roro, but not merely as such. At key turns in the narratives of d'Albertis and Monckton, we have seen how Europeans perceived and wielded their weapons, not just as instruments of corporeal violence but as spiritual resources precisely in the same way that Mekeo and Roro villagers perceived and deployed indigenous and introduced weaponry.

References

Bayliss-Smith, Tim

2005 Fertility and depopulation: Childlessness, abortion and introduced disease in Simbo and Ontong Java, Solomon Islands. In *Population, Reproduction and Fertility in Melanesia*, ed. Stanley J. Ulijaszek, 13–52. Oxford: Berghahn Books.

Bergendorff, Steen

1996 *Faingu City: A Modern Mekeo Clan in Papua New Guinea*, vol. 2. Lund Monographs in Social Anthropology. Lund, Sweden: Lund University Press.

Blayney, J.A.

1898a Report of the Resident Magistrate for the Central Division. In *British New Guinea Annual Report 1896–97*, 51–3. Victoria: Government Printer.

1898b Report of the Resident Magistrate for the Central Division. In *British New Guinea Annual Report 1897–98*, 86–91. Victoria: Government Printer.

1900 Report of the Resident Magistrate for the Central Division. In *British New Guinea Annual Report 1898–99*, 66–70. Victoria: Government Printer.

1901 Report of the Chief Medical Officer, Port Moresby. In *British New Guinea Annual Report 1899–1900*, 111–2. Victoria: Government Printer.

Bramell, Bertram W.

1898 Report of the government agent for the Mekeo District. In *British New Guinea Annual Report 1896–97*, 62–4. Victoria: Government Printer.

British New Guinea Annual Report

1898a Central Division. In *British New Guinea Annual Report for the Year 1897–98*, xxii-xxiv. Brisbane: Queensland Parliamentary Papers.

1898b Report of the Resident Magistrate for the Central Division. In *British New Guinea Annual Report for the Year 1896–97*, 51–3. Brisbane: Queensland Parliamentary Papers.

1898c Report of the Resident Magistrate for the Central Division. In *British New Guinea Annual Report for the Year 1897–98*, 86–93. Brisbane: Queensland Parliamentary Papers.

1898d Sanitary. In *British New Guinea Annual Report for the Year 1897–98*, xxxiv–xxxvi. Brisbane: Queensland Parliamentary Papers.

British New Guinea Colonial Report

1898 Report of the Resident Magistrate of the Central Division. In *Annual Report for 1896–97 (No. 237)*, 26–7. London: Colonial Reports.

1899a Remarks on climate and diseases existing in the possession. In *Annual Report for 1897–98 (No. 258)*, 58–60. London: Colonial Reports.

1899b Report of the Resident Magistrate for the Central Division. In *Annual Report for 1897–98 (No. 258)*, 39–40. London: Colonial Reports.

1900 Report of the Resident Magistrate of the Central Division. In *Annual Report for 1898–99 (No. 292)*, 19–26. London: Colonial Reports.

Chalmers, James

1887 *Pioneering in New Guinea*. 2nd ed. London: Religious Tract Society.

Chalmers, James, and William Wyatt Gill

1885 *Work and Adventure in New Guinea 1877 to 1885*. London: Religious Tract Society.

Chatterton, Percy

1969 The history of Delena. In *The History of Melanesia*, ed. Ken S. Inglis. Papers from the Second Waigani Seminar, 283-95. Canberra and Port Moresby: Australian National University; University of Papua and New Guinea.

Clune, Francis

1942 *Prowling through Papua*. Sydney: Angus and Robertson.

D'Albertis, Luigi M.

1881 *New Guinea: What I Did and What I Saw.* 2nd ed. Boston: Houghton.

Denoon, Donald, Philippa Mein-Smith, with Marivic Wyndham

2000 Depopulation. In *A History of Australia, New Zealand and the Pacific*, ed. Donald Denoon, P. Mein-Smith, and M. Wyndham, 72–9. Oxford: Blackwell.

Douglas, Bronwen

1989 Autonomous and controlled spirits: Traditional ritual and early interpretations of Christianity on Tanna, Aneityum and the Isle of Pines in comparative perspective. *Journal of the Polynesian Society* 98: 7–48.

Dupeyrat, André

1935 *Papouasie: Histoire de la mission (1885–1935).* Paris: Dillen.

Godelier, Maurice

1991 An Unfinished Attempt at Reconstructing the Social Processes which May Have Prompted the Transformation of Great-men Societies into Big-men Societies. In *Big Men and Great men: Personifications of Power in the Pacific,* eds Maurice Godelier and Marilyn Strathern, 275–304. Cambridge: Cambridge University Press; Paris: Editions de la Maison de Sciences de l'Homme.

Haddon, Alfred C.

1901 *Headhunters: Black, White and Brown.* London: Metheuen.

Hau`ofa, Epeli

1981 *Mekeo: Inequality and Ambivalence in a Village Society.* Canberra: Australian National University Press.

Jolly, Margaret

1996 Devils, holy spirits, and the swollen god: Translation, conversion and colonial power in the Marist Mission, Vanuatu, 1887–1934. In *Conversion to Modernities: The Globalization of Christianity*, ed. P. van der Veer, 231–62. New York: Routledge.

Kowald, C.

1893 Report of the government agent for the Mekeo District. In *British New Guinea Annual Report 1891–92*, 90–1. Victoria: Government Printer.

1894 Report of the government agent for the Mekeo District. In *British New Guinea Annual Report 1891–92*, 58–60. Victoria: Government Printer.

1897 Report of the government agent for the Mekeo District. In *British New Guinea Annual Report 1895–96*, 77–80. Victoria: Government Printer.

Lutton, Nancy

1972 C.A.W. Monckton's trilogy of his adventures in New Guinea: Fact or fiction? BA Hons thesis, University of Papua New Guinea. Australian National Library Manuscript No. 3894.

MacGregor, William

1890a Despatch reporting visit of inspection to the St. Joseph River District. In *British New Guinea Annual Report 1889–90*, 76–83, 87–91. Victoria: Government Printer.

1890b Despatch reporting means undertaken to effect capture of certain murderers from village of Nara, etc. In *British New Guinea Annual Report 1899–90*, 83–6. Victoria: Government Printer.

1890c Despatch in further reference to visit of inspection to the St. Joseph River District. In *British New Guinea Annual Report 1899–90*, 87–91. Victoria: Government Printer.

1892 Despatch reporting visit of inspection to the Mekeo (Upper St. Joseph) District. In *British New Guinea Annual Report 1890–91*, 19–21. Victoria: Government Printer.

1893a Despatch reporting visit of inspection to the Mekeo District. In *British New Guinea Annual Report 1891–92*, 15–20. Victoria: Government Printer.

1893b Despatch reporting further visit to Mekeo District. In *British New Guinea Annual Report 1891–92,* 20–2. Victoria: Government Printer.

1893c Annual report, 1891–92. In *British New Guinea Annual Report 1891–92*, v–xxxii. Victoria: Government Printer.

1894a Despatch reporting visit of inspection to country west of Port Moresby, as far as Freshwater Bay. In *British New Guinea Annual Report 1892–93*, 15–23. Victoria: Government Printer.

1894b Annual report, 1893–94. In *British New Guinea Annual Report 1892–93*, v–xxxi. Victoria: Government Printer.

1894c Despatch reporting visit of inspection to the Mekeo District. In *British New Guinea Annual Report 1893–94*, 43–4. Victoria: Government Printer.

1897a Annual report, 1895–96. In *British New Guinea Annual Report 1895–96*, v–xxxv. Victoria: Government Printer.

1897b Despatch reporting visit of inspection to Mekeo District. In *British New Guinea Annual Report 1895–96,* 56–60. Victoria: Government Printer.

1898a Annual report 1896–97. In *British New Guinea Annual Report 1896–97*, v–xxvi. Victoria: Government Printer.

1898b Annual report 1897–98. In *British New Guinea Annual Report 1897–98*, v–xxvi. Victoria: Government Printer.

Monckton, Charles Arthur Whitmore

1920 *Some Experiences of a New Guinea Resident Magistrate*. New York: John Lane.

Monsell-Davis, Michael

1981 Nabuapaka: Social change in a Roro community. PhD thesis, Anthropology, Macquarie University.

Mosko, Mark

1973 Leadership and social integration: A prospectus for ethnographic research among the Roro. Unpublished doctoral research prospectus. Department of Anthropology, University of Minnesota.

1985 *Quadripartite Structures: Categories, Relations, and Homologies in Bush Mekeo Culture*. Cambridge: Cambridge University Press.

1991 Yali revisited: The interplay of messages and missions in Melanesian structural history. *Journal of the Polynesian Society* 100: 269–98.

1992 Other messages, other missions; or, Sahlins among the Melanesians. *Oceania* 63 (2): 97–113.

1997 Cultural constructs versus psychoanalytic conjectures: Comments on "the 'man of sorrow'". *American Ethnologist* 24 (4): 934–9.

1999 Magical money: Commoditization and the linkage of *maketsi* ("market") and *kangakanga* ("custom") in contemporary North Mekeo. In *Money and Modernity: State and Local Currencies in Melanesia*, eds David Akin and Joel Robbins, 41–61. Pittsburgh: University of Pittsburgh Press.

2005 Peace, war, sex and sorcery: Nonlinear analogical transformation in the early escalation of North Mekeo sorcery and chiefly practice. In *On the Order of Chaos: Social Anthropology and the Science of Chaos*, eds. Mark S. Mosko and Frederick H. Damon, 166–205. London and New York: Berghahn Books.

Nelson, Hank

1976 *Black, White and Gold: Gold Mining in Papua New Guinea, 1878–1930*. Canberra: Australian National University Press.

Oram, Nigel

1977 Environment, migration and site selection in the Port Moresby coastal area. In *The Melanesian Environment*, ed. John H. Winslow, 74–99. Papers from the Ninth Waigani Seminar, Port Moresby, 2–8 May 1975. Canberra: Australian National University Press.

Papua Annual Report

Dysentery. *Report for the Year Ended 30th June, 1912.* Victoria: Parliament of the Commonwealth of Australia.

Sahlins, Marshall

1981 *Historical Metaphors and Mythical Realities: Structure in the Early History of the Sandwich Islands Kingdom.* Ann Arbor: University of Michigan Press.

1985 *Islands of History.* Chicago: University of Chicago Press.

1995 *How "Natives" Think: About Captain Cook, for Example.* Chicago: University of Chicago Press.

Scaglion, Richard

1996 Chiefly models in Papua New Guinea. *The Contemporary Pacific* 8 (1): 1–31.

Seligmann, Charles G.

1910 *The Melanesians of British New Guinea.* Cambridge: Cambridge University Press.

Souter, Gavin

1963 *New Guinea: The Last Unknown.* London: Angus and Robertson.

Stannard, David E.

1989 *Before the Horror: The Population of Hawai`i on the Eve of Western Contact.* Honolulu: University of Hawai`i Press.

Stephen, Michele

1974 Continuity and change in Mekeo society, 1890–1971. PhD thesis, Australian National University.

1979 An honourable man: Mekeo views of the village constable. *Journal of Pacific History* 14: 85–99.

1995 *A`aisa's Gifts: A Study of Magic and the Self.* Berkeley and Los Angeles: University of California Press.

1996 The Mekeo "man of sorrow": Sorcery and the individuation of the self. *American Ethnologist* 23 (1): 83–101.

Waldersee, James

1983 *A Grain of Mustard Seed: The Society for the Propagation of the Faith and Australia, 1837–1977.* Kensington, NSW: Chevalier Press.

Waldersee, James, in collab. with John F. McMahon

1995 *"Neither Eagles nor Saints": MSC Missions in Oceania 1881–1975.* Sydney: Chevalier Press.

Winter, Francis P.

1896 Annual report 1894–95. In *British New Guinea Annual Report 1894–95*, vii–xxvii. Victoria: Government Printer.

1898 Report of visit to Mekeo, &c., by the Hon. F.P. Winter (acting as Deputy Administrator). In *British New Guinea Annual Report 1897–98*. Victoria: Government Printer.

Zelenietz, Marty, and Shirley Lindenbaum

1981 Sorcery and Social Change: An Introduction. In *Sorcery and Social Change in Melanesia*, eds Marty Zelenietz and Shirley Lindenbaum. *Social Analysis* 8: 3–14. Special issue.

Notes

[1] This chapter is based on some dozen ethnographic fieldtrips totalling nearly four years among Mekeo and Roro beginning in 1974. I am greatly indebted to the many Maipa, Ioi and Waima villagers as well as others who have so generously provided me with their knowledge, insights and hospitality. Numerous archives have also allowed me access to documentary materials which have proven to be critical in my efforts to understand Mekeo/Roro contact history, including the Melanesian Archives at the University of California at San Diego, the Papua New Guinea National Archives, the National Library of Australia, the Seligmann Papers at the London School of Economics, and the Pacific Manuscripts Bureau in the Research School of Pacific and Asian Studies at The Australian National University. Funding for these endeavours has been generously provided by the Hartwick College Board of Trustees, the University of Auckland Research Committee, the National Institute for the Humanities, the Wenner-Gren Foundation for Anthropological Research, the Marsden Fund of New Zealand, and the Research School of Pacific and Asian Studies at The Australian National University. I have benefited also from the comments and suggestions provided by Hank Nelson, Margaret Jolly, Paul van der Grijp and other participants in the CREDO–RSPAS *Pacific Encounters* workshops in Marseilles and Canberra, and also members of the RSPAS Pacific and Asian History Seminar. All mistakes and omissions remain, of course, my own.

With regard to the colonial history of other Melanesian settings, I have elsewhere (Mosko 1991, 1992) characterised these complex interplays more generally in terms of plural, competing "messages" and "missions." Here I focus upon similar working misunderstandings between Mekeo and Roro villagers and colonial agents over the effect of the latter's use of Western armaments.

[2] Interestingly, while they cite d'Albertis and Monckton, neither Stephen (1974, 66, 81n, 82n, 101n) nor Bergendorff (1996) have drawn upon them as historical sources, except in the most cursory of fashions, apparently because elements in those accounts – elements on which I rely heavily in the following analysis –conflict with those two authors' conclusions.

[3] Stephen (1974, 63–82) presumes that from 1891 to 1896, when Kowald was killed in an accident, relations between Mekeo/Roro and government agents continued to improve. The evidence here suggests that relations had been deteriorating for some time, culminating in the near-complete breakdown of colonial order.

[4] Ironically, if the dysentery was introduced by the prospectors who had gone up the Angabunga River into the mountains, it would appear likely that it was from that source that the disease was transmitted to Mekeo and Roro living downstream.

[5] Other investigators have noted how the Sacred Heart missionaries came to be seen by villagers as sorcerers. Hau`ofa emphasises how Bishop Vangeke, the first Papua New Guinean priest and later bishop, was widely regarded as a sorcerer by his parishioners. Stephen (1974) and Bergendorff (1996) have noted how early priests endeavoured to learn the ritual of sorcery from the sorcerers so that they could understand it. My village friends insist that the only reason one would want to have such knowledge is to use it in one's own personal projects. In my own discussions with several priests over the years and combing through Sacred Heart archives, I was surprised to learn that since the beginning the priests have argued with villagers – not that their beliefs in the spirits of the dead or the deity Akaisa were false, but that those spirits did indeed exist as devils or the minions of the devil. The priests thus declared that it was a sin to pray to Mekeo or Roro spirits, which of course was required to perform all

indigenous ritual actions, especially sorcery. Also, the missionaries devoted considerable time from the beginning to cure villagers of any ailments that they could, some of which were regarded as caused by sorcerers and, thus, could only be cured by sorcerers (cf. Jolly 1996). Monckton notes how he himself would frequently practise surgery on villagers, and that MacGregor was also a medical doctor, as was the colony's Resident Magistrate at the time, Blayney (Monckton 1920, 10, 113, 131–2). Also, Monckton gives a very lively account of the shooting parties of the priests, their inferior guns, etc. He mentions as well how the priests were adept at hunting with packs of dogs, which to Mekeo similarly requires considerable secret ritual knowledge involving spirits, medicines, etc. – ingredients amounting to sorcery. But the point is, it was not only the government officials and police who monopolised firearms; even the missionaries were included among the proficient gun sorcerers.

[6] To counter those who have dismissed Monckton's account out of hand for his tendency to sensationalism and bravado (e.g. Stephen 1974, 101n), I believe that Monckton's candid seeking of counsel from his assistant, Basilio, at this critical juncture lends certain credibility to his account of these events.

[7] It is interesting to consider the extent to which Seligmann's classic description of Mekeo and Roro cultures elicited mainly from the Sacred Heart missionaries was conditioned by the fact that he had arrived on the scene in the immediate aftermath of the 1898 dysentery epidemic. It is therefore unsurprising that he would have gained the impression, as noted above, that Mekeo and Roro were sorcery-ridden to such an extraordinary extent – without appreciating the contributions to that development which Europeans including d'Albertis, Monckton, and the missionaries whom he was interviewing had made and were still making.

[8] This trajectory of Roro and Mekeo transformation is rare, if not unique, in Melanesia. According to Zelenietz and Lindenbaum (1981), it is the *breakdown* of "in-group authority" that has typically accompanied the inflation in sorcery and hostile magic, and usually it has been sorcery suspicion of hostile neighbours that has been emphasised. The Mekeo case would seem to parallel instead the classic case of Hawai`i, where, in Sahlins' (1981, 1985) account, the initial rise in chiefly ritual authority was closely tied to Hawaiians' perceptions of the spiritual powers of Captain James Cook and members of his crew. Nonetheless, Zelenietz and Lindenbaum note that novel fears about sorcery and magic may follow new patterns of disease transmission, which is, I think, clearly the case with Mekeo and Roro, as some have argued for Hawai`i and elsewhere in the Pacific too (Douglas 1989; Stannard 1989; Jolly 1996; Denoon et al. 2000; Bayliss-Smith 2005).

Chapter 10

A Measure of Violence: Forty Years of "First Contact" Among the Ankave-Anga (Papua New Guinea)

Pascale Bonnemère and Pierre Lemonnier

I have now patrolled all the Kukukuku area except that part within the Eastern Highlands District. This southwesterly fringe of the Kukukuku in the Ivori/Swanson area is the most primitive and uncontacted that I have encountered

(P.G. Whitehead, Assistant District Officer; PNGNA 1966–67a, 8).

After approximately 70 years of control in the Gulf District, this must be the most uncontacted and under-developed area of the inland tribes of any District

(R.S. Bell, District Commissioner).[1]

The Kukukuku, as an informant, is most unreliable

(K.I. Chester, Patrol Officer; PNGNA 1950–51a, 3).

For anyone who has hiked through the Anga country of Papua New Guinea, it is remarkable and obvious that the various groups that comprise the 80,000 strong people who inhabit the area do not share a similar view of modernity. Straddling the borders of the Eastern Highlands, and the Gulf and Morobe Provinces, this territory and its people have long been penetrated by colonisation. However, although these areas were "explored" at about the same time, the Ankave ("contacted" in 1937 or 1938 by A.T. Timperley and then in 1951 by K.I. Chester) and the Baruya ("contacted" in 1951 by J. Sinclair), for instance, show striking differences in their interactions with the agents of the state, church and market. In the Baruya valley of Wonenara, there was an airstrip, a patrol post, and a German Lutheran pastor as early as 1961. By contrast, the Ankave were still being "contacted" in the early 1970s and, as far as we know, they have still *never* seen the patrol officer from Kotidanga who is supposed to look after this northernmost part of the "Ankave-Swanson Census Division" of the Gulf Province of Papua New Guinea, although they have often met police from Menyamya (see figure 10.1).[2] Whereas coffee-bean shellers were common among the Baruya in 1978, as late as 2002 Ankave people still broke coffee beans between two stones, or even with their teeth, and sold a few dozen kilos of dried beans in the Suowi valley (also called Ikundi valley, after the name of the main hamlet). In 2004 white missionaries had yet to install a church and a school in this valley.

Figure 10.1 The Anga groups in Papua New Guinea

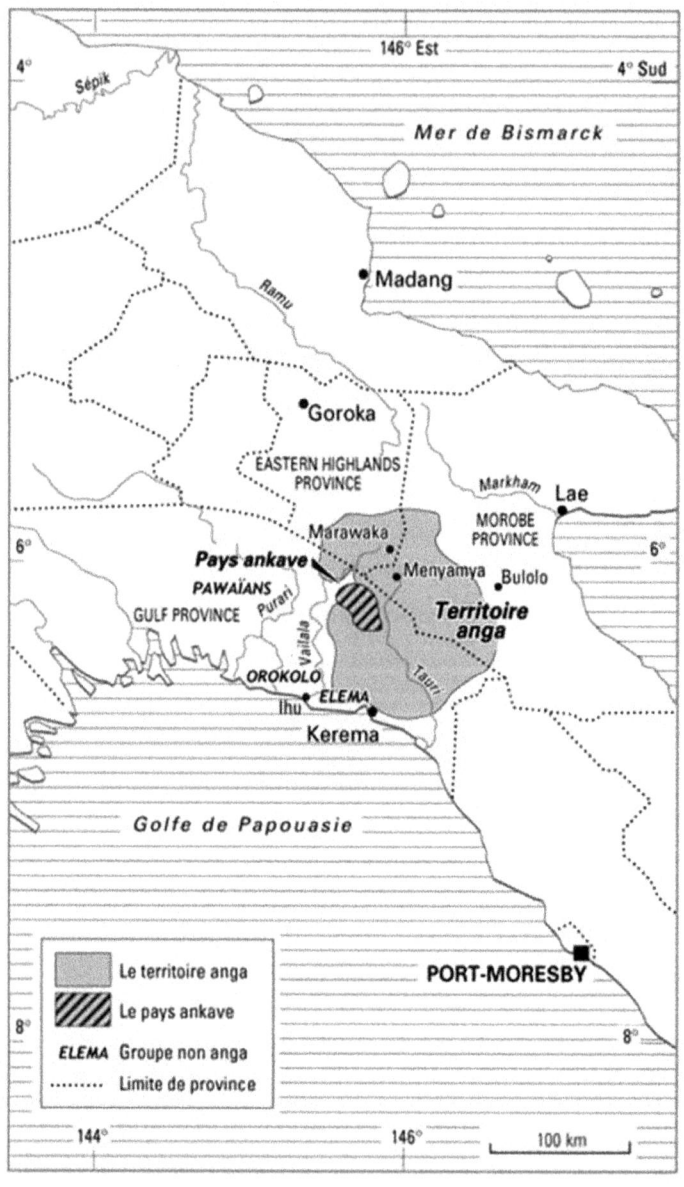

Figure 10.2 The Ankave country

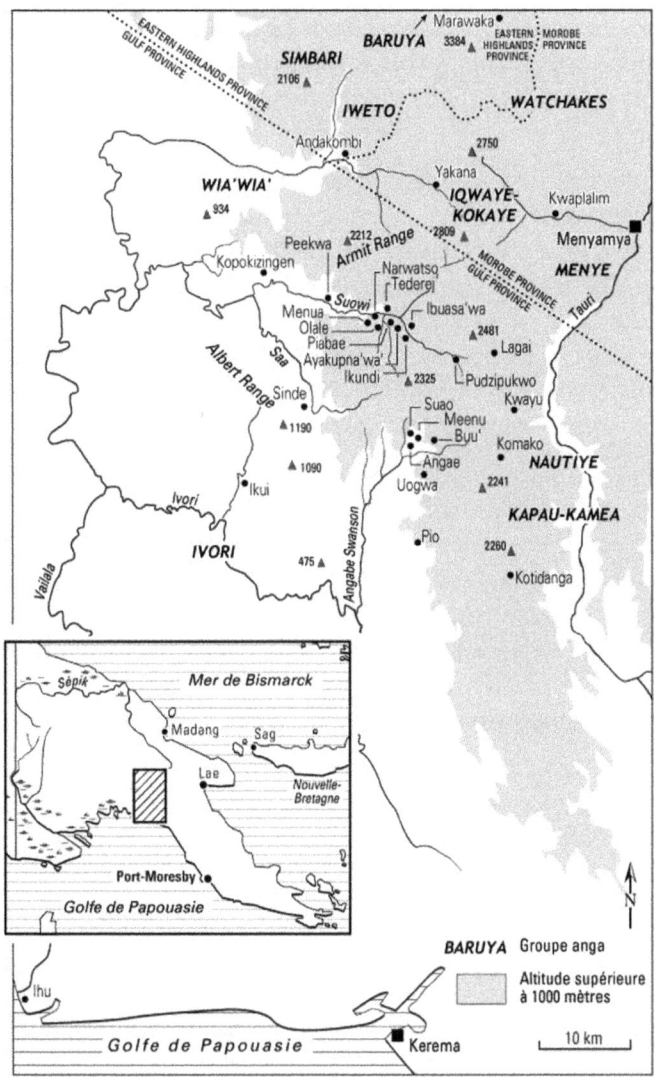

Unlike the Baruya, the Ankave have no bush stores in their valley. Children around Ikundi hope to see a school before they are adults, and their cousins around Angae, near the Ankave-Swanson River (see figure 10.2), miss the *tok ples skul* "school in the local language" (Tok Pisin), which was closed around 1995, three years after the missionary from the Summer Institute of Linguistics departed following a twelve-year stay (1980–92). Similarly, a mere twelve-minute helicopter flight (or a one-and-a-half day walk up and down the mountain) away from computers, co-operative stores, coffee buyers, missions and the health centre at Menyamya (a patrol post opened in November 1950), one is struck by the absolute respect for food taboos, ongoing male initiations, fear of invisible cannibal witches and the semi-annual need to drive away the ghosts of the recent dead, which are all still strongly embedded in everyday Ankave life in sets of representations and practices that were theirs long before they discovered the Australian patrol officers, their carriers, policemen and belief in modernity, fifty years ago.

Such sharp contrasts between areas "contacted" at roughly the same time calls for explanation. As Thomas puts it, in most places in Oceania "there came a time in each place ... when [the] incursions [of the West] ceased to be manageable. The histories subsequent to that time cannot be seen in terms of the increments and extensions of an indigenous cultural logic. The stream of outside offerings ceases to be a matter of contingent events which internal structure selectively receives and accommodates, and the structural aspect of what is external itself impinges on the local system and its contingencies" (1989, 114).

The Ankave have not reached that point yet. Furthermore they have dozens of "reasons" not to be excited by many aspects of modernity. Notably, they still share representations, a worldview and ways of interacting that are linked in some way or another in what we will call a "culture." For instance, in light of their ongoing will to associate the origin of humanity with male initiation, or mortuary rituals with the necessity of chasing away the ghosts of the recent dead, their lack of interest in Christianity comes as no surprise.

On the other hand, there is no doubt that the limited relationship the Ankave entertain with the outside world is related to their sparsely populated valleys, lying well away from the main axes of development in the Highlands and at the intersection of three provinces, each as uninterested in their lot as the next. However, it should be noted that some remote Anga valleys (such as those of Yakana and Andakombi for the Iqwaye, a two-day walk north of the Suowi/M'Bwei valley, see figure 10.2) are home to foreign missionaries, New Guinea teachers, airstrips, aid posts and so on, and such circumstances of "contact" need to be somehow explained.

One particular way to look at the problem raised by Ankave disinterest in modernity is to posit that it derives *partly* from the very form of the series of first contacts — "first contact" needs a plural here — with white people and other New Guineans (Neumann 1994, 113). One factor that may have restricted Ankave interactions with the agents of the state, the church, the school and the market derives from the very characteristics of their first encounters with the strangers who penetrated their valleys roughly between 1938 and 1970. The use of new forms of violence for dealing with internal problems or with conflicts involving people from the two main Ankave valleys is another aspect of today's local life that may have originated in the violence of the encounters. This explains why, although we had no *particular* interest in "first" contacts, we decided to put together the fragments of information regarding the passage of the first Australians, Papuan carriers and police in the area.

Few Sources, So What?

Compared to other areas of Papua New Guinea, the sources for Ankave encounters with the Europeans are few. The area was clearly off the path of the "great patrols," and, as far as we know, no *kiap* ("patrol officer") ever published an account of his explorations in the Ankave-Swanson, Saa'/New Year Creek or M'Bwei/Suowi valleys.

There are two main sources: patrol reports in the PNG National Archives (PNGNA) and the oral history we have collected since 1982. Numbering thirty or so, the patrol reports consulted were written first by pre-World War II administrators who were not based in the Anga region proper (but at Ihu, Salamaua and Kerema), then by *kiaps* after World War II at new patrol posts within that region, at Menyamya, a two-day walk from the Ankave valleys, and at Kaintiba, which is at least four days away from the Ankave (i.e. more than a week at the time of the patrols which were walking through "unknown country").

The Ankave people we have interviewed, or listened to in the last twenty years,[3] belong to three generations:

(1) The first generation comprises old women and men who were 65 or more in 1987 – more precisely, we have a detailed oral account by one man, Idzi Erauje (recorded in 1990), and shorter ones by two women (recorded in 1987).

(2) The second generation comprises people now in their 50s or 60s: a highly detailed account in 1990 from Abraham, a man from Lagai[4] (in Iqwaye country); and interviews of two women done in 2002 about (a) what they knew of encounters with Europeans and (b) what they told their children about them.

(3) The third generation comprises young men and women without children yet, or those with children not yet old enough to be told or comprehend stories: twelve or so of these young people were interviewed in 2002 about what they knew of encounters with white people and unknown New Guineans.

Since the Ankave numbered altogether fewer than 1,000 in three valleys at the time, not many people can have seen the coming of the Australians. Only half a dozen witnesses to the 1938 patrol were still alive when we started to work on "first contact" in 1987, only three of whom talked to us. In the 1980s, there were probably around twenty men and women who remembered more recent events, notably the 1960s patrols, but we actually worked with only a dozen of them. Some important information was also merely mentioned in passing during ordinary conversation. For instance, commenting on the arrival of steel tools in the area, one interlocutor said – in one short sentence – that this was when the first white men came up the valley. For us, notably because we have long been looking for a trace of that party in the archives, this short statement has been an important piece of information. Such a statement is not an account of "first contact," but a mere comment indirectly referring to early encounters.

Since we were dealing with the everyday life of the Ankave (e.g. gender relations, male initiations, land tenure, mortuary rituals, etc.) when we began our long-term fieldwork among the Ankave in 1987, "first" contacts were not our primary concern. Questions that were not asked at the time will thus forever remain unanswered. Yet, because we felt that the violence in these first encounters with white people paved the way for some important aspects of today's life in the Suowi valley, we finally undertook a systematic enquiry.

This chapter compares information derived from the colonial archives with what people "know" about these events, either because they witnessed them or heard about them. It also reports what we can decipher of the consequences of these contacts both before and since we started our fieldwork. In many cases, matching Ankave remembrances with administration reports permitted us to pin down some quite important dates, which were previously only approximate because they were based on the age and memory of the informants (see also Gammage 1999, 4): the first departures for plantation work; the arrival of Seventh Day Adventist New Guinean catechists; and, of course, the violent events that "disrupted" the people we work with.[5] The "matching" also shows how both Ankave and whites have selected specific information to be memorised or transmitted to subsequent generations. In particular, the minimising of all forms of violence in the colonial archives we have consulted so far would be worth an in-depth study. However, and notwithstanding the differences in the meaning of "dates" for the Ankave and for European historians, which we are well aware of, dates are important here. First, as relative time markers ("This took place before or after that"), they are part of Ankave narratives. Second, the people of the Suowi valley are as much interested in the order of the incoming patrols as we are. This is a way for them to relate the chronology of their own violence – namely of wars and vendettas – to that of the whites and their followers, notably because vendettas were used to enforce the ban on armed warfare. These temporal landmarks also have political implications, because people remember fairly well who was living where at the time of these outstanding events. The departure of the young men for plantation work is another historical process in which the sequence of events matters – Who went away first? With whom? For how long? What happened while they were away? Did some co-initiates stay home at that time? What did they bring back?, etc.

Written sources include published books by *kiaps* narrating their own or their colleagues' encounters with the Kukukuku (as the Anga were previously known), especially McCarthy (1963, 90–125) on "The wild men of Menyamya" and Sinclair (1966, 24–75) on the discovery of the "Batiya" (Baruya) salt-makers. Historical publications were used to provide the general context of the "exploration" of Anga country, but they also proved invaluable for us in locating essential archives (Simpson 1953; Sinclair 1966; Souter 1974; Nelson 1976; Fitzpatrick 1999).

There are probably traces of explorations in the SDA or Lutheran mission files in Menyamya, but we have not consulted them, primarily because the mission explorations do not seem to have concerned the Ankave area. Although the Lutheran pastor A.P.H. Freund, (who arrived in Menyamya early in 1951) often made exploratory patrols from Menyamya (with his rifle, the Iqwaye man Abraham recalls, see endnote 4) in areas where the *kiaps* had not yet gone, as far as we know, it seems that none went into the Suowi or Ankave-Swanson valleys. A Lutheran mission was opened at Kwaplalim by Reverend Russel Weir in September 1957 (Fitzpatrick 1999, 191), but we have never heard his name among the Ankave. In 1990, Abraham remembered well that "Rasol Wua" had come to the neighbouring valley of Lagai around 1957, but not to the Ankave area. There were SDA personnel from Menyamya[6] at Buu' in the Ankave-Swanson valley as early as 1966, that is, at a time when the region was still "restricted."[7] They were people from Menyamya, and not Australians, and we doubt that they left reports; however, if they did, these would of course be worth their weight in gold. In the Suowi (Ikundi) valley, mission work proper did not start before 1972, a few years after young men started to go to work on the plantations.

Gold and Order: The General Context of the Explorations among the Anga (Kukukuku)

The bulk of the exploration of the Kukukuku country was concomitant with the first discoveries of gold ore, before 1910. In 1906, Monckton (a resident magistrate)[8] descended the Lakekamu River (Simpson 1953, 15; Souter 1974, 85; Gash and Whittaker 1975, 242–3), and gold was found midway down the river in 1909 by prospectors who had first explored the Tauri (Simpson 1953, 15; Gash and Whittaker 1975, 260, 263; Nelson 1976, 194–8, 224). In 1907, the first two Australian officials posted to the new Gulf "division" (Captain Griffin, then Higginson) successively went up the Lohiki River, which is the first important tributary of the Vailala as one goes inland (Souter 1974, 98–9).[9] In September 1909 two German explorers, Dammköhler and Oldörp, ascended the Watut River from the Markham and were attacked by thirty natives armed with spears, bows and arrows – they were possibly Kukukuku. Dammköhler died from his numerous wounds (Souter 1974, 112–3; Burton 1996, 2). In 1910, an Australian prospector illegally sneaked into German New Guinea, went up the Waria River, then the Watut and discovered gold in Koranga Creek, a tributary of the Bulolo River (Demaître 1935, 44–6; Simpson 1953, 25). Although it was a one-day walk from the nearest Anga village, Nepa was for many years the only government station in Anga country (Nelson 1976, 216). In 1912, two Lutheran missionaries crossed the northeast corner of the Kukukuku region during an extraordinary trek from the Watut to the Markham.[10] World War I was the time of the long wanderings of German Captain H. Detzner, who refused to surrender to the British in 1914 and walked through New Guinea until 1918, including part of that same region between Watut and Markham, though doubts remain about the exact Anga area he went through (Detzner 1935, 57–61, 177; Burton 1996, 8–12; Gammage, pers. comm. 2004). In 1916 and 1917, patrols from Kerema reached the Lohiki and even the Ivori, that is, the tributary of the Vailala River immediately south of the Ankave territory (Skelly 1919). Both Skelly, around the Ivori, and Griffin, on the Lohiki, describe Anga men and women fainting with terror and excitement at the sight of white people (Simpson 1953, 16). Although an important mountain range in Ankave country is called "Staniforth," it is unlikely that the administrator of Papua, Staniforth Smith, who headed the Kikori expedition in 1910–11, actually passed nearby, for the area in which he wandered was at least 150 kilometres west of the Vailala as the crow flies (Smith 1911).

It is mostly from camps of gold prospectors or miners that, in the pre-World War II period, Europeans penetrated Anga territories lying far in the interior of the island. This penetration mainly concerned the valleys immediately west of the gold fields of Wau and Bulolo. The prospectors who explored the region between the Watut and the Markham were usually followed by Australian *kiaps* chasing Kukukuku who had attacked these prospectors.[11]

Administration exploration of Ankave territory proper did not start until late 1929, when Middleton reached its westernmost part (PNGNA 1929–30). But there are indications that gold miners may have penetrated the Ankave country from the Vailala. First, Nelson (1976, 219) mentions that Pryke led prospectors 120 miles up the Vailala in December 1911. They reached the Iova (a right-bank tributary of the Vailala, some 15 kilometres downstream from the spot where the M'Bwei/Suowi flows into the river), "and then walked east" – that is, probably toward the lower Fore/Sambia country. On the way back, the party – including Pryke, who was badly wounded in the chest by a Kukukuku arrow – explored the Ivori and the Lohiki. These areas are located north and south of Ankave territory, but the miners may have been quite near places like Ikui, a tiny Ankave hamlet a few hours' walk north of the lower Ivori, from which people have reached Esu (Ihu) by raft or canoe possibly since the 1950s. It was during the patrol led by the Assistant Resident Magistrate E.C. Skelly on the Ivori in 1917 that the Angabe was named "Swanson River" after a Mr. Swanson (Skelly 1919, 72).[12]

And so, administration explorations reached the western tip of the Ankave country for the first time in late 1929. Four years later, on the site of the present-day district offices of Menyamya in the Tauri valley, located a mere two-days' walk from the northeastern part of the same territory, McCarthy opened a patrol post in the middle of a huge, flattish savannah. Several Anga groups believed this to be close to the spot where humanity originated and where their languages and cultures started to differentiate. A first aeroplane landed there on 2 September 1933, but the post was rapidly abandoned because of the absence of gold and also, because the Kukukuku regularly attacked the patrols (McCarthy 1926–52, 1963: 90–113; Sinclair 1966, 8; Gammage 1998, 21–22). McCarthy explored the Tauri valley, and several prospectors – namely, Yeomans, Jensen, Lewis, Lorenz – "extended their journey to the headwaters of the Vailala River" (Sinclair 1978: 210, 2001: 152). According to the patrol reports (PNGNA 1933–34, 29–41), the area they explored at that time was the Iqwaye country, that is, the valley just north of the Ankave territory. They do not seem to have entered the high Kuowi or Suowi valleys, nor any part of the Ankave country (PNGNA 1933–34). Exploration stopped during World War II, but a hundred kilometres east of the Ankave territory, the building of the Wau-Bulldog track in 1942–43 employed more than two thousand New Guinea labourers and a thousand soldiers on the border with the Kapau country (Powell 2003, 34–37).[13]

Europeans in Ankave Country

The documented contacts with the Ankave are summarised below in Table 10.1. As one can see, twelve years passed between the last pre-war and the first post-war patrol in or near the Ankave valleys. Another fifteen years (1950–65) elapsed between Chester's and O'Brien's patrols. Exploration and law-and-order were still the main goals of these administrative penetrations of the area until 1970, when Coles led "the first patrol of a non-punitive type."[14] Without exception, the reports dealing with the period we are investigating here speak of "contacting" people, making census, "spreading government influence," and explaining what the Australian administration was willing to and could offer. Coles' 1970 patrol actually had nothing to do with "law-and-order" problems, but it appears to be an exception: fighting on the Ivori/Ankave border continued at least until 1972.[15] We will see that tensions between the main Ankave valleys soon developed into non-lethal but very violent encounters in which the administration was enrolled, if not manipulated. The main change here was that fights were between Papuans, whereas pre-war patrols elsewhere in the Kukukuku country often dealt with attacks on gold miners or *kiaps*.

Table 10.1 Administrative patrols in or around Ankave country (1929–72)

1917–18 E.C. Skelly, 20 October to 9 November 1917, ascended the Ivori as far as the Angabe, which he named the "Swanson" (Skelly 1919, 72).

1929 S.G. Middleton (PNGNA 1929–30), 29 November 1929, to 26 January 1930, went up the Vailala and lower Ivori River, including a section of the stream that the Yoye Amara of Sinde (Ankave speakers) used for their trade expeditions. [16]

1937–38 Together with Patrol Officer A. Timperley and nine policemen, the Australian geologist S.W. Carey walked from the Upper Vailala River to the Tauri (along the Mbwei river that flows between the Staniforth and Armit ranges) on an exploratory patrol for the Oil Search Limited company (Murray 1937–38, 27; Carey 1990, 20–21; Sinclair 2001, 198). Having departed from Kerema on 27 October 1937, Timperley came back on 14 January 1938 after having gone through the Mbwei valley between 8 and 21 December 1937. This was a long and very difficult trip during which it is reported that first contact was made. Several violent conflicts occurred between the population and members of the prospecting expedition which ended with casualties on both sides as well as repeated desertions from exhausted and frightened carriers (Murray 1937–38, 27; PNGNA 1937–38). [17]

1951 K.I. Chester (PNGNA 1950–51a), 3 January 1951 to 29 February 1951, coming from Menyamya, descended the M'Bwei River as far as the Vailala River, including Yoye Amara territory (also called New Year Creek, Saa' River). [18] Chester estimated the population in the M'Bwei valley at 500 persons, but the valley was "unpopulated for most of its length." Before they left, instructions had been given to the members of the party about the thieving habits of the Kukukuku. They were consequently warned not to leave any axes or knives lying around. On February 13, it is noted that "people were not very enthusiastic about us." As Patrol Officer O'Brien comments some fifteen years later, "This patrol happens to have been just passing through the area to obtain an idea of the population living there" (PNGNA 1965–66a, 25).

1951 L. Hurrell (PNGNA 1950–51b), 20 June to 8 July 1951, patrolled the Iqwaye valley of Peemdzerwa, crossed the range that separated the valleys converging toward Menyamya from those at the "Vailala Headwaters." He visited the Iqwaye valley around Yakana, a two-day walk due north of the Ankave territory, but he did not enter the M'Bwei/Suowi valley. He met "refugees from the Iakoi River villages" and "brought from the Vailala several old men to see the Kokaia [Iqwaye of the Iakoi River, west of Menyamya] people and have a reunion" (PNGNA 1950–51c, 7,

9). It seemed that word of this may have reached the Lagai valley where many other Iqwaye refugees, those living on the upper the Kuowi (a large tributary of the M'Bwei), came from.

1951 O.J. Mathieson (PNGNA 1951–52b), 1 August to 7 September 1951, coming up from Kerema, went through the Yoye Amara village of Pipidawa, whose inhabitants took him to the Ivori River, where he met a SDA catechist. Further on, he reached the Swanson but stayed in Ivori country without entering the Ankave area. [19]

1953 W.M. Purdy (PNGNA 1953–54), 23 October to 9 November 1953, walked from the Iakwoi valley to Yakana, around the "Vailala Headwaters." As a result of patrols by Hurrell and Purdy, the Iqwaye who had been settled on Ankave territory for almost ten years were safely brought back to their homeland.

1965 K.G. O'Brien (PNGNA 1965–66a), 18 September to 23 October 1965, ascended the M'Bwei River, cutting across Saa'/New Year Creek; stayed around Ayakupna'wa', then went to the Swanson valley, up to Meenu. This was a "joint patrol" with Weber (PNGNA 1965–66b). [20]

1966 P.G. Whitehead (PNGNA 1966–67a), 24 November to 23 December 1966, enquired about murders in the Ivori River area, near Pio, and looked for Ankave witnesses at Buu' ("The area is primitive and uncontrolled, and many villages were entered for the first time" (1966–67a, 7)). This was a joint patrol with R.A. Deverell (PNGNA 1966–67b).

1967 G.C. Connor (PNGNA 1966–67c), 23 June to 23 July 1967, walked from Kaintiba via Komako to the Ankave-Swanson (Buu' and Angae) and the Suowi (Ikundi) valleys, "to contact people in Swanson and M'Bwei River regions" ("Object of patrol"). This is a well-remembered patrol, notably because some six policemen searched the area for twenty days, trying to capture a man who had shot a carrier.

1969 A.M. Didlick (PNGNA 1969–70a), 22 August to 2 September 1969, enquired about alleged murders at Manteba and Famba, on the upper Ivori River. In "fact," it appeared that the two dead people had drowned. [21] The bulk of the patrol stayed in the Ivori country, but two policemen went to the Swanson area (Uogwa), looking for escapees from the Kerema jail (PNGNA 1969–70a, 1, 3).

1970 R.S. Coles (PNGNA 1969–70b), 3 to 25 March 1970, enquired about a murder in Buu'. However, the assistant district commissioner in Kerema notes: "After 60 years, the last of the Kerema inland areas is now administratively settled." [22] The *kiap* writes that "the main idea of this [patrol] is to demonstrate that the Administration can do something for the people besides chasing them up hill and down dale"; "Some 50 adults

(15 men and the rest women) claimed that they had not previously seen a European at close quarters before. All had heard of Europeans before and all the men and about half of the women had seen patrols passing through the area, but they had remained hidden and watched from a distance" (PNGNA 1969–70b, 1).

1970 R.S. Coles (PNGNA 1970–71), 8 October to 11 November 1970, went to Uogwa, Buu', Meenu in the Ankave-Swanson valley with only three policemen, one medical orderly and two interpreters. "The majority of the population are still wary of administrative patrols. At least part of this wariness would be due to the mistreatment given to these people by some members of former administration patrols and village officials from other areas" (PNGNA 1970–71, 5).

1972 A.J. Meikle (PNGNA 1971–72), 1 to 18 May 1972, apropos of raids between Pio/Famba and Sinde, did not go into the Ankave-Swanson nor the M'Bwei/Suowi but descended the Ivori River. "At Sande [Sinde] on New Year Creek two men were found who could speak pidgin (of sorts) which they had picked up whilst working on 'big line' in Menyamya" (PNGNA 1971–72, 3) – this is the place where a Belgian TV crew met "Stone Age people" twenty-one years later [23] (Lemonnier 2004).

Fragments of Ankave Memories

We do not know much about the general impressions the whites made on the Ankave. Some thought the Europeans were dead people coming back, as they were as clear-skinned as dead bodies are after being rubbed and anointed with grey or white clay. But others clearly explain that the *kiaps* or Catholic missionaries looked like the *pisingain awo'* ("bush spirits") and not like the *pisingain siwi* ("spirits of the recent dead"). They called the Australians *ange wietange'* ("people from elsewhere") or *wauze* ("strangers"). The Australians were tall, and so were their Vailala carriers, truly immense compared to the Anga. They had dogs; they had firearms; the police were violent; and they asked to clear a piece of forest in a certain place, right on top of the present anthropic savannah of Ayakupna'wa'; a woman who remembers that the "strangers" did not eat the grease, skin and bones of the pigs they killed, but only the meat.

In the Ankave accounts, three main points are underlined: the violence; "the cowrie shells that fell from the sky"; and the identity of the people who had a house next to the place where the patrol cleared the forest in view of this airdrop. The last is important, because it is now proof that some members of the Idzadze clan already had a right to live on this piece of land belonging to the Nguye clan, which will become the pathway for modernity entering the valley, when the airstrip is completed, if ever. In other words, this event (the 1965 patrol, see below) is immediately linked with the present: new forms of violence involving the police and tensions over land surrounding the future airstrip, which the Ankave equate with access to regular health services, the coming of a schoolteacher and, more generally, a door opening onto modernity. The modification in the exchange rates due to the sudden abundance of cowrie shells is not commented upon, but the money falling from the sky – and the view of a plane circling in low passes over rugged terrain – is still remembered as part of these extraordinary events.

As already mentioned, part of the information about these first encounters derives from very short statements made in passing during conversations or interviews dealing with other topics.

The first patrol known to have entered the Suowi (that is, the first ever in Ankave territory) was that of Carey and Timperley in December 1937 (see Table 10.1). It is said to have killed two Ankave men, and a "policeman" was shot in the eye. In fact, as already mentioned, five carriers from this exploratory patrol were killed and eleven went "missing." An old woman remembers:

> I was married and had several children when a white man came with many other people from Ihu. He killed a man from here. Several men took bushknives belonging to the white man. Back then, we had only stone axes. When the white man woke up, he killed Toatto Ngudze, who was not the culprit. He was not the one who stole the bushknife; other men did it. Everybody was very frightened and went back home. The white man stayed six days (Iwasi Rwej, an old woman; recorded on 26 June 1987, at Ayakupna'wa').

But a few days later this old woman, Iwasi Rwej, denied that Toatto Ngudze was killed by the Australian patrol officer and said instead that he had been the victim of a local man, after a dispute about an adultery. Abraham, the Iqwaye man who was a refugee along the Upper Suowi River until an early 1950s patrol took his family back to his own valley of Lagai, spoke of the killing a few years later. He was a child in 1950, but the fairly well-documented account he gave us of that first, and violent, patrol had been told to him when he was a young man:

> The white people had left some of their cargo in order to prepare the next step of their patrol. At that time, another man, Ikundi Onaxo, stole a machete and ran away. When they realised that, they shot the first man they encountered, and that was Toatto Ngudze. The women were hidden nearby with their children. They gave no steel tools or shells because they were cross. That [stolen machete] was the first gained by the Ikundi people.
>
> At the place where the Tsigigni [stream] flows into the Kuowi [river], above Ikundi near Pudzipukwo, Abe Nguye akwije, one of the victim's

> brothers, shot a Papuan policeman in the eye with an arrow. They [the patrol] wanted to retaliate, but the attacker(s) ran away. The patrol's dogs did not find [the man who had shot the arrow]. The policeman did not die on the spot. They carried him. The two whites walked in the lead. After Pudzipukwo, they met a man from Lagai named Wewo ognorwa [of the Akwirele clan] who was out walking. It was the first time this man saw white people because no one had come from Menyamya yet to this place [the Suowi valley]. He was looking from a distance, and they killed him because they thought that he was preparing an ambush. They went on and made a camp, at the place where Maadze Angapatse ulakwa had the last [Ankave] gardens in the valley. They had left some supplies in Ikundi. Their patrol boxes were empty. The next day, they went through Kwaye[24] to take the track that goes up [to Komako]. The policeman died on top of the ridge; they left his body there, under some leaves, together with a patrol-box that was too heavy (recorded on 21 July 1990, in Ayakupna'wa').

According to Carey, who mentions that bushknives were "coveted" (1990, 22), only one native was killed – by Carey himself – because he was aiming an arrow at him. Carey knew that this person "belonged to the next valley over the Vailala–Tauri divide," so he was probably Wewo ognorwa.

Violence was also part of the second patrol remembered, which was clearly that of Chester, in February 1951. Some members of the patrol stole sugarcanes from a garden and shot a big male pig.

> At the time I had a child. A white man came with several policemen from the lowlands, stopped at Pudzipukwo and returned following the same road. People from here stole their knives. The white man tied Iwadze Erwanguye up with a rope for he wanted to take him with him. But Iwadze Erwanguye broke the rope and told his dog to kill this man. But they finally did not fight. The patrol looked for a man from here to bring him back with them. These knives were the first we ever saw. We gave food to the whites and they gave us a few machetes. We bought beads, but we did not give them cowries. Before, there were no cowries; we only had many when they fell from the sky (Igete wiej, a woman of 70 or more, Ayakupna'wa', October 1987).

The only other data we have of this patrol is an oral account given by Abraham:

> Nguye Omadze stole a steel axe. The patrol threatened the people by saying that they would burn the houses if the axe was not brought back.[25] At some stage, they captured Erwa Nguye and tied him up with a rope, but he pretended he wanted to go to the toilet and freed himself with a bamboo knife. But, when the next patrol entered the area, coming

from Menyamya via Lagai, Iqwaye carriers told their Ankave affines not to behave "badly" [i.e. not to steal], because the whites had given them beads and cowries in exchange for food. The Ankave did not bring food to the patrol, a good reason for Chester to just pass through (Abraham; recorded on 21 July 1990, in Ayakupna'wa').

Fifteen years later, the carriers accompanying the next patrol in the area (coming from the coast) – the patrol of O'Brien (1965–66) and seven policemen accompanied by two Catholic priests from Kavava (Ihu) (PNGNA 1965–66a)[26] – had to point to their belly so that the Ankave of the Suowi would understand they wanted food. People who agreed to bring tubers were given beads, razors, matches and salt. That was the time "when cowries fell from the sky" – as an old woman once told us, that is, when a plane circled above Ayakupna'wa', where people had cut trees to prepare "a helicopter site" on which cargo (food, tools, beads and cowries) was dropped. If one can judge by the precision of the memory, that event was a watershed:

> The whites gave us axes so that we could cut trees, then they installed a radio. We did not know what it was. They stayed one day and told us that a plane was coming, but we did not understand, except that we had to hide. He wanted everybody to gather in one place so that the supplies would not fall on our heads [during the airdrop]. The plane came from the west, from Kerema.[27] I wanted to go to Lagai in order to fetch Abraham to translate what the whites said. On my way I met someone [a man named Wamdze, who was still alive in 1990] who could do that. So, that man acted as an interpreter.

> So we hid. We heard the noise of the plane circling above Ayakupna'wa' without seeing where the people were. The carrier lit a great fire; the plane came down circling and dropped patrol boxes and big bags full of different kinds of shells. The bags broke [there were five bags] and one of the three patrol-boxes too. There was rice, *girigiri* [Tok Pisin, "small cowrie shells"], tins, sugar, coconuts. No axes or machetes, those had been brought by the carriers. There was a bag missing. People from here [Ayakupna'wa'] had hidden it under some leaves. The white man gathered us to sort out what was going on. The translator explained where he had seen the bag fall and it was found. There was frozen meat, rice. He [the Australian] gave some to the people and asked where the translator came from. He said he lived in Lagai and had come to help the people from here. He had gone to school in Wau with Abraham. The white man and his carriers spent the night here and said they wanted to kill a pig. So we gave him one we had previously killed.

> Before he ate, the white man gathered the young men: he designated some of them, those he wanted to go to school: Apatse, Maadze Nguye,

Maadze Angapatse akwije, Ngwadze akwije [who was dead by the time of the interview], Apatse Wadzo [deceased], Ngwadze Nguye [deceased] and Mark. All were already initiated. They were afraid, but they went. Their parents killed a pig and the white men stayed one more night. The next day, they destroyed their shelter and off they went. Maadze Erauje [deceased] joined the group of youths. They followed the Kuowi up to its headwaters and decided to spend the night up there, on the border between Angae and Ikundi. The young men tried to run away. They had been sent to fetch firewood, and they escaped (Idzi Erauje, a man aged 70 or so in 1990, living in Ikundi; recorded in July 1990 in Ajakupna'wa').

When Asaia [the narrator's son, born around 1975] was still young, I told him that the whites had thrown *girigiri* and beads. We took them: they had fallen all around and we gathered them up. It was the first time we saw that. The women gathered the shells and the men cut the trees. They gave axes and machetes. We used this *girigiri* until the [Australian] money came. Now we use it as body decorations. We wear shirts and trousers and we do not use shell money anymore. The time of Independence, we call it *Keba'ya*. The whites came from down below and came up the Suowi. There were five white people[28] and very tall people from Papua [Pawaïans are, indeed, very tall]. They took me into their house. I was [staying] with my future in-laws [at the time]. They told me: '*Yu stap na harim long redio*' [Tok Pisin. 'Stay there and listen to the (shortwave two-way) radio']. I was with my father-in-law and they gave me beads, salt and matches. I listened to the radio. My father was dead. The women were afraid. I myself was worried, but I did not cry because I was already grown up [12–13 years old]. I told that story to my children, and only that one. I did not see which track they took when they left. They gave us shells, which we ground down on stones and made into *kama'a*. I do not remember the stories suggesting fights [with the Australians]. I do not remember that a man shot a carrier. After this patrol, no one came [no other white].(Ikundi Beri, a woman aged 50 or so; recorded in July 2002 in Ajakupna'wa').

I was young and I had no children yet. Angeri Wadze akwije's mother had just given birth. She was frightened and ran away with her baby. There were a lot of people: two white men with tents, which they installed on top of the "airstrip" [that is, the area where the future airstrip is projected to be]. People from here cut trees at the whites' request. The next day one plane, only one, circled and dropped *kama'a* and *sinangwen'* shells. The patrol boxes fell. One fell in a tree and broke. We had never seen *girigiri* before. We cleaned them ourselves. There were beads. They had told us before that these shells were going to fall from the sky, together with rice and tinned fish. We gathered only the shells. Everyone had come back to gather them – men, women and children. The beads were given by the whites in exchange for some food. They were so kind and so tall. ... We gave them sugarcane, bananas and greens, and we got beads in exchange. They stayed five days; they slept five nights and went on the road to Buu'. They slept at the head of the Kuowi River (Onorwa'e, a woman aged 50 or so; recorded in July 2002 in Ajakupna'wa').

Cowries fell down in great amounts at the time [or shortly afterward] these whites came [see the Igete wiej's account above, of the patrol by Chester in 1951]. They had built a house at the top of the "airstrip" site. They stayed quite a bit of time; in their bags, they had *buai* [Tok Pisin, "lowland areca nut"] and *girigiri*. They gave us small and big knives as well as axes (Igete wiej, a woman aged 70 or so; recorded in October 1987 in Ayakupna'wa).

Igete wiej showed one of us (Pascale Bonnemère) a very old knife and said that the whites ate only the meat of the pigs that had been killed for them and discarded the grease, the skin and the bones, which they threw away anywhere around. A woman who was seated next to her added:

They made me sit down on a patrol box, because I had brought food to them. I thought they wanted to take me with them. They raped a woman, Ngudzi abenaxej, and left after four nights (Nguye onexej, a woman aged 70 or so; recorded in October 1987 in Ayakupna'wa').

Sometimes the ethnography complements the patrol reports fairly well. In a patrol report from 1967, for instance, it is noted in passing that, while searching in the upper M'Bwei (Suowi) valley for a man from Angae who had shot a carrier, the party that stayed there for one week met three men from Ikundi who "had recently returned from a 12-month labouring expedition to Rabaul" (PNGNA 1966–67c, 3–5).[29] Matching that report with information scattered in our notes enables us to ascertain the dates of a series of departures, when some thirty-five men went to plantations between the 1960s and 1975 (that is, at a time when most of the Ankave area was still considered "uncontacted"!).[30]

During one of the last "exploration patrols," the victims of violence were on the government side only:

On the morning of Friday June 30th [1967], the Village Councillor from Kwayu [in Kamea territory, a day's walk east of the Swanson River] informed us that he had previous knowledge of the Meenu people [an Ankave hamlet in the Swanson area] and that he understood their local dialect, and that he would like to go with a group of men from his village to try and contact the Meenus. He stated that he would go alone, without a police escort as he believed that the people had run away yesterday because they were afraid of the police as well as myself.

Upon coming to Meenu they saw one man working in his garden and they approached him. The man turned, saw them, and evidently became afraid, as, before they could talk to him he picked up his bow and arrows and fired one arrow which struck one of the carriers above the right breast and penetrated to a depth of about 6 inches. The man who fired the arrow then ran off into the bush and was not pursued.[31]

A police party was sent, which searched unsuccessfully for the Ankave man who had shot the carrier for 20 days in a 30-mile radius.[32] While the policemen were in the M'Bwei [Suowi] valley, '1930 [i.e. 7:30 p.m.] report comes that Constable Yan who is with the search party in the M'Bwei River area, has fallen over a rock face and is unable to walk.'[33] The carrier and the policeman were picked up by a helicopter on July 2nd and July 17th respectively and 'it is felt that money, time and effort cannot be spent on these small pockets of semi-nomadic hunters, who do not wish our presence.'[34]

Seen from the Ankave side (that is, the tape-recorded life story of Peter Saapitso from Angae as well as various indications scattered in our notes), the story runs like this:[35] As usual the carriers recruited in Kaintiba or in the Vailala area were "supplemented as required by local Kukukuku carriers on a village to village basis" (PNGNA 1966–67a, 11). In fact, the attacked carrier was previously known to the people around Meenu and Angae: he was a Naotiye (i.e. a Kapau) from Kwayu, who had previously raped the wife of Iwadze Toatto, the man who shot him. As for Constable Yan, it happens that he fell on the slippery river rocks while running after Ibua Akwoningi, then a young woman. Iwadze Toatto took refuge with a brother-in-law at Sinde – the main hamlet on the banks of the Saa'/New Year Creek river valley, some fifteen kilometres long, where some forty to fifty people live. According to what Peter Saapitso was told when he was young,

> Iwadze Toatto was hiding and one of his brothers-in-law living in Ikundi helped him to hide. Two men from Lagai, who had come to Angae in order to buy bark capes, had their hands tied too and they were asked where the fugitive was. The young man [from Lagai] denounced Iwadze Toatto and said that, if the handcuffs were removed, he would show the way. The fugitive, therefore, fled farther. The members of the patrol caught the people they found here [Ikundi] and tied their hands because they refused to talk. They burned the houses and the gardens and killed all the pigs, which were left to rot. They destroyed the place and raped the women. People from here went to get people from Kwaplalim. They ran after the fugitive. Ibua Akwoningi ran away and a black policeman

ran after her. In his flight, he fell into the We'ne River, near Ikundi, and drowned. A helicopter searched for him and he survived [he was not totally drowned then!]. He was half dead, but kept on shooting his gun to let the other policemen know of his presence.

They chased the fugitive to the Kogan River, then came back empty-handed and took a bunch of people [but not Idzi Erauje or Ibua Akwoningi] back to Angae. There the whites made a big speech: "It's all your fault if they wrecked your villages, etc. Don't do it again." They sent the people of Ikundi back home, except for three persons, all of whom are dead today [Apatse Iwadze, Maadze Erauje and Iwadze Sandze]. These three went to work at the Kaintiba airstrip; in reality they were responsible for the firewood only. They came back on foot [it's a long walk] after two weeks. An old man from Lagai came back with his handcuffs still on his wrists and his hands were swollen (Peter Saapitso, a man born around 1965; recorded in July 2002 in Ikundi).

Violence and Shells: A Process of Selective Remembrance?

Analysing the oral accounts of Ankave people from three different generations apropos encounters with the whites offers an opportunity to think about the way these people construct their own memory of these events. This also points to how violence is told, or not told, as well as to what is transmitted to children and young people.

The interviews took place at different times. In 1987 and 1990, two fieldwork periods when our line of research was not particularly focused on encounters with outsiders, older women came to Pascale Bonnemère to tell stories about these events. As we have seen, when Iwasi Rwej spoke about the first patrol that ever entered the Suowi valley in 1937–38 (by Timperley and Carey, described above), she mentioned the name of one of the two men killed, but, when asked again a few days later about what she had previously said, she denied that he had been killed by a white man, attributing his death to an internal vendetta instead. She added that she did not want to say more about this because she did not remember the events well. Whether this change of mind is to be attributed to memory failure or to an uncomfortable feeling toward the white ethnographer is not possible to tell. But it must be noted that in 1990, when Abraham from Lagai gave Pascale Bonnemère a detailed account of this event, Idzi Erauje – passing by – told him that it was not a good idea to tell her all this, that "the whites could take revenge." He was, of course, talking about the shooting of the policeman in the eye with an arrow. The older people, who had witnessed these violent encounters, were thus clearly not at ease with these extremely violent events.[36]

What Igete wiej and Abraham related about the next patrol (by Chester in 1951) also concerns a violent event: what was emphasised by both were the theft of knives and seizing of a man. In 2002, by contrast, no one talked of the first and violent encounters that had been spontaneously mentioned fifteen years before. As mentioned previously, two categories of people were interviewed: women aged 50–60, of whom two (Ikundi beri and Onorwa'e) gave quite detailed accounts (see above), and several younger men and women. All of them talked about the patrol led by O'Brien, which involved the airdrop. We may infer that, as time passed, these informants did not talk about events that did not concern them. In 1937/38, when Timperley and Carey's patrol entered the valley, the older women were not even born. In 1951, they were very young girls. As for the youngest people, they were not yet born at the time.

It is as direct witnesses that, in 2002, when systematic interviews were undertaken, the middle-aged women gave personal accounts with details about events that they themselves had experienced (Ikundi beri being asked to come with her future father-in-law to listen to the radio when she was 12–13 years of age) or which occurred when the white people approached the campsite (Onorwa'e remembering that a woman who had just given birth fled in terror with her newborn child when she saw them). For some reason, mothers' personal experiences have not been transmitted to younger generations. The accounts that the children of Onorwa'e gave do not contain details of this kind, and only the main lines of what happened were told. On the whole, what is firmly known by the younger people is restricted to: first, the general geographical direction from which the patrol came; and second, the airdrop that followed a few days later, with all the goods being scattered on the ground and people picking them up.[37] Compared to the older generations' recall and comments, the violence of the first encounters is strikingly absent.

The one event mentioned briefly but repeatedly is the airdrop of all sorts of supplies, including beads and shells. It has been described at length above from accounts given by two old people (Nguye onerej, a woman, and Idzi Erauje, a man) in 1987 and 1990, and by two rather younger women, aged fifty and sixty years in 2002. Moreover, this is something young generations spoke of as well.

To sum up, two points have to be emphasised, both of which are related to the status of violence in regard to encounters with the whites and the memory of them. The first concerns the obliteration of any mention of violence, the second the relation of gender to memory.

As far as we can tell, no transmission to younger generations has been made of the violent events that occurred during the first patrols. Apparently, people who were reluctant to speak to us of the violence of the 1937 and 1951 encounters did not talk more freely about them to other Ankave either. There has not been any cultural elaboration of violent past encounters with Australians, since all the younger people inhabiting the Suowi valley in 2002 simply do not know about them.

This would match the findings of previous analyses dealing with the question of transmission. Edward Schieffelin notes that the "stories of the [Strickland–Purari] patrol were not often told by the people amongst themselves and were not particularly well known to the younger generation" (Schieffelin and Crittenden 1991, 9). It might also be the case that the Ankave situation parallels that of the Huli, about which Chris Ballard writes that those narratives told by the women were for women only (2003, 124).

Can we, therefore, say that the first violent encounter with the whites is something that Ankave people simply want to forget? It seems that this may be the case. The only image of these strangers in people's minds today is that of a provider of goods that one day dropped from a plane and scattered on the ground. Some of these goods were new to people at the time, but they are now part of the landscape. It is well known that, in other parts of what is now Papua New Guinea, the giving of shells (identical to the ones they already had through inter-tribal exchanges) by the Australians has been interpreted as a mark of their human nature (Strathern 1992, 251; Ballard 2003, 130). It was only when such an exchange gesture was made that local people could determine the identity of these strangers. Among the Ankave people, while the violence of the first whites entering their valleys has been forgotten for lack of transmission, it seems probable that, like elsewhere in the country, the image of them as providers of shells will be transmitted to future generations, and become an enduring one.

The second point that can be made concerns gender and memory. When comparing the accounts of the same event given by a man (Idzi Erauje) and by two women, it becomes possible to propose hypotheses about who transmits information to younger generations and what kind. The event in question is the encounter with O'Brien and his carriers, immediately followed by the airdrop. In July 1990, Idzi Erauje told Pascale Bonnemère in great detail what happened during this patrol (see above). Although the events occurred twenty-five years prior to the interview, his memories were quite vivid. He rendered them in chronological order and, on the whole, with great clarity. He remembered the names of the young boys (all initiated at the time) whom the white man wanted to take away to school but who finally fled. In short, his account was quite factual. When, in 2002, his young adult son was asked what he knew about the encounters, nothing similar came out, although he is one of the most talkative young men in the valley. He clearly did not know this story in detail.

Now, for some reason (including demographic ones – e.g. "my father died without telling me this story") we were told many times that young men and women had heard about the first contacts from their *mothers*. Women, rather than men, are the ones who talk to their children about these events. And, as we have seen, the women's narratives of encounters have a more personal tone than the men's, which are more factual and detailed. Comparing what the women told us with what they seem to have transmitted to their children, it also appears that, together with violence, what has disappeared from the accounts are the women's first impressions of whites (tall, not eating pigs' grease) and what happened to them personally.[38]

In any event, violence during the first encounters has become a "blind spot" in the present-day memory of that event. And this is reason enough to go back to the place of violence, which was intrinsically central to the reciprocal view the Ankave and the Europeans had of each other during the twenty years or so of their "first" encounters.

"Killers in Bark Capes": Epitomising Stone Age Cannibals

The raids by the "diminutive but ferocious mountaineers" (Souter 1974, 97) against the coastal populations around Kerema are a leitmotif of reports from "British New Guinea" (Papua) at the turn of the previous century (Blayney 1901, 57–60, quoted by Gajdusek et al. 1972, 18; Higginson 1908, 50–5, quoted by Gajdusek et al. 1972, 32; Murray 1912, 170–2, quoted by Gajdusek et al. 1972, 35). To officially put an end to their attacks, a new "division" was created in Papua (Gulf Division) and a new patrol post opened in Kerema in 1906 (Murray 1908, quoted by Hallpike 1978, 4). The capture of a Kukukuku, the day before Christmas 1907, who was carrying the leg of a victim killed and cut up near a coastal village did not help their reputation (Simpson 1953, 13). The only relations the Anga had with the coastal populations were hostile, which explains why the Australian administration noted the impossibility of recruiting non-Anga interpreters speaking an Anga language (Murray 1926, cited in Hallpike 1978, 5). In 1919, the peaceful visit of a Kukukuku to Kerema was therefore a rather remarkable event (Simpson 1953, 19).

The stories published by the patrol officers who approached the Anga country between the two World Wars mention attacks on their camps (Humphries 1923, 50–63; Hides 1935). The general tone of the prospector's autobiography is similar (Sinclair 1979, 104–34, who narrates J. O'Neil's prospecting efforts on the Upper Watut; Leahy and Crain 1937, 106–26; Leahy 1991, 23–48). To be brief, the expedition by the Pryke brothers and Crowe between the Tauri and the Lakekamu was attacked in 1909 (Nelson 1976, 219–20; Simpson 1953, 15; Souter 1974, 99). In 1910 Darling was hit by five "Nautiya" (Kapau) arrows, and several of his carriers were wounded while discovering the Bulolo goldfields (Simpson 1953, 25). In early 1923, Patrol Officer George Ellis conducted the first patrol on the Upper Watut, during which "they came into conflict with the fierce little Kukukuku bowmen" (Sinclair 1998, 35). In 1927, District Officer S.S. Skeate and Patrol Officer Jim Taylor patrolled the Upper Watut (Gammage 1998, 9). Two years later, Patrol Officer Alan Roberts had made "the first extensive contacts with the Kukukuku of the Upper Watut" (Sinclair 1998, 127), but the German prospector Helmuth Baum, who accompanied him, was killed, beheaded (and eaten) by Kapau people from Kareeba, along with eight of his Buang carriers (Simpson 1953, 34–7; Sinclair 1966, 8; Souter 1974, 178–9). Between July 1930 and March 1931, Patrol Officer Jack Hides, who was walking from Kerema on the coast to Wau and back, investigated the attack on a mining camp near the Lakekamu by some Kukukuku, cutting diagonally across the southern part of the Anga country at the same time (Nelson 1976, 249–50; Gash and Whittaker 1975, 261; Schieffelin and Crittenden 1991, 46–7).

In April 1931, some time before the Leahy brothers made the Highlands patrols recalled in the film and book *First Contact* (Connolly and Anderson 1983, 1987), Mick Leahy was attacked and wounded by Langimar people, an Anga group now known as Angaatia, while rescuing Assistant District Officer N. Penglase (Sinclair 1966, 8; Leahy 1991, 37–40; Souter 1974, 178–79; Gammage 1998, 12). In 1932, a patrol post was opened at Otibanda by M. Pitt and K. Bridge to protect the gold miners on Surprise and Slate Creeks, that is, near the border of the Langimar and Kapau territories (Blackwood 1978, 8; McCarthy 1963, 91). In January 1933, prospectors Clarius and Naylor were killed by Kapau, together with six of their Buang carriers (Sinclair 1978, 206; O'Neil, quoted by Sinclair 1979, 112; Townsend 1968). McCarthy arrested the murderers, but he too was attacked and seriously wounded in March 1933.[39] Six months later he returned to the area and opened the first patrol post in Menyamya. The local Kukukuku were still hostile. On 12 September 1933, "an arrow hit John [Black] over the left eye, splitting the bone and jamming in his skull. ... Next morning, John was flown to Salamaua" (Gammage 1998, 22). The Menyamya patrol post was closed a few weeks later. The next month, during their exploration to the west of Menyamya (i.e. toward the Vailala headwaters), McCarthy and the three prospectors he accompanied together with fourteen policemen were heavily attacked and the Kukukuku were killed (Sinclair 1998, 131).

Many administrators probably shared Hides' view that the Kukukuku were "probably the lowest type we have in Papua, and it will be a long time before they are civilized people" (Hides 1936, 202). In the early 1950s, a *kiap* entering the valley of Marawaka had quite a poor opinion of its inhabitants (Baruya speakers): "Their faces are not attractive, being of a glowering cast, and even when they smile there is nothing of the open, hearty cheerfulness of the Pinatas and Onei-Biras [in the Lamari River valley]. One instinctively distrusts them" (PNGNA 1951–52a, 18). At any rate, the reputation of the Kukukuku as warriors was well established. They were dangerous killers who "attacked" the patrols. For instance, whereas the people of the Suowi give an account of the pre-war patrol according to which two men were killed on the spot soon after a steel machete was stolen, the comments by the Australian speak of "attacks" by the local people, to which they could only retaliate.

Needless to say, the carriers too considered that the Kukukuku were dangerous people.[40] As one *kiap* wrote in 1925 about a patrol in the lower Tauri area, "the behaviour of the carriers on this patrol [was] difficult to describe. Their fear of the Kukukuku was beyond all reason" (PNGNA 1925–26, 10). Forty-five years later, a patrol officer wrote that "even with the increased pay and allowances offered to carriers, there is a growing reluctance to act as carriers among the more sophisticated groups in the Kaintiba/Kaiberope areas. In the case of this patrol the reason for this may have been an underlying fear of going into the "unknown" territory to the west of the Swanson River, which seems to form the natural boundary to the Kamia [Kamea]-speaking people" (PNGNA 1971–72, 2). In passing, Pierre Lemonnier saw a government interpreter and a medical orderly from Ihu run away from the lower Ivori area for fear that the *kiap*, who was somewhere in the bush trying to reach the Ankave hamlet of Sinde, had been "killed and eaten by the Kukukuku." That was in 1979. Even the possibility that the Anga practised "ritual murders" linked with initiations was present in some Australian minds.[41] At the time of the last exploration patrols among the Ankave, the "Yaba murders" (twenty-three Kamea people killed in one fight in a single hamlet by a neighbouring group) was in everyone's minds and, together with exploration, restraining violence was always an official aim of patrols (PNGNA 1961–62, sec. 1). In any event, for decades, most non-Angan people would have agreed that "when the Kukukukus came from the hills, it was to kill" (Zimmer 1969).

Anga carriers themselves would have shared the same view about the supposed aggression of the remote "uncontacted" Anga peoples they visited. Aside from warfare and intergroup trade, which involved relations between individual partners or "friends" on both sides of a border, Anga locals had only limited contacts with each other. People of the next valley were known, but those a range further away were usually not. In 1987 our oldest informants insisted that, prior to the 1950s patrols, they had never been to Kwaplalim or Menyamya, a mere fifteen-hours' walk from the Suowi. As a result, for those Anga who had long been in contact with Australians but lived days or weeks away from the patrolled area, the inhabitants of the valleys they entered were dangerous "bush kanakas" ("country bumpkins"). As for carriers belonging to a neighbouring group, they probably had a better idea of who they were going to meet. Yet, tension and violence were most probably part of the encounters, as any two Anga groups had a high probability of being former or present enemies.[42]

Violence is Good for the Others

Angan "treachery" and "savagery" are a product of the Australian imagination, but there is no doubt that inter-group warfare and intra-group vendetta was part of their everyday life. Patrol Officer Weber's view apropos the headwaters of the Ankave-Swanson, for instance, is most probably right: "The people in the Kwinyi area, except for one or two who had been to work at Menyamya, have had no contact with Europeans, and are living and fighting in their traditional manner. The houses are all guarded by a network of fences to prevent sneak attacks – this practice has ceased in the Kaintiba area. There were reports of many killings in the past, all between hamlets living an hour or so walk apart" (PNGNA 1965–66b, n.p.).

Indeed, the idea that the Ankave were fighting each other a lot was not simply an Australian administrator's view about "primitive" Kukukuku. It is still that of the Ankave themselves, when they refer to the period of their encounters with the agents of the state. On the northern frontier, the war with the Iweto (Iqwaye people in the Yakana and Andakombi valleys, who were the Ankave's traditional enemies) ceased in the early 1950s, almost as soon as the *kiaps* from Menyamya passed through. At that time, the situation between the Ankave of the Suowi and the Kamea speakers of Kwayu was tense, because three Kamea had been killed (possibly in the late 1940s) after they themselves had murdered Ikundi Onarada. But no revenge has been taken yet, nor any compensation paid.[43] Things were even worse on the southeastern border, between the Ankave of the Swanson and New Year Creek valleys and the Ivori speakers of Pio and Famba. There was still fighting in 1972 (PNGNA 1971–72, 3). As one man from Ikundi explained to us:

> When you leave Uogwa [the last Ankave hamlet to the south], people do not attach their *ass-maro* [barkcloth loincloth that covers the buttocks] with a rope hanging from the neck; it is only held by a belt. That's the reason why they react as brutes, without thinking of what they are doing. For instance, when you give them a woman in marriage, they send arrows to their brothers-in-law instead of thanking you! (Erauye Nguye, a young man around 30; recorded in July 2002 in Ayakupna'wa').

As for the people of Uogwa, they were on good terms with the Kamea of Komako, but on bad terms with their fellow Ankave-speakers of Angae and Buu'.

The shattering of their shields (and killing of pigs) by Lee Enfield bullets during the "firearms demonstrations" organised by the patrol officers surely accounted for the cessation of inter-group warfare and intra-group vendetta.[44] In a hamlet that would host eighty people only on special occasions (e.g. a mourning ceremony, in time of war, or during the initiation rituals), a column of two *kiaps*, sixty carriers, six policemen and two interpreters was quite a shock. Indeed, something to keep away from. Up to now, people refer to the policemen with something like terror.

Fear of the police was so strong that one woman remains famous for the incredible joke she played in the 1970s on her family by donning the pants, shirt and shoes her husband had brought back from plantation work. With a hat on her head, a backpack, a cane in her hand and chattering a pseudo-pidgin, she so frightened her own brother that he ran away and left the game he was cooking in the fire of his garden shelter. The history goes on to say that her father was so angry that he broke a bamboo pipe over her head and her husband wounded her with an arrow to the chest.

Rather than the fear of death in a fight, which any Ankave man would deny, it is the fear of jail and that of the bad manners of the police that men emphasise (women do not say much about these things, because women are not supposed to kill people with whom they disagree). Several times we heard statements like "I won't kill this guy because I do not want to go to jail, when you are in jail, you cannot see your kids. And the police beat you." The striking thing is that, notwithstanding their fear of the police, the Ankave almost immediately adopted the state's view of how to deal with culprits. That is, they very rapidly decided to refer problems to the police of Menyamya that they would previously have handled with bows and arrows (Lemonnier 1998). And they do it on at least two levels: to deal with inter-valley collective problems and, more recently, on an individual basis.

In 1982, together with two Baruya friends and a dozen men from Angae, Pierre Lemonnier was walking in the thick mountain bush that separates Angae from Ikundi, when he saw a lone woman some fifty yards down the track. She stared for a second at the "patrol" and immediately jumped into a ravine and disappeared. The Angae men burst into laughter, yelled and searched for the woman, who did not reply or reappear. In other words, the mere sight of an unknown European travelling with unknown carriers (two of Pierre Lemonnier's Baruya friends) had made the woman flee and run for her life. It took us a dozen years to realise that she had good reason to avoid encounters with unknown people coming from Angae. We also know, from experience, that in 1985 people from Ikundi walking with us to Angae would not stay alone in that village, but would take refuge in the house of the missionary from the Summer Institute of Linguistics who was based there at the time, or stay within a few metres of us, the anthropologists. Surely, there was some sort of quarrel going on.

For decades, indeed probably a century, relations between Ikundi and Angae were good. By contrast with the thirty-nine deaths resulting from warfare or vendetta in the Suowi valley, tensions between Ikundi and Angae resulted in only three deaths, probably in the late 1890s. At the time of the "contacts" (1953–70), the 1,000 or so Ankave speakers would more or less react as one political body and, at least in theory, all enemies were common to both valleys. In fact, until the mid-1970s, all of the boys were initiated together, either in Angae or in Ikundi. In the 1960s, internal fighting was rapidly fading away under the double pressure of the Iqwaye people from Lagai (who explained to their neighbours how good it was to be peaceful) and that of the first *tultul* or *luluai* ("local headmen") appointed by the *kiaps* as a sort of local agent of the state. It was at this time that something unheard of happened: many people (twelve adult men and eleven adult women) suddenly died en masse in *several* hamlets *simultaneously*. For us, this was a consequence of what *we* know to have been a flu epidemic. An influenza epidemic had spread into the inland in 1969. But the Ankave had a different interpretation.

Unlike the *ombo'* invisible cannibals, whose main action is to cut or block organs so that the circulation of blood, the key life substance, is lethally hampered, *ayao'* sorcerers exercise a remote negative action characterised by flows of bodily fluids, usually pus, blood or mucus. *Ayao'* sorcery is usually performed to protect personal belongings, to punish a thief, but also to steal something from someone. The many deaths occurring in the late sixties were attributed to *ayao'* sorcerers, who were supposed to have taken revenge after some wrong. And since no hamlet was spared in the same valley, there was no doubt that the sorcerers belonged to the neighbouring valley. For some reason no enemy group was involved.

Whereas we now have a good view of the various wars and vendettas that killed respectively twenty-seven and twelve people in the Suowi valley between 1920 and the mid-1960s, the details of the tensions between the two main Ankave valleys are still unclear to us, notably because things are still not settled. But at least we know what kind of events, factors and agents were involved.

In the 1960s, a man from Suao (Omeri Iwadze) allegedly used *ayao'* sorcery to kill a man from Ikundi (Olale hamlet), whose wife (Toatsi) he wanted to "steal." Omore Dzadze, the brother of the sorcerer's victim, in turn, killed the alleged sorcerer. The people from Suao, we were told, were quite happy with that, since they had already killed Erwato Apitse, the sorcerer's brother, because he himself was supposed to be a sorcerer. At that stage, things were dealt with in a highly conventional way. Clearly, Chester's and Purdy's patrols had not been enough to convince the Suowi people that they should report their law-and-order problems to the *kiaps* and the Menyamya police.[45]

Years later, around 1972–74, a man from Ikundi killed his wife's lover, and the police from Menyamya were called in to arrest the murderer. At that time, there was some fighting between Angae and Meenu in the Swanson valley. For some unknown reason, Witi Yaye "cut" two men (Iwadze Apitse Akwije and Wite Akwonengo) with his machete. The Meenu people went to Ikundi, met their in-laws, and they all walked to the *kiap*'s or police office in Menyamya. The police went to Angae, captured the troublemakers and jailed them for two months (some say four months). On their way back to the station, the police apparently also arrested a young man from Ayakupna'wa' (Ngwaje Akwije) for adultery with Ibua Akwoningi.

Some time after all the men had come back from their stay in prison, Ngwaje Akwije died, together with another twenty-two adult men and women.[46] His mother was from Meenu, a hamlet then at odds with Angae. Also, people now say that the population from Angae was unhappy that Ikundi had helped Meenu to call the police to Angae. At any rate, it was thought at the time that Ngwaje Akwije had died from an *ayao'* attack by some Angae sorcerer, acting on behalf of his own hamlet but also on behalf of Rotabie Erauye, a man from Ikundi whose affines were from Buu'. Rotabie Erauye, it was said, was looking for revenge after some people laughed when his young son died. The sorcerer from Buu' was identified as Erwa Namo.

Ayao' sorcery is totally imaginary in the sense that, although its effects might be dangerously real once people believe they are under magical attack, we have no reason to think that any Ankave ever manipulated some substance or pronounced formulae in order to harm someone else. For this reason, no one will ever know what was the real aim of those "people" who allegedly asked a supposed sorcerer to exterminate part of the population of the Suowi valley. What matters here is that fearing for the life of Erwa Namo (remember that two sorcerers from Suao and Angae had been killed in Ikundi in the previous ten years or so) the Angae people asked the police from Kaintiba[47] to come and, as a precaution, arrest their opponents in Ikundi. Around 1978 (we are missing the patrol reports for that time) the police *and* the men from Angae burned the houses, beat everyone on their hands with rattan canes, killed "all" the pigs and raped the women in a house, under the floor of which their husbands, fathers or brothers had been put away. Some people were sodomised with rattan sticks. Captured in the forest, Moregni Dzadze was left "half dead," hanging from a tree with rattan ropes. Memory of this event obviously inspired the flight of the Ikundi woman Pierre Lemonnier met in 1982.

A year or so later, some men from Angae stole some eels and pigs in Ikundi. They also raped some women. A man from Ayakupna'wa' wounded one of the assailants, and the policemen from Menyamya were asked to intervene. The people from Ikundi went to Angae with the policemen and took revenge. The hamlet was surrounded "and we did the same thing to them!" Hence the tense atmosphere in Angae in 1985, when Pierre Lemonnier stopped there on the last stage of a patrol from Ikundi via Sinde and the lowlands.

As far as we know, that was the last of the collective punitive expeditions the Angae and Ikundi people organised against each other with the help of the police. It is noteworthy that two patrol posts located in two different provinces, Menyamya and Kaintiba, were approached. The main result of these new ways of handling tensions – the old caused by adultery and the new caused by large scale *ayao'* sorcery – was the separate organisation of the first stage of the male initiations, which, unlike the second and third stages, used to gather all the boys from the three valleys (Ikundi, Angae, Sinde) for more than a month. However, in 1987, there was some co-operation between the two valleys because a new type of witch hunter (called *boss sangguma* in Tok Pisin and specialising in finding *ombo'* ("cannibal witches")) was introduced from the Kamea-speaking area of Komako, but the subsequent killing of two women in Angae resulted in the Ikundi people losing interest in the experts from Buu' or Angae. In 1990, Angae organised its own rituals; in 1994, only two men from Angae took part in the rituals in the Suowi (both friends of the authors, by the way); in 2002, a ritual expert from Angae was called for the third-stage initiations in Ayakupna'wa'. Stay tuned ...

At some stage in the mid-1990s the use of police in local affairs shifted from an inter-community scale to a local one. Not only were the police asked to enforce the law in the case of homicide, brawling, theft or adultery, but they have also been used as a weapon in personal or vaguely clan affairs. Personal ties are involved between those few Ankave men who now act as radio operators or *komiti* (a local representative of a valley, elected or not) and the police they meet in Menyamya and make friends with. The policeman usually comes alone, without a colleague or any patrol officer, and rattan beating is the only violence involved. It is unclear whether the money often given to the policeman is some sort of fine or a gift under the cover of an "offending fee." At any rate, violence is still present. No one is killed by the police anymore, but a man unduly accused of murder in 1996 or 1997 lost a tooth after being beaten with a rattan cane by a policeman. He was (he is now dead) one of the last living members of the Nguye clan that owns the strip of land on which the future airstrip is currently being constructed; and the police were called in by an Idzadze man who has been sneaking into Nguye territory for the last fifteen years. Fear of the police is such that a young man who had insulted them from afar in Ikundi literally fainted when he was recognised by one of the constables a year later in Menyamya; that was in 2000. The story and history of this mixture of bribery and local policy remains to be written. But, clearly, if one "agent" of modernity has been manipulated by the Ankave more than any others, it is the police.

Conclusion

It is well documented that, although repetitive and spanning a long period of time, "first contacts" durably paved the way for the future relationship of the Ankave with modernity in two ways. They determined the relations between their two main valleys; and, for at least forty years (1953–93), during which the administration was equated with law-and-order problems, they shaped the image of the people from the "Ankave-Swanson Census Division" in a way highly compatible with the basic view of the Anga as Kukukuku, that is, as fearless warriors.

For the Ankave, the irruption of the *kiaps* and their constables has been integrated into local and regional (inter-tribal) history. At the time of contact the relation between the Ankave valleys proper was rather even: wars were a thing of the past, marriages were ongoing and both male initiations and enemies were shared. However, this peaceful but quite fragile equilibrium was destroyed by two concomitant and related novelties brought by the Australians: the end of inter-tribal warfare, which stopped immediately after the first glimpse of the power and destructive capacity of the police weapons, and the epidemic spread of illnesses that – for some reason – were interpreted as a large-scale *ayao'* sorcery, as a magical vendetta, rather than a magical war.

As for the Australians, they had "known" for a long time that the Kukukuku were dangerous people as well as troublemakers. When the *kiaps* penetrated the Ankave rivers, the Kukukuku had long since stopped raiding the coastal people, but McCarthy's difficulties and, later, the Yaba "murders" were in everyone's minds. At the very end of the 1960s, the supposed Anga violence and resistance to colonisation was stressed in the orders given to the patrol officers who were in charge of contacting these indomitable holdouts. As a result, violence was part of the programme. And three Ankave men were killed in the Suowi valley, a rather high figure in relation to the overall population concerned (300 people, and less than a total of 1,000 in the three valleys at that time).

In turn, the Ankave interpreted this violence as a new but perfectly normal way of dealing with problems. It took more than two decades (1950–72) before they stopped running away at the sight of a white man, but they have been quick to enrol the police in their own ongoing tensions. The use of arms was forbidden, but the violent beatings and the rapes by the policemen and foreign carriers had become part of their new arsenal. And it is clear that the manipulation of the police plays an important part in the strategies linked with the incipient individualism now observed in Ikundi or Ayakupna'wa'.

References

Ballard, Chris

2003 *La fabrique de l'histoire: événement, mémoire et récit dans les Hautes Terres de Nouvelle-Guinée*. In *Les rivages du temps: Histoire et anthropologie du Pacifique*, eds Isabelle Merle and Michel Naepels, 111–34. Cahiers du Pacifique Sud Contemporain no. 3. Paris: L'Harmattan.

Blackwood, Beatrice

1950 *The Technology of a Modern Stone Age People in New Guinea*. Occasional Papers on Technology 3. Oxford: Pitt Rivers Museum.

1978 *The Kukukuku of the Upper Watut*. Oxford: Pitt Rivers Museum.

Blayney, J.A.

1901 Report of resident magistrate for the Central District, British New Guinea. In *Annual Report for 1899–1900*, App. I, 57–60.

Burton, John E.

1996 Early colonial contacts among the Upper Watut and Biangai Peoples from 1895 to the First World War. In *Hidden Valley Social Mapping 1995/96*. Hidden Valley Project, Working Paper no. 6. Canberra: CRA Minerals.

Carey, S. Warren

1990 Fifty years of oil research. In *Petroleum Exploration in Papua New Guinea: Proceedings of the First PNG Petroleum Convention, 12–14 February*, eds. George J. Carman and Zina Carman. Port Moresby: PNG Chamber of Mines and Petroleum.

Connolly, Bob and Robin Anderson

1987 *First Contact*. New York: Viking.

Demaître, Edmond

1935 *L'enfer du Pacifique: Chez les cannibales et les chercheurs d'or de la Nouvelle Guinée*, trans. H.D. Beaumont. Paris: Grasset.

Detzner, Hermann

1935 *Moeurs et coutumes des Papous: Quatre ans chez les cannibales de Nouvelle-Guinée, 1914–1918*. Paris: Payot.

Fisher, N.H.

1936 Amongst the Kukukukus. *Walkabout* 2 (7): 13–20.

Fitzpatrick, Philip

1999 The A.P.H. Freund collection of New Guinea artefacts held by the South Australian Museum. *Records of the South Australian Museum* 31 (2): 181–214.

Gajdusek, D. Carleton, Peter Fetchko, Nancy J. Van Wyk, and Steven G. Ono

1972 *Annotated Anga (Kukukuku) Bibliography*. Bethesda: National Institute of Neurological Diseases and Stroke, National Institutes of Health.

Gammage, Bill

1998 *The Sky Travellers: Journeys in New Guinea 1938–1939*. Carlton, Vic.: Miegunyah Press/Melbourne University Publishing.

Gash, Noel, and June Whittaker

1975 *A Pictorial History of New Guinea*. Milton, Qld: Jacaranda Press.

Hallpike, Chris R.

1978 Introduction. In *The Kukukuku of the Upper Watut,* ed. Beatrice Blackwood. Oxford: Pitt Rivers Museum.

Hides, Jack Gordon

1935 *Through Wildest Papua*. RNB geography of the Pacific series. London: Blackie and Son.

1936 *Papuan Wonderland*. RNB geography of the Pacific series. London: Blackie and Son.

Higginson, Charles B.

1908 Annual Report, Gulf Division. In *Papua: Annual Report for 1907–1908*.

Humphries, Walter Richard

1923 *Patrolling in Papua*. London: Fisher Unwin.

Leahy, Michael J.

1991 *Explorations into Highland New Guinea, 1930–1935*. Tuscaloosa: University of Alabama Press.

Leahy, Michael J., and Maurice Crain

1937 *The Land that Time Forgot: Adventures and Discoveries in New Guinea*. RNB geography of the Pacific series. London: Hurst and Blackett.

Lemonnier, Pierre

1998 Showing the invisible: Violence and politics among the Ankave–Anga (Gulf Province, Papua New Guinea). In *Common Worlds and Single Lives: Constituting Knowledge in Pacific Societies*, ed. V. Keck, 287–307. Oxford and New York: Berg.

2004 Hunting for authenticity: Stone Age stories out of context. *Journal of Pacific History* 39 (1): 79–98.

McCarthy, John K.

1926–52 Patrol reports and other papers.

1963 *Patrol into Yesterday: My New Guinea Years*. Melbourne: F.W. Cheshire.

Murray, J.H.P.

1908 *Papua: Annual Report 1907–1908*.

1912 *Papua: Annual Report 1911–1912*.

1926 *Papua: Annual Report 1924–1925*.

1937–38 *Territory of Papua: Annual Report*.

Nelson, Hank

1976 *Black White & Gold: Goldmining in Papua New Guinea 1878-1930*. Canberra: Australian National University Press

Neumann, Klaus

1994 "In order to win their friendship": Renegotiating first contact. *The Contemporary Pacific* 6 (1): 111–45.

Pilhofer, G.

1915 Eine Durchquerung Neuguineas vom Waria- zum Markhamfluss. *Dr. A. Petermanns Mitteilungen aus Justus Perthes' Geographischer Anstalt* 61 (21–25): 63–66.

PNGNA (Papua New Guinea National Archives)

1925–26 W.R. Humphries, Kerema Patrol Report no. 2

1929–30 S.G. Middleton, Kerema Patrol Report no. 12

1930 E.R. Oldham, Kerema Patrol Report no. 29

1933–34 J.K. McCarthy, G.E. Ballam, and J.R. Black, Salamaua Patrol Report no. 15

1937–38 A.T. Timperley, Kerema Patrol Report no. 7

1950–51a K.I. Chester, Kerema Patrol Report no. 3

1950–51b L. Hurrell, Menyamya Patrol Report no. 6

1950–51c A.L. Hurrell Menyamya Patrol Report no. 2

1951–52a G. Linsley, Kainantu Patrol Report no. 6

1951–52b O.J. Mathieson, Kerema Patrol Report no. 2

1953–54 W.M. Purdy, Menyamya Patrol Report no. 2

1955–56 R.R. Haviland, Menyamya Patrol Report no. 8

1960–61 J. Jordan, Kerema Patrol Report no. 3

1961–62 A.J. Carey, Kerema Patrol Report no. 9

1965–66a K.G. O'Brien, Ihu Patrol Report no. 3

1965–66b R.E. Weber, Kaintiba Patrol Report no. 2

1966–67a P.G. Whitehead, Ihu Patrol Report no. 3

1966–67b R.A. Deverell, Kaintiba Patrol Report no. 3

1966–67c G.C. Connor, Kaintiba Patrol Report no. 6

1969–70a A.M. Didlick, Kaintiba Special Report no. 3

1969–70b R.S. Coles, Kaintiba Patrol Report no. 15

1970–71 R.S. Coles, Kaintiba Patrol Report no. 1

1971–72 A.J. Meikle, Kerema Patrol Report no. 1

Powell, Alan

2003 *The Third Force: Angau's New Guinea War, 1942–46.* Melbourne: Oxford University Press.

Riley, Ian D., Deborah Lehmann, and Michael P. Alpers

1992 Acute respiratory infections. In *Human Biology in Papua New Guinea: The Small Cosmos,* eds Robert D. Attenborough and Michael P. Alpers, 281–8. Oxford: Oxford University Press.

Schieffelin, Edward L.

1991 Introduction. In *Like People You See in a Dream: First Contact in Six Papuan Societies,* eds Edward L. Schieffelin and Robert Crittenden, 1–11. Stanford: Stanford University Press.

Schieffelin, Edward L. and Robert Crittenden

1991 The Strickland–Purari patrol: Starting Out. In *Like People You See in a Dream: First Contact in Six Papuan Societies,* eds Edward L. Schieffelin and Robert Crittenden, 44–57. Stanford: Stanford University Press.

Simpson, Colin

1953 *Adam with Arrows: Inside New Guinea.* London and Sydney: Angus & Robertson.

Sinclair, James

1966 *Behind the Ranges: Patrolling in New Guinea.* Melbourne: Melbourne University Press.

1978 *Wings of Gold: How the Aeroplane Developed New Guinea.* Bathurst: Robert Brown & Associates.

1979 ed., *Up from South: A Prospector in New Guinea* by Jack O'Neill. Port Moresby: Robert Brown & Associates.

1998 *Golden Gateway. Lae and the Province of Morobe.* Bathurst: Crawford House Publishing.

2001 *Mastamak: The Land Surveyors of Papua New Guinea.* Adelaide: Crawford House Publishing.

Skelly, E.C.

1919 Report of a patrol made by acting assistant resident magistrate, Upoia, to the Albert Mountains (Ivori valley) from the 20th October to 9th November, 1917. In *Papua Annual Report for 1917–1918,* App. C, 68–74.

Smith, Staniforth

1911 Sketch from fragmentary notes. Showing approximately the route followed by the Hon. M. Staniforth Smith, Administrator, 24th November 1910 to 26th January 1911. In *Papua Annual Report,* App. G.

Souter, Gavin

1974 [1963] *New Guinea: The Last Unknown.* Brisbane: Angus and Robertson.

Strathern, Marilyn

1992 The decomposition of an event. *Cultural Anthropology* 7 (2): 244–54.

Thomas, Nicholas

1989 *Out of Time: History and Evolution in Anthropological Discourse.* Cambridge: Cambridge University Press.

Townsend, George W.L.

1968 *District Officer: From Untamed New Guinea to Lake Success, 1921–1946.* Sydney: Pacific Publications.

Zimmer, G.F.W.

1969 When the Kukukukus came from the hills, it was to kill. *Pacific Islands Monthly* 40 (11): 85–93.

FILMOGRAPHY

Connolly, Bob and Robin Anderson

1983 *First Contact.* Part of *The Highlands Trilogy.* Produced and directed by Bob Connolly and Robin Anderson in association with Institute of Papua New Guinea Studies. Colour, 54 min.

Notes

[1] This chapter owes much to Chris Ballard, Bill Gammage, R. Grieve, Hank Nelson and James Sinclair, who patiently gave of their time and knowledge, so that we could contextualise both our ethnography and the patrol reports dealing with the area in which we work.

Letter from R.S. Bell, district commissioner, Kerema, to A.M. Didlick, assistant district commissioner, Kerema, 18 September 1969, attached to Kaintiba special patrol report (PNGNA 1969–70a).

[2] Here, our use of the ethnographic present corresponds to the time of one of our last periods of joint fieldwork in Ayakupna'wa' (Suowi or "M'Bwei" valley, Gulf Province) in July 2002.

[3] Pierre Lemonnier started fieldwork among the Ankave in 1982. Since 1987 the ethnography of the Suowi valley has been carried out conjointly with Pascale Bonnemère. Among other institutions, such as the French Ministry for Foreign Affairs and the Fyssen and National Geographic Foundations, the three main institutions supporting our research – the French National Centre for Scientific Research (CNRS), the Papua New Guinea Institute of Medical Research at Goroka and the Papua New Guinea National Archives at Waigani – deserve special thanks.

[4] Like other Iqwaye refugees, Abraham was living on the Upper Suowi River until the early 1950s patrols in Iqwaye country enabled his family to go back to his own valley of Lagai. At some stage he became one of those people officially entitled by the administration to settle land disputes and, indeed, the Ankave relied on him to solve some of their own land problems. In 1990 he gave Pascale Bonnemère a whole set of accounts of the encounters with white people in the Suowi valley. He had heard about

them from his parents when he was a young boy. As an adult, he developed a great awareness and knowledge about all these events involving white people in the region, in part because he is very concerned about the poor situation in which the Ankave have always been left by government authorities. From the 1960s onward, he has been considered by the Ankave as an intermediary and a translator, when necessary, in encounters with Australians.

[5] "The present policy of raising spasmodic patrols will not achieve anything except the heavy expenditure of patrol funds, exhausted patrol personnel, and disrupted inhabitants" (PNGNA 1966–67a, 14).

[6] Peter Rayapo from Angae in his tape-recorded life story; also R.A. Deverell (PNGNA 1966–67b, 3, 7).

[7] There were also SDA Australians (a family) in the valley northwest of Menyamya in 1966 (Gammage, pers. comm.).

[8] Resident Magistrates were the Papuan equivalent of District Officers. They were later called District Commissioners. See also Mosko (this volume) on Monckton.

[9] Souter writes Lahiki, but there is no doubt about the identification of that stream on the left bank of the Vailala.

[10] i.e. G. Pilhofer and L. Flierl (Pilhofer 1915; see also Burton 1996; Gash and Whittaker 1975, [plates 548, 555] 244, 247; Souter 1963, 114).

[11] They were also followed by anthropologists. Sent to New Guinea by the Pitt Rivers Museum, Beatrice Blackwood took up residence in a hamlet comprised of Kapau (Nauti) and Langimar (Manki) in order to study "the technology of a modern Stone Age people" (Blackwood 1950). This woman from Oxford was forty-seven years of age at the time and had already a year of fieldwork experience (1929–30) on "both sides" of the Buka passage, in the Solomons, when she undertook an eight-month study on the Upper Watut in 1936/37. First contacts in the Upper Watut are also dealt with by Burton (1996).

[12] This prospector may have been either James Swanson or his son, with whom he previously "went up the Vailala and the Tauri" in 1909 (Nelson 1976, 195). His son was probably H. Swanson, the prospector who, in company of E. McGowan, discovered oil on the lower Vailala in June 1911 (Sinclair 2001, 167). Twenty years later, an H.T. Swanson (who is probably the same man) tried to reach the Lakekamu from Kerema, and a party led by Resident Magistrate Oldham was sent to look for him (PNGNA 1930, 1–3). We do not know yet if Swanson was really lost then. H.T. Swanson is not to be confused with A.P. Swanson (who was a "chainman" in the Morobe Goldfield in August 1934 (Sinclair 2001, 153)), nor with P.M. Swanson, mentioned in the May 1936 *Walkabout* issue (Fisher 1936) (who is said to have accompanied Patrol Officer K.W.T. Bridge on a patrol in the Kapau River area; see also Sinclair 2001, 227 for details about P.M. Swanson's activities during World War II).

[13] This track was designed to enable trucks and troops to cross the ridge and fight the Japanese in case they progressed beyond Wau, which they did not.

[14] Letter from N.C. McQuilty, assistant district commissioner, to the assistant district commissioner, Kerema, 3 June 1970, attached to Kaintiba patrol report (PNGNA 1969–70b).

[15] In 1972, A.J. Meikle still mentions the Ivori "raiders" coming from Famba and Pio into Ankave territory (PNGNA 1971–72, 3).

[16] Reports about patrols from Kerema into the *lower* Kukukuku country are: Kerema no. 6, 1928–29; no. 12, 1929–30; no. 1, 1934–35; no. 8, 1935–36; no. 5, 1936–37; no. 8, 1937–38; no. 11, 1937–38 (Ivori River).

[17] It is only in 2007 that we had access to a copy of the report about this prospecting patrol for the Oil Search Limited company (OSL), that was accompanied for exploratory and security reasons by the Kerema patrol officer, Alan T. Timperley, who wrote the report. It was thus too late to include an analysis of this very detailed piece (34 pages) and so a forthcoming paper will be devoted to this first contact, which was followed by a long period without any visit in the Mbwei valley.

[18] On 2 January 1930, Middleton (PNGNA 1929–30, 23) named "New Year Creek" a tributary of the Ivory, which according to Patrol Officer Mathieson, whose demonstration is clearly correct (PNGNA 1951–52b, 11), was not the tributary of the M'Bwei/Suowi River named "New Year Creek" on the maps (until now). The "New Year Creek" referred to here is that tributary of the M'Bwei/Suowi River (locally known as Saa') on which the hamlet of Sinde is located.

[19] As far as we know, Vizard only patrolled the Ivori River (PNGNA 1950–51a).

[20] In the meantime, Jordan (PNGNA 1960–61), 24 July to 27 September 1960, came from Menyamya (and not from Kerema, where he was based) and looked at the Swanson from afar.

[21] We mark this fact with quotation marks, because we know of "accidentally" drowned people who were killed before being thrown into the river.

[22] Letter from J.B. Quinn, Assistant District Commissioner, to the District Commissioner, Kerema, 22 June 1970, attached to Kaintiba patrol report (PNGNA 1969–70b). At the same time, Abraham (the Iqwaye man) had attended school for two years in Wau and could discuss with his "cousins" in Ikundi the (still unsolved) question of which district (now province), the Gulf or Morobe, they would like to belong to.

[23] A Japanese film crew working in the Kamea area definitely passed through the Ankave country in 1970 or so. Pierre Lemonnier saw their film once, twenty years ago, but we have not been able to locate it thus far.

[24] The last hamlet at the head of the Kuowi River; not to be confused with Kwayo, which is a Kamea village, east of the Ikundi valley and south of Komako.

[25] In his report, K.I. Chester writes for 10 February 1951: "we climbed to the Aweia–Mwei Divide, 7600', which was reached at 0907 hrs. Here, as Const. Tauvailogo was off colour, I gave his swag to our guide, who had volunteered to carry it. Fifteen minutes later I was to regret this action, as, when our guide rounded a bend out of sight, he suddenly disappeared into the scrub. We called to him, but received no answer. Const. Erapa tracked him, and a few minutes later returned with the swag minus a tomahawk" (PNGNA 1950–51a, 14). However, nothing is said about the seizing of a local man, as the Ankave and Abraham mentioned to us.

[26] This patrol was unofficially accompanied by two Catholic priests. Archbishop Paul Marx confirmed to us the route followed. The patrol left the Vailala a few kilometres downstream from where the Ioua flows into it. They had to walk for six days before reaching New Year Creek (Saa') and another six days to get to Subu, near Ikundi (map attached to the patrol report).

[27] Kerema and the coast are due south, but the Ankave locate both in the west.

[28] At least two patrol officers and two Catholic priests, as we know.

[29] Led by Constable Felix, the search party stayed in the Suowi valley from July 11 to 19.

[30] It seems that the SDA catechists from Menyamya played some role in the very first departures. Around 1973, recruiters from Lae were active in the Suowi. Plantation work declined rapidly at the time of Independence. In the early 1980s, the Australian patrol officer in Menyamya enforced the law and asked for a legal contract to be signed between the companies and the workers (D. Thompson, former *kiap* in Menyamya, pers. comm.), and no Ankave left for plantation work for at least ten years.

[31] PNGNA (1966–67c, App. A).

[32] "Once the word spread that we were searching for the character that did the shooting, people whom we possibly would have contacted fled, no doubt carrying the word further that their judgement day had arrived, causing others too, to flee" (PNGNA 1966–67c, 4).

[33] PNGNA (1966–67c, diary: 4).

[34] Letter from B.W.P. Burge, assistant district commissioner, Malalaua, Gulf District, to the district commissioner, Kerema, 19 August 1967, attached to Kaintiba patrol report PNGNA (1966–67c).

[35] Recorded in Tok Pisin in 2002, Peter Saapitso's life story is currently being edited by Pierre Lemonnier.

[36] As for ourselves, we had no clue at the time about the Ankave and Iqwaye attacks on the carriers, and we did not enquire more about the crucial but seemingly forgotten first patrol. This was clearly a mistake.

[37] However, a few other sketchy things about the white men and the Ankave were recounted to Pascale Bonnemère by young people and not mentioned by older ones; e.g. that some people thought the first plane they saw was an eagle, and that an old man tried to shoot it. The noise resembled that of a big insect.

[38] These remarks would of course need to be thought over and refined, for example, by comparing systematically young men's and women's accounts.

[39] His cook Boko firing his Winchester and his corporal Anis charging with his bayonet saved his life. McCarthy walked back to Mumeng after being wounded by two arrows (McCarthy 1963, 106–13; Sinclair 1966, 8).

[40] Carriers were recruited around the post from which the patrol started and also on a village-to-village basis. In Chester's patrol, eleven carriers were Keuru prisoners, that is, people from around Ihu (PNGNA 1950–51a, 3: summary).

[41] "Although this was not admitted, I consider this was a ritual murder in the initiation of [so and so]" (PNGNA 1966–67a, 10).

[42] Hurrell's comment about encounters between Iqwaye living on both sides of the range separating Menyamya from the Vailala headwaters in 1953 is worth quoting here: "The Iakoi people on more than one occasion on entering a hamlet and having the villagers crowd around too closely would shout 'Keep clear you Kanakas, don't bring the smell of your women to us. We've been alone for many days'" (PNGNA 1950–51b, diary: Thursday, July 3, 1951).

[43] Until today, no Ankave from the Suowi would walk to Kwayu, a two-day walk west of Ikundi, unless they walked behind us, the anthropologists; at least, that was the case in 1988.

[44] During a patrol in 1967, two pigs were purchased from the Ankave "for use in firearms demonstrations" (PNGNA 1966–67c, 3).

[45] Interestingly, Haviland's "medical" patrol was also said to be the first time the Australians were considered as people friendly enough to be called for help (PNGNA 1955–56; see n. 69). This fits well with the common opinion that the *kiaps* of the 1950s were those whose presence allowed the Iqwaye and the Ankave inhabiting the eastern side of the Vailala–Tauri divide to cross the range toward Menyamya.

[46] We have not yet found any record of this epidemic. Whatever the case, epidemics were not uncommon among the Ankave at the time of "contact." In May 1956, Patrol Officer R.R. Haviland led a medical patrol in the "Vailala headwaters." He estimated that a flu epidemic had killed forty to sixty people in the previous ten months in the Iqwaye valley right north of the Suowi. However, this epidemic seems to be too early to be the one the Ankave are referring to. Another influenza epidemic spread through the southern part of Papua New Guinea (Riley et al. 1992, 284–5), but this seems too early as well.

[47] They may have reported in Kotidanga, near Kanabea but, as far as we know, there were no policemen in Kotidanga at the time.

Subject Index

Note page references to figures and tables are in italics.

Artifacts, not just objects but embodiments of ancestral power 20–1; Oceanic material culture as sources of history 20
Australian settlement, Port Jackson as penal colony 203; Watkin Tench's depiction of Port Jackson 199ff

Beach, "beach crossings" in diverse locales 96–7; Greg Dening's concept of xii, 60
Beachcombers, as teachers of writing in Tonga 166; claims to superiority over missionaries 165; in Tonga 165–6
British voyages, Cook in New Zealand, Aotearoa 138; Wallis in Tahiti 139; Cook in Vanuatu (New Hebrides) 79–93; Hamilton in Tonga 136–8

Cannibalism (anthropophagy), d'Entrecasteaux on Kanak 187; Obeyesekere on 18; Sahlins on 35–6
Cartography 3, 24, 26; Anga groups in Papua New Guinea *296*; Ankave country territory *297*; in travel fictions of Papua and New Guinea 234–5, *236*, *237*, *241*; maps of Australia and the Pacific *28*, *Océanie 24*, *Terra Australis Incognita 3*, Vanuatu *58*; of site of *La Nueba Hierusalem 66*; voyage tracks of Bougainville in Vanuatu *75*; voyage tracks of Cook in Vanuatu *80*; voyage tracks of d'Entrecasteaux *177*; voyage tracks of Quirós in Vanuatu *63*
Colonial imaginary, in Africa, the Americas, and Papua New Guinea 223, 231, 243–5

Dance, "dancing with strangers", concept of Clendinnen 13, 93–9, 200; *hula* of Hawai`i 13, 145, and *heiva* of Tahiti, 13

Discovery, as norm binding scientific community 242–3; European claim in relation to Indigenous presence 113; European invention precedes discovery 161–4

Encounter, concept of 1; encounters as "double deeds" 245; events of 8; Indigenous encounters 2; power in 3
Enlightenment, the 12, 14, 59, 73–4, 71, 79, 84, 162–3, 166, 183, 187, 190–1, 204, 222
Ethnography and history, Ankave-Anga 299; in analysing Mekeo 260–1; relation of 16 17, 19
Europeans, indigenous perceptions as gods, ghosts and humans 2, 10–11; ni-Vanuatu and Maori conceptions of 94, 96–7
Exchange, as constitutive of humanity 22; Australian exchanges with Ankave-Anga 307–11; on Bougainville's voyage in Vanuatu 74–5; on Cook's voyage in Vanuatu 87, 90; on d'Entrecasteaux's voyage in Admiralty Islands 178; on Quirós' voyage in Vanuatu 64–5, 70

Fiction, travel fiction in relation to "real" 4, 8, 221ff; verisimilitude in travel fictions 223–34, 255
First contact, first contacts in Tonga 161ff; forty years of, among Ankave-Anga 295–324; problems with concept 1–4, 12, 13, 59–60
French voyages, de Bougainville 74–9, 115, 123–35; d'Entrecasteaux 175–98; La Pérouse 115–19, 121–3; Marchand 138

Ghosts, ancestral spirits, bush spirits; Europeans allegedly seen as 11, among Ankave-Anga 306, in Hawai`i 59, in Papua New Guinea 59, in Vanuatu, 84ff

History, distinction from pre-history, critiqued by Hau`ofa 15

Illness on Quirós voyage 67, compared with Cook's voyage 109; epidemics among Mekeo 263, and Roro 264, 270, 274–6; Mekeo aetiologies of 263–4; smallpox in Port Jackson 211, 215

Indigenous Australians, Clendinnen's writing in relation to 211–12; representations of people of Van Diemen's Land on d'Entrecasteaux' voyage 182–4; settler interactions with Indigenous Australians in Port Jackson 209–15; Watkin Tench's representations of Indigenous Australians in Port Jackson 207–9

Indigenous agency, articulation in language 1–2, in appropriation of foreign powers 10, in European texts 19, in material objects 20, 61; as "countersigns" in colonial texts and images 19, 175, 179, 188

Kidnap of indigenous people, by Benjamin Morrell in New Guinea and their exhibition in United States 228; on Quirós' voyage in Vanuatu 67, 109; of Tongan chiefs by d'Entrecasteaux 198

Labour trade ("blackbirding") 42, 49; and the development of pidgins 49; ni-Vanuatu memories of 59, 94

Languages, distribution of languages in the Pacific 37–39, indigenous language contact 1–2, 43–8; in diasporic communities 52; difficulties of translation in Vanuatu 84–5, 110, 111; "foreigner talk" 37, 48; indigenous languages, Papuan and Austronesian 1–2; metropolitan languages in the Pacific 51–2; mission languages 51; multilingualism in Oceanic languages 37; oral/aural communication in encounters 12; Polynesian outlier languages 39, 43; sign languages 37; translations of Bible 51

Men and Indigenous masculinity, European representations of, in Vanuatu, in portraits by William Hodges 81, *6*, *7*, on Bougainville's voyage 74–6, on Cooks voyage 81ff, on Quiros' voyage 69–70; on d'Entrecasteaux's voyage in the Admiralty Islands 179–80, 181, Van Diemen's Land 183–4, *185*; Tongatapu 185–6, *185*, New Caledonia 188, 190, *189*

Naming of islands of Vanuatu by Europeans 57, 85, 106, 109; New Hebrides, Papua and New Guinea, etc 256–7

Narrative conventions, on d'Entrecasteaux's voyage 177ff; "I" and "we witnessing in Watkin Tench's writing; in Tench's journal 200ff; in the travel fictions of Trégance 232–4; in travel fictions of Lawson 234–3; Tench's travel writing and audience 203–5

Observation, European Enlightenment stress on 73, 201, 204; as source of truth 204; detailed "observations" in travel fictions 224–5

Oceania, concept of 22–5; map of *Océanie* 24; relation to Melanesia, Polynesia, Micronesia 23–5; self-identifications and contemporary globalisation 25

Oral history 10, 16; eye-witness versus later accounts in Ankave-Anga history 299ff; of Ankave-Anga 299 ff; of ni-Vanuatu in relation to place 59, 93–6

Other, changing European conceptions of 57, 71; as akin to Europe's past 74; as part of European self 84; Clendinnen on Indigenous Australians 214; denial of co-eval presence (Fabian) 73, 79; in Enlightenment period 79; in indigenous constructions of Europeans 96

Pandanus red textiles in Vanuatu, 20, 76, 77, 78
Pidgins and creoles, 37, 42, 49, 51

Race, concepts of 8, 79, 81; emergent from events of encounter 179ff, 187, 197, 198; from eighteenth to nineteenth century 8, 157, 176; on Quirós voyage 109; race in travel fictions 227, 229, 238
Reality effects, in Tench's narrative 213; verisimilitude in travel fictions 223–4
Religion, Christian conversion 10; Christian missionaries and the Bible 20, 42, 51, among the Ankave-Anga 295, 297, among Baruya 295, among the Mekeo 270, 273, in Tonga 164–6, 167–9; in Quirós' world view 61–2, 64, 66–7, 69; Judeo-Christian and ancestral 10
Renaissance, the, 5, 59, 61, 71, 107

Sandalwood trade, 40
Savage, concepts of noble and ignoble savages 162–3, 177, 188–9, 207
Sexuality, and violence 14; and Polynesian beliefs of conception and pubescence 141–5; critique of model of sexual hospitality 113–47; explicit discussions in French sources 134–5; from ritual to sexual commerce in Tahiti 132–4; marriage of virgin girls in Polynesia 114–15, in Samoa 119–23, in Tahiti 123–32; ritual defloration 120, 129–32, 137, 140–3, 156, 158; the myth of the French lover 135; Western myths of Polynesian sexuality 115, 147
Sign language 37, 64, 69; and use of green boughs in Vanuatu 89-90; green boughs in Tahiti 131, and sign language more generally 156; in Admiralty Islands 192; in Van Diemen's Land 184
Sorcery, European performances of sorcery 277–81; Mekeo concepts of 263, 266, 269; missionaries as sorcerers 292; sorcery as magical war among the Ankave 324; suspicions of European sorcery 91, 110
Spanish voyages, esp. Quirós 60–71, 163; European commemoration of Quirós in 2006, 106, 111; later European views of Quirós 107–8, 110, 111

Taio, translation as "friend" 12–13
Tapa (barkcloth) 5, 21, 131, 133, 144
Teleology, avoidance in writing history 13
Terra Australis 3, 61, 163; and *Terra Austrialia del Espiritu Santo* 106
Theft, by Europeans on Quirós' voyage 67; by Admiralty Islanders during d'Entrecasteaux's voyage 178; by Tongans during d'Entrecasteaux's voyage 190, 198; from missionaries by Tongans encouraged by beachcombers 165; theft of d'Albertis' belongings by Mekeo, 269
Time, in events of encounters 13–15
Tomarr, problematic translation of Malakulan word 13, 84, 86–9

Venereal diseases, 15
Verisimilitude, 9; in travel fictions 223-224
Violence in encounters 1, 14, 21; and memory 22; European violence against Mekeo 266ff, 272, 276–86; occlusion of violence in Australian colonial archives 300; on Bougainville's voyage in Vanuatu 74–5, 109; on Cook's voyage in Vanuatu 79, 89–93; on d'Entrecasteaux's voyage in Tonga 187; on Quirós voyage in Vanuatu 65–7, 58; pacification and police for contemporary Ankave-Anga 324; reciprocal views of violence of Ankave-Anga and Europeans 316ff; representations of indigenous violence in Vanuatu 74–5; selective remembering of violence of encounters by generation and gender among Ankave-Anga 313–15;

spearing of Governor Phillip as ritual payback 212–13; violence as spiritual efficacy among Mekeo 259, 286

Vision, and realism 5; as privileged sense for Europeans 3–5; "double vision; in Oceanic philosophies, in relation to concepts of invisible agency 11

Visual sources (European drawings, engravings, paintings) 5, 81, 180–2; La Billardière and Piron 184, 188–91, 197

Voyages, European voyages: Bougainville in Tahiti 117–18, 123–33ff; Bougainville in Vanuatu 74–9; Cook in Vanuatu and Aotearoa 79–93, 138; d'Entrecasteaux in Admiralty Islands, Van Diemen's Land, Tongatapu and New Caledonia 175–98; La Pérouse in Samoa 115–16, 119, 122–3; Marchand in Marquesas 138; Quirós in Vanuatu 60–71; Wallis in Tahiti 139; map of European voyages 1788–1840, 41; of Oceanic peoples 25

Whaling, sealing and beche-de-mer trade 40

Women, La Billardière and d'Entrecasteaux on women in Van Diemen's Land and Tonga 186–7; position of Indigenous Australian women as mark of "primitive" society 208; representations of ni-Vanuatu women, by Bougainville 76, 78, by Cook 79, by Quirós 64, and by William Hodges 82; representations of women in travel fictions 227, 238; "women" and girls and sexual relations with European men 113–60; women in transmission of oral history among Ankave-Anga 314–15

World War II, 51, 88, 260, 299, 303, 331

Writing, beachcombers as teachers of literacy in Tonga 166; Bible translations 51; Christianity and 20; Indigenous graphic forms 20; missions and literacy 168–9; Oceanic texts 19; writing as cosmic power, secreted by Europeans 20, 164, 170, 172; writing as rupture 164

People and Places Index

Note page references to figures and tables are in italics.

Abraham, 299, 301, 307–9, 313–14, 330, 332
Africa, xv, 8, 222–3, 226–7, 231, 234, 243, 256
Ahutoru, 129–30, 135–6
Akwije, Ngwaje, 321–2
Akwoningi, Ibua, 312–3
Americas, the, 8, 61, 68, 162–4, 219, 223–4, 231, 234, 238
Ankave-Anga (Kukukuku), xiii, xiv, 16, 21–2, 295–333
Arabanoo, 206, 209, 211, 215
Arioi, 144, 156, 158
Asia, 8, 9, 39, 109, 226, 231, 234, 238, 255
D'Auribeau, Alexandre d'Hesmivy, 184–5
Australia, xv, 12, 13, 14, 20, 23–5, 40, 52, 59, 68, 73, 94, 96–7, 106, 156, 166, 172, 192, 197, 230–1, 232–3, 234, 242, 271; Administration of New Guinea, 16, 298–9, 301–4, 306–10, 314–19, 324, 331, 332, 333; New South Wales, 40, 106, 165, 172, 199, 208, 257 (Port Jackson, 5, 15, 24, 199–216; Sydney, 5, 23, 24, 40–1, 97, 168, 199–200, 204, 210–11, 234); Queensland, 41–2, 49–50, 242; Tasmania (Van Diemen's Land), 8, 15, 24, 41, 175–6, 182–6, 190–2, 198, 257 (Recherche Bay, 183–4, 198)
Australian National University, The (ANU), ix, xi, xiii, xiv, xv
Austronesian languages, 1–2, 24, 39, 43, 44, 46–8, 259

Ballard, Chris, 4, 8–9, 16, 23, 256, 315, 330
Baneelon, 206, 209, 211–15
Banks, Joseph, 135, 146, 158, 198, 204
Baruya, 22, 295–7, 301, 317, 320
Basilio, 279–80, 283, 293

Beach, Charles, 229–30, 256
Beer, Gillian, 229, 243
Bell, R.S., 295, 320
Bergendorff, Steen, 261–2, 285, 292
Bligh, Captain William, 141–2, 144
Boileau, Nicolas, 221
Bonnemère, Pascale, 11, 16, 18, 21–2, 311, 313, 315, 330, 332
Bougainville, Louis Antoine de, 13–15, 17, 57, 59, 71, 73–8, 93–4, 109, 113–14, 116–17, 123–4, 126–7, 130, 131–5, 146, 155, 156, 204, 207, 256
Bravo, Michael, 224

Carey, S.W., 304, 307–8, 313–14
Centre de Recherche et de Documentation sur l'Océanie (CREDO), ix, xiii, xiv, xv
Centre National de la Recherche Scientifique (CNRS), ix, xi, xiii, xiv, xv
Chaillu, Paul du, 242
Chester, K. I., 295, 303–4, 308–9, 311, 314, 321, 328, 332
China, 2, 9, 39, 40, 51, 225, 238; Canton, 40–1, 167
Clarke, Marcus, 231, 256
Clendinnen, Inga, 13, 200–1, 206, 211–14
Colbee, 206, 209, 211, 213, 215
Cole, Edward, 230
Coles, R.S., 303, 305–6
Collins, Judge-Advocate David, 199–200, 211–6
Commerson, Philibert, 127, 146, 155
Cook, Captain James, 5, 10–11, 13, 15, 17–18, 24, 35, 57–9, 69, 71–4, 79–97, 106–7, 108, 109, 110, 111, 114, 116, 127, 135–6, 138, 144, 146, 157, 158, 164, 182, 187–8, 190, 198, 201–4, 210, 219, 228, 262, 293
Cook Islands, the, 35, 41
Copia, Jaques-Louis, 19, 176, 180–1, 185, 188–9, 197
Coulter, John, 228–9, 230, 256
Crocker, Henry, 232, 136, 257

339

D'Alais, Vairasse, 163
D'Albertis, Luigi Maria, 9, 16, 21, 226, 244, 257, 262, 264–71, 273–4, 278, 282, 285–6, 292, 293
Dampier, William, 4, 208, 224
Debrett, John, 202
Defoe, Daniel, 4, 222, 224, 227–8, 229, 245, 256
Dening, Greg, xii, 5, 60, 107, 155, 201
D'Entrecasteaux, Antoine Raymond Joseph de Bruni, 8, 15, 19, 24, 175–92, 197, 198
Douaire-Marsaudon, Françoise, x, 3, 15, 20, 157, 158
Douglas, Bronwen, 8, 15, 19, 24, 221
D'urville, Dumont, 8, 17, 23–4, 145, 158, 176, 178, 182–3, 186, 188, 190–2, 197
Dutch, 4, 9, 11, 134–5, 137, 161, 225, 238, 257

Earl, George Windsor, 230, 233, 238, 242, 257
École des Hautes Études en Sciences Sociales (EHESS), ix, xiv, xv
Edwards, Gavin, 204
English language, ix–x, 12, 23–4, 37, 40, 42, 48–52, 61, 74, 86, 107, 132, 155, 157, 159, 173, 197, 202, 210, 257, 270
Erauje, Idzi, 299, 310, 313–15
Europe, 13, 20, 117–18, 136, 146, 173, 202–4
Europeans, 1–4, 8–22, 24–5, 35–6, 37, 42, 43, 48–9, 51, 57–60, 65, 67, 71–4, 78–85, 88–9, 90, 92–7, 106, 110, 111, 113–27, 155–6, 157, 161–70, 172, 175, 177–8, 179, 186–8, 190, 192–3, 198, 207–9, 222–7, 232, 245, 255, 256, 259–86, 293, 299–306, 316, 319, 320

Fabian, Johannes, 57, 71–3, 79, 84, 86
Fesche, Félix, 93–4, 117, 123–35, 139, 141, 144, 155, 156, 157
Fiji, 1, 2, 10, 12, 15, 20, 35, 39–42, 48–9, 178, 182; Suva, xi, 25, 40
First Fleet, the, 24, 199–202, 214
Fitzhardinge, L.F., 199, 204, 205, 219

Forster, Johann Reinhold, 4–5, 12, 74, 81, 85, 89, 91, 110, 111, 138, 182, 191
Forster, Georg, 4, 13, 69, 79, 89, 91–3, 107, 109, 110, 111, 187, 190
Foucault, Michel, 11
France, ix–x, xi, xiv, xv, 17–18, 22–3, 73–6, 106, 114–24, 126–36, 138–41, 144, 146, 155–6, 157, 175–80, 182, 183–4, 186–8, 191–2, 198, 201, 224, 232; Paris, 114, 115, 146, 155, 197, 199
Franciscan Order, 62, 69, 108
French language, 24, 42, 48, 51–2, 107, 131, 132, 146, 155, 159, 197, 201, 202, 204, 219, 223

German language, 24, 42, 51, 202, 223, 257
Germany, 13, 49, 106, 182, 295, 301, 302, 317
Glen, David, 242
Great Britain, xv, 2, 17–18, 22, 40, 73, 83, 91, 110, 128, 135, 146, 163–7, 173, 176, 178, 199, 202–3, 205–7, 209–13, 224–5, 230, 232, 243, 257, 273, 302; London, 40, 199, 202–3, 205, 213, 215, 238, 243–4
Greenblatt, Stephen Jay, 221

Hamilton, George, 136–8
Handy, Edward C.S., 139–40
Hanson, Alan F., 123, 158
Hau`ofa, Epeli, 15, 25, 292
Hawai`i, 10–11, 13, 15, 19–20, 40–1, 52, 96–7, 106, 114, 134, 136, 143, 144, 145, 155, 157, 158, 167, 210, 262, 293
Hawkesworth, John, 146, 157, 158, 202, 204
Henry, Teuira, 142, 158
Hides, Jack, 317
Hindi, 24, 48
Hobbes, Thomas, 163, 203
Hodges, William, 5–7, 13, 35, 81–3
Huli, 15, 315
Hunter, John, 199, 202, 214–15, 219
Huxley, Thomas, 225–6, 230, 235

Igete wiej, 308, 311, 314
Ikundi beri, 310, 314
Indigenous Australians, xv, 8, 23, 24, 182–6, 192, 200–1, 203, 205–15, 219, 234; Abaroo, 211, 214; Nanbaree, 211, 213
Indonesia, 23, 38–9, 52, 197, 256
International Program of Scientific Collaboration, ix, xi
Iqwaye, 298–9, 301, 303–5, 307, 309, 319–20, 330, 332, 333

Jack-Hinton, Colin, 61, 106, 107
Jacobs, Thomas Jefferson, 228, 231–2, 256
James, Henry, 239
Jolly, Margaret, 4, 11, 15, 156, 158, 292
Jukes, Joseph Beete, 225, 230

Kamea, 311, 318–9, 323, 332
Kame`eleihiwa, Lilikala, 15, 20
Kanak, 19, 48, 187–91
Kaon, Bumangari, 95, 96
Kelly, John, 12, 108

La Billadière, Jacques-Julien Houtou de, 176, 178–88, 191–2, 197, 198
Lamlam, 233, 257
Langimar, 317, 331
La Pérouse, Jean François de Galaup, 14–15, 17–18, 113, 115–17, 119–23, 141, 147, 155, 156, 176–8, 187, 198
Las Casas, Bartolomé de, 162, 172
Lawson, John A., 8–9, 16, 31, 227, 232, 234–45, 277
Leahy brothers, 317
Lemonnier, Pierre, 11, 16, 18, 21–2, 318, 320, 322, 330, 332
Levasseur, Emile, 23–4
Lindstrom, Lamont, 35, 110, 111
London Missionary Society, the, 42, 51, 162, 164–5, 168, 270
Lono, 10, 59, 97, 106
Luque, Miguel and Carlos Mondragón, 61–2, 66, 68, 71, 106, 107, 108, 109

Ma`afu, 2
MacGregor, Sir William, 244, 273–6, 282, 293

Maison de l'Asie–Pacifique, ix

Makahiki, 10
Malaysia, 9, 23, 39, 197, 226, 234, 238, 242, 256, 257
Maori, 11, 13, 25, 52, 73, 81, 97, 136, 138, 157, 168, 191
Marchand, Captain Etienne, 138–9, 155, 157
Mariner, William, 17, 166–7
Marquesas Islands, 40–1, 61, 114–15, 134, 138–9, 145, 155
Marra, John, 86–90
Marryat, Frederick, 225, 234, 255–6
McCarthy, John K., 301, 303, 317, 324, 332
Mead, Margaret, 117, 140–1, 145, 147, 157
Medieval period, 5, 59, 71, 162, 172
Mekeo, xv, 16, 21, 279–313
Melanesia, xv, 8, 23, 25, *38*, 118, 156, 158, 176, 182, 188, 191, 261, 270, 292, 293; Languages of, 2, 39, 40, 42–3, 46–9, 51–2
Mendaña, Álvaro de, 61–2, 107, 108, 138
Merle, Isabelle, 5, 15, 24
Micronesia, 2, 23, 25, *38*, 182; Languages of, 39–40, 42, 43, 51–2
Monckton, C.A.W., 9, 16, 21, 244, 262, 271–3, 276–86, 292, 293, 301, 321
More, Sir Thomas, 69, 163, 224
Moresby, Captain John, 9, 16, 234, 239–40, 242, 244, 257, 259
Morrell, Abby and Benjamin, 228, 230, 231–2, 256
Morrison, 17, 142
Mosko, Mark S., 9, 16, 21, 106, 110, 331
Motu, 43, 51

Nanggu, 46–7
Nassau, Prince of, 74, 113, 123–8, 130–1, 144, 155
Nauru, 40, 51
New Caledonia, xv, 8, 12, 15, 19, 23, 24, 40–2, 48, 51–2, 176, 187–91, 257; Loyalty Islands, 41, 42, 51
New Zealand, Aotearoa, xv, 11, 17, 20, 23, 25, 41, 45, 52, 73, 79, 96–7, 133–4, 143, 155, 168, 192, 197, 233, 257
Ngudze, Toatto, 307
Norfolk Islands, 41, 51

Obeyesekere, Gananath, 10–11, 18–19, 35, 97, 108
O'Brien, K.G., 303–5, 309, 314–15
Oliver, Douglas L., 142, 158
Onorwa'e, 311, 314
Orangwŏks, 8–9, 232–4, 236, 241, 257

Pagden, Anthony, 177
Papua New Guinea, xiii, xiv, xv, 1, 8–9, 11, 15,16, 18, 20, 21–2, 23, 24, 35, 41, 59, 68, 106–7, 110, 176, 178, 182, 190, 197, 221–35, 236, 237, 238–45, 255, 256–7, 259–86, 292–3, 295, 296, 297, 297–324, 330–1, 332, 333; Admiralty Islands, 8, 15, 24, 176, 178–84, 192, 197 (Angae, 297, 305, 310–13, 319–23, 331; Buu', 301, 305–6, 311, 319, 322, 323); Ankave-Swanson valley, 297, 299, 301, 305, 306, 309; Bismarck Archipelago, 38, 42, 228, 232 (Bougainville, 2, 38; New Britain, 2, 38–9, 49, 228, 256; New Ireland, 1–2, 38–9, 49, 228, 256, 265); British New Guinea, 49, 242, 259, 262, 271–3, 306; German New Guinea, 49, 51, 256, 301; Highlands, 1, 15–16, 21–2, 59, 107, 244, 295, 298, 317; Ihu, 299, 302, 307, 309, 318, 332; Ikundi, 296–7, 307–8, 310–14, 319–24, 332, 333; Ivori River, 295, 302–6, 318–19, 331; Kaintiba, 299, 305, 312–13, 318–19, 322, 330, 331, 332; Kerema, 299, 302, 304–5, 309, 316–17, 330, 331, 332; Komako, 305, 308, 309, 323, 332; Kwaplalim, 301, 312, 318; Kwayu, 311–12, 319, 333; Lagai valley, 299, 301, 305, 307–9, 312–13, 320, 330; Languages, 1–2, 24, 37–9, 42–3, 46–51, 55 (Äiwoo, 2, 43, 46–8, 55; Nendö, 2, 43, 46, 48, 55; Tok Pisin, 49, 297, 309–11, 323, 332); Meenu, 305–6, 311–12, 321–2; Menyamya, 295, 297, 299, 301, 303, 304, 306, 308–9, 317–23, 331, 332, 333; Morobe, 16, 295, 331, 332; Pio, 305–6, 319, 331; Port Moresby, 43, 270, 274, 276–8, 284; Saa'/New Year Creek valley, 299, 304, 305, 312, 331, 332; Sinde, 304, 306, 312, 318, 322–3, 331; Suao, 321–2; Suowi valley, 296–313, 315, 317–24, 330, 331, 332, 333; Tauri valley, 301, 303–4, 308, 321, 323; Uogwa, 305–6, 319;Vailala River, 301–6, 308, 312, 317, 331, 332, 333; Veifa`a, 271, 273, 278–80; Watut River, 301–2, 316–17, 331; Wau, 302–3, 309, 317, 331, 332; Yakana, 298, 304, 305, 319; Yule Island, 265–6, 270, 273
Peru, 61–2, 108, 109
Philip III, 62, 68–9, 108
Philippines, the, 23, 39, 61, 109; Manila, 40, 68, 227, 229–30
Phillip, Arthur, 199–200, 202, 206, 209–14, 219
Pileni, 46–8
Piron, 19, 176, 178, 180–2, 188–9, 197, 198
Poe, Edgar Allan, 230
Pohnpei (Ponape), 40–1
Polynesia, xiii, xv, 2, 5, 8, 10, 12–13, 15, 21, 23, 25, 38, 40, 84, 107, 113–18, 128, 131, 132–6, 138–45, 147, 155–6, 157, 158, 161, 163–4, 182, 188, 190, 191, 197, 265, 270, 273; Languages, 39, 42–3, 46–8, 51–2, 85
Portugal, 61–2, 69, 108, 163
Prado y Tovar, Don Diego, 62, 66, 69, 108, 109
Pratt, Mary Louise, 245
Pritchard, William T., 121, 135, 156
Purdy, W.M., 305, 321

Quirós, Pedro Fernández de, 1, 4, 15, 18, 57, 59, 60–79, 94, 106, 107, 108, 109–10, 111, 163

Rome, 61–2, 71, 107
Roro, 16, 259–76, 278, 281–2, 284–6, 292, 293
Rose, Deborah Bird, 94
Rossel, Elisabeth-Paul-Edouard de, 179, 190, 197
Rousseau, Jean-Jacques, 163, 183, 207, 215, 222
Rwej, Iwasi, 307, 313

Saapitso, Peter, 312–13, 352
Sacred Heart Missionary, 273, 280, 282, 284, 292, 293
Sahlins, Marshall, 10, 11, 15, 19, 35, 84, 97, 114, 155, 158, 261, 262, 286, 293
Said, Edward, 221
Salmond, Anne, 11, 81–5, 87, 89, 96, 107, 110, 111, 155
Samoa, xv, 11, 14–15, 17, 18, 19, 20, 41, 42, 49, 51, 52, 113–17, 119–23, 134–6, 138, 139–40, 143, 145, 147, 155, 156, 157, 158, 167, 177
Schieffelin, Edward, 315
Seligmann, Charles G., 116, 284, 292, 293
Selkirk, Alexander, 4, 224
Shapiro, Karl, 223, 255
Sia Raga, 20, 93–6
Silva, Noenoe, 19
Singapore, 23, 39
Skelly, E.C., 302, 304
Smith, Bernard, 5, 8, 11, 14, 19, 60, 73, 104, 109, 177, 180, 182, 195–8, 207, 217
Smith, Keith Vincent, 212
Solomon Islands, 2, 15, 35, 38, 39, 41, 42, 43, 46, 48–9, 51, 62, 156, 331; Reef Islands, 46–7, 54; Santa Cruz Archipelago, 2, 44–8, 64, 107, 108 (Taumako, 46, 64, 69, 107, 108, 109; Tikopia, 46–7, 55, 64, 109; Vanikoro, 46, 48, 55, 156)
Souter, Gavin, 223, 256, 272, 331
Spain, 4, 8, 18, 22, 60–5, 67–71, 73, 106, 107–8, 109–10, 138, 156, 172
Spanish language, 42, 51, 107, 108, 156
Sparrman, Anders, 65–6, 87–8, 92–3, 111
Spate, Oskar, 60–2, 68, 107, 108
Stanley, Owen, 225, 233, 255
Stephen, Michelle, 260–2, 269, 285, 292

Tahiti, 12, 13–15, 17, 19, 35, 40–2, 75, 76, 78, 79, 81, 85, 90, 109, 113–18, 123–4, 126–36, 138–44, 146, 155–6, 157, 158, 165, 167, 198; Language, 51–2
Taiwan, 2, 39
Tapa, 5, 21, 131, 133, 142
Taylor, John P., xi, 20, 59, 93–6, 106, 108, 109, 111

Taufa`ahau, 168–9, 173
Tcherkézoff, Serge, ix, x, xi, 10–15, 17–20, 106, 107, 156, 157, 158, 256
Tench, Watkin, 5, 15, 24, 199–216, 219
Thomas, Nicholas, 2, 3, 84, 97, 155, 278
Timperley, A.T., 295, 304, 307, 313–14, 331
Toatto, Iwadze, 312
Tonga, xiii, 1–2, 8, 15, 17, 19–21, 25, 35, 41, 48, 114–15, 134, 136–8, 139, 142–3, 161–2, 164–70, 172–3, 179, 182, 184–93, 197, 198; Tongatapu, 24, 176, 184; Vava`u, 166–7
Torres, Luis Vaez de, 62, 64, 67–9, 106, 108
Torres Strait, 23, 234, 239, 284
Trégance, Louis, 8–9, 16, 227, 232–4, 236, 241, 244–5, 257
Tryon, Darrell, xi, 1–2, 15, 24, 39, 158
Tsing, Anna, 12
Tupaia, 12, 85

Ulukalala, Finau, 167, 170
United States of America, 20, 42, 88, 97, 107, 138, 147, 172, 202, 228–30, 259

Vanuatu (New Hebrides) xiii, 2, 4, 11, 12, 15, 18, 21, 39, 40–2, 43, 48–9, 51, 57, 58, 59, 63, 64–97,106, 107–8, 109–11, 156; Ambae, xi, 57, 65, 74–8, 109; Banks Islands, 51, 63, 64, 70, 74 (Gaua, 64–5, 70, 75, 109); Erromango, 40, 57, 79, 81, 84–5, 89–90, 91–3, 110; Espiritu Santo, 1, 4, 57, 65, 66, 68, 70, 78–9, 106, 107, 109, 110, 111 (Big Bay, 65, 68, 70–1, 107, 109, 111); Malakula (Mallicollo), 5, 21, 57, 79–92, 110 (*Man of the Island Mallicollo*, 5, 6–7, 81); New Jerusalem, 4, 60, 65, 70, 109; Pentecost, 35, 57, 65–6, 74, 93–6, 110; Tanna, 12–13, 21, 35, 57, 79–85, 89–93, 109, 110, 111
Vaujuas, 122–3, 139
Vibart, Eric, 163
Voltaire, 146, 158, 203

Wales, William, 85, 93
Wallis and Futuna, xiii, 51
Wallis, Samuel, 13–14, 17, 134, 139, 157, 204
Wallace, Alfred Russel, 9, 23, 226, 238, 242, 243, 244, 256, 257
Wesleyans, 164, 168, 171
White, John, 199, 202, 213
Whitehead, P.G., 295, 305, 328
Williams, John, 120–1, 158
Williamson, Robert Wood, 116–17, 147
Wyss, Johann, 225, 234, 255

www.ingramcontent.com/pod-product-compliance
Lightning Source LLC
Chambersburg PA
CBHW041248240426
43669CB00034B/2990